☞ **W9-BEW-393**

ADVANCED PRAISE FOR *SCHOOLS THAT CHANGE: EVIDENCE-BASED IMPROVEMENT AND EFFECTIVE CHANGE LEADERSHIP* BY LEW SMITH, CORWIN PRESS (2007)

"Few things in life pack the punch of a good example. It is hard to make excuses about what cannot be accomplished when we confront a concrete example of what has been accomplished. Lew Smith's book offers educators a variety of inspiring examples of schools that beat the odds and improved teaching and learning. What I appreciate most about Smith's approach is the fact that he thinks like a designer rather than a problem solver. Problem solvers concentrate on eliminating things—problems; designers focus on creating things—in this case, exciting new learning environments. For my money, the hopes of our neediest young people are better vested in the dynamics of designers than the predicaments of problem solvers."

Daniel L. Duke, Professor and Research
Director of the Partnership for Leaders in Education;
Author, *The Challenges of Educational Change* (2004)

"Lew Smith's patient attention to developing a framework that captures the dimensions of successful school improvement has paid off handsomely. The school portraits in Schools that Change *are based on deep familiarity, and are inspiring because they lead to important conclusions. Three of these stand out: There are many paths from failure to success, all take a longtime, and all involve nimble local adjustments to evolving circumstances rather than adherence to a fixed program or strategic plan. Both researchers and school administrators will gain insight into the theory and art of change leadership from this book. More important, readers will come away with many ideas about how to create the conditions that Smith identifies as critical to substantive change for teachers, students, and families."*

Karen R. Seashore (Louis), Rodney S. Wallace
Professor, Educational Policy

"Schools surely do change each autumn when a new group of students arrives—whether the schools' faculties like the good and bad habits that each group of kids inevitably bring with them. Some schools, however and in addition, take the initiative for change, looking for a 'better way' to serve their constituencies. Lew Smith has given us a revealing and important glimpse of some of these latter, remarkable schools."

Ted Sizer, Chairman Emeritus, Coalition of Essential Schools;
author, *Horace's Compromise* (1984), and *The Red Pencil* (2004)

"Replete with comprehensive reviews of the literature on change and leadership and in-depth portraits of eight schools with histories of failure that became high performing, Schools That Change *makes the often ignored powerful connections that bridge research, policy, and practice, enabling those in all three fields to make decisions to effect systemic improvement of teaching and learning in America's schools. It is refreshing to have this timely book, which not only makes the case for change and improvement in America's schools but also provides evidence on how to do it."*

Thomas W. Payzant, Professor of Practice,
Harvard University Graduate School of Education;
former superintendent of Boston Public Schools

"Lew Smith has written about how eight schools (four elementary and four secondary) have changed from schools of mediocrity to schools of excellence. He presents the story of each of these schools, with in-depth reviews of the progress from those involved in making it happen. He concludes his study with practical suggestions of how to accomplish the same results through the essential elements of context, capacity, and conversation. The book has a scholarly foundation but has a practical focus reflecting the author's own experiences as a successful high school principal."

Frank J. Macchiarola, President, St. Francis College;
former Chancellor of the New York City Public Schools

"School people . . . and their schools . . . have shown themselves to be gifted and talented at resisting and subverting change. Lew Smith hands to us the keys to the storehouse of insights about how schools changed . . . really changed."

Roland Barth, founder, Harvard's
Principals Center and noted author

"As the former superintendent of two large urban school districts, I know first-hand of the challenge to dramatically improve underperforming schools. I also understand that within every district there are schools that beat the odds and excel. Schools that Change *provides educators and policymakers with eight such schools that now serve as exemplars. There is much we can learn from these stories drawn from Lew Smith's extensive research."*

Dr. Arlene Ackerman, Christian A. Johnson Professor of
Outstanding Educational Practice, Teachers College,
Columbia University, Former Superintendent,
Washington DC & San Francisco, CA

"Remember when it was change, *then* reform, *later* restructuring *and even re-*engineering, *the more syllables the better, it seems. But Lew Smith's new book captures real "school change" where it counts most: in schools and classrooms—for children, teachers, and communities. A must-read!"*

Bruce Cooper, Professor, Educational
Leadership, Fordham University

"*Schools That Change is an engaging, practitioner-friendly, examination of successful school improvement that locates its perspective from inside the school's walls. Smith provides eight vivid portraits of schools that were once seen as failures, but have subsequently pulled themselves together and dramatically improved. By blending theories of change with the actual policies and practices that have enabled success across a variety of educational contexts, this book provides both instruction and hope to educators, parents, policymakers, and aspiring school leaders. It should make the short list of required reads for all school stakeholders.*"

Steve Jacobson, Chair, Educational Leadership,
University at Buffalo, State University of New York

"*In a thorough review of the literature, Lew describes both the beauty and the challenge of change. However, he does [not] stop there. What makes* Schools That Change *an important book is the fact that the messages, the lessons learned, are grounded in the stories of real schools and the paths they took to work their way from the bottom to laudable positions as high-performing schools. The stories of struggling schools that find their way from the bottom to the top will resonate with school leaders everywhere, particularly urban educators. The book is a great contribution to the field and is needed now more than ever.*"

Beverly L. Hall, Superintendent,
Atlanta Public Schools

"Schools That Change *is the fruit of the National School Change Award program, which examined 474 nominated schools between 2000 and 2005. The author selected eight of the forty-two winning schools for detailed portraits, describing the schools' contexts, capacities, the conversations that took place within them, the leadership exercised by both principals and teachers, and of course the messy process of change. But while the book acknowledges how hard the process of change can be, its essential message is optimistic: schools can change to improve the achievement of all students, and there's nothing magical about the process. Along the way,* Schools That Change *provides every school a great many valuable strategies to consider.*"

W. Norton Grubb, David Gardner Chair in
Higher Education Faculty Coordinator, National Principals
Leadership Institute, University of California, Berkeley

"*At last, a book that provides practical guidance to schools on how to improve by focusing on schools that have.* Schools That Change *offers sound insights from experienced educators on what it takes to create the schools we need to educate America's children.*"

Pedro Noguera, Director, Metro Center
for Urban Education, and Professor, New York University

"Schools That Change *is a rich guide for educators interested in nuts and bolts tools and resources to support the journey from low performance to high performance. The thoughtful discussion of change and leadership provides school leaders with access to well-documented school change efforts gathered over seven years of methodical study by Lew Smith. The book is practitioner friendly as it includes material that can be applied in the schools of leaders seeking to improve student outcomes. Lew Smith has powerfully captured the lessons learned in his magnificently colorful portraits of eight schools selected for the National School Change Award. Practitioners will find* Schools That Change *to be wonderfully grounded in evidence-based research and documented best practice. The accomplishments of these award winning schools are honored in the work of Lew Smith."*

Larry Leverett, Executive Director,
Panasonic Foundation, and former school
superintendent, Plainfield, NJ, and Greenwich, CT

"Schools That Change *captures that rare combination of intellectual rigor, challenging vision, and the passionate teaming that has come to characterize the National Principals Leadership Institute that Dr. Smith has directed for the past ten years. I have been eagerly awaiting this book to share with our board and with all of our educators. Beyond the mechanistic change processes that are observed all too often, Lew helps us locate the work squarely where it resides; in the messy, organic world of human organizations where leaders must understand and work though the change essentials of context, capacity, and conversations. In addition, by telling the stories of courageous school leaders, who have led schools of all sizes and levels throughout the United States, Lew has written a singular work that not only teaches . . . it inspires and informs all of us who dream of sustained excellence in our schools that yes—it can be done!"*

Duane Brothers, superintendent and CEO,
Sunrise School Division, Manitoba, Canada

Schools That
CHANGE

Evidence-Based Improvement
and Effective Change Leadership

LEW SMITH
Foreword by MICHAEL FULLAN

CORWIN PRESS
A SAGE Company
Thousand Oaks, CA 91320

Copyright © 2008 by Corwin Press

All rights reserved. When forms and sample documents are included, their use is authorized only by educators, local school sites, and/or noncommercial or nonprofit entities that have purchased the book. Except for that usage, no part of this book may be reproduced or utilized in any form or by any means, electronic or mechanical, including photocopying, recording, or by any information storage and retrieval system, without permission in writing from the publisher.

For information:

Corwin Press
A SAGE Company
2455 Teller Road
Thousand Oaks, California 91320
www.corwinpress.com

SAGE Ltd.
1 Oliver's Yard
55 City Road
London EC1Y 1SP
United Kingdom

SAGE India Pvt. Ltd.
B 1/I 1 Mohan Cooperative Industrial Area
Mathura Road, New Delhi 110 044
India

SAGE Asia-Pacific Pte. Ltd.
33 Pekin Street #02-01
Far East Square
Singapore 048763

Printed in the United States of America.

Library of Congress Cataloging-in-Publication Data

Smith, Lew, EdD.
Schools that change : evidence-based improvement and effective change leadership / Lew Smith.
    p. cm.
Includes bibliographical references and index.
ISBN 978-1-4129-4951-4 (cloth)
ISBN 978-1-4129-4952-1 (pbk.)
    1. School improvement programs—United States—Case studies. 2. Educational change—United States—Case studies. 3. Educational leadership—United States—Case studies. I. Title.

LB2822.82.S645 2008
371.010973—dc22   2007031657

This book is printed on acid-free paper.

08 09 10 11 10 9 8 7 6 5 4 3 2

Acquisitions Editor:	Elizabeth Brenkus
Editorial Assistants:	Desiree Enayati, Ena Rosen
Typesetter:	C&M Digitals (P) Ltd.
Proofreader:	Victoria Reed-Castro
Indexer:	Sheila Bodell
Cover Designer:	Michael Dubowe
Graphic Designer:	Lisa Riley

Contents

List of Figures

Foreword

Lew Smith's *Schools That Change* is based on seven years of careful, engaging work. It integrates equal parts of passion and intellect. It is a success because it respects and reveals the enormous accomplishments of eight schools going from awful to good and great performance. The book weaves brilliantly from complex individual cases to the wider knowledge base. It captures the messiness of change with a few powerful insights that greatly advance our understanding not only of success but also, more significantly, of *how* it is accomplished.

Smith's model of change is derived from a weaver's immersion in the cloth of reality over many years. The effort culminates with the emergence of powerful concepts that enable the reader to understand how success can occur and how it might be guided. The result is an elegant 3 × 3 model. The three essential elements—context, capacity, and conversations—are there, and the three catalytic variables—internal dissonance, external forces, and leadership—bring the dynamism to interactive life. If you want to know about school success under diverse, difficult, challenging circumstances, it is between the covers of this impressive book.

Ever reflective, *Schools That Change* gives us maximum clarity but warns against acting too quickly on this new knowledge. The ten traps listed in the final chapter furnish a sober reminder that if we are to understand and do something about change then we need to do the in-depth, immersive work of getting inside the problem as Smith has done. His warnings are apposite: if you think this is a cookbook, go back to the bookstore; if you are arguing whether it's product or process, you lose; if you're future focused, you've got it one third right; if it's quick and easy, consider it a failure (and six more of these wise warnings).

This is a book that is carefully crafted. It is interesting and insightful. Each of the eight school portraits can be used as mini case studies to understand change. The 3 × 3 model allows us to see the forest and the trees. Many of us have been working toward how to accomplish success on a large scale in a sea of reform better known for its disasters. We think we are getting somewhere identifying the deep problems, and some of the powerful ways out. We can add Lew Smith's book to this small but growing field that we now know, as Smith concludes, that although it is difficult work, "It can be done!" *Schools That Change* is a well-crafted contribution to the literature on successful reform—a sophisticated and nuanced book that should be read with care.

—Michael Fullan, Ontario Institute
for Studies in Education (OISE), University of Toronto

Preface

You are reading this book because you care about schools. You share my concern, and that of many others, that an unacceptable number of schools in America are not living up to their potential. You believe good schools can be great ones and low-performing schools can also become great. In this book, I discuss why and how they can change.

Concern about American schools has been a constant theme throughout our history, and it continues in the twenty-first century. Critics and reformers have a litany of complaints.

National attention has focused on the "achievement gap" between White students and students of color, between middle-class students and those who come from lower socioeconomic backgrounds, between students who have special needs or who are English language learners and those who are not. But not enough has been done to address this inequity.

Many schools in poor urban areas lack certified and trained teachers, textbooks, computers, and facility upgrades needed to provide a quality education. Some observers, like Jonathan Kozol (2005), argue that, as a result, school segregation is now worse than ever.

The emphasis on increasing reading, writing, and math scores has, in many cases, led to regimentation and a sole focus on raising test results. Critic Alfie Kohn (1999) argued that schools need to encourage students to think widely and deeply, not to memorize facts but instead to explore ideas and challenge assumptions. Psychologist Robert Sternberg (2006) calls creativity a habit and is disturbed that because of conventional standardized tests, which have only one "right answer," schools today are treating creativity like a *bad* habit.

Other educational reformers contend that important educational goals, such as the need to develop students who can think critically, problem solve, and work in teams, have been tossed aside. Furthermore, in some schools, foreign language, physical and health education, art, and music have virtually disappeared. Character education has been forgotten.

Despite a technological revolution and widely spreading globalization, American high schools are described as remarkably similar to what they were nearly a century ago. The December 2006 issue of *Time* magazine calls for bringing U.S. schools out of the twentieth century, noting that "American schools aren't exactly frozen in time, but considering the pace of change in other areas of life, U.S. public schools tend to feel like throwbacks"(Wallis, Steptoe, & Miranda, 2006, ¶ 2). American students must have twenty-first-century skills. They need to have good people skills, become global trade literate and "out-of the-box" thinkers. In an age of unlimited and overwhelming information access, students need to "rapidly process what's coming at them and distinguish what's reliable and what isn't . . . Students must know how to manage, interpret, validate, and use the overflowing information coming their way" (Wallis et al., 2006, ¶ 8).

Nonetheless, there is good news. The same *Time* magazine article quoted above gives examples of schools that require fluency in a second language, college-level research papers, and real-world service projects; schools that combine core knowledge with making connections across academic disciplines; schools that choose depth over breadth and have students discuss challenging topics, such as "the elusive nature of truth."

Some major urban school districts, such as Atlanta and Boston, have seen dramatic increases in student achievement. In Atlanta, between 1999 and 2005, the number of fourth-graders who met or exceeded English and math standard scores increased from 47% to 83% and 43% to 79%, respectively (Panasonic Foundation, 2006). According to an analysis conducted by an advocacy group and independent researchers, a pilot network of sixteen autonomous schools, collaboratively designed by the Boston school district and the teachers union, were "paying off in higher test scores, attendance, and college-going rates" (Manzo, 2006, p. 9).

Education Week, in nearly every issue, focuses on an education victory, such as an innovative after-school program, a successful community outreach project, a powerful business/school district partnership, a set of nontraditional strategies used for school improvement. For example, the San Francisco school district emphasizes assistance for low-performing schools, rather than mandating particular teaching models or conducting wholesale school restructuring. The goal is to remove barriers to good instruction by providing full-time substitute teachers, more teacher planning time, experts to provide feedback on lessons, and a master teacher to lead schoolwide training (Archer, 2006, p. 36).

The small learning community concept, although difficult to implement, has produced numerous small schools, characterized by more individual attention for students; staff growth; and thematic, interdisciplinary teaching. There are innovative schools where teachers are treated as professionals and collaboration has replaced isolation; schools where creative classes become the norm; schools where the teachers go to summer school to learn how their teaching can correlate with the demands of technology, scientific research, or financial companies.

This book does not disparage or dismiss these important examples of school improvement and innovation, but it does question why these examples are the exception rather than the rule.

Schools That Change asks us to consider how some schools, that were once disappointments and failures, were able to become exemplary. We will look at what these schools were; what they became; and, most important, *how* they made significant change. What I call "lessons to be learned" are included throughout this book. These are lessons drawn from harsh realities. However, these are also lessons that generate hope and demonstrate how we can bring schools seen as dismal to schools that serve our children and adolescents in meaningful ways.

Dramatic school improvement—significant school change—is challenging, but, as this book details, it can be done. It has been done, and, you as an educator, student, parent, community activist, researcher, advocate, concerned citizen, or policymaker can help create many more school success stories. Your commitment to the children and adolescents, who attend PreK–12 schools, requires you to be a dreamer, a realist, a leader, and an agent of change.

Change involves a journey, filled with promise and perils. This book presents portraits of eight schools that took that journey and in doing so experienced poor travel conditions, accidents, missed landmarks, and maps filled with errors. Sometimes, they had to change drivers or rest along the way. Sometimes, they got lost and doubted they would complete their trip. Nonetheless, they continued and finally reached their destination, transforming schools that desperately needed to be changed.

More schools can successfully navigate a similar journey, and it is my hope this book will help. *Schools That Change* is organized into six parts. The first part is called "The Dynamics of Change," and it reflects what we have experienced as individuals who initiate and feel the impact of change. The ideas and concepts, the definitions and terms, will be familiar to you. Often, you will shake your head in agreement because you can relate to the examples and anecdotes.

Parts II and III tell wonderful stories of elementary and secondary schools. They present portraits of eight schools that turned the dynamics of change in their favor. These are schools that took on the challenge of change—and won. These are schools that serve as exemplars.

Similar to the schools described in this book, the particular school *you* care about is at a different place all its own. It is idiosyncratic. It has its own history and players, its own circumstances and conditions. In reading this part of the book, you may find a school that seems a lot like a school you attended, worked in, or studied. Make the comparison and learn from that story. But don't stay there; the other school portraits also have important lessons to teach.

This part of the book provides data and documentation. It depicts what happened in real schools; it does not use hypothetical case studies. You will meet dynamic characters and dramatic plots. Certainly, you may read as many of these portraits as you wish. I urge you to read all of them so you can identify the common themes.

My research has suggested common variables, which are pieced together in a conceptual framework. See if you agree with my interpretation. In Part IV, I explain what I term *essential elements*, and in Part V I talk about *catalytic variables*. Although these sections are free standing, they flow from the portraits. Finally, in Part VI, I synthesize the lessons and present traps to avoid.

As you read, ask yourself whether the conceptual framework and lessons make any sense. Can you use them—and in what ways? Can you relate—and why does that matter? Can you look at schools in different ways, for what they are and what they could be? Can you unleash the energy that is within yourself and others? Can you make a difference?

Answers are important, but questions are more important. John Dewey wanted us to relate learning experiences to the real world, to learn by doing, to construct our knowledge. But even more critically, he wanted us to reflect on what we were learning and doing. He wanted us to see the world anew.

Acknowledgments

This book is in memory of **Molly Maloy**, whose leadership enabled George Washington Carver Academy in Waco, Texas, to significantly change and become an exemplary middle school.

In salute to the other principals and school communities whose wonderful and inspiring portraits fill the pages of this book, I thank the following: **Bill Andrekopoulos**, Gustav Fritsche Middle School, Milwaukee, Wisconsin; **Joanne Cockrell**, Louis W. Fox Academic and Technical High School, San Antonio, Texas; **Rob Carroll**, South Heights Elementary School, Henderson, Kentucky; **Michele Hancock**, John Williams School No. 5, Rochester, New York; **Doug Law**, Niles High School, Niles, Michigan; **Sandy Stephens**, Government Hill Elementary School, Anchorage, Alaska; and **Chris Zarzana**, Skycrest Elementary School, Citrus Heights, California.

I also recognize the six doctoral students who worked with me in creating the National School Change Awards: **Lois Colletta**, **Cesar Espineda**, **Winsome Gregory**, **Marlyn Lawrence**, **Frank Melia**, and **Matthew Murphy**.

I express gratitude to the two special assistants who propped me up, provided assistance and support, and tried (unsuccessfully) to remove the clutter from my desk, **Yvette Colon** and **Francesca Sinatra**. I extend thanks to Francesca as well for correcting the charts, repaginating the book, composing the figures, and completing dozens of book-related tasks.

A special thank-you goes to **Alison Benowitz**, who researched faster than a speeding bullet, and **Fred Stokley**, who hovered over every page, providing advice I typically ignored.

I extend many thanks to the team who conduct the National School Change Awards and National Principals Leadership Institute, especially **Juan Fonseca**, **David Kroun**, and **Mary Rivera**, three esteemed colleagues and close friends.

I express heartfelt appreciation to those who believed in this book and who mentored me, worked with me, and set examples of what it means to be a gifted and caring educator and leader: **Ben Canada**, **Beverly Hall**, **Barbara Jackson**, **Frank Macchiarola**, and **Grayson Noley**.

I offer a special tribute to **Frank Smith**, whose beliefs, ideas, and passion run through these pages. In many, many ways, this is Frank's book.

I also express my appreciation of **Martha Graham** and **Michael Feller,** who led the Chase Manhattan Foundation's initial sponsorship of the National

School Change Awards and to the others who followed: **Gene Carter**, Association for Supervision and Curriculum Development; **Joe Small**, Pearson Education; and **Paul Houston**, American Association of School Administrators.

Finally, with great respect and recognition, admiration and appreciation of two exceptional educators who have passed away, but who have left their indelible stamp on me and on thousands more, I recognize **Colman Genn** and **George Shebitz**.

Corwin Press gratefully acknowledges the contributions of the following individuals:

Thomas Alsbury, Assistant Professor
Educational Research and Leadership Program
North Carolina State University
Raleigh, NC

Randel Beaver, Superintendent
Archer City Independent School District
Archer City, TX

Raymond Lowery, Associate Principal of Instruction
Alief Hastings High School
Houston, TX

Anthony Przeklasa, Associate Professor of Leadership
Concordia University Chicago
River Forest, IL

Gina Segobiano, Superintendent
Harmony Emge District 175
Belleville, IL

Dana Trevethan, Principal
Turlock High School
Turlock, CA

About the Author

 **Lew Smith** received his BA, MA, and School Administration/ Supervision Certificate from Brooklyn College and his EdD from Teachers College, Columbia University. He began his career as a social studies teacher in New York City high schools, where his interdisciplinary course in American History, titled "The American Dream," became a textbook published by Scott Foresman and adopted nationwide. Dr. Smith has served as the principal of a New York City high school; the executive director of America's first settlement house, a multisocial service agency; and the principal of a suburban junior– senior high school.

Dr. Smith conceived and directed the New York City Middle School Initiative, which ultimately launched middle school reform in twenty-six of New York City's thirty-two community school districts. He facilitated the creation of eighty-two school-based leadership teams for the Newark, New Jersey, school system.

Dr. Smith has served as Associate Professor in Educational Leadership and Associate Dean, Program Development and Outreach, at the Fordham University Graduate School of Education. As a member of the educational leadership faculty, Dr. Smith directed the revision and expansion of the Master's Program in Educational Administration, which generated more than 200 well-prepared school administrators between 2000 and 2003. Dr. Smith, working with a Fordham team and external partners, conceived and directed a Critical Issues in Education Conference Series, the National School Change Awards, and the National Principals Leadership Institute.

Dr. Smith's research and teaching focus is on leadership development and school change. He has presented papers and conducted workshops in numerous school districts, at regional conferences, and at national conferences conducted by the American Association of School Administrators, the American Educational Research Association, the Association for Supervision and Curriculum Development, and the University Council of Educational Administration. Four commentaries authored by Dr. Smith have appeared in *Education Week.*

Dr. Smith has been involved in extensive school restructuring and school design work, including the creation of three small New York City high schools dedicated to the themes of public service and social justice. Additionally, he helped with the restructuring of four K–8 schools and two high schools in Paterson, New Jersey; the design of a middle school in Baltimore, Maryland; and the redesign of four secondary schools in Newburgh, New York. He prepared educators in Milwaukee, Wisconsin, for the redesign of all eighteen high schools in their district and facilitated a new Aspiring Principals program for the San Francisco, California, Unified School District. Dr. Smith is married, with four children and one grandchild, all of whom have attended public schools. He is an avid reader, cook, and vegetable gardener.

For my wife, Jann Coles,
My partner, my soul mate, my best friend
And for our children,
Lindsay, Eric, Sabrina, and Whitney and our granddaughter Jaelyn

Introduction

THE CHANGING WORLD WE LIVE IN

This book is about change. It will explore the human dynamics of change and consider how these dynamics impact change efforts in schools.

As of January 2006, Amazon.com reported the availability of 60,805 books on change; Barnes&Noble.com listed 37,823. Google cited 1,490,000,000 (nearly 1.5 billion!) hits on change. One hundred forty-four movies had *change* in their titles. Between 2000 and 2005, a total of 866,071 patents reflected entrepreneurial endeavors and a wide range of inventions. No doubt, by the time you read this, these numbers will have skyrocketed.

We live in a society that promotes and rewards change. Bookstores contain dozens of volumes about self-improvement. Daily newspapers routinely report new technological advances. Our newly purchased computers become second rate within months as more sophisticated models are released.

Look at what has unfolded recently. We now walk around with cell phones literally attached to our ears and, if we have Bluetooth, we talk into thin air. We cannot live without access to the Internet. Daily, dozens—if not hundreds—of e-mails hit our computer screens or Blackberries. Mailing a letter is passé; instant text message responses are expected. We can shoot photographs and within minutes transmit them to the other side of the world.

We unlock our cars with passive alarm transmitters; we have a remote control for everything. Floppy disks, videos, and audiocassettes are ancient history. *Digital* is now the word that describes how we view things, communicate, compute, and complete our work. We can bring our own movies on airline flights. iPods, popular and impressive when they could store hundreds of songs, can now store thousands. The speed and breadth of change worldwide is astounding; its place in the fabric of America is significant.

THE AMERICAN DREAM

America has stood as a symbol of change, "the world's last best hope." Essayist Frederick Gentles put it this way: "The mystique of the American Dream has captured the imagination of the world, for it has created a glamour and a dynamism that make this country stand in vivid contrast to [what some see as] less vital societies" (Gentles & Steinfeld, 1971, p. 3). America became a "nation that considered itself unique because it seemed to be the place where dreams could be fulfilled" (L. Smith, 1977, p. 9).

Benjamin Franklin called America the place where it is always morning. Historian Daniel Boorstin captured the sprit of America when he wrote, "The United States thus became . . . a place of second chances, opportunities, revivals, revisions, and rebirths. A place for trying out what elsewhere was only imagined, or could not even be imagined elsewhere because it could not be tried" (Boorstin, 1972, p. 9).

In 1960, when John F. Kennedy accepted the Democratic Party's nomination for the presidency, he used the image of pioneers overcoming hazards and hardships as they conquered the West:

> Today some would say that those struggles are all over—that all the horizons have been explored—that all the battles have been won—that there is no longer an American frontier. But I trust no one in this vast assemblage will agree with those sentiments. For the problems are not all solved and the battles are not all won—and we stand today on the edge of a New Frontier—the frontier of the 1960s—a frontier of unknown opportunities and perils—a frontier of unfulfilled hopes and threats . . . I believe the times demand new invention, innovation, imagination, decisions. I am asking you to be pioneers on that New Frontier. (Kennedy, 1960)

THE DREAM DEFERRED AND DENIED

Unfortunately, the dream, in the words of poet Langston Hughes, had, for some, been a "dream deferred." Rev. Martin Luther King Jr., in his 1963 "I have a dream" speech, made it clear that the dream could no longer be deferred, as he referred to President Abraham Lincoln's signing of the Emancipation Proclamation "as a great beacon light of hope to millions of Negro slaves . . . a joyous breakthrough to end the long night of captivity." However, as King affirmed:

> But one hundred years later, we must face the tragic fact that the Negro is still not free. One hundred years later, the life of the Negro is still sadly crippled by the manacles of segregation and chains of discrimination . . . so we have come here today to dramatize an appalling condition. In a sense we have come to our nation's Capital to cash a check . . . we refuse to believe that the bank of justice is bankrupt. We refuse to

believe that there are insufficient funds in the great vaults of opportunity in this nation. (King, 1963)

Because America allegedly provides unlimited possibilities to advance and unprecedented opportunities to change, its failures and contradictions provoke considerable anger and disappointment. However, despite the contradictions, each year millions still choose to come to America in search of something better, something new, something hopeful. This country remains the crucible of change, improvement, and advancement.

EDUCATION AS THE EQUALIZER

To become successful in America requires hard work, perseverance, and determination. Nonetheless, in the United States one could advance and succeed, with American schools serving as the means to securing the American dream. In the words of Horace Mann (1842), "Individuals who, without the aid of knowledge, would have been condemned to perpetual inferiority of condition and subjected to all the evils of want and poverty, rise to competence and independence by the uplifting power of education" (p. 44).

In his Pedagogic Creed, published in 1897, John Dewey, America's most prominent philosopher and educator, stated:

I believe that education is the fundamental method for social progress and reform. I believe that all reforms which rest simply upon the enactment of law, or the threatening of certain penalties, or upon changes in mechanical or outwards arrangements are transitory and futile. (p. 129)

As progressive reformer Herbert Croly expressed in 1909:

The real vehicle of improvement is education. It is by education that the American is trained for such democracy as he possesses; and it is by better education that he proposes to better his democracy. Men are uplifted by education much more surely than they are by any tinkering with laws and institutions, because the work of education leavens the actual social substance. (p. 214)

AN UNFULFILLED MISSION

Americans have recognized the importance of a good education and have presumed that schools will do their job in providing that education. Ironically, despite the fact we expect much from our schools, we are often discouraged about the ability of public schools to serve as the route to success. This disappointment is not new.

One hundred years ago, Dewey (1899) pointedly said:

> Nothing would be more extraordinary if we had a proper system of education than the assumption, now so commonly made, that the mind of the individual is naturally adverse to learning, and has to be either browbeaten or coaxed into action. (p. 255)

More than twenty years ago, John Goodlad, in the very first sentence of his highly respected book *A Place Called School* (1984), stated in no uncertain terms, "American schools are in trouble. In fact, the problems of schooling are of such crippling proportions that many schools may not survive. It is possible that our entire public educational system is nearing collapse" (p. 1).

For Linda Darling-Hammond, things had not sufficiently changed as recently as 1997:

> Although the right to learn is more important than ever before in our history, schools that educate all of their students to high levels of intellectual, practical, and social competence continue to be, in every sense of the word, exceptional. Although many such schools have been invented throughout this nation's history, they have lived at the edge of the system, never becoming sufficiently widespread for most young people to have access to them. (Darling-Hammond, 1997b, p. 2)

THE CHALLENGE OF CHANGE

With each scathing review of American education comes a different attack on what schools currently do. Depending on the timing, the setting, the speaker, and the audience, the problem shifts. It could be poor test scores, inadequate preparation for college or the world of work, poor quality of teaching, or a general lack of public confidence in schools. Along with each outcry comes a demand for renewal, reform, restructuring, reinvention. Something must be done! All this implies change: moving schools from what they are to something better. But many individuals, including educators, do not believe something can be done. They are wrong.

Peter Senge, a leading advocate of learning organizations, tells the story of a session he conducted with educators, instead of businesspeople. He asked those present whether significant change occurs only as a result of crisis. In business groups, typically three quarters will respond affirmatively. This group of educators responded differently. Very few raised their hands. Puzzled, Senge went on to ask, "Does that mean you believe significant innovation can occur without crises?" No one raised a hand. Now exasperated, Senge asked, "Well, if change doesn't occur in response to a crisis and it doesn't occur in the absence of a crisis, what other possibilities are there?" A soft voice from the audience responded, "I guess we don't believe significant change can occur under any circumstances" (Senge, 2000, p. 33). The implications of Senge's anecdote are dramatic, but not shocking.

Consequently, there are two sets of critical issues for us to consider:

1. What do we mean by significant school change? How might we define it? How would we know when it has taken place?

2. What does it take to move a school from below par to acceptable and even exceptional levels of performance?

There is no doubt that the pace of progress and the speed of change in U.S. society is astounding. Our way of living has been dramatically transformed in nearly all arenas. The world is not the same. Yet many schools (and, some would contend, most schools) have not been sufficiently reactive, much less proactive.

In writing this book, which is based on seven years of extensive research, my assumption is that we can more effectively serve as facilitators and supporters of change if we can describe change, measure change, and explore change; look at schools that have dramatically improved; and use a conceptual framework to suggest what it takes to bring about significant school change.

THE PURPOSE OF THIS BOOK

This book looks at schools that have significantly changed for the better. Ironically, in a society that applauds change, many individuals believe these school success stories are the exception, not the rule. Despite reports that have complained about the United States being "a nation at risk" or initiatives that feel compelled to remind us that "no child should be left behind," many American schools just coast along, doing what they have always done. Despite studies that announce embarrassing comparisons of American students with their counterparts in other nations, too many American schools do not get better. It can be argued the vast majority of schools in America deny they have to change, do not know how to change, or are unsuccessful in their attempts to change.

This book draws from a eight-year national research project, which looked at data and documentation from 601 schools from forty-four states. Using sixteen criteria that measure significant school change, each of these schools was nominated for the National School Change Awards. Eight of the forty-eight award-winning schools (six per year for eight years) were selected for deep and rich portraits, multilayered stories complete with plots, actors, and themes.

Each of these portraits is about a school that once had been considered a failure or major disappointment. These are schools that had been rated in the bottom quartile (or worse) in terms of student achievement, quality of teaching, and parental approval. These are schools that had terrible reputations.

However, these are schools that brought themselves up by their bootstraps to become some of the best schools in their districts and states. These are schools that had symbolized much of what is wrong with American schools and transformed themselves to be models of what is right about American education. These are schools that demonstrate successful change efforts are within our reach.

THE PLAN OF THIS BOOK

This book is organized into six parts.

Part I is titled "The Dynamics of Change"; its three chapters provide a foundation and framework for the book. In Chapter 1, "Describing Change," we examine the *human phenomenon of change* and apply it to school change. We consider reasons why the exhilarating and exciting sense of change is frequently met with resistance. We look at how school change is sometimes threatening and why it is often difficult. We explore specific descriptions of change and consider how these influence our ability to change a school. For example, some contend change cannot be precisely predicted; it does not proceed in a logical and linear manner; it involves multiple factors, seemingly unrelated to each other. At the same time, change can attack our assumptions and disrupt our routines.

On the one hand, these change descriptions can be applied to life itself. On the other hand, they can help us to better appreciate the complexity and difficulty of changing schools. I believe we can better understand change through the lens of human dynamics. We may wish to change organizations, such as schools, but these entities are not inanimate objects; they are filled with people who have a full range of psychological, emotional, and physiological needs, and reactions. As James and Connolly (2000), in their book on school change, stated:

> We might like to think that we have at some time a period of stability but change carries on nonetheless. Change can be minor, low key and easily handled. It can however be substantial, very significant and imposed upon us, or we may initiate it and carry it through ourselves. (p. 16)

Chapter 2 addresses the issue of *how to measure change.* It explains how the National School Change Awards were created and provides the research base for the four domains used to identify and measure significant school change.

Each of the four domains addresses a fundamental question about school change. First, how meaningful is the change? Is it substantial rather than superficial? Second, how deep and broad is the change? Is it systemic rather than isolated? Third, how is the change focused? Is it student centered, looking at teaching and learning? And, fourth, how is it measured? Is it solution or outcome oriented?

Chapter 3 describes our effort at *exploring change* by looking at the research methodology used to conduct this deep study of eight of the school change award-winning schools. Although each of the eight schools was idiosyncratic, a number of common themes emerged, themes that led to my design of a comprehensive conceptual framework.

Part II, Chapters 4 through 7, contains the portraits of four elementary schools.

Government Hill Elementary School in Anchorage, Alaska, posed a unique set of challenges. For example, it's not every principal who has to go on moose patrol, checking the playground before the students have their recess. And it's not every principal whose school is slated for closing because of falling enrollment. Principal Sandy Stephens took on both challenges. A growing limited English proficiency population at Government Hill affected all classes, and teachers did not know how to adjust. By 1991, large numbers of students had transferred to other schools, and the school was down to 156 students; it was the end of Government Hill. However, in 2001, there were 475 students, and on registration day the cars with families who wanted to enroll their children stretched around the block. The school's achievement scores consistently rose to the city's top ten.

John Williams Elementary School No. 5, in Rochester, New York, is in the city's poorest and most dangerous neighborhood. The first thing that Michele Hancock did when she was appointed John Williams's new principal in June 1999 was to bring together her family, friends, and colleagues to paint the common areas of the uninviting elementary school. Michele's new message was that expectations should be high for the students in this urban high-poverty area and, with hard work, school improvement was possible. Over the next four years, the Grade 4 English language arts passing scores went from 13.3% to 63.2%, and the math scores rose from 30.7% to 78.8%. Science scores jumped 39 points, to 70%, and 83% of students passed the new social studies exam.

Skycrest Elementary School in Citrus Heights, California, was considered the worst elementary school in the San Juan School District. As one teacher put it, "I hated coming to work because the school was out of control and no one was doing anything about it." Deciding to take on the challenge, Chris Zarzana moved to Skycrest from leading a successful elementary school in the district. She first restored order. With her credibility established, the focus shifted to reading, reading, and reading. Over three years, the student population rose 20%, to 740 students; children living in poverty climbed from 52% to 82%; and the percentage of English language learners jumped 300%, to comprise one third of Skycrest students. Nonetheless, Skycrest students from this multicultural community secured gains of seven percentage points in reading and four percentage points in mathematics.

South Heights Elementary School is in Henderson, Kentucky, a rural area hundreds of miles from any professional hockey team. Nonetheless, principal Rob Carroll used the feature length film *Miracle* to show his students and staff that miracles could happen. The film tells the story of Herb Brooks, the untraditional hockey coach who announced to American Olympic officials he was going to create a hockey team that would beat the Soviet Union, the legendary powerhouse. Months of grueling practice built on rigorous discipline transformed the players; they became gold medal winners in 1980. The South Heights miracle was equally dramatic. In 1997, only 41% of South Height's fourth- and fifth-graders averaged a proficient score in reading, writing, mathematics, science, social studies, the arts and humanities, and practical living. In 2002, it was 66%.

Part III, Chapters 8 through 11, contains the portraits of the four secondary schools.

Gustav Fritsche Middle School in Milwaukee, Wisconsin, was led by Bill Andrekopoulos, a "troublemaker" who is now the superintendent of the Milwaukee Public Schools. As a middle school principal, Bill would constantly challenge the status quo with simple questions like "Why does it have to be this way?" Mr. A, as he is called, and his teachers dared the state of Wisconsin to designate Fritsche as a public charter school that would report directly to the state rather than to the district's bureaucracy. They got their wish. Bill used a participatory model, visits to exemplary middle schools, and data-driven decision making to involve the entire staff. By 2000, Fritsche's sixth-graders outperformed other district students by two times in writing and four times in mathematics.

George Washington Carver Academy in Waco, Texas, is literally down the road from President George W. Bush's ranch and retreat. Upon entering this one-story middle school, one steps on a large blue carpet that announces "Texas Blue Ribbon School of Excellence." But it was not always this way. Located in a neatly kept African American community, the school had a previous life as the district's only sixth-grade school. That effort to deal with a federal desegregation court order missed the mark on two counts: It did not lead (1) to racial integration or (2) to academic excellence. The district's strategy shifted, and Carver was converted in 1992 to a Grades 6–8 magnet school. Principal Molly Maloy assembled a staff that truly wanted to be at Carver. She asked the teachers to hire their new colleagues, create their own curriculum, and think through "what's good for kids." From 1994 to 2000, Carver students increased their reading scores by twenty-seven percentage points, mathematics by forty-seven percentage points, and writing by twenty-two percentage points. Furthermore, in the 1999–00 school year, 46% of the students were African American, 32% were Hispanic, and 21% were Anglo.

Louis W. Fox Academic and Technical High School in San Antonio, Texas, is only a mile away from the Alamo, where Texas freedom fighters refused to yield to the overpowering forces of General Santa Ana's Mexican troops. More than 150 years later, surrender to the forces of despair and defeat was not an option. Unfortunately, in 1985, Fox Tech had been defeated, declared by the Texas State Department of Education to be "disestablished." New principal Joanne Cockrell was firm as she told the reconfigured staff that she expected them to like kids and not watch the clock, because there was much work to be done. The large school was reorganized into four theme-based schools within a school; successful alumni were brought back to inspire the students; tutoring in reading was remarkably successful. Soon, many students were being prepared for the SATs because college admission had become their goal. Fox Tech lowered its dropout rate in seven years from 14.2% to 2.6%. Sophomore state mathematics results went from 22% passing to 92% passing. From the "worst high school in Texas," the school rose to national recognition by *Time* magazine in 2001.

Niles High School, in Niles, Michigan, is located in Michiana, an area hovering near the Michigan–Indiana state border. This comprehensive high school was neither a "knock your socks off" school nor a disaster. It just coasted along until dozens of alumni reported they had to drop out of college because they were ill prepared. Other graduates came back and complained that they could not get decent jobs. New principal Doug Law revitalized a school leadership team and created a climate for change. The critical question that drove the effort was "Why are we here?" The Niles High School team increased graduation requirements, created a strong (and nationally recognized) school-to-careers program, implemented block scheduling, developed approaches for ninth-graders to successfully transition to high school, and provided support for at-risk students.

Part IV, which includes Chapters 12 through 14, focuses on a conceptual framework I propose—three essential elements required for significant school change: context, capacity, and conversations. Part V, Chapters 15 through 17, continues to look at the conceptual framework. It describes three catalytic variables that influence the aforementioned elements, these being internal dissonance, external forces, and leadership.

Finally, in Part VI, I attempt to create meaning from the extensive data and the emerging themes. The question I raise is, what are the lessons we can learn?

PART I

The Dynamics
of Change

"Tell me, Mr. Mott: have you tried any experiments with any of our new educational systems? The modern kindergarten methods or the Gary system?"
"Oh. Those. Most of these would-be reformers are simply notoriety-seekers. . . . what these faddists advocate—heaven knows what they do want—knitting, I suppose, and classes in wiggling the ears!"

—Sinclair Lewis, *Main Street* (1920)

Life is full of challenges. And we measure ourselves and our success in life by how we meet those challenges . . . Challenge validates our aliveness and often disturbs the order of our lives.

—Barbara Jordan

An innate, searching curiosity about all around us—What do we not *know? How can we do it* differently? *How can we do it* better? *is at the heart of excellence. Then human progress and excellence comes when someone goes beyond "why" to "why not?"*

—John Glenn, U.S. senator, astronaut

This book is concerned with why some schools can significantly change, while most schools cannot or do not. To begin, we consider the human dynamics of change. In Chapter 1, I describe change, taking into account theoretical models and human reactions; look at the reluctance to embrace change and the resistance it can cause; and consider the implications of change being described as unpredictable, nonlinear, and chaotic. I discuss the importance of routines being disrupted, assumptions being attacked, and the emotional nature of change.

In Chapter 2, I present the criteria for measuring the degree to which a school has significantly changed. In Chapter 3, I present the conceptual framework developed through the study of eight schools that changed from unacceptable to exemplary.

Questions we might ask include the following:

- Why is change appealing, exciting, and motivating to some people and not to others?
- What is the significance of the following point of view? "People like change but don't like being changed."
- How might an understanding of the human elements and dynamics of the change process help a principal charged with the task of significantly changing a school?

1

Describing Change

A chapter called "Describing Change" is, by its very nature, an oxymoron. Change, whether personal or professional, large or small, local or global, is a concept that defies definition or description. Although change can be tangible and obvious when we hold a cell phone or iPod in our hands, it is also intangible and elusive when policies and practices are changed. Change involves emotions and often defies logic. It is complicated and complex, yet much of the time most of us, as individuals, manage to deal with it. Organizations, such as schools, are not so fortunate; few are able to significantly change. Consequently, we need a better appreciation of change, as it plays out in schools.

There is no question change can be rewarding, even joyous. Frequently we seek change and fight hard for it. We celebrate change. We mark achievements. We are in awe of progress. The eight school portraits in this book symbolize the beauty and essence of change: determination, passion, and triumph.

Change frequently feels daunting, however. It can be difficult, very difficult—at times it can seem virtually impossible. Change endeavors can involve the practical and political, the rational and emotional, the subtle and the obvious. The impact can be immediate or distant. The desires of some individuals may be anathema to others; what is viewed as progress may be seen as a setback. We all do not view or react to change the same way; change involves an individual endeavor and experience and can feel like a struggle, a battle.

Looking through the lens of human dynamics, in this chapter I review how change and the change process have been described, particularly in regard to schools; consider the range of reactions to change; and reflect on what this means, in general, for leaders who try to change schools and, in particular, what it meant for the principals of the eight schools described in this book.

As we explore each of these descriptions of change, you might consider the efforts to change (or not change) in your personal and professional lives. Consider, in particular, the attempts at change in schools you and your family have attended, schools you have worked in, and schools you have observed or heard about.

A RELUCTANCE TO CHANGE DIRECTIONS

Roland Barth is a noted educational reformer and a highly skilled sailor. His love of the sea and his ability to navigate choppy waters have compelled him to use sailing as a metaphor for school change. He tells of a transmission of a U.S. Navy radio conversation:

Transmission:	Please divert your course fifteen degrees north to avoid a collision.
Response:	Recommend that you divert your course fifteen degrees south to avoid a collision.
Transmission:	This is the captain of a U.S. Naval ship. I say again, divert your course.
Response:	No, I say again, divert *your* course.
Transmission:	This is the aircraft carrier Enterprise. We are a large warship of the U.S. Navy. Divert your course now!
Response:	This is a lighthouse. Your call. (Barth, 2001, p. xxiv)

Reprinted with permission of John Wiley & Sons, Inc.

Changing direction is not easy, especially for warships—and schools. Ogden and Germinaro (1995) believed we can understand the reasons for this reluctance to change by looking at the "essence" of a school, its underlying values and beliefs and how they are translated into practice. They looked at how schools define what they do, make decisions, and respond to parents and the community as well as how instruction is delivered, accountability is defined, and principals do their jobs. In their view, American schools can be classified in one of three categories: (1) conventional, (2) congenial, or (3) collegial.

Conventional schools were characterized by teacher autonomy and isolation, very little conversation among staff, and a feeling research and professional development are unnecessary. "These are schools that have no common goals, no collective sense of what they are trying to accomplish as a whole, as a school" (Ogden & Germinaro, 1995, p. 4). The principal served as a manager, keeping things moving along: Supplies were delivered, parent complaints were handled, discipline was maintained. Teacher evaluation was considered to be an intrusion, an unfortunate bureaucratic requirement, and a waste of time.

Positive assessments of conventional schools were generated by what was *not* happening—no major complaints or crises, no disruptions or violence, no staff grievances. If standardized test scores were low, it was because of the problems students brought to school. It was inevitable that some students would fail. In the eyes of the school, "a good year is one in which there have been few calls for change" (Ogden & Germinaro, 1995, p. 5). In conventional schools, administrators and teachers did not look at what they were doing or for a moment consider they could change direction.

The second category of schools was labeled *congenial*. They were very similar to the conventional schools, except the teacher isolation had broken down. These teachers did talk to each other; however, the conversations were about social activities (e.g., When are we having the staff holiday party?), not about student progress, teaching methods, or school success. The focus was on the adults, improving the school climate, and relieving their stress. The overriding concern was having a school where people were happy. There was little, if any, thought given to changing direction.

The third category was the *collegial* schools (also called *effective* or *professional* or *student outcome-based* schools). In these schools, "satisfaction is derived from professional work accomplished together and from the achievement of students" (Ogden & Germinaro, 1995, p. 7). In these schools, the principal served as an instructional leader, making sure everyone understood the message that all students could achieve. Conversations about students, teaching, new ideas, and vision were encouraged and valued. The staff welcomed research findings and found great merit in professional development. Time was provided to ask the hard questions, research and reassess, and take risks. These collegial schools constantly raised the bar for all students and staff. They believed data frequently had to be collected, disaggregated, and analyzed so continuous improvement could take place. The collegial schools were committed to changing direction.

Unfortunately, in the view of Ogden and Germinaro (1995), the vast majority of schools were conventional or congenial. Few were collaborative. Few had a commitment to change.

INEVITABLE RESISTANCE

American colonists in the 1770s were divided into three almost equal-sized groups. About one third was firmly committed to remaining British colonists, loyal servants of the king. In light of their political, economic, and social status, it was in their interests to maintain the status quo.

On the other end of the spectrum were the revolutionaries, who desperately wanted freedom from England. They were determined to do what it took to win independence. They would not be deterred. In the middle stood a third group, whose members were not sure which side to join. This metaphor speaks to the range of responses to proposed change: refusal to change direction, reluctance to change direction (To which side do I turn? What's in it for me?), and a passion to bring about the change.

The same range of responses will exist in organizations, like schools, that are initiating change or responding to change. It is important to recognize and respect these different perspectives and responses. Principals who wish to be effective facilitators of change need to think carefully how to handle these reactions. For example: What is motivating the resisters? How can we gather more information about this resistance? Once we know more, what do we do? As for the change proponents, how do we reward and support them so we can keep them in our camp? Perhaps the most critical group is the middle group, intrigued by the change but reluctant to commit. Here we need to ask: How can we show them the proposed change is in their interests? What frightens them? What can we do to overcome their wariness?

The big question I address in this book, and critical to my research, is: Why do people firmly stay on their usual course, ignoring warnings (or incentives) to do otherwise? Whether it is personal change or organizational change, why do people resist? Reich (2000) wrote about resisters in the corporate world, but these reactions to proposed change will be familiar to educators. In both the worlds of business and education, change involves moving people to a new place, and often they don't want to go there. The excuses many people use include "That seems risky . . . let's go back to basics . . . it worked before . . . we're just fine the way we are . . . there will be unforeseen consequences" (Reich, 2000, p. 150).

Seymour Sarason (2002), in looking at educational reform, wrote that "resistance to change is as predictable as death and taxes" (p. 30). Therefore, as students of change, we must recognize and understand the many possible forms of resistance, how subtle resistance can be, and the depth it can reach. More disturbing for Sarason (2002) is that he has "never known an instance, or heard about one, where the new reformers *seriously and sincerely* sought to elicit the diagnoses of those who are now being asked to change their thinking and actions" (p. 31).

Conner (1995) outlined the main reasons for resisting change by noting that the initiation of change will be both rational and irrational, and the responses to it likewise will be rational and irrational. People do not trust impending change or those who would initiate such change; they believe change is unnecessary or not feasible; they resent interference. There is fear of failure and threats to values and ideals. People are being asked to leave their comfort zones, and naturally they will resist.

What Kotter (1996) found amazing is how change facilitators and managers do not take the time to think about who might resist change and why. In his view, organizational change will inevitably run into some form of human resistance, which will sometimes go underground and emerge again at a strategic time. Consequently, it is essential to understand the range of reactions to change, sometimes obvious, sometimes subtle, that may emerge. The problem is that leaders have not been prepared for transformational challenges (Kotter, 1996).

Nonetheless, resistance to change is not automatic. In fact, the onset of change can produce a variety of responses. As Tyack and Cuban (1995) put it,

"Educators have variously welcomed, improved, deflected, co-opted, modified, and sabotaged outside efforts at reform" (p. 7). Furthermore, when there is resistance, not all of it is uncalled for, irrational, or bad. It may be needed. "Resistance to change is sometimes dismissed as the result of popular ignorance or institutional inertia, but that oversimplifies. Often teachers have had well-founded reasons for resisting change, as have parents" (Tyack & Cuban, 1995, p. 7).

CHANGE IS UNPREDICTABLE

In August 2005, nature's fury and man's folly fused together as Hurricane Katrina uprooted the lives of hundreds of thousands. Packing the energy of a ten-megaton nuclear bomb, exploding every ten minutes, the hurricane devastated the Gulf region, leaving in its wake physical destruction and loss of life not experienced in the United States for more than a century (Thomas, 2005). The days leading up to the hurricane, the storm itself, and the aftermath provided insights about the unpredictable nature of change.

Tropical storms, including hurricanes, have been forecasted for decades in terms of when they will occur, where they will strike, and their anticipated force. We have sophisticated software models, satellites beaming critical information, and complex mathematical formulas. With all our technology, human error is supposed to be virtually eliminated. Hurricane Katrina's approach was being tracked, with initial predictions that the storm would slam directly into the historic city of New Orleans. Then, the predictions were changed; New Orleans would be spared. Finally, both predictions proved wrong. The hurricane did not frontally smash into New Orleans; however, it did take a furious swipe at the city, causing damage and loss of life that defied expectations and explanations.

Life defies predictability. Whether a monstrous act of nature, a terrible family tragedy, or a sweeping and drastic change in an organization, no one knows for sure how things will unfold.

Loss of life is certainly far different than changes in routines or attacks on assumptions, yet we cannot escape the unpredictability of our daily lives. In reflecting on school change, Fullan (1993) noted that "Complexity, dynamism, and unpredictability, in other words, are not merely things that get in the way. They are normal!" (p. 20).

The professional lives of educators are, for the most part, predicated on predictability. The students arrive in September (or late August) and depart with the onset of summer. Classroom activities in elementary schools are centered on the seasons and holidays, with Halloween, Thanksgiving, Christmas, Valentine's Day, Easter, and Memorial Day serving as reliable markers. Routines and rules for students are assumed and expected. The school day begins and ends at the prescribed times. Unlike most other professionals who control their schedules, such as doctors, lawyers, and scientists, teachers typically report to the same location, at the same time of the day, teaching in the same ways. Consequently, changes in schools that deviate from that predictability are hard to acknowledge, accept, or appreciate.

THE NONLINEAR NATURE OF
THE CHANGE PROCESS

Perhaps one of the most ambitious initiatives of the 1990s was Bill and Hillary Clinton's effort to radically change health care in America. Although the former President and his wife understood that the reform would not be easy to achieve, they counted on a rational and logical sequence of steps: Dramatize the need, bring together experts to suggest solutions, develop a plan, build favorable and supportive public opinion, and have the new plan adopted. The health care reformers, led by the Clintons, did not realize how differently people would feel about the need, how resistant opponents would be, or how hard it would be to develop a consensus. Their campaign took one step forward and two steps back. It was sideswiped, detoured, and had to shift gears. As logical as it seemed to be to provide health care to Americans who could not afford it, their attempt to change the health care system failed in 1994.

As Hillary Clinton, chairwoman of the President's Task Force on National Health Care Reform, looked back, she noted,

> Our goals were simple enough. We wanted a plan that dealt with all aspects of the health care system rather than one that tinkered on the margins. We wanted a process that considered a variety of ideas and allowed for healthy discussion and debate . . . Almost immediately, we hit turbulence. (H. Clinton, 2003, p. 153)

Clinton remembers being advised that the proposed reform was massive and would take at least five years. She was urged to learn from the efforts of previous presidents who had advocated health care reform, such as Harry Truman, Lyndon Johnson, Richard Nixon, and Jimmy Carter. Furthermore, she later realized that personal passion and enthusiasm for change were not enough.

We can learn many lessons about the nonlinear nature of change from this case study. First, some people may oppose a proposed change because they believe the change contradicts their value system. In this case, many conservatives felt the proposed health care plan would give too much control to the government and cost too much. Second, public support for an idea can become derailed. When it became known that increased costs for health care would impact most families, public support (once quite strong) evaporated. Third, required partners might have competing interests. In this case, members of Congress were dependent on major campaign funding from the private health care industry, and most legislators could not risk cutting those ties. Fourth, opponents to a proposed change can launch a powerful fight against it. In this case, lobbyists and special interest groups opposed to a national health care program used multiple strategies, including designing effective advertising, conducting massive mailings, forming coalitions, and applying pressure everywhere (Laham, 1998). Fifth, individual self-centered interests can overshadow a plan to help others; the fundamental question becomes "What's in it for me?" Neither members of Congress nor the majority of Americans were willing to set aside their own interests to support health care for the minority of Americans. As Dougherty (1996) put it, "The failed attempt at reform by the Clinton administration is the long-standing and significant mismatch between the value aspirations of most Americans for universal coverage combined with a reluctance to accept the tax increase necessary to pay for it" (p. 10). Finally, initiating and implementing a change requires a careful look at how others might react. In this case, that was not done. Change did not move ahead, logically, step by step.

Change has traditionally been interpreted as a rational, linear, and neat process. Starting in the late 1980s and 1990s, researchers and practitioners challenged that view. Adams (1991) offered a distinction between *rational* and *interactive* models by calling the former "basically sequential, observable, and capable of being evaluated[, while] interactive models, on the other hand, reflect an emphasis on the human dynamics of decision making" (p. 8).

In effect, the linear model fails to consider what is important to the "players" in a change process: how they interpret what is happening, how they react to that process, and what they will do to support or oppose the changes being proposed or implemented. As Hamilton (1991) put it, "If it is people who give an organization meaning and if it's people who actually do the planning, then it is people, not abstract models, who need to be understood through planning actions" (p. 43).

Burke (2002) pointed out that change leaders will frequently plan change as if it were a linear process, with one neat step following another, only to discover that neither planning nor implementation is linear, neat, smooth, or rational:

> The implementation process is messy: Things don't proceed exactly as planned; people do things their own way, not always according to plan; some people resist or even sabotage the process; and some people who would have been predicted to support or resist the plan actually behave in the opposite way. In short, unanticipated consequences occur. (p. 2)

As Tyack and Cuban (1995) pointed out, "Reformers who adopt a rational planning mode of educational reform sometimes expect that they will improve schools if they design their policies correctly" (p. 83). It's not that simple. We never start completely from scratch; we never leave everything behind; we never move in neat and precise steps:

> Innovations never enter educational institutions with the previous slate wiped clean . . . Rational planners may have plans for schools, and may blame practitioners if they think that the plans are not properly implemented, but schools are not wax to be imprinted. (Tyack & Cuban, 1995, p. 83)

CHAOS THEORY

Chaos theory is an attempt to make sense of what doesn't seem to make sense. When Burke (2002) talks about chaos theory, he reminds us "even though not apparent when in the midst of change, patterns do exist" (p. 288).

In the mid-1990s, dire predictions were being made about crime, especially with regard to teenage crime, which was expected to rise by as much as 100% over the following decade. "The smart money was on the criminals" (Levitt & Dubner, 2005, p. 4). However, these forecasts were very wrong. Instead of crime going up, it dramatically and persistently fell and continued to fall in every crime category, in every section of the United States. For example, between 1995 and 2000, teenage crime did not rise by 100% as predicted; it fell by 50%!

Criminologists, sociologists, politicians, and the public wanted to know why. A set of logical theories was suggested. The decline was due to a robust economy, the proliferation of gun control laws, more sophisticated policing strategies. However, Levitt and Dubner (2005) contended that the cause of the crime decrease took shape twenty years earlier and involved a young woman in Dallas, Texas, named Norma McCorvey: "Like the proverbial butterfly that flaps his wings on one continent and eventually causes a hurricane on another, Norma McCorvey dramatically altered the course of events without intending to. All she wanted was an abortion" (p. 5).

McCorvey was 21, poor, uneducated, unskilled, and addicted to drugs and alcohol. She had already put two children up for adoption, and abortion was illegal in Texas. Advocates seeking the legalization of abortion adopted McCorvey and made her the lead plaintiff in a class-action lawsuit. McCorvey became Jane Roe, whose legal rights were contested by Henry Wade, the Dallas County district attorney. Ultimately, the *Roe v. Wade* case reached the U.S. Supreme Court which, on January 22, 1973, ruled in favor of McCorvey.

What did this have to do with the dramatic decrease in crime? Decades of studies had shown that "a child born into an adverse family environment is far more likely than other children to become a criminal" (Levitt & Dubner, 2005, p. 6). Levitt and Dubner (2005) contended that "because of *Roe vs. Wade* these children *weren't* being born. This powerful cause would have dramatic, distant effect years later; just as these unborn children would have entered their criminal primes, the rate of crime began to plummet" (p. 6). One change (legalization of abortion), on its surface, seemed to have nothing to do with the other (decrease in crime).

Similarly, supposedly random phenomena in the school world can converge and cause unexpected and unwanted results. For example, a decision to end social promotion for eighth-graders and instead prevent them from entering the ninth grade has several unanticipated consequences. Under the *No Child Left Behind (NLCB)* federal legislation, the school loses funding, which further impairs the school's ability to serve students with weak skills. By including the eighth-grade students who have been held back, the size of eighth-grade classes increases the following year. This same social promotion decision leads to tracking and lowered expectations for the students who did not advance to the next grade. Behavior problems in the school increase, time is diverted from instruction, and teacher morale plummets. Academic performance gets worse, not better.

In response to the concept of chaos theory, Senge (2006) advanced the concept of *systems thinking*, which suggests that we should view things not as snapshots (e.g., a decline in student attendance) but instead as a system, which takes into account actions taken at different places and times (e.g., state policy changes the way school attendance is calculated; an economic recession keeps students at home, taking care of siblings; dangerous schools discourage attendance, etc.).

CHANGE DISRUPTS OUR ROUTINES

What if you were told that if you did not change, you would die? Ninety percent of the individuals who received that "change or die" warning *did not change* (Deutschman, 2005). According to research completed by physicians, psychologists, and neuroscientists, when patients received their instructions after bypass surgery, almost all of them did not follow the prescribed advice. They did not change their diet, begin to exercise, or return for regular checkups. A large number of these patients suffered a heart attack, and some did die. Why didn't these vulnerable individuals change? In the words of Dr. Edward Miller, dean of the medical school at Johns Hopkins University, "Even though they know they have a very bad disease and they know they should change their lifestyle, for whatever reason, they can't" (Deutschman, 2005, p. 52). Even though their habits were literally and figuratively deadly, these individuals resisted the disruption to their routines.

As mentioned previously, the nature of schools in America is quite predictable because the routines have been set in place for years, perhaps decades, for both teachers and students. In Sizer's (1984) words,

> the basic organizing structures are familiar. Above all, students are grouped by age (that is freshman, sophomore, junior, senior), and are all expected to take precisely the same time—around 720 school days over four years, to be precise—to meet the requirements for a diploma. (p. 78)

These are not new routines for American high schools; one can find them in "The Seven Cardinal Principles of Secondary Education," promulgated in 1918 by the National Education Association (Raubinger, Rowe, Piper, & West, 1969). Disrupting those routines has not been impossible; neither has it been easy.

Barth (1990) lamented about the routine nature of education:

> For most [school staff] there is little to do this September except what they did last September—more of the same. Same books, same room,

same colleagues, same curriculum. Only pupils are different from one year to the next. But the burden for the professional health of adults in schools should not rest with the students. (Barth, 1990, p. 12)

CHANGE CHALLENGES OUR ASSUMPTIONS

The *Concise Oxford American Dictionary* (2006) defines the noun *assumption* as "a thing that is accepted as true or as certain to happen, without proof" (p. 48). The *American Heritage Dictionary of the English Language* (2006) defines it as "the act of taking for granted . . . *the assumption of a false thing*." Moreover, the dictionary adds "presumption; arrogance" (p. 110). In a study of change, we must pay special attention to assumptions, because they drive what we do, whether or not they are "true."

The following are two examples. In the late 1400s, Christopher Columbus had a hard time convincing people the world was round, not flat. Columbus argued he could sail east and not fall off the edge of the world. He challenged the existing assumptions about the shape of the earth and travel routes. He was right. Christopher Columbus literally and figuratively opened new worlds.

Five hundred and fifteen years after Columbus won his argument in 1492 that the world is round, Thomas Friedman (2005) challenged our assumptions about how work is completed because he contends (metaphorically) that "the world is flat." For example, we assume that our accountant in New York or Los Angeles is calculating our tax returns, but that is not true, because a worker in India is doing the grunt work. Or we expect CAT scans completed in American hospitals to be interpreted and diagnosed by radiologists at these hospitals; however, radiologists in Australia are interpreting them.

Friedman (2005) made the case that the world is flat, and he wants us to let go of the ways we have traditionally seen things. From Friedman's perspective, the twenty-first century world is flat because communication between any two (or more) parts of the world can be accomplished in seconds, via new networks. A level playing field opens opportunities in ways never imagined before; knowledge no longer stays within narrow domains but can be accessed with ease and speed. Friedman contends that

> it is now possible for more people than ever to collaborate and compete in real time with more other people on more different kinds of work from more different corners of the planet and on a more equal footing than at any previous time in the history of the world—using computers, e-mail, networks, teleconferencing, and dynamic new software. (p. 8)

The world is round; the world is flat. Are we being forced to dramatically change our assumptions, our perceptions, beliefs, and attitudes? Yes. Will this be easy? No. Are educational decisions and practices based on assumptions? Absolutely.

The New York Times headline read, "Stressed. Scared. Nauseous. Sick." These sound like the reactions of educators to proposed change. Instead, these are words used by nine- and ten-year-olds to describe how they felt about an impending fourth-grade reading test. To allay their fears, social workers at their public school in Brooklyn introduced the students to the "Test Monster," an art exercise designed to enable these students to express and manage their fears. The students knew much was at stake because this examination, spurred on by the *NCLB* federal legislation, would determine whether they would be promoted from the third grade to the fourth grade and whether their school would be labeled as failing (Herszenhorn, 2006, p. B1).

Consider the educational assumptions revealed by this anecdote.

- First assumption: Teachers would commit to guaranteeing "no child would be left behind" only if there were serious sanctions for their schools, such as a loss in federal funding.
- Second assumption: Student achievement could best be measured by performance on state-designed tests.
- Third assumption: Children could (and should) be prepared for high-stakes tests by reducing their anxiety level.
- Fourth assumption: Requiring students to repeat a grade will enable those students to bolster their academic skills.

In looking at assumptions, what are the implications for change facilitators? It doesn't matter whether assumptions are believed to be well founded, based on experience, or data driven. It often does not matter if certain assumptions are outdated. What does matter is that assumptions drive what we do. As Wagner and his research team noted, "It is not easy to call into question and alter the assumptions we have taken as truths . . . Habits of mind can be as intractable as habits of behavior" (Wagner et al., 2006, p. 167).

In terms of change efforts, consider the impact of attacks on assumptions. For example, if a large number of teachers believe academic achievement can best (and perhaps only) be measured by mandated testing, then "teaching to the test" will probably be central to their instructional practices. For the veteran teachers, this assumption may have driven what they did and how they did it for many years. However, a new school reform program could declare that teaching to the test is "wrong." Instead, the teachers could be urged or required to teach differently, focusing on constructivism, inquiry, and student projects. Telling these teachers their assumptions are wrong will be experienced as a threatening, even devastating, attack. We need to understand that possible reaction and be prepared to deal with it.

CHANGE IS STRESSFUL

On the face of it, Robert Sapolsky, an anthropologist and biologist, who won one of the MacArthur "Genius" awards, has nothing in common with Spencer Johnson, a physician who became a popular author with *Who Moved My Cheese?* (1998). Johnson's parable, translated into 25 languages, has sold more than 3 million copies and has been used in hundreds of workshops that focus on change. Sapolsky's (2004) informal biology text, *Why Zebras Don't Get Ulcers*, on the other hand, is a mainstay among academics and popular with the general public. However, the two authors are joined by a fascination with rodents (real and imagined) and reactions to change.

Sapolsky (2004) looked at the physiological consequences of stress and described the dilemma of zebras. He asked us to think like a zebra as he pointed out,

> For animals like zebras, the most upsetting things in life are *acute physical* crises. You are that zebra, a lion has just leapt out and ripped your stomach open, you've managed to get away, and now you have to spend the next hour evading the lion as it continues to stalk you. (p. 4)

You, to say the least, are quite stressed.

Using numerous studies of rats, Sapolsky (2004) contended that the second cause of stress is *chronic physical challenges,* and the third way to get upset, most germane to this book, are *psychological and social* disruptions. Unlike rats and zebras, social primates such as baboons and humans do not need physical dangers to cause stress. We can imagine it. We can "experience wildly strong emotions (provoking our bodies into an accompanying uproar) linked to mere thoughts" (Sapolsky, 2004, p. 5).

Johnson (1998), recognizing how change produces stress, used the metaphor of two mice and two "littlepeople" and their experiences in a maze. In this case, there is a disruption to feeding patterns: The cheese disappeared; it had been moved. Sniff and Scurry, the two mice, quickly moved on to find out where the cheese was, but the "littlepeople," Hem and Haw, were flabbergasted. As Johnson (1998) described it, "No one had warned them. It wasn't right. It was not the way things were supposed to be" (p. 35). Hem and Haw were immobilized, angry, frustrated, and in a state of denial. They blamed each other for their troubles and finally realized "We keep doing the same things over and over again and wonder why things don't get better" (p. 43). These two littlepeople were seriously stressed and had much difficulty embracing change.

Understanding that change can be very stressful is important for leaders of school change. As Hall and Hord (2006) pointed out,

> Although everyone wants to talk about such broad concepts as policy, systems, and organizational factors, successful change starts and ends at the individual level. An entire organization does not change until each member has changed. Another way to say this is that there is an individual aspect to organizational change. (p. 7)

Evans (1996) was concerned with the "human side of school change" and, as such, he addressed the issue of stress. He used a medical metaphor to make his points about pressure, stress, and the ability to adjust and cope. Treatment of a medical symptom will be affected by the person's overall health, including that individual's ability to handle the additional stress that comes with the cure itself. Furthermore,

American schools, trapped between rising demands and limited resources, have become textbook cases of stress . . . In everyday speech we refer to stress almost as a kind of infection that we can catch. To medical researchers, stress is internal, the reaction within an organism when the demands of the external environments tax its ability to cope. (Evans, 1996, p. 130)

In the early 1990s, Day and his colleagues used case studies of twelve schools in England to discover the roles of headteachers (i.e., principals) in implementing change (Day et al., 2000). They considered how these school leaders affected change and how the change effort affected them. These headteachers worked very hard and had to cope with high levels of stress. Although these leaders handled the stress in different ways, such as going to the gym, relying on family, pursuing an active social life outside of work, and becoming active in union activities, "stress was a constant feature of their work" (Day et al., 2000, p. 71).

THE EMOTIONAL ARENA

It is clear that we enter the emotional arena when we deal with change, as either the initiators of that change and, even more so, when we are impacted by the change. As Kotter (1996) pointed out, all of us experience some turmoil. Even when the change appears to be rational or positive, change involves loss and uncertainty. Resistance is virtually inevitable for one (or more) of these reasons: "A desire not to lose something of value, a misunderstanding of the change and its implications, a belief that the change does not make sense for the organization, and low tolerance for change" (Kotter, 1996, p. 31).

For example, when Mayor Michael Bloomberg took control of the New York City school system in 2001, all four forms of Kotter's (1996) theory of resistance were quite evident. Thirty-two community school district school boards were upset because they perceived (correctly) they would *lose power*. Thirty-two community school district superintendents *misunderstood* why the mayor, and his new chancellor, Joel Klein, reorganized the system into ten regions for the purpose of implementing more direct accountability. Central office bureaucrats, desperate to keep their jobs during a far-reaching organizational shakeup, tried to justify their positions, claiming that the *changes did not make sense*. Finally, teachers who were required to adopt one standard literacy curriculum had *low tolerance* for this prescribed shift in teaching methods. Previously, teachers were free to teach as they saw fit and they did not have to "march to the beat of the same drummer." Officials in the newly named Department of Education knew resistance was inevitable, but they had underestimated the fears it would generate.

Fears take many different forms. "Will I be able to handle this?" is a frightening, but not uncommon, question. With both personal and professional changes, new attitudes, skills, and behaviors will be required. At the same time, all of us have limits, and some may find the new requirements overwhelming. In the worst-case scenario, the changes simply may demand too much, too quickly (Kotter, 1999).

There is also fear of the unknown. In Zimbalist's (2005) words, "Many teachers who have developed personal styles and curriculum bases feel comfortable where they are. Perhaps fear of the unknown feeds their reluctance to embrace a new direction" (p. 115).

James and Connolly (2000) conducted a study of 32 schools in South Wales in the late 1990s and looked at the "reactions, the successes and failures and the accounts of those involved in bringing about change" (p. 14). They concluded that

> Change is complex because it is inextricably linked to our emotions. Imposed change [in particular] can call up a whole range of emotions: anger at the imposition and the denial of personal autonomy, sorrow at the sense of loss of the old, and anxiety at the uncertainties that the new will bring. (James & Connolly, 2000, p. 17)

Goleman (1995) wrote that "I take *emotion* to refer to a feeling and its distinctive thoughts, psychological and biological states, and a range of propensities to act" (pp. 289–290). Entering the emotional arena does not mean only difficulty, pain, and suffering. Psychologists point to both "positive" emotions (e.g., joy) and "negative" emotions (e.g., anger). Both types will be generated by substantial change.

Brooke-Smith (2003) felt that the literature about change has ignored or downplayed the role of anxiety, which she felt is at the heart of the change process. In her view, anxiety can at times work as an asset in the change process. Leaders, to create a felt need for change, may welcome a certain level of anxiety in the organization.

> On the other hand, anxiety, if unrecognized, unappreciated, or misunderstood could rise to "out of control" levels. Too much anxiety will be experienced as a significant threat; the existing system may become dysfunctional and unstable; and oppositional political activity may be created. The change endeavor will become derailed. (Brooke-Smith, 2003, p. 106)

In effect, if change generates anger, fear, sorrow, or loss, it becomes painful. Perhaps it has to be that way. Sizer (1991) contended that meaningful change in schools is, by necessity, painful: "To get the needed gains for kids, we adults must expect and endure the pain that comes with ambitious rethinking and redesign of schools. To pretend that serious restructuring can be done without honest confrontation is to create an illusion" (p. 34).

SO MUCH TO DO, SO LITTLE TIME

Bringing about school change has been described as trying to change a flat tire when the car is in motion. From 1995 to 1998, Hargreaves, Earl, Moore, and Manning (2001) looked at twenty-nine teachers in Toronto, Ontario, Canada, who were implementing integrated curriculum reform in their seventh- and eighth-grade classes. They wanted to know how these teachers were adjusting to a mandated curriculum policy. Were they able to accept and apply the changes to their daily practice? What conditions and support were needed for them to be able to do so? Was there a preferred process for bringing about these changes? One of their most important findings relates to the changing-tire analogy:

> The teachers we studied were not just trying to implement single innovations, one at a time. They were facing multiple and multifaceted changes to their practice . . . moreover, this set of changes could not be addressed in isolation from other aspects of their work in their schools. (Hargreaves et al., 2001, p. 23)

Linda Darling-Hammond (1997b) described the problem in another way:

> It might be said that Americans are always fixing their schools. Each decade another set of fads emerges (often recycled ideas with new names) . . . Schools are usually asked to adopt these fads as single ideas laid on top of old structures. Such ideas are poorly assimilated and quickly rejected. Schools chew up and spit out undigested reforms on a regular basis. This creates a sense within schools, that whatever the innovation, "this too shall pass"—and that it probably should. (p. 22)

Consider what we have discussed in this chapter. Schools are asked to continue functioning; schools are asked to change. Teachers are counted on to do their jobs; teachers are encouraged or required to reconsider what they do. Principals are asked to be managers, maintaining the status quo and making sure all runs smoothly; principals must look beyond the status quo in an effort to initiate, implement, and sustain change.

Change brings good things; change is resisted. Organizational and institutional change is a logical, step-by-step process; change is irrational and nonlinear. Precise things are forecasted; change, by its nature, is unpredictable. Change is presumed to be a fresh start; we bring our past to the present. Change is neat; change is messy.

We celebrate change; we fear it. Change produces joy; change produces anxiety. Change is easy; change is difficult. Change is contradictory. Our actions are grounded in our fundamental assumptions and our familiar routines; however, impending change may attack those assumptions and disrupt those routines. What we believe in may be challenged.

Although Niccolo Machiavelli (1910/1992) is often cast as a cynical political advisor, he is also viewed as an astute student of human nature, with insights that 16th-century rulers found useful. Writing about change, Machiavelli noted, "It must be considered that there is nothing more difficult to carry out, nor more doubtful of success, nor more dangerous to handle, than to initiate a new order of things" (p. 13).

2

Measuring Change

Filmmakers have generally not been kind to American schools. The 1950s classic *Blackboard Jungle* warns about the dangers of juvenile delinquency as it shows students out of control, overwhelming their teachers. Frederick Wiseman, in his award-winning 1960s documentary *High School*, portrayed a school that is centered on the adults and the status quo, not on the students and their growth and development. *Dead Poets Society* stars Robin Williams as John Keating, an inspirational English teacher scorned by his colleagues because they are threatened by his mission to have students think for themselves.

Teachers, starring Judd Hirsch as an ineffective and self-centered high school assistant principal, gives us an unforgettable cast of characters: the school psychologist who packs a pistol; the social studies teacher who decides to teach radiator repair; the teacher who falls asleep behind his newspaper while his students routinely complete worksheets; the alumnus, now an attorney representing a graduate who contends he learned nothing in the school.

Even when a teacher is portrayed as dedicated and competent, like Jaime Escalante in *Stand and Deliver*, he has to fight a culture of low expectations and no accountability. Escalante's students go from basic math to calculus, despite school administrators who insist the students' poor background cannot be overcome.

Some common themes emerge from these films. They depict schools in trouble, schools where the dedicated few have to fight against the tide, schools that are rudderless. These are failing schools. These are schools that desperately need to radically improve, to significantly change. These are schools that need more than quick fixes and cosmetic changes. These are schools whose values, beliefs, and practices have to dramatically change.

Assume a serious effort is made to significantly change one of these failing schools. Several questions become quite important. How would we know whether significant change has taken place? Are there specific measurements and benchmarks that can tell us the degree to which the school has changed? Will identifying the degree to which change has taken place help us understand what assists or impedes significant school change?

CREATING THE NATIONAL SCHOOL CHANGE AWARDS

Fullan (2001) contended that school and school system change is *not* rational, seamless, and linear. Second, as Fullan (2001) is frequently quoted, "Change is a process, not an event." It is a messy and unpredictable process. It is a journey, which often goes astray, takes a backward spin, or experiences natural ups and downs. Therefore, to move a school from Point A (where it is) to Point B (where it wants to go) is an incredible endeavor, especially if the change is substantial (rather than superficial), is sustained, and has meaning.

As Figure 2.1 depicts, when we look at school change, there are three things on which to focus: (1) Point A, (2) Point B, and (3) the journey to go from Point A to Point B. This task seems simple, but it is not. It is essential that we appreciate and understand the three parts of a successful change story: where we are, where we want to go, and how we will get there. Otherwise, in my opinion, significant change will not unfold.

POINT A

Every school in America is at Point A, which represents where the school is right now. Some schools may be in a good place in terms of the quality of teaching and learning, student achievement, and the development of the whole

Figure 2.1   An overview of the school change process

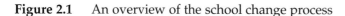

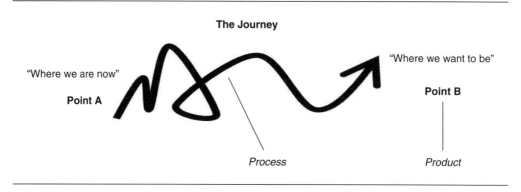

child. These schools may be fine in the eyes of parents and the community at large. These schools might be considered good, but is that enough? They could be great schools. However, a sense of comfort and complacency has stalled that, *good is the enemy of great.*" leap forward. In fact, Collins (2001) argued that "good is the enemy of great." After completing a five-year detailed analysis of corporations, Collins noted:

> That good is the enemy of great is not just a business problem. It is a *human* problem. If we have cracked the code on the question of good to great, we should have something of value to any type of organization. Good schools might become great schools. Good newspapers might become great newspapers. Good churches might become great churches. Good government agencies might become great agencies. And good companies might become great companies. (p. 14)

This book, however, is not about good schools. In the sections that follow I present portraits of schools that were considered very far below the designation of *good*. These schools were failures. In the business world, these would be stories of corporations that went bankrupt and went out of business. These schools were bankrupt, and it can be argued they should have gone out of business.

In looking at Point A, we need to consider five things about the school. The first and foremost is *instruction*: how teachers are teaching and how students are learning, the methods and materials being used, how students are engaged, and so on. The second concern is *organization*, meaning how the school uses its resources, such as personnel, time, funding, and space. The third concern is *governance*, which includes studying how decisions are made, how leaders conduct themselves, and how power is distributed. The fourth concern is *accountability*: How does the school define and measure its success? Finally, we need to understand the *culture* of the school, the underlying values and beliefs (L. Smith, 2001a).

Most schools do not look at themselves. They do not understand "where they are." At best, they may accept or reject someone else's views of how they are doing. Principals, teachers, students, and parents typically are not asked to examine where they are, or they do not have the inclination, power, skills, or experience to complete the task. Therefore, how can a school move to another place without understanding where it has been?

POINT B

Corporate consultants, government agency evaluators, and school reformers ask the same questions of the organizations they serve: "What do you want to be?"; "Where do you want to go?"; "What is your destination?"

In general, we would not jump into our cars and drive away to a mystery location. Perhaps as a way to relax, we might take such a ride for pleasure, but our driving is usually more purposeful as we drive to work, complete a chore, or take a vacation. Most people would not tell others that they do not know where they are going; however, most schools do not engage in thinking about their destinations. Schools tend to go about their business in the same and familiar ways and do not realize there could be a new destination.

This book looks at eight schools that knew where they were and refused to stay there. They developed a vision of what they wanted to be, where they wanted to go. They considered the same five elements used to describe Point A: (1) instruction, (2) organization, (3) governance, (4) accountability, and (5) culture. Then, each of them embarked on their journey.

THE JOURNEY

If a school reaches an understanding of where it is (Point A) and can envision where it wants to be (Point B), the obvious question becomes "How do we move from Point A to Point B?" In effect, we need to look at both product and process. The product is clearly central to our work; Point B is the product. However, many school reformers and researchers argue that the process might even be more important than the product. If we do not understand the complexities of change—its nonlinear and chaotic nature, its unpredictability, its emotional component, its attacks on our assumptions and disruptions to our routines—then our design of a change process (to the degree that we can design one) will be limited, incomplete, and probably unsuccessful. If we neglect to understand the human dynamics of change, we will not complete our journey from Point A to Point B. Or, our arrival at Point B may be a temporary stay, frustrating the "travelers" who have invested so much physical, psychological, and emotional energy in the endeavor. Those who have been on the trip may simply have "run out of gas." They will lose their faith in the driver/leader, turn back, and refuse to venture forth again.

SUCCESSFUL JOURNEYS

In the fall of 1999, I organized a team of six doctoral students in educational leadership who expressed a strong interest in studying school change. We wanted to know about schools that implemented theories of organizational change. We wanted to document how schools moved from embarrassment to being exemplary. We wanted to know about the "before" stage of a school's life and level of success (Point A) and compare it with the "after" stage, when there was much greater success (Point B). Even more important, we wanted to know about the journey from Point A to Point B. What was the process the school community experienced? How did that process bring about significant school change? What were the variables and factors that made a difference?

As Fullan (2001) pointed out, "it is necessary to contend with both the 'what' of change and the 'how' of change. Meaning must be accomplished in relation to both these aspects" (p. 8). Furthermore, Fullan (2001) noted, "more and more, the evidence [about school change] points to a small number of key variables" (p. 71). At the heart of the matter, Fullan (2001) argued, is that we need to understand the variables connected to successful teaching and learning in what is a complex and dynamic change process.

My students and I decided to create an award, the first of its kind, that would look beyond a school's blue ribbon status and focus on the school's previous status as a failing school and look at how it dramatically changed.

THE SCHOOL CHANGE AWARD CRITERIA

Each of the four dimensions addresses a fundamental question about school change. First, how meaningful is the change? Is it substantial rather than superficial? Second, how deep and broad is the change? Is it systemic rather than isolated? Third, how is the change focused? Is it student centered, looking at teaching and learning? Fourth, how is it measured? Is it solution or outcome oriented?

The rationale for four dimensions, and the requirement that a nominated school meet at least two criteria in each dimension, was to guarantee a school addressed all four distinct yet interlocking concerns (see Figure 2.2). Without asking schools to address all four dimensions, it would be possible for a school to point to Dimension 1 and provide data and documentation that it had substantially changed, but the change did not affect teaching or learning. Or, a school could claim its changes were deep and broad; yet again, with little attention paid to teaching and learning.

In other words, nominated schools had to demonstrate that the changes were meaningful (substantial rather than superficial) *and* that they were deep and broad (not isolated) *and* that these changes were focused on teaching and learning *and* that the changes led to measurable outcomes.

DIMENSION 1

How Meaningful Is the Change?
Is It Substantial Rather Than Superficial?

In dozens of workshops I have conducted nationwide, I have used the same opening exercise. Parents, teachers, and school administrators were asked to list their associations with the phrases *superficial change* and *substantial change*. The responses came quickly. Superficial change was defined as illusory, temporary, cosmetic, "a passing fad," mandated or top down, on the surface, not making a difference. Substantial change, on the other hand, was linked to having an impact, affecting teaching and learning, changing what people actually do, led by practitioners, involving a sense of ownership, leading to measurable outcomes (L. Smith, 2001a).

The frustration with superficial change, which participants almost always declare to be the dominant variety (in their view, substantial change infrequently took place), reminds me of the elementary school principal in the Midwest who worked in a large school district that gave much autonomy to each school. For example, when a new district initiative was announced, it

Figure 2.2   National School Change Award criteria

Criteria			
Dimension 1	Dimension 2	Dimension 3	Dimension 4
How meaningful is the change? Is it substantial rather than superficial?	*How deep and broad is the change? Is it systemic rather than isolated?*	*How is the change focused? Is it student centered, looking at teaching and learning?*	*How is the change measured? Is it solution or outcome oriented?*
A. There has been a measurable change in attitudes, beliefs, and values.	A. The change is not merely affecting one classroom or grade; it is more widespread (systemic) in the school.	A. The overall quality of teaching has improved, as measured by observations, peer evaluations, self-assessments, student feedback, parent comments, etc.	A. There has been a sharp increase in student achievement as measured by in-school assessments such as portfolios, student grades, exhibitions, etc.
B. The practices, especially in classroom instruction, dramatically changed.	B. The changes in school have been felt in decisions about instruction, organization, governance, and accountability.	B. Innovative teaching practices, such as problem-based learning, interdisciplinary teaching, cooperative learning, etc., have been initiated, adopted, and sustained.	B. There has been a sharp increase in student achievement as measured by "outside" evaluations, such as district, state, or national norm or criterion and/or standards.
C. The changes have been driven by the teachers; they "own" the change.	C. There is a perception in the school among stakeholders (administrators, teachers, students, parents) that positive change has taken place.	C. There is an alignment of curriculum, instruction, assessment, and standards.	C. There are documented increases in measurable outcomes such as promotion rates, graduation rates, acceptances into prestigious schools, job placements, number of visitors to the school, etc.
D. Students and staff want to come to school, enjoy being in school, and they often stay beyond normal hours.	D. There is a perception in the larger community that positive change has taken place, as reflected in a higher number of applicants, registrations, visits, etc.	D. The school culture promotes inquiry, use of research, professional development, growth, and the idea of a "learning organization."	D. The school has won recognition and awards for improved performance.

would be up to the principal to decide whether her school would participate. This principal followed the "three-year rule": If the initiative was still around for a third year, then she seriously considered enrolling her school. In effect, this principal was tired of the *reform de jour* syndrome.

Several researchers have used the concepts of first- and second-order change to distinguish superficial from substantial change. Watzlawick, Weakland, and Fisch (1974) saw first-order (superficial) changes as continuous within stable systems. Second-order (substantial) changes are discontinuous and cause instability because they transform fundamental properties or states of the organization.

Levy (1986) contended that first-order changes occur naturally as an organization grows. They are "minor improvements and adjustments that do not change the system's core" (p. 10). Although K. K. Smith (1982) agreed that first-order changes are embedded in the natural developmental sequence, he also contended that they can be seen as changes that "enable things to look different while remaining the same" (p. 318). I see second-order changes as those that are thoroughly integrated into the organization and transform its very essence.

Cuban (1988) built on these interpretations and, in doing so, he popularized the first-order/second-order distinction. For Cuban, first-order changes merely seek to take what is in place and make it more efficient. No new ground is broken; no new practices are adopted. The way that adults and children perform their roles is not altered.

For example, one middle school faced a fairly typical problem: Students were consistently tardy in getting to their classes. The response, mandated by the principal, involved reminding all the teachers they had to be more diligent in the hallways during passing time in moving students quickly to their classes. This "solution" falls into the category of first-order change; the change involved making existing practices more efficient. Additionally, it was not a change that was designed by those who would have to implement it; it was not well conceived; it ignored incentives for either the teachers or students. In many respects, it was cosmetic.

Second-order changes, on the other hand, entail a shift in values, beliefs, and practices. Underlying assumptions are challenged. The fundamental way that organizations are put together is changed; goals, structures, and roles shift. Fullan (1991) stressed the shift in belief systems. When people "understand conceptually what and why something should be done, and to what end, [this] represents a much more fundamental change" (Fullan, 1991, p. 42).

Returning to our example of lateness to class, a second middle school decided that tardiness was a symptom of something more deep and fundamental. The teachers asked the students why they were late. They discovered two things. First, the students felt there was no reason to be in class on time because the classes were boring, irrelevant, and not connected to their lives. Second, the students needed and wanted opportunities to socialize with their friends. In response, the staff looked at their teaching practices and revised the daily schedule to provide an opportunity for students to join clubs, explore individual interests, and learn how to work with their peers.

Figure 2.3 Theories of superficial versus substantial change

Theorist	Superficial (first order)	Substantial (second order)	Year
Watzlawick, Weakland, & Fisch	Continuous within stable systems.	Discontinuous, transforming fundamental properties of the organization or system.	1974
K. Smith	Embedded in natural development sequence; enables things to look different while remaining the same.	Thoroughly integrated into the organization and transforms its very essence.	1982
Levy	Minor improvements that do not change the system's core.	Challenges the existing conditions.	1986
Cuban	Improves the efficiency and effectiveness of what is already in place without disturbing the basic organizational features or altering the way children and adults perform their roles.	Fundamentally alters the ways organizations are put together, in terms of goals, structures, and roles. Challenges the existing assumptions.	1988
Conley	Renewal: Helps the organization to do better or more efficiently what it is already doing. Reform-driven: Organization adapts to new rules, circumstances, or requirements without culture change.	Restructuring: Changes fundamental assumptions and relationships. Reform-driven: Could lead to second-order change if process changes assumptions and culture.	1993
L. Smith	Band-Aid, cosmetic, fad, illusory, imposed, irrelevant, mandated, no buy-in, no impact on core values, not taken seriously, quick fix, *reform du jour*, temporary, waste of time	Challenges assumptions; dramatic change in practices; lasting, meaningful, measurable change in outcomes; meets needs; sense of ownership; shift in attitudes, beliefs, and values; teacher driven	1999

Second-order changes call for suspending assumptions and looking beyond symptoms to the causes of a problem. Risks are taken as new approaches are initiated. Second-order changes involve looking at values and priorities. In regard to the tardiness issue, questions were raised about what the school valued most. Previously, the school staff had valued punctuality over performance, efficiency over engagement, and conformity over creativity. That significantly changed.

Conley (1993, pp. 7–8) saw school change activities as falling into one of three categories. *Renewal* activities are those that help the organization to do better and/or be more efficient in what it is already doing—first-order changes. *Reform-driven* activities alter existing procedures, rules, and requirements to enable the organization to adapt to new circumstances or requirements. If the adaptive activity means probing deeper with a serious reshaping of what the school does for and with students, then the reform-driven activity could become substantial (i.e., second order). Meanwhile, *restructuring* activities change fundamental assumptions, practices, and relationships, both within the organization and between the organization and the outside world, in ways that lead to improved and varied student learning outcomes for essentially all students.

To sum, the first dimension of measuring significant change raises questions about the fundamental nature of the change. Is the change attempt just another top-down whim of the moment, or is it something that challenges the actual rhythm of a school, something that asks people to seriously look at what they believe, what they value, what they hold dear—and, in the end, what they do? As Albert Einstein once pointed out, "we cannot solve our problems with the level of thinking that got us the problems in the first place. We need a paradigm shift. We need to look at things in a different way" (Einstein, 2002).

DIMENSION 2

How Deep and Broad Is the Change?
Is It Systemic Rather Than Isolated?

College football has been played the same way for close to a century. It has traditionally been a punishing game, with massive and strong offensive linemen opening up holes for a player to run through. Even when "passing the football" won some acceptance, starting in the 1970s, the game still relied on passing for yardage a little bit at a time.

For Mike Leach, the coach of Texas Tech, which plays in one of the highest-ranked college divisions in the country, the traditional way wasn't working. The team lost game after game. Consequently, Leach significantly changed the team's strategy; the team stopped running. "Synergy, in Leach's view, doesn't come from mixing runs with passes but from throwing the ball everywhere on the field, to every possible person allowed to catch a ball" (M. Lewis, 2005, p. 58).

Almost every play involved passing for long yardage, with the team's offensive line spread out. Leach upset the ordinary rhythm of the game, bewildering opposing teams, who did not know what to do. The new strategy took Texas Tech from second-rate status to a national ranking, with their quarterbacks and receivers breaking or challenging passing yardage records for a single game and a single season. This deep and broad change did not involve only the quarterback and two receivers; every offensive player had his field position changed, his role redefined, his priorities shifted.

Deep and broad change in football, police work, business, and education involves the change striking at the most fundamental approaches (deep) and affecting more than a few individuals (broad). For example, in 1993, the New

York City Police Department completely revamped what police officers did and how they did it (deep), with nearly all officers involved in the changes (broad). As I discussed in Chapter 1 when I looked at chaos theory, many variables affected the subsequent dramatic decrease in crime. Nonetheless, the deep and broad changes in the police department were an important factor.

Unfortunately, for schools and the families they serve, it is rare that deep and broad changes take place. There are exceptions, of course, including the 601 schools from 44 states nominated for the National School Change Awards between 2000 and 2007. However, as Debbie Meier (1995) argued:

> School change of the depth and breadth required, change that breaks with the traditions of our own schooling, cannot be undertaken by a faculty that is not convinced and involved. Even when teachers are engaged, it's tough to change the habits of a lifetime, embedded as such habits are in the way we talk about schooling and the way our students and their families expect it to be delivered. (p. 107)

In the late 1970s and early 1980s, Popkewitz, Tabachnick, and Wehlage (1982) conducted a four-year study of the Individually Guided Education (IGE) program. Initially, they were interested in how a new educational program is introduced, that is, what happens when new ideas about curricula, use of time, instructional practices, and administrative support make their way into the real world of schools. They wanted to know "what values and meanings are transmitted by reform programs into schools" (p. xi). However, they discovered much more and summarized their findings in their book, *The Myth of Educational Reform: A Study of School Responses to a Program of Change*.

For the Popkewitz research team, true reform involves substantial change, a deep questioning of what is currently in place instead of what is typically passed off as change. Although the IGE reform was accepted in different ways at different schools, in all cases the individual school reinterpreted and reshaped the reform strategy more than the strategy shaped the school. The IGE reform was interpreted as making school efficient (*technical schooling*), or exploring ways of knowing (*constructive schooling*), or creating an image of substance (*illusory schooling*). In all cases, how the reform was interpreted and implemented was a reflection of the existing values and beliefs in the particular school. There was little questioning of what was already in place. Each school's "new ways" were aligned to how the school was already approaching teaching and learning. Change in these schools was not deep and broad; few teachers changed what they did. They merely used the new language to label what they had always done.

Deep and broad means a complete look is taken at what is done, why it is done, and how it might be done differently. More than a decade ago, Sarason (1990) predicted the failure of educational reform because of its timidity. For Sarason (1990), it was "time to stop tinkering around the edges. Isolated and narrow efforts would simply not matter" (p. 120).

The second dimension, then, asks whether the change attempt is limited to an isolated case of an ambitious teacher doing creative things in her or his classroom. When change is deep and broad, changes unfold in many classrooms. The changes are not centered on only one aspect of school; instead, important decisions are made about instruction, organization, governance, *and* accountability. Also, the tinkering has ceased; a system has been moved; a school has become a very different place, which is obvious to all those who live within it (administrators, teachers, students, and parents) and to those in the larger community (F. Smith & L. Smith, 1993).

DIMENSION 3

On What Is the Change Focused? Is It Student Centered, Looking at Teaching and Learning?

Drawing from his study of large urban school systems in Chicago, San Diego, Boston, and Chicago, Simmons (2006) emphasized school reform must have one primary focus: the quality of instruction. For Simmons, exemplary school performance means changing the structure and culture, creating new leaders, involving parents, and strengthening funding—all with a common purpose: changing the way students learn and increasing their academic achievement.

Tucker and Coddings (1998) made it clear that instruction is the core business of schools. As they pointed out, today, principals are expected to raise student achievement, which involves understanding what good instruction looks like, knowing how to mobilize resources on behalf of the instructional design, convincing a faculty that all students can achieve, and providing the appropriate knowledge and skills for those teachers.

However, many school reformers have argued that what a principal does is not enough; the adoption of innovative teaching practices is not enough; an alignment of curriculum, instruction, assessment, and standards is not enough. Without a doubt, these are important elements for a school committed to significant school change, but there is another essential element. A new collaborative and collegial culture, one committed to the growth of both the students and the adults, needs to be created.

Among the names given to schools that possess this culture are *learning-enriched schools, teacher learning communities,* a *more professional culture, learning organizations,* and *centers of inquiry.*

Hawley and Valli (1999) pointed to research, which argues that the improvement of schools requires the improvement of teaching, which in turn is dependent on the quality of professional development. They advocated learning-enriched schools, which support teacher learning, have shared goals, and are marked by a collaborative culture.

Little (1999) used the term *teacher learning communities* to convey the same idea. In her view, this means schools "solve the problem of the closed classroom door"

(p. 255). Instead of teachers wanting no interference with what they do, a culture of inquiry is created. Teachers visit each other's classrooms, aims and practices are frequently and honestly examined, and risk taking is encouraged. In Little's words, "Teachers live with one another through the messiness of genuine discovery" (p. 255).

Lieberman, Saxl, and Miles (1988) attacked the current structure of schools by contending they "infantilize" teachers because the typical school "makes it hard for teachers to act like adults. Rather than work collectively on their problems, everyone must struggle alone" (p. 151). Instead, they argued that collegiality must be strengthened to create a more professional culture.

Senge's (2006) work on *learning organizations*, applied initially to the corporate world, quickly became an approach adopted by government agencies, nonprofit organizations, and some schools. Senge and his colleagues believed learning organizations are "more than just an imperative to work and talk together" (Senge et al., 2000, p. 5). They contended that every organization is a product of how its members think and interact. They urged school administrators and teachers to look at the quality of their interactions and conversations and ask themselves some difficult questions: Do people listen to each other? Do they advocate their views so loudly that others cannot hear? Do they blame others for the school's problems or engage in team problem solving? Are they open to talking about the differences between and among them? Are they genuinely interested in creating something new? (Senge et al., 2000, pp. 19–22).

Sergiovanni (1996) wanted schools to become *centers of inquiry*, with organizational structures, teaching environments, and working conditions that allow and encourage teachers to became researchers of their practice and to become reflective practitioners.

Therefore, the third dimension asks whether the change endeavor is focused on what and how students are learning, on how teachers are teaching, and on how both students and teachers are engaged in an ongoing growth process.

DIMENSION 4

How Is Change Measured? Is It Solution Or Outcome Oriented?

If you want to start a passionate argument, join a group of educators or parents (or both) and announce that state educational achievement standards are to be strengthened—or eliminated. That will get everyone's attention. Controversy about the standards movement, which greatly grew in the 1990s, continues today.

In his 2002 book, *The Leader's Guide to Standards*, Douglas Reeves bluntly commented:

> We do not have to like standards, but we must recognize our alternatives are limited. Rejecting standards as the method for student evaluation

leaves us with an evaluation system based on comparison of one student to another, a system that is inconsistent, unfair, and ineffective. (p. 5)

Reeves offered the example of airline pilots: We would not certify and license one prospective pilot over another merely because the first prospect scored better on examinations, unless the first pilot (and perhaps the second) met proficiency standards. We expect pilots to meet the appropriate standards; if not, we will not fly.

Tucker and Coddings (1998) stated it another way: "Abandon immediately the idea that we are doing our job by sorting youngsters into winners and losers and instead dedicate ourselves [to] the idea that all students can and must achieve at internationally benchmarked levels" (p. 23).

Hundreds, if not thousands, of books and articles have posed questions about how to measure student performance. In a self-labeled "action guide" entitled *Raising the Standard,* Doyle and Pimentel (1997) posed arguments that would later be given national attention by the *NCLB* legislation: "Even if your school system by all indications is performing well in the aggregate, some students are not succeeding at high levels" (p. 7).

This discussion about results centers on what externally set standards and tests seek to measure. Schools can no longer hide from that data—and data provide one way to look at outcomes.

Fullan (2007) recounted England's National Literacy and Numeracy Strategy, a comprehensive plan launched in 1997 to raise the literacy and numeracy achievement of all students up to age 11, involving seven million students in 20,000 primary schools. Fullan was involved in monitoring and assessing the ambitious program and noted that the results were astounding. For example, the percentage of 11-year-olds reaching Levels 4 or 5 (the highest achievement levels) in literacy rose from 63% in 1997 to 75% in 2000; the numeracy proficiency increase rose from 62% to 73% in the same time period (Fullan, 2007, p. 244). Although the results reached a plateau in 2001 and 2002, with literacy proficiency staying at 75% and numeracy proficiency advancing one percentage point, getting thousands of students to be literate and numerate who otherwise would not be so is not a bad day's work and is bound to make a difference in many lives. In this case, not just one school, but an entire national school system, won recognition for improved performance.

Some educators want to look at outcomes inside their schools with standards and measurements they create. For example, Debbie Meier pioneered the ideas of portfolios, demonstrations, and exhibitions. In her view, if a student could demonstrate (alone or with a team of students) how to do something meaningful, then learning had taken place. At Central Park East, before high school seniors could graduate they had to complete fourteen portfolios, including seven major presentations made to a graduation committee of teachers and students. Meier (1995) contended:

This process . . . creates a series of tasks that require a wide range of performance skills, habits of work as well as mind: the sheer ability to put the material together for their committee to review, to arrange and schedule meetings, to make oral presentations and answer unexpected questions with poise and aplomb! (p. 60)

Several times in the last ten years, I have asked principals in attendance at the National Principals Leadership Institute to describe what they wanted their elementary, middle, or high school graduates to "look like," meaning: What did they want these students to believe, know, and be able to do? In turn, the principals had to design the learning experiences of their students so these end products could be achieved.

Wiggins and McTighe (2005) called this approach *backward design*. They contended educators must plan everyday activities on the basis of how those activities will enable students to reach desired goals. Furthermore, teachers must continually look for evidence of the desired results. In their words, "we are referring to evidence gathered through a variety of formal and informal assessments during a unit of study or a course. We are not alluding only to end-of-teaching tests or culminating tasks" (Wiggins & McTighe, 2005, p. 19). In their view, the collected evidence can include traditional measurements (quizzes, tests, performance tasks and projects, etc.) and student self-assessments.

Although the emphasis on academic achievement, measured by both internal and eternal criteria, remains strong, some educators and reformers ask for more. Peter Cookson (2006) lamented that American schools have moved away from being child centered to primarily being driven by number crunching. He advocated remembering the importance of the "softer aspects of education—spontaneity, creativity, humor, and risk" (p. 32). To make his point, Cookson turns to his role model, Socrates. He explained:

Socrates, the original ideal teacher, asked questions, questioned the answers, and then moved on to deeper questions. If PowerPoint had been available, would Socrates have skipped the questions altogether and moved on to a colorful digital display of the answers? Did his curriculum need to be stamped "scientific" by government bureaucrats? Did Plato, for that matter, need an "exit" exam? (Cookson, 2006, p. 32)

Cookson's (2006) concern about the "whole child" echoes the beliefs of other education reformers. For example, physician and educational pioneer James Comer created the Yale School Development Program, which

puts the development of the child at the center of the educational process. All of the adult stakeholders—administrators, teachers, support staff, parents and the young people themselves—above elementary school—are involved in developing an environment that nurtures adults and the students. (Comer, 1997, p. 216)

Comer schools, as they became known, foster the physical, social, and emotional health of students; the meaningful involvement of parents; and shared decision making. The Yale School Development Program is predicated on six developmental pathways: (1) physical, (2) ethical, (3) social, (4) language, (5) psychological, and (6) cognitive. Within each pathway are specific expectations, such as ethical, involving "making choices based on self interest and the collective good"; social, including "empathy and appropriate conduct"; and language, incorporating "competency in expressive and receptive language and serving as a bridge for relationship building" (Joyner, Ben-Avie, & Comer, 2004, p. 11).

Although these outcomes are difficult to precisely measure, Comer schools are characterized by lower dropout rates; fewer disciplinary referrals; decreased incidents of violence; more parents who are involved with the school; lowered absenteeism due to medical problems (quantitatively measured); and a change toward a healthier climate, engaging classroom discussions, adults and children treating each other with respect, and emotional management (qualitatively measured). In my view, the qualitative measurements are no less important than the quantitative indicators.

Mike Schmoker, in his research about results, also goes beyond test scores. He shared an anecdote about a popular current affairs television show, featuring opposing points of view, which was not a forum for reasoned arguments. Schmoker (2006) argued that "A more literate populace won't abide such nonsense. It will have lower tolerance for stupid, distorted political talk and advertisements, a growing appreciation for clarity and accuracy" (p. 74). To enable students to distinguish between propaganda and facts requires using the twelve years of school to "cultivate such a disposition, to provide hundreds of opportunities for students to read, think, discuss, question, and write in a more intellectually charged classroom" (Schmoker, 2006, p. 74). The development of dispositions can be determined by what teachers require and expect, what students are able to do, and the types of measurements a school uses.

In the fourth dimension, the inquiry is aimed at results, results, results. What are the measurable outcomes in terms of academic achievement, social/emotional heath, citizenship, creativity, critical thinking, and so on?

LOOKING AT ALL FOUR CRITERIA

As illustrated in Figure 2.4, the four dimensions are connected to each other. For example, outcomes are tied to teaching and learning. As Schmoker (2006) contended, "a focus on *learning*, on assessment results, becomes the leverage for improvements in *teaching*, which is only as good as its impact on learning" (p. 126). Hargreaves, Earl, Moore, and Manning (2001) explained it this way:

> Clearly defined learning standards or outcomes can transform how teachers think about curriculum, teaching, and learning, steering them into considering not just what they will teach but precisely what their students will learn and what they as teachers will need to do to ensure that such learning is achieved. (p. 44)

Labeling school change as *substantial* means little if the change has not focused on teaching and learning—for the students and for the adults. Furthermore, if the improvement is limited to a few classrooms, we will not have change that is deep and broad. We cannot claim "better teaching" and meaningful learning without some evidence, some measurements. We will not move beyond today's results—as good as they might be—without creating a different belief system that values student achievement and growth.

This book is founded on the belief that significant change in schools is rarely found but not impossible to achieve. Some schools in America have changed, some quite significantly. In my view, a school that meets at least two of the four criteria in each dimension and has satisfied ten or more of the sixteen criteria presented in Figure 2.2 is a school that has achieved significant change.

Figure 2.4   The interlocking relationship of the four dimensions of significant school change

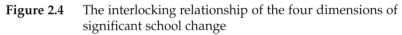

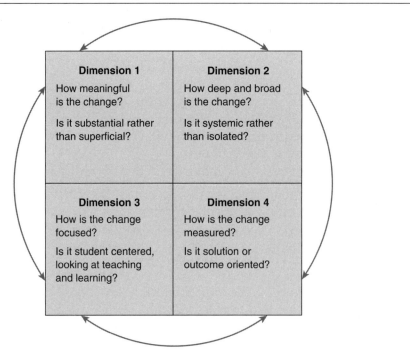

3

Examining Change

The study of change has been a constant for centuries. To better understand the phenomenon, philosophers ponder, mathematicians calculate, futurists predict, sociologists survey, psychologists interpret and guide. The effort seems endless.

The American obsession with change is intimately linked with our commitment to self-improvement. Just walk the aisles of any large bookstore, such as Barnes & Noble or Borders. The self-help section will have more books than anthropology, biology, psychology, and sociology *combined*. These books will tell you how to launch into change, handle change, deal with change, embrace change. They suggest where to go and how to get there.

Paperbacks will urge you to unlock the hidden dimensions of your life (Chopra, 2004); take seven steps to living at your full potential (Osteen, 2004); and discover the secrets of creative visualization, which in turn will transform your life (Cooper, 1999). You can change your life in seven days, heeding the advice of a hypnotist (McKenna, 2004), or plot a year to success, following the path of a businessman and inspirational speaker who amassed a fortune of more than $20 million by the time he was twenty-nine (Bennett, 2004).

In the world of education there are many books about school renewal, restructuring, and reform; many studies and research findings; many tales of schools, which have succeeded or failed. However, there is not enough. Fullan (1991) argued that we know a great deal about what change is but far too little about how to successfully facilitate it. This book taps the extensive research on school change and provides new insights through portraits of eight schools that significantly changed and the conceptual framework growing out of those portraits.

THE AWARD WINNERS

Between 2000 and 2007, 601 schools from forty-four states were nominated for the National School Change Awards. The nomination packets from each of the schools contained considerable data and documentation, requiring a close examination of the submissions. An average of seventy-five nominations were screened each year, with twenty-four finalists selected. (One hundred twenty-seven schools were nominated in 2007!) The finalists' materials were sent to judges from across the United States, with nine judges (in teams of three) reviewing each nominated school. Each year, the judges, who later convened as a group for one day to select the six winners, included graduate students; university professors and deans; retired and currently serving public school teachers, principals, and superintendents (including some from schools that previously had won the National School Change Award); directors of national education and arts organizations; corporate and foundation officers; government officials; community activists; and high school students.

As a result of this rigorous process, forty-eight schools were selected over the first eight years of the award. Each school was recognized at a special local ceremony at their school and at a national awards ceremony in New York City, which involved the U.S. Department of Education and the award sponsors: Fordham University's Graduate School of Education and, starting in 2003, Pearson Education and the American Association of School Administrators. The Chase Manhattan Foundation and the Association for Supervision and Curriculum Development served as sponsors in the first three years of the award. Starting in 2008, the awards program will be sponsored by The Panasonic Corporation of North America and The Panasonic Foundation. Additionally, each winning school received a $5,000 grant; the school's principal was a guest at the National Principals Leadership Institute, conducted at Fordham University in July; and the school became involved in this national research project focusing on significant school change.

During the visit to each winning school, data were collected about the "before" and "after" stages of the school's climate, culture, and conditions (including statistical data about student achievement); the critical moments in the school's change process; the interplay of various variables; and the role of the school principal.

SCHOOLS THAT CHANGE: THE PORTRAITS

Eight of the winning schools were selected for detailed portraits. Multiple visits were made to the following schools: elementary schools in Alaska, California, New York, and Kentucky and secondary schools in Michigan,

Figure 3.1   Nominations have been received from these states (2000–2007)

SOURCE: Panasonic National School Change Awards (n.d.)

Wisconsin, and Texas (one middle school and one high school). One of these schools is in a major metropolitan area, one is in a large city, three are in mid-sized cities, one is urban/suburban, one is rural, and one considers itself rural/urban.

THE RESEARCH LENS

The intent of the field research was to compose portraits of eight schools that had significantly changed. The methodology was qualitative, leaning heavily on the portraiture techniques advanced by Sara Lawrence-Lightfoot.

Lawrence-Lightfoot and her colleague, Jessica Hoffman Davis, see portraiture as a genre of inquiry and representation that joins the fields of science and art. On one hand, it calls for scientific rigor, with an objectivity and systematic attention to detail; on the other hand, it draws from the ability of art to express emotions, inspire, and be interpretative. The science side intends to inform and

Figure 3.2   National School Change Award winners, 2000–2007

Year Won	School	Level	City	ST
2000	Allenbrook Elementary	Elem	Charlotte	NC
2000	Daniel Boone Elementary	Elem	Chicago	IL
2000	G.W. Carver Academy	MS	Waco	TX
2000	Niles High School	HS	Niles	MI
2000	Rosemont Middle School	MS	Charlotte	NC
2000	Skycrest Elementary	Elem	Citrus Hts	CA
2002	Belmont Elementary	Elem	Lincoln	NE
2002	Bensley Elementary	Elem	Richmond	VA
2002	Henry W. Grady High	HS	Atlanta	GA
2002	Liberty Elementary	Elem	Valley Cottage	NY
2002	Shreve Island Elementary	Elem	Shreveport	LA
2002	Waren Travis White High	HS	Dallas	TX
2004	Blackstone Valley Reg. Voc. Tech High School	HS	Upton	MA
2004	Dr. Michael Conti, PS #5	Elem	Jersey City	NJ
2004	Ridgecrest Elementary	Elem	Houston	TX
2004	Rolling Hills Elementary	Elem	Orlando	FL
2004	South Heights Elementary	Elem	Henderson	KY
2004	Westminster Academy #26	Elem	Eizabeth	NJ
2006	Brighton High School	HS	Brighton	TN
2006	Brockton High School	HS	Brockton	MA
2006	Chicora Elementary	Elem	Charleston	SC
2006	Heather Hills Elementary	Elem	Indianapolis	IN
2006	Oil City Elementary	Elem	Oil City	LA
2006	Roosevelt Elementary	Elem	Long Beach	CA

Year Won	School	Level	City	State
2001	Chase City Elementary	Elem	Chase City	VA
2001	Government Hill Elementary	Elem	Anchorage	AK
2001	Gustav A. Fristsche	MS	Milwaukee	WI
2001	Hallandale Elementary	Elem	Hallandale	FL
2001	La Mesa Dale Elementary	Elem	La Meda	CA
2001	Louis W. Fox Tech High	HS	San Antonio	TX
2003	First Avenue School	Elem	Newark	NJ
2003	Havencroft Elementary	Elem	Olathe	KS
2003	Hillcrest High School	HS	Jamaica	NY
2003	John H. Williams School #5	Elem	Rochester	NY
2003	North Twin Lakes Elementary	Elem	Hialeah	FL
2003	Sussex Tech. High	HS	Georgetown	DE
2005	Comelia F. Bradford, PS 16	Elem	Jersey City	NJ
2005	Don Pedro Albizu Campos	Elem	New York	NY
2005	Keith L. Ware Elementary	Elem	Ft. Riley	KS
2005	Maplewood Elementary	Elem	Indianapolis	IN
2005	Norview High School	HS	Norfolk	VA
2005	West Jasper Elementary	Elem	Jasper	AL
2007	Anna F. Booth Elementary School	Elem	Irvington	AL
2007	Dreamkeepers Academy	Elem	Norfolk	VA
2007	Chalkley Elementary School	Elem	Chesterfield	VA
2007	P.S. 196	Elem	Brooklyn	NY
2007	Signal Hill Elementary School	Elem	Signal Hill	CA
2007	World of Inquiry School	Elem	Rochester	NY

Elem = elementary school; MS = middle school; HS = high school

Figure 3.3   National School Change Award–winning schools selected for portraits

Demographics	Grades	School	Location	Principal	Year
Rural	Elementary	South Heights	Henderson, KY	Rob Carroll	2004
Mid-sized urban	Elementary	John Williams	Rochester, NY	Michele Hancock	2003
Mid-sized urban	Elementary	Government Hill	Anchorage, AK	Sandy Stephens	2001
Suburban/urban	Elementary	Skycrest	Citrus Heights, CA	Chris Zarzana	2000
Large urban	Middle	Gustav Fritsche	Milwaukee, WI	Bill Andrekopoulos	2001
Mid-sized urban	Middle	Carver Academy	Waco, TX	Molly Maloy	2000
Urban/rural	High	Niles HS	Niles, MI	Doug Law	2000
Major urban	High	Fox Tech HS	San Antonio, TX	Joanne Cockrell	2001

offer the arena of intellect; the art component sees things as layered, influenced by imagination and offering a humanistic sensibility (Lawrence-Lightfoot & Hoffman Davis, 1997). "The portrait, then, creates a narrative that is at once complex, provocative, and inviting, that attempts to be holistic, revealing the dynamic interaction of values, personality, structure, and history. And the narrative documents human behavior and experience in context" (Lawrence-Lightfoot & Hoffman Davis, 1997, p. 11).

For Lawrence-Lightfoot and Hoffman Davis, to function as a portraitist places the researcher in a unique and special position. The idea is to document and illuminate the complexity and detail of a unique experience and place, hoping the audience will relate, will see themselves reflected in it. The goal is to have the readers identify with the portrait. This, in effect, becomes an eclectic, interdisciplinary approach, shaped by the lenses of history, anthropology, psychology, and sociology. It blends "the curiosity and detective work of a biographer, the literary aesthetic of a novelist, and the systematic scrutiny of a researcher" (Lawrence-Lightfoot & Hoffman Davis, 1997, p. 15).

In writing about narrative research, which has been conducted since the 1950s, Clandinin and Connelly (2000) pointed out that a purpose of narrative is to have the readers of the research raise questions about their own practices and their own ways of knowing (p. 276). Lawrence-Lightfoot and Hoffman Davis (1997) echoed the same sentiment. They, too, want the reader involved in serious reflection.

The portraiture focus places the researcher as an active participant in the drama and helps to connect research and practice. From the perspective of the practitioner, this is long overdue (Meier, 1995). For myself as a researcher, it has meant living the life of a school so I could better understand where it is and where it has been. Louis, Toole, and Hargreaves (1999) urged researchers looking at school change to grapple with the dimensions of why and how change can impact how students learn. They want us to understand schools as a dynamic and uncertain environment for change, to distinguish between planned change and autonomous developmental processes, and to appreciate the impact of a school culture on change efforts. Portraiture can help us meet these objectives.

As Lawrence-Lightfoot and Hoffman Davis (1997) concluded in *The Art and Science of Portraiture*, they see portraiture as a seamless endeavor. It is "enriched by carefully constructed *context*, expressed through thoughtfully modulated *voice*, informed by cautiously guarded *relationships*, and organized into scrupulously selected *themes*" (Lawrence-Lightfoot & Hoffman Davis, 1997, p. 274). To understand the context, hear the voice, experience the relationships, and identify the themes requires a trust between the researcher and the participants in the study.

Because the National School Change Awards program includes a visit to and ceremony at each winning school, an unusual opportunity emerged for me to establish trusting relationships with a range of individuals at each site, including the principal, school staff members, students, parents, district office personnel (including the superintendent), and community members.

Interviews, focus groups, participation in school activities, observations, and document review were used during multiple visits to each of the eight schools selected for this study. Most focus group sessions included a drawing exercise. The adults were asked to visually portray their versions of the change process that unfolded at their school. The students were asked to draw pictures that described their school. With both the adults and the students, these representations were shared and explained to other members of the focus group, provoking additional discussion.

A CONCEPTUAL FRAMEWORK
FOR LOOKING AT SCHOOL CHANGE

My research has identified three critical and overlapping elements for significant school change: (1) context, (2) capacity, and (3) conversations. Each of these essential elements requires an understanding on three levels. First, what does the element, such as context, mean? Second, how can it be described at a particular school? Third, why is it important for this element to be changed, and how can this be accomplished?

By *context*, I mean the interplay of climate, messages, environment, and culture. By *capacity*, I mean strengthening a school's ability to plan, teach, assess, work in teams, and learn. And by *conversations*, I mean constant and meaningful dialogue about teaching and learning, students, the school's vision, and the school's progress. In the eight schools that were studied, the

Figure 3.4   Conceptual framework for looking at change

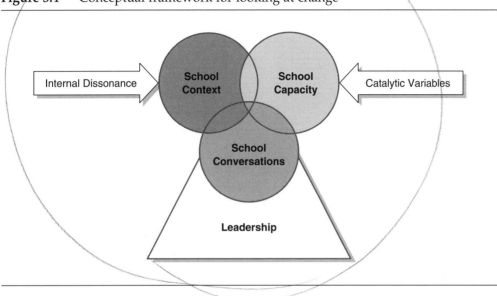

principals understood the importance of context, capacity, and conversations; were able to describe how these three essential elements operated in their schools; and took deliberate steps to change each of the three.

The eight principals also appreciated the three catalytic variables that influence a school's success at significantly changing: (1) internal dissonance, (2) external forces, and (3) leadership.

Internal dissonance involves school stakeholders, such as teachers and parents, reaching the point of no return. They can no longer accept the unfortunate condition of their school. They are upset with the inadequate leadership, the embarrassing low level of academic achievement, the chaos, the unsafe conditions, and so on.

External forces take two forms. They can be *push-in* forces, which are imposed on a school, such as state intervention or a court order, or they can be *reach-out* forces, which involve the school reaching out to take advantage of an opportunity, such as a grant.

The third, and perhaps most important, catalytic variable was *leadership*. Each of the principals of the eight schools I studied were different in terms of personality, previous experience, and priorities. Five of the eight came from other schools; three of them had been in the National School Change Award–winning school for a number of years. For half of them, it was their first principalship. Nonetheless, these eight principals shared nine common characteristics: They were *focused* on teaching and learning and academic achievement, they set a *vision* for their schools, and they had a remarkable *understanding of change*. These eight principals also were *strategic, learners, relational, communicators, empowering,* and *courageous*.

PART II

The Elementary Schools

Now, what I want is Facts. Teach those boys and girls nothing but Facts. Facts alone are wanted in life. Plant nothing else, and root out everything else . . . Stick to the Facts, sir!

—Charles Dickens, in
Hard Times (1854/1961)

When I hear the term critical thinking, I am reminded of my son, Christopher, who came home from first grade excited but exhausted. I said, "Christopher, what in the world did you do today to make you so tired?" He replied, "Mrs. Newton made us think all day long." Not thinking, I said, "Oh that's too bad." Christopher quickly responded, a little miffed that I had missed the point, "No Mom, thinking is fun!"

—Anne L. Sweaney

GIANTS, WIZARDS AND DWARFS was the game to play . . . Organizing a roomful of wired-up grade-schoolers into two teams, explaining the rudiments of the game . . . all this is no mean accomplishment . . . You have to decide now which you are—a GIANT, a WIZARD or a DWARF! . . . A small child stands there looking up, and asks in a small concerned voice, "Where do the Mermaids stand?" . . . Well, where DO the mermaids stand? All the "mermaids"—all those who are different, who don't fit the norm and who do not accept the available boxes and pigeonholes? Answer that question and you can build a school, a nation, or a world on it.

—Robert Fulghum

W hen we watch kindergarteners at the beginning of the school year, we can be overwhelmed by their enthusiasm, curiosity, and joy. They are in school to explore new worlds, frequently question, and sometimes even challenge. Their energy is boundless.

Yet, in some schools, by the time many of these children reach the second or third grade (if not sooner), their enthusiasm is gone, their curiosity is denied, and there is little joy. What happened? This is not to say that all elementary classrooms are devoid of inspirational teaching. But even if there were one such classroom in each school across America (and there are more), it would be too many. Fortunately, the staffs of our award-winning schools brought back the joy.

Questions tackled in this section include the following:

- What had happened to the joy of learning for many students? Why?
- Thinking back to the descriptions of change presented in Chapter 1, which ones played a role in each school portrait presented in the chapters in this section?
- The portraits of the four elementary schools have many things in common. What are they? What are the implications of the similarities?

4

"We're Closing This School"

Government Hill Elementary

Anchorage, Alaska

Sandy Stephens, Principal

The 2001 official Anchorage Visitors Guide offers a proud welcome, calling Anchorage "a modern city in the middle of mother nature's finest work" and noting that "Anchorage provides plenty of opportunities to see Alaskan wildlife in its natural setting." This claim sets the tone for sightseers and frames the duties of an Anchorage elementary school principal.

At Government Hill Elementary, it is 11:00 a.m., and student recess on the playground will start in ten minutes. Principal Sandy Stephens puts on her jacket and goes outside to complete her daily moose patrol. After Sandy signals the "all clear," the children rush out, taking a break from their rigorous and engaging dual-language instruction. At Government Hill, the moose have always been around, but the excitement of learning is new.

FEET DO THE WALKING AND THE TALKING

When families have a choice about where to send their children to school, quality (or the lack thereof) will eventually have an impact. So it was with Government Hill. The school served two populations: (1) students from new families in the area, referred to as *yuppies* (young upward professionals), who were conspicuously middle class, and (2) a set of transient, low-income families, many of whom did not speak English as their primary language.

Embarrassing academic results and a terrible school reputation drove families to switch schools or not enroll their children at Government Hill. In 1988, 350 students attended Government Hill. In 1990, the student body was down to 158 students, spread over six grades.

Teachers told their Anchorage colleagues: "You're going to Government Hill? What did you do to deserve that?" "I would not send my own child to Government Hill." For Anchorage teachers, the assignment to Government Hill was at best a respite before retirement, because few demands would be made. At worst, the assignment carried a stigma. "We had a reputation—a bad one—and at the same time, internally we had no identity." The school had no identity, not even a sign outside the building. If you wanted to find Government Hill, you needed very explicit instructions.

New teachers who were assigned to Government Hill were not welcomed. In the words of one teacher, "The tension and discomfort [were] intense." As soon as they were eligible to transfer, most new teachers opted out.

No one seemed to care. There was no cohesiveness, little discipline, and no sense of purpose. Teachers went to their individual rooms to escape the tough kids and the general disorder. In one large room, two teachers divided the space and drew a line on the floor to serve as a boundary. One teacher told the other teacher, "Keep your children and parents on your side of the line." No one stepped over that boundary; each teacher had her own very guarded turf.

The decisions about what to teach were left to each teacher. Everyone did his or her own thing. No grade-level consultation, much less sharing across grade levels, took place. It was possible for third-graders to learn about animal habitats and then have the same unit repeated in fourth and fifth grade.

Parents had little faith in their school. As one parent activist put it, the teachers were just counting down the days until they could leave. Great movement—out of the school by teachers, students, and even principals—was apparent. Government Hill was figuratively and literally at the bottom. Its test scores were last; sixty of the sixty-one Anchorage elementary schools had better results. In 1996, California Achievement Test scores for fourth-grade students who met required standards ranked at the 40th percentile in reading, the 38th percentile in language arts, and the 61st percentile in math.

One parent described her dilemma by recalling her very serious choice when, in 1993, her daughter was approaching kindergarten age: "Although I wanted to support our neighborhood elementary school, it was a disaster . . . the school's poor reputation had driven most of the middle class students in the area from Government Hill and into optional schools."

There was one clear way to keep Government Hill open: enroll more students. The problem was that the school was not appealing to anyone who was free to make a choice. The district turned to mandated busing as the answer, with families in the low-income Mountain View school having no say in the decision to send their children to Government Hill. The new students arrived without any preparation by the staff, who simply did not know how to serve a more needy population. The increased enrollment at Government Hill deepened the school's internal dissonance: disorder, poor student achievement, faculty discontent, uninvolved parents. The staff and students remained needy and neglected.

The second strategy imposed by the district office called for a Spanish immersion program. Although well intentioned, the program had limited success in the beginning, because the principal didn't endorse it and the veteran teachers didn't care about it. Furthermore, there was no understanding of what was to be done and how teachers would know how to do it. Except for serving a few kindergarten and first-grade children, the immersion program became a label, not a reality; it did little to change the school's reputation.

Government Hill was caught in a downward spiral. Some teachers described the situation: "There was no consistency"; "We had negative feelings about the school as a place to be"; "We felt isolated, downtrodden, and stagnated"; "There was no real vision for the future." New leadership was needed, and it arrived with Sandy Stephens.

ALWAYS LEADING A PARADE

When Sandy Stephens was a nine-year-old fourth-grader, she and her friends went to a Seafair Parade in her native Seattle, Washington. Motivated by that experience, Sandy decided she ought to organize a similar parade in her neighborhood. Within days, her friends were dressed in homemade costumes, and banners were constructed. To the delight of the parents, the parade was a smashing success.

Asking "why not?" and making things happen—with others—became Sandy's way to channel her energy. After college, Sandy's restlessness could not be contained; she had to leave Seattle. Intrigued by the education world, Sandy traveled to Wrangle, a small town of 3,000 residents on Wrangle Island in southeast Alaska, to take a job as an art teacher. After two years of teaching, Sandy fell ill and had to take some time away from teaching. When she was ready to return to work, she took a job as secretary to the Wrangle city manager. The books were in shambles, and Sandy was asked if she could balance them. Sandy replied that she balanced her personal checkbook, so why not? Six months later, she replaced the city accountant and stayed in the job for three and half years, until a fourth-grade teaching job became available in Wrangle. She stayed for twenty-one years, holding a variety of teaching jobs, including special education, reading, math, and kindergarten and getting to know nearly everyone in this ethnically diverse logging and fishing community.

Dr. Mary Francis, the Wrangle superintendent, adopted Sandy and assigned her every job that principals either did not want to do or did not know how to do. Consequently, over the years, Sandy, serving as an unofficial assistant to the superintendent, conducted staff development, coordinated vocational education, wrote grants, took charge of special education and Title I, and learned about the needs of migrant families and Native Americans. Mary became Sandy's role model, especially in terms of how she thought through problems. For both Mary and Sandy, it was the challenge of the unsolved problem that intrigued them. How many different ways could this problem be approached? Was it sometimes necessary to switch strategies? What would be the short- and long-range consequences? Sandy made a connection between her literary tastes and her problem solving; she became a Sherlock Holmes, fascinated with putting the pieces of a puzzle together.

In 1994, Sandy went to Anchorage to become the district's elementary school special education supervisor, a job that required her to visit all sixty-one elementary schools. For many educators, being elevated from a school-based assignment to the district office represents a promotion and a chance to have impact on a wider scale. Not for Sandy Stephens. Although she appreciated her opportunities as a supervisor to theoretically reach more students, most of her time was spent putting out fires. Sandy credited the experience with teaching her a lot about mediation, conflict resolution, and how to bring about change, but it was frustrating and draining. There was little ongoing contact with specific teachers or students and too few opportunities to make a difference. In Sandy's words, "It was a job from hell." After two years, Sandy Stephens wanted out.

Sandy realized that her variety of experiences and her knowledge of all the Anchorage elementary schools had given her a rich repertoire of skills and, as she said, "I wanted to see if I could put it all together as a principal." In 1996, Sandy arrived at Government Hill Elementary to become its third principal in seven years.

"YOU HAVE TO MAKE SURE THEY KNOW YOU'RE IN CHARGE"

Through her work as the district's elementary special education supervisor, Sandy Stephens already knew Government Hill. Naturally, she made comparisons with the other sixty-one Anchorage elementary schools and understood some of the reasons why Government Hill ranked last. In her mind, Sandy began to see possibilities, and in her heart she knew things could be much better.

The 1995–96 school year offered an opportunity for Government Hill. The district decided to pursue a $1 million Title VII grant, which would fund the continued development of the two-way language immersion program and impact all Government Hill students. The funding was important, but the process played a more critical role. The grant required a school-based steering committee, composed of parents and teachers who would work with district specialists in devising a plan. Sandy Stephens was asked to be on that team, and she soon asserted herself in the discussions. The question that drove the process was "What would you do if you could do anything?" Team members were asked to be imaginative and creative, to think out of the box, and not be saddled with a "This is the way it has always been done."

In the spring of that school year, Sandy was officially named Government Hill's principal. She took advantage of the timing; she spent May and June in the school, visiting classrooms and observing lessons. She invited all staff members to schedule a conversation with her so each could share impressions of the school. Many did, and through those conversations Sandy learned the adults, as well as the students, were quite needy.

Sandy also had the chance to assess her own leadership style. She tells the story of how an eager parent emerged as the PTA president. The woman was excited, full of ideas as to what parents could do to make the school better. However, a more experienced administrator took Sandy aside to tell her not to let the reins of power out of her hands. Sandy didn't understand at first. Wasn't it a good thing to have such parental enthusiasm? No, Sandy was told, it was more important to let everyone know that Sandy Stephens, as the new principal, was in charge.

This was not Sandy Stephens. As Sandy describes herself, she is constantly thinking about the situation she is in, who the players are, and how things can be moved forward. It is a mental process, deliberate yet sensitive. Sandy anticipates reactions to her thoughts and plans, and she is willing to adjust according to how others react. But her eyes are always on the prize, never losing sight of the goal. Leading a school means knowing yourself, and for Sandy this means not being in control all the time. In her words, "I like to be involved, but I don't have to be in charge."

SEVEN STRATEGIES, FROM THE START

If your school is last in the district, there is only one direction to march: forward. Sandy Stephens led the parade by adopting seven strategies: (1) putting the kids' interests first, (2) showing she meant business, (3) forging important alliances, (4) building on success, (5) providing support to teachers, (6) creating a new climate and culture, and (7) engaging parents.

It did not take Sandy long to understand that some of Government Hill's teachers were not serving their students. These students needed and deserved better. In one case, Sandy asked the unhappy teacher if she had considered a transfer. The teacher replied yes, but she did not know how to maneuver the system. Sandy said she would help. It turned out there were no positions available at other schools. The teacher reacted by saying that if she had known that, then she would have taken the new retirement incentive. Alas, it was too late to secure the $10,000 incentive. Sandy told the teacher she would try to take care of it. She did; the teacher got her $10,000, and a vacancy was created at Government Hill, a spot Sandy filled with a talented third-year teacher. The incident conveyed three important messages: (1) Students would be served; (2) Sandy meant business and knew how to get things done; and (3) new, energetic teachers would be welcomed at Government Hill.

The most unusual, yet critical, alliance Sandy forged was with the teachers' union. Sandy had been president of the teachers' union in Wrangle and had established a reputation for fairness, honesty, and a concern for students and teachers. One of Sandy's first steps as Government Hill's principal was to visit the Anchorage teachers' union president. Sandy was forthright in asking for his help and told him to check her out with Wrangle's union activists. An alliance was born. As Sandy summarized, "I never had a problem with the union because I always asked what steps I could take to help a particular teacher." Frequently, the union would step in and also work with the teacher. The fundamental question for both the principal and the teachers' union became whether a teacher was hurting the kids. Personnel decisions were neither arbitrary nor capricious, and the union leaders were Sandy's partners in solving personnel problems.

Not all was lost at Government Hill. Despite an awkward and poorly supported start, the two-way language immersion program, which began with the kindergarten and first-grade students, had great promise. However, it needed to be strengthened and expanded. The school received the $1 million, five-year Title VII grant, the application for which Sandy had helped write. This meant additional teachers needed to be trained that first summer of Sandy's tour of duty. Sandy joined the teachers for the professional development, and subsequently she facilitated discussions about how to reach the goals and objectives spelled out in their successful grant proposal. The strategy was simple: Build on small successes, which in this case was winning the grant.

Things changed at the school with the arrival of Sandy Stephens. She built trust. The focus and level of conversations dramatically shifted. Teachers who were doing their job began to feel appreciated. As one teacher put it, "We no longer felt we were alone." Sandy knew teacher isolation—which had intensified at Government Hill—had to be broken down. She knew she had to provide support for teachers, in the form of supplies, coaching, and advice.

Creating a new climate and culture was not easy. As Sandy noted, "I had to make it safe to change." At her very first meeting with the Government Hill staff, she used role playing. She asked volunteers to act out a scene that could take place in the front office; each scene would involve a staff member and a visiting parent. Through the different versions of the scene, the staff saw how first impressions in the front office send out a powerful message. Sandy explained that in her visits to all the district's elementary schools, she had experienced very different climates. Government Hill had one of the worst reputations in the district, but the power to change their image was in their hands.

Sandy's efforts to change the culture took more time. At the same initial staff meeting, Sandy asked everyone to think of one short phrase that described

Government Hill. Upon Sandy's signal, a Babel of voices shouted out. No one could be understood. It was clear that there was no common view, no agreement, and no unity. Six months later, after the staff struggled to compose a mission statement, the shouting exercise took on a new flavor. The chorus of voices sang the same song. Government Hill now stood for something positive and praiseworthy.

Parents joined the choir, becoming involved in new and varied ways. A range of activities and services brought them to the school: parenting workshops, English language classes, social activities, parent–teacher conferences, community events, a school leadership team, a parent center, volunteer duties in the classrooms, and so on. Sandy shared the story of the father of a fourth-grader who worked in the oil industry. His schedule took him out of town for two-week stretches, followed by two weeks at home, without any work responsibilities. During his two-week stints at home in Anchorage, he became a fixture at Government Hill.

GARDENING AS THE METAPHOR AND BOOKS AS THE TOOLS

In harsh Alaskan falls and winters, plants are greatly valued. Daylight is scarce, and moods can also turn dark. Sandy Stephens maintains her sanity and spirit in her greenhouse. She needs to grow flowering plants. As days get shorter, her grow lights take over. When outside temperatures drop to ten below, heaters take up the slack. Working as a principal in a challenging school and serving as a committed change agent is draining. For Sandy, the evening retreats into her greenhouse provided both calm and new energy.

Sandy describes her school mission by saying "I try to grow things others say are impossible to grow." Her greenhouse—in which forty orchids live among a kumquat tree, a coffee plant, a fig tree, hibiscus, banana tree, bougainvillea, Mandeville, and hoya (wax flowers)—attests to that claim. As in her greenhouse, Sandy plants, waters, weeds, nurtures, and celebrates the new blossoms at Government Hill. Gardening is not easy work. Neither was transforming Government Hill.

Sandy left her garden tools at home, but not her many books. These volumes inspired Sandy, and she used many of them with the staff in voluntary book talks. Spencer Kagen's *Cooperative Learning* became the vehicle for inspiring teachers to give students more responsibility for their learning. *Habits of Mind*, by Art Costa and Bena Kallick deepened the staff's understanding of how students learn. To help teachers master dual-language instruction, Sandy used *Languages and Children* by Helena Curtain, *Learning Through Two Languages* by Fred Genesee, and *Teaching With the Brain in Mind* by Eric Jenson.

The Jensen book was particularly powerful because it provided evidence that students benefit from early dual-language immersion. According to Jensen, as children reach puberty, the brain retools itself for new duties and automatically prunes itself of potential language cells and synapses. The time to seamlessly develop multiple language skills is when children are young. In Sandy's words, "Elementary school students can more quickly learn to speak a new language than anyone older and speak it without an accent."

Sandy's style greatly differed from that of her predecessors. In the past, principals would stay in the principal's office, with the blinds drawn. The principal's secretary would serve as the gatekeeper. Emerging from the office meant a quest to catch someone doing something wrong. Risk-taking was not valued; the emphasis was on not rocking the boat. Parents were not welcomed.

PARENTS AND PROGRAMS: DUAL-LANGUAGE EDUCATION

Conditions changed for parents as the middle-class yuppies won. These parents enrolled their children at Government Hill, because a language immersion program attracted them. However, the immersion initially was a label, not a meaningful teaching/learning approach. In fact, some staff and administrators did not see the value of elementary school students learning Spanish. One even thought not speaking English was rude.

The new middle-class parents at Government Hill were upset because the school's alleged language immersion program was not being supported or sustained. As one parent activist put it, "Immersion parents are at [Government Hill] by choice and those that took the initial risk of enrolling their kids had a huge stake in making the program work." In 1996, with the principal's forthcoming retirement, they insisted the new principal have more concern and compassion for the lauded approach. Sandy Stephens provided that commitment.

Dual-language programs have been built on previous attempts to meet the needs of multicultural populations. As U.S. Secretary of Education Richard Riley noted in 2000, the programs "are challenging young people with high standards, high expectations, and a curriculum in two languages" (Department of Education, ¶32). Foreign language study was incorporated into the Goals 2000 statement of the National Education goals, with dual-language programs centered on four interrelated goals: (1) gaining knowledge of other cultures, (2) connecting all academic subjects, (3) developing insights into the nature of language, and (4) participating in multilingual communities.

There are several models of dual-language programs. In some, there is a 90–10 distribution of time spent learning in the targeted language and learning in English, whereas other programs have a 50–50 split. The Government Hill team selected the latter, meaning that 50% of each student's day was taught in Spanish and 50% was taught in English. The Government Hill program, called *Exito!*, placed an equal number of English speakers and Spanish speakers into each class. When the instruction was conducted in Spanish, the Spanish-speaking children were at an advantage; they were leading and showing the other students. Consequently, they developed self-esteem and pride in their native language and culture.

The Government Hill program was based on the latest research. The model emphasized social interaction for language learning (Rogoff, 1991), was predicated on the consistent integration of language with content (Genesee, 1993), and used bilingualism to advance literacy skills (Collier, 1992). Entry level for the program was kindergarten and first grade for English speakers and any grade level for Spanish speakers.

The program was built on ongoing strong professional development for teachers, paraprofessionals, parents, and volunteers. The staff developers, when delivering the training, modeled the teaching methods teachers used with the children: cooperative learning, inquiry-based learning, and team building. The training connected school personnel with parents as they completed joint activities. All course participants became grounded in second-language acquisition theory and application.

Community involvement was assured through a PRINT connection (Partners Reading In Needed Tutorial) with volunteers, primarily from the Alaska Railroad, a corporate sponsor. High school and university students majoring in languages were engaged and rewarded through a credit-bearing program sponsored by the local high schools and the University of Alaska. This tutoring component was conducted after school, in the early evenings, and on Saturdays. At Government Hill one readily saw how all students were involved with dual-language learning. That was not the case with special education, however.

"I CAN'T FIND THE SPECIAL EDUCATION STUDENTS"

When one walks around Government Hill and visits classrooms, one sees that students are actively engaged. After leaving the room, visitors are often asked to identify the classified special education students. They cannot.

Sandy Stephens brought many years of experience in special education to Government Hill. In her view, there is excessive overplacement of students in special education. For Sandy, the inclusion model is preferred. Classifying children as special education students means labeling them and driving down expectations in the eyes of students, their parents, and the staff. Large special education populations might be the norm in most schools but, as Sandy put it, "Not at Government Hill; not on my watch."

Sandy told the story of a third-grader who was falling behind his classmates. The staff persevered, as did the student. Reading skills and math results wavered near the passing level; nothing spectacular, but there was achievement. With a great deal of individual attention, tutoring, and emotional support, the child was definitely learning. A year later, an IQ test was administered, and the student scored only 75 but had standard scores in the 90s for all academic areas. If everyone had known about the score of 75 in advance, the staff would have had lowered expectations for this student, and the child's performance would have probably matched those expectations.

Changing the special education program required the same elements used with the two-way language immersion program: first, a shift in attitudes and beliefs; second, discussion of the latest research; third, ongoing staff development; and, finally, in-classroom support.

THE CARS ARE LINED UP AROUND THE BLOCK

Issue 24 of *The Nanuq Newsletter* appeared on April 29, 2001, announcing on its masthead "Government Hill Elementary School, A safe, positive, friendly, multicultural school with high standards for students." The two-sided photocopied family newsletter was filled with announcements and news in Spanish and English. The contents ranged from the mundane ("Use the overpass when coming and going to school"; "Breakfast to honor school volunteers"; "Soaring school lunch prices") to the marvelous ("The artists in residence will be teaching the ancient Japanese art of Taiko drumming to all our students"; "Join the annual city-wide clean up crew"; "Air Force band assembly"). The "Coming Events" column mentioned the Saturday Diversity Fair, a student mediation meeting, the "How Does Your Garden Grow?" musical, National Teachers Day, mobile mammography, a PTA meeting, an annual bike trip, and a field day.

Today, parents fight to get their children into Government Hill. The enrollment roller coaster ride was dramatic: Enrollment had plummeted from 350 (in 1988) to 175 (in 1991) and rocketed back up to 300 (in 1996) and then to 473 (in 2001). On registration day, cars circled the block, waiting their turn. As one parent described the school, "This is a great place to walk into. It feels like things are happening. There is a sense of energy."

James Blasingame, vice president for corporate affairs at the Alaska Railroad Corporation, explained how their involvement with Government Hill was motivated by self-interest. As one of the largest employers in Anchorage, they were unhappy with the skill level of job applicants. They understood that an upgrade in those skills had to start in the early grades. Consequently, when Sandy Stephens came for help for the Government Hill students, Alaska Railroad organized volunteer tutors who went to the school on company time. In Blasingame's words, "This quickly became an instant hit with our employees because they believed, as a corporation, we were doing the right thing by stepping forward to donate employee time and company resources for such a rewarding purpose."

Times changed. Government Hill got on the right track. As one staff member put it, "Teachers are here now because they want to be." Among the words and phrases used by teachers and parents to describe the new Government Hill are the following: *shared vision, focus, consistent, collaborative, pride, enriched, stable, open, welcoming*, and *happy*.

EXPLAINING WHAT HAPPENED

Timing is everything. By 1995, something had to happen with Government Hill. Declining enrollment triggered cosmetic changes—more students bussed in and, later, a district-mandated program. However, fundamental things did not change. A disconnect between district demands and school sentiment remained. Values and assumptions were frozen in place. The school stood still at a time when it needed to reinvent itself.

Sandy Stephens stepped in and had an unusual opportunity to take on the challenges. First, with her deep knowledge of special education and her commitment to diversity and dual-language programs, she had experiences unique to the Government Hill setting. Second, Sandy had worked with some Government Hill staff members for a full year before she was assigned to be the principal. Third, Sandy's formal assignment came early, and she had the opportunity to be at Government Hill for two months without having school authority and responsibilities. Those two months gave her important insights. She saw first hand how teachers taught, staff interacted, parents were treated, and students were served. Sandy Stephens did not have to make decisions based on second-hand information.

For the staff, Sandy Stephens provided a new outlook. In the words of one teacher, "I think it's the vision thing. Sandy knows where she wants the school to go." Another teacher quickly added, "Sandy is a good communicator, very approachable, accessible, and visible." Sandy Stephens understood her new school and the forces around it.

External pressure for change came in different forms. The state emphasis on test scores, coupled with public announcements of school rankings, made it impossible for Government Hill Elementary to hide. Middle-class parents in the immediate geographic zone would not accept an inferior school. School district officials welcomed and supported serious change initiatives.

The Title VII School Restructuring grant provided a different external force. It was hard to say no to a possible $1 million; consequently, the financial incentive was there. The grant process required a steering committee involving district officials, school staff, and parents; a "school family" had to be created. The grant demanded research-based strategies and measurable projected outcomes. The purpose of the grant was to reject what had failed; the school had to be fundamentally restructured. Cosmetic change would no longer be tolerated.

The December 24, 2000, issue of the *Anchorage Daily News* published a major article titled "Schools make strides; efforts bring big gains in test scores" (Shinohara). Government Hill Elementary was one of the three schools featured, with the article noting that Government Hill's "fourth grade reading and writing scores doubled in five years, making it the city's most improved elementary school, based on five years of California Achievement Test scores" (Shinohara, 2000, ¶ 3).

The Shinohara (2000) article also noted the following:

> Successful schools are guided by principals who pay attention to educational research and to what works elsewhere in the country. The schools have goals, a plan for getting better, and experienced teachers. Teachers at these schools engage in ongoing discussions about lessons and frequent training sessions. (¶ 11)

To explain what happened, one teacher created a diagram that depicted stages of change at Government Hill. At the start, Government Hill was a neighborhood school with low scores and some violence. The new language immersion program created uncertainty for staff and parents. With a new principal, the immersion program began to solidify, and the staff began to work cohesively. With a more active PTA and a new look at diversity, the "us and them" way of thinking changed. Test scores began to rise, the school's reputation strengthened, and the demand for the school made a waiting list necessary. An upward spiral was created with an enhanced school reputation and recognition, increased parent participation, and the fine-tuning of programs (see Figure 4.2).

The Title VII grant proposal, written in 1996, contains a line that captures the spirit of Government Hill Elementary: "It is centered on the child. It is driven always by its purpose of academic achievement." This goal, philosophy, and outlook translated itself, over five years, from vision to reality.

Figure 4.1   Demographics for Government Hill Elementary School, 2001

Grades: K–8	No. staff: 31
No. students: 459	Size of district: 50,000 students; 76 schools
White: 35% African American: 7% Hispanic: 37% Asian: 6% Native Alaskan: 10% Other: 5%	Elementary schools: 60 Middle schools: 9 High schools: 7

Figure 4.2 One teacher's interpretation of the school change process at Government Hill Elementary School

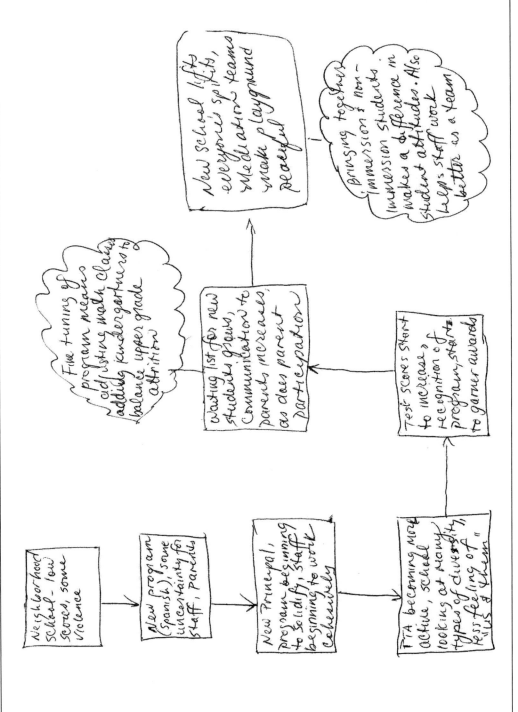

Drawing done by Melissa Abbott

5

"This School Must Be a Sanctuary"

John Williams School No. 5

Rochester, New York

Michele Hancock, Principal

The first thing Michele Hancock did was buy some paint. Then she recruited her husband, Charles, her younger son, Brandon, and his friend, a colleague, and three of her new staff to a painting party; they were going to spend the summer changing the look and feel of the John Williams School No. 5. For Michele, it was a "no-brainer": She had just been appointed principal of this failing elementary school and was determined to turn the school around. She knew it would be hard work and had to start somewhere.

PAINTING AS MESSAGE, MILESTONE, AND METAPHOR

Michele deliberately selected the physical structure because it emanated a sense of failure. Walls were scarred; the cafeteria, with its smell of melted ice cream, was repelling; the bathrooms were unacceptable. Graffiti, sometimes crude, marked the desks. The message was clear: "We do not care about you or about ourselves." As Michele put it, "The school wasn't right for the children. A school should be a sanctuary for the children it serves. John Williams School No. 5 wasn't a sanctuary. It was a disgrace."

To document the need for change, Michele asked her husband Charles to come to school and take photographs of the school's exterior and interior. She sent a letter with these pictures to the Deputy Superintendent for Operations. He was away and his secretary, as a matter of course, opened his mail and found these shocking photographs. Word quickly spread throughout the district office; the situation could not be ignored.

Michele believed that if she didn't upgrade the physical environment, she would not be able to move an agenda for change. And change was desperately needed. School No. 5's academic achievement ranked in the bottom 10% of Rochester's schools. Only 13.3% of the fourth-graders passed the New York State English Language Proficiency examination in 1999; fewer than one third passed the mathematics examination, and only 41.5% passed science. This was unacceptable.

Even with an increased awareness at the district office, they did not send painters to School No. 5. Michele and her crew had to do the painting. Charles told his wife that it was impossible; even with 18-hour days they could never get it done. Michele refused to give in. She engaged the head secretary, who was working in the school that summer. She recruited the school's parent liaison, who was thrilled to be involved. She called the school's art teacher, who joined Brandon and his friend in painting murals in the back of the cafeteria. Michele and her team attacked the hallways, main office, faculty lounge, and cafeteria with paintbrushes, motivational posters, and photographs of smiling children. Plants were placed in the entranceway. Michele inspired the school's custodial staff to clean the building in ways that had not been done before. When the head custodian complained he had no cleaning supplies, Michele simply told him to make a list. She got what he needed.

THERE IS NO "I" IN *PLATOON*

That 1999 summer was hot, much too hot to paint. Although the Hancock family and friends thought about quitting, they could not disappoint Michele, who inspired confidence and generated loyalty. Michele Hancock grew up in Chicago, coming from a family of five children where high expectations and helping others were core elements of the family value system. One of Michele's earliest memories is turning to her mother and saying she and her siblings couldn't have what the other kids had because the others were White. Her parents quickly squashed that thought, as did teachers in Michele's schools, who recognized the spark in her eyes.

As Michele put it, "I always knew I wanted to be a teacher because teachers expected a lot of me and helped me." From her youth, Michele became the leader, the helper, and the one in whom peers confided. Her professors at the University of Illinois, where she earned her degree in early childhood education, told her she had a natural gift for leadership.

Upon graduating from college, Michele enlisted in the Army Reserves, where she spent six years. She learned the importance of people working together toward a focused goal. She watched different styles of leadership and concluded that effective leaders knew how to directly and honestly deliver a message, something they modeled. In Michele's view, there is a big difference between appearing to complete a task and actually doing something that makes a difference.

In the Army, it was emphasized that there was no "I" in *platoon*. You preserved your individuality but committed it to a larger cause. As Michele insisted, "It is always bigger than you." The Army experience inspired Michele to think about Colin Powell and his determination to clearly tell who he was and what he represented. As an educator, Michele would do the same.

Michele Hancock started her educational career as a Head Start teacher in Chicago and was soon promoted to Infant Head Development teacher, which meant supervising teachers, developing an integrated curriculum that tied different subjects together, and training parents. In 1986, she arrived in Rochester and spent eight years as a primary teacher, teaching kindergarten through third grade in the city's schools. In 1994, Michele was named the cofacilitator of a teacher-run, Grades 3–5 primary school.

In 1998, she was tapped to help administer the James Madison School of Excellence, a new middle school. As her husband Charles remembers, "it became a year of hell," because Michele's energy and enthusiasm were threatening to others. But Michele did not let the petty jealousies bring her down. Her assignment was to create an interdisciplinary curriculum for young adolescents, and she found willing administrators and teachers to help plan and launch the new instructional approach.

BRINGING NEW LEADERSHIP TO SCHOOL NO. 5

The James Madison experience prepared Michele well for the challenges of School No. 5. Student achievement was abysmal. The teachers were quite unhappy with the school's leadership and filed grievance after grievance. Many parents complained. Nearly everyone believed School No. 5 was destined for failure and could not be changed.

Consequently, Michele took the time over the summer, in between painting sessions, to meet with groups of School No. 5 teachers. She discovered a high level of dissatisfaction centered on school conditions and practices. Michele moved ahead with a deliberate plan and sent each person on the entire staff a copy of *Who Moved My Cheese?* by Spencer Johnson (1998). This bestselling book uses the metaphor of two mice and two "little people" reacting differently when their cheese is moved. It is a tale of dealing with change and moving ahead, overcoming the challenges. Johnson's advice is to understand that change happens, anticipate it, monitor it, and adapt quickly. He urges us to enjoy change, rather than fear it. Michele saw the book as a way to introduce her to a school staff who cried out for change and, at the same time, feared what it would bring.

When the staff reported for the new school year on August 31, they walked around the refurbished school for an hour before the opening day staff meeting. They could not believe what they saw. When Michele walked into the auditorium to greet the staff, the group burst into applause. One teacher rose and said. "I am embarrassed that we allowed the school to be this way. Never again!" Michele told them that the school's physical transformation over the summer had been the work of only a few persons. Imagine what all of them could do!

After the staff meeting, Michele took a representative group around the building to see the physical changes. As one teacher stepped into the "new" cafeteria, she looked around and began to cry. It was clear School No. 5 needed change, could change, and had started to change.

Michele Hancock brought more than energy and paintbrushes to School No. 5; she also brought insights and critical experiences. Over several years, Michelle visited Kansas City, Missouri, to watch her sister-in-law, Audrey Faye-Bullard, in action. Audrey was an excellent teacher who became principal of one of the worst schools in that district. Using an Afrocentric curriculum, staff collaboration, and tough discipline, she brought her school from the bottom to the top. Audrey trail-blazed a path Michele would soon take in Rochester.

Michele Hancock didn't do it alone. She had her books with her. A voracious reader, she had been influenced by the writings of Marian Wright Edelman, Max DePree, Robert Quinn, and others. The common theme among those authors was gathering the strength to be a leader who empowers others. Michele fondly remembers those books: "They taught me not to be afraid to have people see me for who I am . . . that it was OK to show my vulnerability, to make mistakes and own up to them, to embrace people and to explain why I was doing what I was doing."

A SCHOOL IN DENIAL

There was much to change at School No. 5. The building was filthy and emanated a feeling of gloom and doom. One didn't feel safe in the community—and in the school. As Michele explained, "This was the school where they found a body in the Dumpster; where 22 years ago a teacher was shot in the building." The school was out of control, and the teachers felt abandoned, without the support of the school's administration.

Teachers worked in isolation, with each teacher driven by her or his personal view of teaching. Special-interest groups vied for control of the master schedule each year; self-interest ruled. With a teacher's contract that said the teachers' workday ended when the students were dismissed, many adults left the parking lot before the school buses departed. Generally speaking, there seemed to be no sense of community or commitment. In a state of denial, many teachers in School No. 5 did not admit or confront the school's problems and faults.

On her first day with the full staff, Michele's distributed a questionnaire, which asked the staff to name the two best things about School No. 5 the new principal should know about. The overwhelming responses were that the staff cared about the students and saw the diversity of the students as a strength. Furthermore, the survey results declared, "The staff is really committed. They are willing to try many things for the good of students, willing to share ideas, and seek change."

The survey also included the following item: "to become a successful educational institution, list two things that we need to work on or change at School #5 *right now.*" The three most repeated responses centered on resources (textbooks, computers, supplies), schoolwide expectations (discipline policy, recognition of accomplishments), and the improvement of staff morale. Only one person said to improve reading scores, and only three mentioned inclusion or effective integration of subject content.

The survey results for Michele were useful for what they showed and for what they did not show. She saw the staff did not take responsibility for the school's dismal performance. She knew that with a sense of order and accountability, instruction and student achievement could improve. Michele understood that everyone would not like her, but she was determined to win their respect by taking decisive actions. It started on the very first day the teachers reported back, when Principal Michele Hancock told the staff they could do better. It continued on the first day of school for the children, when Michele demonstrated her enforcement of school rules as she suspended two students who were misbehaving in the cafeteria, renamed the "Sunshine Cafe." The school needed new leadership; it got it.

OVERCOMING RESISTANCE AND MOVING FORWARD

Michele Hancock's message was stated early and repeated often: "Accept responsibility for the school situation, regardless of the circumstances that got the school to that point." After restoring order and dramatically changing the school's physical environment, Michele focused on how the school programmed its teachers and students. For example, there were fifteen special education self-contained classes, which caused many in the district to say "Oh, you work in that special education school." Michele and her supporters reorganized those students into eleven inclusion classes and only four self-contained classes. Second-language learners also were mainstreamed.

Michele encountered resistance; there were determined blockers. Some teachers did not want to meet as grade-level teams. Others resented Michele's insistence on feedback. The English language learner teachers did not want their students to move into inclusion classes, and they contacted the district coordinator of their program. He took their side and told Michele to halt her proposed change. However, Michele Hancock would not be deterred. These teachers might be angry with her, but she responded quietly and professionally. Slowly, she won over all but three nay-sayers by sharing articles on the latest research showing that inclusion worked for English language learners.

It is fortunate Dr. Clifford Janey was the superintendent of the Rochester Public Schools. Janey had a low-key style, and he supported Michele behind the scenes. He was accessible. When Michele faced a particularly difficult situation, she would call, and he would visit her at the school. He consistently asked her to think through the situation and move from an emotional reaction to a reasoned and logical response. To reinforce his suggestions, Janey added to Michele's personal library books like *Leading Change* by John Kotter (1996), which outlines how change was successfully conducted in the corporate world.

With the change in the master schedule, common planning time was created for grade-level teams to meet twice a week. These forty-five-minute meetings enabled teachers to analyze student work, align curriculum goals, share best instructional practices, and discuss professional articles. Michele Hancock asked for written feedback about each meeting, summarizing the discussion and the follow-up plans.

Michele then began to raise the bar, beginning with the first-grade teachers. She discussed articles with them. She modeled lessons. She sent them to visit other schools (while she covered their classes). In effect, Michele was creating a community of adult learners, much of it built around the ideas of reformer Richard DuFour, nationally known for his research about professional learning communities and collaborative teams. Michele's goal was to have her teachers ask themselves whether they were making a difference.

During her first year as principal, Michele took three of her staff to a conference in Chicago conducted by DuFour so they could hear him and visit a troubled Chicago school that had turned around using his strategies. Michele's team took photographs at that school and made several presentations back at School No. 5. The staff now understood that a school located in a depressed area, such as theirs, could make a difference for kids if administrators, staff, parents, and children worked together.

During her second year, Michele took the five grade-level facilitators to an urban education conference in Las Vegas. DuFour's message was reinforced as speaker after speaker insisted that urban kids should be seen as resolute and filled with their own strengths, not as empty vessels needing to be filled with adult wisdom and knowledge. The follow-up at School No. 5 involved a dinner meeting with the entire staff, at which time the grade-level facilitators began their turnkey training with the rest of the staff.

CHANGE INCREMENTALLY, YET DECISIVELY

Michele Hancock posed challenging questions; at the same time, she tried to be nonjudgmental. She understood her teachers, who had complained of never being supported, needed to be brought along slowly. She knew she had to show an interest in their professional lives and, as she put it, "in their lives as human beings." That attitude, she hoped, would trickle down to how her teachers would view and interact with their students.

Michele organized teams to learn about, adapt/create, and implement a series of research-based approaches focusing on student behavior, support for students, and teaching/learning. At the same time, Michele and some volunteers created a new School No. 5 Instructional Handbook, which summarized the school's philosophy.

The staff-authored instructional handbook explicitly (and visually) connected expectations and norms for students, teachers, curriculum, and the environment. Students would work independently and collaboratively, be able to demonstrate what they were learning, and answer essential questions. Teachers would bring high expectations to their roles as coaches, vary activities, pose essential questions, develop rubrics, use student assessments for planning instruction, and share with their colleagues. The curriculum would align strategies with standards, be built around essential questions, and be developed horizontally and vertically. Finally, the environment would encourage active learning and display clear expectations, essential questions, and student work.

To provide structure, set limits, and strengthen a sense of order and discipline, a series of student behavior programs were created for the students. The first disciplinary strategy was the "Second Chance Intervention Room," set up as a "pre-crisis location to provide students with a safe location to analyze their feelings with appropriate adult engagement." In other words, it was a time-out room or, as Michele Hancock put it, "a place and a time to chill out." Students could be in the room for no more than 30 minutes and couldn't be sent to the room more than once a day.

Peer mediation became the next disciplinary strategy. As its guidelines state, "School No. 5 has an ongoing commitment to assist our students in becoming 21st century problem solvers." In 2001, the school's physical education teacher and social worker initiated the school's peer mediation program, with help from the Center for Dispute Settlement, a local nonprofit organization. Twenty-one third- and fourth-graders were trained in conflict resolution strategies and given their own room in which to mediate with students. The number of disciplinary referrals dropped dramatically while students learned how to handle themselves and help others.

The final disciplinary approach took the form of an alternative out-of-school suspension program, which included literacy development and community service. Called the "Community ConnecTime program," it assigned intermediate students (Grades 3–5) to community service activities, such as FOODLINK, which provided meals to the hungry. As the volunteer coordinator of FOODLINK wrote, the John Williams School No. 5 students enabled the organization "to efficiently move food to the programs that directly serve people in need within our community." The hungry were fed, while at the same time students learned that they could make a difference in someone else's life.

The support systems for students and their families took several forms. The idea for a Strategic Intervention Team was adapted from another Rochester elementary school. Children were referred to this team, which included the principal, assistant principal, a social worker, and two teachers. It was not a referral for special education but a proactive program dedicated to preventing problems from worsening. Each child was reviewed, with strengths identified and goals set. Then, strategies were planned for the classroom (e.g., pair the child with another student who could help with sentence structure assignments), schoolwide (create opportunities for this student to complete art projects), with the family (provide closer supervision with homework), and in the community (enroll the child in a summer recreational program).

The staff created the "Bobcat Kids College," which provided courses in an extended day program. These opportunities enabled students to improve literacy skills through drama; master computing skills, such as word processing, using spreadsheets, and completing graphic designs; practice reading and math problem-solving strategies; develop math skills through playing golf; learn science through cooking; and play sports by integrating reading and fine motor skills. Each instructor was called "professor"; so, for example, it was Professor Michele Hancock who taught an economics course, which integrated reading, writing, and mathematics.

Michele Hancock's younger son, Brandon, was responsible for one of the support systems. He was a senior at McQuaid Jesuit High School, and he needed a project to complete his community service requirement. He asked his mother if he could organize a team of tutors who would spend one day each week at School No. 5. Michele said yes, and the McQuaid Student Tutors program was born. It paired fifteen successful high school students with School No. 5 students who needed help in specific subjects, such as mathematics, and in general learning skills, such as organizing time.

IN THIS ROOM, YOU WILL FIND . . .

It was June 7, 2003. I was at School No. 5 to present the National School Change Award. Before the ceremony, I walked the halls and visited classes with Michele. A large hand-made poster outside a classroom caught my attention. It announced the name of the teacher who taught in that room and explained her special expertise. Outside the next room, a similar poster appeared. As we walked, we read about one teacher, who was recognized for her skills in cooperative learning, and others who were "expert" in direct instruction, student grouping, balanced literacy, and so on. On all the posters, the methodology was briefly explained, and teachers and visitors were invited to see teachers in action and learn more about a particular methodology.

These posters did more than decorate a hall. They sent a clear message how at School No. 5, teaching and learning were important for both the students and the staff. Other posters around the school celebrated the school's success in reaching goals, told about the rising scores, and announced the state standards that were being met. However, these posters were different; they attested to the various ways individual teachers could motivate and move their students to higher levels of success. These posters announced teacher learning and growth. They made it clear that School No. 5 was a professional learning community.

Teachers visited each other. They learned from each other and celebrated their new learning. Teachers taught their colleagues and felt good about what they were able to show. Students were proud of what they were learning and could explain how that learning unfolded. The conversations about teaching and learning became richer. As one teacher put it, "I never appreciated how excited students could become when working in teams. I saw it and found out from my colleague how to plan and organize these worthwhile activities. Then, I did it!" To make these intervisitations a reality, someone had to take over classes while teachers saw a colleague in action. Michele Hancock taught those classes and, in doing so, she emphasized the importance of these class intervisitations. It was clear Michele Hancock was an instructional leader who would assist, model, and provide resources. She "walked the talk."

WALLS THAT TELL STORIES

John Williams School No. 5 sits in a traditional gothic-styled brick building built in the 1890s. The entrance has limestone sculpted flowers overhead. The front door is massive, and it is locked. You have to ring a buzzer to be let in. Fortunately, the inside is much more inviting. The security desk posts a prominent welcome sign. Color is everywhere.

A poster portrayed two sculpted figures: one a teacher, one a parent. It mirrored the poster next to it, which said "When parents and teachers collaborate on behalf of children, they create windows of light for the generation that follows." A homemade poster declared "I know I can be what I want to be, if I work at it, I'll be where I want to be." A gigantic calendar announced holidays and major events: final exams, Flag Day, field day, Father's Day, moving-up ceremonies, report cards. Student work was displayed next to the state standards the work satisfied.

Another poster told about a trip to the amusement park Darien Lake. It announced the skills that had to be applied so funds could be secured for the trip. The list read: organizing and conducting a bake sale and a candy sale, using Excel to plan a pizza sale, solving word problems, creating "superman equations," and working in teams to plan the activities.

It used to be a standard school hallway, circling around the second floor. Not anymore. Not for those three days. While other corridors at John Williams School No. 5 could boast student achievements, celebrate academic projects, announce school goals, display photographs of active learning, tell about special activities, and proclaim teacher specialties, this was different. This was an art gallery, filled with student work. Every grade was represented with a display of paintings, drawings, printmaking, self-portraits, masks, fiber projects, still-life drawings, paper sculptures, three-dimensional clay projects, and line drawings. Students in their finest attire welcomed and escorted parents and other guests through a gallery walk. Many visitors inquired about the prices of the artwork and returned to School No. 5 the next week to pick up their purchases. Adding to the celebratory atmosphere, a "Cultural Food Tasting" was conducted in the auditorium.

THE CHANGE JOURNEY CONTINUES

The rhythm of the John Williams school year now includes time to reflect, revise, and recharge. A voluntary book club brings together staff members who are interested in discussing the latest books on education. Informal conversations unfold between Michele Hancock and individual teachers about their classroom activities and about specific students. Data showing progress toward school goals are posted on wall charts. And then there are the special events for the staff.

For example, two days in March 2004 were devoted to a "teacher exchange." Teachers were matched with a colleague who taught a different grade. Meeting in advance, each pair of teachers discussed "plans for the day and strategies to best address the emotional and management needs of the classroom and individual students." To guide and enrich the experience, teachers were asked to select two of ten reflective questions, which included looking at strategies used to start lessons, developing supports for students not meeting exit standards, using the learning histories of individual students, inserting the content across the curricula, and providing support for families.

The collective conversation continued on May 28, the traditional superintendent's conference day devoted to staff planning and/or professional development. At School No. 5, teams worked on various components of the 2004–05 School Improvement Plan. A wide range of topics were discussed, from interdisciplinary instruction, the classroom integration of technology, and curriculum mapping, on one hand, to academic intervention services, professional development, and parental involvement, on the other hand.

Evaluations of these staff development days revealed much about the state of the school. The majority of responses praised being able to work with a diverse group and generating many ideas. People enjoyed the small groups, felt they were active participants, and appreciated the fact that their ideas/input were valued. When asked to share how the school improvement planning session impacted them as individuals, responses included:

> It was fantastic to be off school property . . . wonderful plans have been created . . . I've learned a lot about the responsibility of providing children with a quality education . . . it has increased my interest in the new reading program . . . very informative . . . it made me think how I can improve in certain areas . . . unfortunate that we were rushed, we could have done this for a full weekend . . . I see how dedicated many of our staff are in creating a good school environment for students and staff.

EXPLAINING WHAT HAPPENED

When I asked School No. 5's staff to visually summarize what had happened at their school, they used different symbols to illustrate the change process. One teacher composed her drawing with a tree in the center. The roots were labeled *professional growth*, *hope*, *structure*, *boundaries*, and *change*. The trunk used the word *strengthen*. The treetop was called *new change*, with "respect, results, working together and happy," pointing to that treetop. A watering can was labeled *nourishment*, and a sun said *life*.

A second person used a bumpy line called *climbing up*. It started with 1997, "Alone—lack of support" and ended with 2004. At one point on the journey upward, a list of words appeared: *standards*, *policies*, *procedures/rules*, *consistency* (with an asterisk next to it to indicate its special importance), *high expectations*, *empowerment*, *professional development*, *organization*, *reflective practices*, and *celebrations*. This led to staff/parents working together. However, in getting from 1997 to 2004, there was a trail labeled "dips in the road" and a jagged line.

A third artist drew a pyramid. The base was labeled "Putting children first." The layers leading to the top were sequenced: grant money and personal funds, set rules and procedures in place and consistently enforced, constant change and reflection, professional development for all, physical environment, developing a family community, all welcomed to every committee, empowerment, and high expectations. Finally, the top layer was called "Knowing that we will never truly get there," and the apex was labeled *achievement* (see Figure 5.2).

What themes emerged? There was an overriding feeling that a journey had unfolded, one that had not ended. A combination of strategies was used: financial, practical (supplies, exterminators, and cleanliness), and professional development. Metaphors centered on growth, with many elements contributing to that growth. There seemed to be an invisible hand, bringing about consistency, clarity, and a new sense of community. There was a decisive new leader, one who unleashed the energies of many. This was not a solo journey. It was difficult, but it was hopeful and ultimately successful.

On one of the walls in Michele Hancock's office, Margaret Mead's words claimed, "Never doubt that a small group of thoughtful, committed people can change the world." That said it all.

Figure 5.1   Demographics for John Williams School No. 5, 2003

Grades: Pre-K–5	No. staff: 120
No. students: 560	Size of district: 34,000 students;
White: 20.6% African American: 48.9% Hispanic: 22.1% Asian: 8.4%	56 schools Elementary schools/middle schools: 40 High schools: 16

Figure 5.2   One teacher's interpretation of the school change process at
John Williams School No. 5

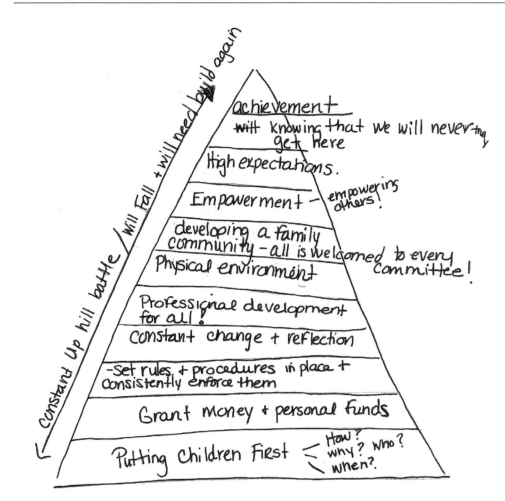

Drawing done by Kelly Bauman

6

"California Dreaming"

Skycrest Elementary

Citrus Heights, California

Chris Zarzana, Principal

It became a family dispute. Chris Zarzana came home and told her husband what had transpired in her meeting with San Juan Unified District Assistant Superintendent Arlene Inglis. She had asked Chris to take charge of the worst school in the district, Skycrest Elementary. Chris was an experienced and highly regarded elementary school principal, leading one of the best elementary schools in the district. She was intrigued with the Skycrest challenge. Her husband, George, also an experienced and accomplished elementary school principal in the district, felt that it would be a great mistake. As he stated, "Are you nuts? Why would you move when you are having a great time, doing what you do so well?"

Chris took the job. Her husband was right; the school was in desperate need of change. There was no sense of discipline or order. Staff morale was at an all-time low. The 12 "portables," each housing two classrooms, were more like military Quonset huts, as if the school were under siege. The place was depressing, as were the test scores. Ninety percent of the children were one or more years below the expected reading level.

A CALIFORNIA STORY OF OPPORTUNITIES AND DISAPPOINTMENTS

For more than a century, California served as a magnet, attracting millions of Americans from across the country and millions of new immigrants. California symbolized the American dream, with its promise and possibilities. But for many families the dreams were denied. Skycrest Elementary School in Citrus Heights exemplified that disappointment.

Like many school districts that sit outside major cities, the district had an urban and suburban flavor. Sacramento, California's state capital, was a twenty-five-minute drive away, and many Citrus Heights residents worked in the city. The area's social–economic characteristics and demographics were similar to many urban centers. Most residents rented apartments instead of owning homes. Yet the dependence on automobiles, the spread of ranch-type homes, and the activity in shopping malls created a suburban flavor.

Citrus Heights was a newly incorporated community that reflected the urban and suburban mix. As Mayor Tom Rainey explained, Citrus Heights became its own entity because the local residents felt underserved and were angry because their tax dollars were being funneled away to fund services in the larger county. In 1991, the residents voted for change. A new formula was created that allowed the Citrus Heights community to tax itself as much as it wanted, with the county and the federal government providing matches in funding. The California State Supreme Court approved the new government structure. The county appealed to the U.S. Supreme Court, which refused to hear the case. Therefore, the county could no longer block the change; Citrus Heights, as an independent incorporated entity, was born.

The Citrus Heights saga served as a metaphor for the Skycrest story. In both cases, there were dissatisfaction with the existing conditions and a perceived need for a new governance structure and dynamic leadership. It was clear that the old ways did not work, and people realized that change was needed. "You take something that is tired and run down and you show there is a better way," is how Mayor Rainey described the changes in the community's status. He described the renewal of Skycrest Elementary in the same terms.

"MY NEIGHBORS TOLD ME NOT TO SEND MY CHILD TO SKYCREST"

When Chris Zarzana arrived at Skycrest as its new principal, she inherited a school in deep trouble. Staff and parents described Skycrest as being rudderless and out of control. There was no direction or vision, as exemplified by previous principals convening staff meetings and not having an agenda. As one teacher saw it, "We didn't have a goal. It was just a matter of trying to get through the day."

In effect, teachers did whatever they wanted, as did the children, who did not respect each other or the staff. Parents were concerned about the name-calling, fighting, and the lack of discipline. As another teacher described it, "The kids did not have problem-solving skills. Instead, they hit or shoved their classmates." There were no discipline guidelines for the school; each classroom had its own set of rules.

The teachers worked in isolation, with little sharing or collaboration. As one teacher stated, "Every teacher was her own island. We were all friends but not teammates. We made no effort to identify or correct the school's problems. To me, I thought that was how all schools operated." Another teacher noted, "We didn't know anything different."

The physical conditions reflected the absence of order and pride; litter was everywhere, and it seemed no one cared about the place. Doors were painted dark colors; there was a somber tone. As Chris Zarzana remembered, the place was "drab, dingy, and dirty." The teaching materials were uninviting and outdated. In the eyes of many parents, the teachers did not care; they were just putting in their time.

Meanwhile, the student population of Skycrest had changed. New immigrants, largely from eastern Europe and Mexico, poured into the district. The need for English language learning intensified. The school's designation as a Title I school started in 1976, and the percentage of students receiving free or reduced-price lunch grew each year.

Skycrest teachers were in a state of denial. As they saw it, the school's low academic performance had nothing to do with them. In their view, these new students weren't the San Juan Unified School District students they had always taught. As one district administrator noted, "The problem was the teachers did not have the strategies to deal with this changing population . . . Furthermore, if you really want a problem solved, you must have the people closest to the problem working to solve it." At Skycrest that was impossible, because the teachers did not understand or accept that there was a problem.

As another assistant superintendent remembered, the sentiment among many teachers was that "they were doing the best that they could with the students they get." No one challenged that attitude. Skycrest was a place that lumbered along as if all was well. Teachers who were close to retirement were assigned to Skycrest. The last five principals before Chris Zarzana had Skycrest as their final assignment before each of them retired. There was no effort to have parents involved, and consequently there was no parental pressure to improve the school. California student achievement standards had not yet been promulgated, so there was no external state pressure to do better.

No one asked the teachers, "What are the kids learning?" There was no standards-based curriculum. There was no way to judge student progress and no effective approach being used to assist the students with weaker skills. For example, the low-performing students (and there were many) were pulled out of their regular classes to be remediated. This meant they were taught a "dumbed-down" version of the same material.

"I hated coming to work" is how a veteran teacher described her feelings about Skycrest. The school was mired in its own familiar sense of failure. Skycrest had become a school with low expectations for students and sense of frustration for teachers. It was a great disappointment for the community. There was no joy at Skycrest. Someone needed to reverse the downward spiral.

THE RIGHT PERSON, AT THE RIGHT PLACE, AT THE RIGHT TIME

When it became known that Chris Zarzana was coming to Skycrest to be its next principal, staff members quite naturally tried to "get the scoop." They learned Chris had a reputation for being a no-nonsense person and that she was tough. She was a leader who got things done. In the view of one of the veteran teachers, "The district was sending in one of the big guns." Chris was described as tenacious, focused, and primarily interested in student learning and achievement. She was known as a strong disciplinarian and someone who set high standards. Although many Skycrest teachers craved strong leadership and knew that something had to be done, they were frightened. As one teacher put it, "When a big change is needed it's very scary. People have to come out of their comfort zone."

Chris Zarzana matched her reputation. But she was more than tough. Chris understood that a strong leader needs to set direction but also needs to involve others in important decisions. She understood that the necessary changes at Skycrest would be difficult to achieve and that teachers needed to be nurtured and cared for. Chris understood that all problems could not be solved at once and that facilitating change was a complex endeavor. With a determined effort, however, it could be done; Chris Zarzana's life demonstrated this.

From the age of four, Chris heard her mother say she was going to go to college, and from the age of five, Chris was a regular visitor at the local library. She became an insatiable reader, with a relentless desire to learn more. At the same time, Chris was instilled with a strong work ethic, one later reinforced by the nuns in her high school. Others saw Chris, as a child and later as an adult, filled with promise, and that perception became Chris's reality. She described her outlook thus: "You can do anything you set your mind to do. But if you are going to do something, do it well."

That attitude drove her educational career and helped explain why Chris refused to accept student failure. She had high expectations for herself and for others, adults and children. However, to help others do better, one had to know more. Chris developed an unusual thirst for knowledge, which in her view made her a research-based person. Of particular interest to Chris were questions about how children learned.

Understanding how to teach reading became Chris's area of expertise. She earned her master's degree in administration and her state certification as a reading specialist. She attended reading conferences across the United States as

" research based person "

both a participant and a presenter. She became fluent in the latest research about reading. As Chris moved through the San Juan school system as a first-grade teacher, reading specialist, vice principal, and principal, she became known as a reading expert. Chris wanted all children to experience the joy of reading, just as she had in her developmental years.

Chris Zarzana was a teenager in the 1960s and was strongly influenced by those times of challenge and change. President John F. Kennedy was one of her heroes because of his vitality and his message. Kennedy's call for a New Frontier, his questioning of the status quo, and his blending of idealism and pragmatism impressed Chris. She adopted a similar attitude. Chris wanted to be part of a new wave of leaders who could make things happen. She got her chance in the San Juan school district.

As late as the mid-1970s, the principals in the district were members of an "old boys" network, with most having a physical education background. In 1976, fifty of the fifty-four principals were men. They were the managers of their schools. Chris Zarzana became a member of a new wave of principals in the San Juan Unified School District. These principals, mostly women (forty-three of fifty-three in 2000), frequently had strong backgrounds in reading. They saw themselves as instructional leaders.

STARTING WITH SMALL BUT SIGNIFICANT STEPS

Before arriving at Skycrest Elementary to serve as its principal in September 1991, Chris did her homework. Over the summer, she mailed a letter to the entire staff, asking each person to meet with her to discuss the strengths and weaknesses of the school. Most of the staff responded to the invitation. As expected, the teachers were most concerned with the children's unruly behavior. They wanted a leader who could clean up the place, literally and figuratively.

Chris first responded with the obvious: She ordered the cleanup of the campus. She painted the inside of the first building, which contained the school's office. Chris's secretary selected the paint; her vice principal pitched in; and a retired painter, who babysat for the vice principal, was recruited. It was a start.

On the basis of staff feedback, Chris formed an advisory group, with one teacher representing each of the seven grades. As Chris described it, she had to first take the "kindergarten steps" of serving as a principal by restoring order. Additionally, Chris created four committees to address major concerns about student behavior: (1) establishing and maintaining rules, (2) rewards and recognition, (3) bus behavior, and (4) cafeteria tone.

Chris responded with a directive approach. After receiving the input from the staff, Chris laid down the law. The school needed a firm hand and strong sense of direction; Chris provided them. In restoring order, Chris accomplished four things. First, she set the foundation for the more important agenda. She knew teachers could not pay attention to new instructional techniques if they were concerned about order and safety. Second, Chris established her credibility.

She could make things happen. The teachers appreciated and respected her initial actions. Third, Chris won the confidence of the parents. Seventy-five percent of the families who sent children to Skycrest were new immigrants, and they did not know what to expect from American schools. Many felt that something was wrong but did not know where to turn. Finally, Chris demonstrated to the district office that their investment in resources for Skycrest Elementary School would be well spent. Even George, Chris's husband, was won over.

IT WASN'T A YELLOW BRICK ROAD

Bringing academic achievement to Skycrest was not easy, but Chris's previous experience as a principal paid off. As she explained, "I learned once you leave the classroom, you are perceived differently. I learned how to set the stage. I learned things come more readily if teacher voices are heard." Chris combined decisive decision making with teacher empowerment. For example, when the new school year began, Chris distributed a new teachers' handbook. Its ideas were drawn from the teachers and reflected their concerns, but it was Chris who brought it together. She announced that this new handbook would be used; this was how things would work. As one veteran teacher observed, "Chris was someone you could respect."

Chris Zarzana won everyone's respect by making the Skycrest commitment clear to students, staff, parents, and the larger community. "At Skycrest, we are a community of learners, with everyone participating in the excitement of learning," is how Chris described the school. Skycrest was transformed into a learning community where lifelong learning was encouraged and rewarded. One teacher thankfully said, "In my 13 years of teaching, I never felt like I was a professional. Now, I feel that way." Chris Zarzana elevated the role of the classroom teacher. She reminded the teachers of their importance, their mission, and their critical role in the life of each and every student. She told them they would see better results—and they did.

Chris patiently and carefully led teachers to a new understanding of how to assess and teach their students. While she played the role of a coach, Chris admitted that sometimes she just wanted to tell some teachers the way they were teaching just wasn't working. Chris knew much needed to be done and that the teachers were the ones who had to do it. They needed to be given new insights, knowledge, and tools.

Extensive professional development was provided for the entire staff. The clerical staff was taught how to use the latest technology. The instructional assistants were trained in writing workshop strategies, using technology in the reading intervention model, and so on. Teachers were taught how to assess student progress, plan interventions, differentiate instruction, and use a range of teaching methods.

There were three ways professional development was conducted. First, it was held on site, with modeling and practice conducted in Skycrest classrooms on topics such as interactive writing, guided reading strategies, and the open-court phonics program. Second, at times it was district mandated, with Skycrest staff receiving training in the assessment of fluency in reading, writing, listening, and speaking. Third, Skycrest staff attended conferences and seminars, which focused on successful strategies designed by nationally recognized organizations such as The Great Books Foundation and reading and assessment experts such as John Shefelbine, J. David Cooper, and Douglas Reeves.

Students were taught to believe in themselves. The story was told of a student who became quite frustrated as he tried to complete a class reading assignment. After declaring, "I can't," his fifth-grade peers responded by yelling back, "Not yet!" Skycrest students had adopted a new attitude. They were working at "getting it"—and with enough effort, they would get it. As one teacher noted, "There isn't a kid at Skycrest who believes she cannot learn."

Students talked about their progress. They knew where they were and where they needed to go in terms of their own achievement levels. They were clear about the number of words per minute they could currently read and about their next reading goal. They were eager readers, and they were determined to improve.

Parents were recognized as instructional partners and providers. As the Skycrest team declared in their school change award application, "Parents will always be their children's first teachers." Consequently, on enrollment, kindergarten parents were given a packet of games and materials to help with the students' transition to school. Parent education workshops were conducted. Second-language translations and frequent contact with parents improved communication and created a strong school–home connection. Parents were welcomed as volunteers, involved in an active parent/teacher organization, shown instructional materials on Family Nights, and surveyed annually about how Skycrest was doing.

At the same time, parents were supported. Multiple social services were made accessible to families. Social workers were housed on campus. Preschool programs were conducted at the school, including an all-day federally funded Head Start program. Chris was entrepreneurial and relentless in gaining resources for the Skycrest students, staff, and parents. She identified district, state, and federal funding sources and secured release time for teacher volunteers to write grant proposals and applications.

The link between and among staff, students, and parents was reinforced through a written contract that detailed each stakeholder's responsibility in the learning process. Because the Skycrest staff never abandoned their concern with student behavior and responsibility, the contract emphasized both academic growth and character building. The school won a Character Education Grant, which focused on encouraging tolerance, celebrating diversity, and teaching problem-solving skills. In effect, the students were taught to respect themselves and each other. The staff were expected to do the same by working together and recognizing the talents each student brought to the table.

The goal was to change the school's culture and, slowly, that happened. In Chris's view, the achievement of the at-risk students (and almost all Skycrest students were at risk) "has nothing to do with who they are or where they come from; it has to do with how we teach them." To facilitate conversations about teaching and learning, Chris distributed abundant data about Skycrest students: test scores, comparisons of academic achievement between and among students, progress (or lack thereof) when students moved from one grade to the next, and comparisons with schools inside and outside the district with similar populations. Chris asked the staff to determine what the data revealed, the implications of the findings, and what ought to be done.

Grade-level meetings took on greater importance as teams of teachers planned how to improve the performance of the students in their grade. In addition, the teachers spoke with the teachers of the previous grade so they would better understand the strengths and needs of the students they would be teaching. At the same time, teachers communicated with teachers of the next grade to better understand their expectations.

As one teacher stated, "We talk more. We plan more. We change things. It is not top down." Discussing research findings and visiting other schools became a regular routine.

As one would expect, not everyone welcomed this new Skycrest life. Therefore, Chris identified a core group of teachers who wanted to change, and she leveraged their enthusiasm and success to bring others into the change effort.

READING, READING, AND READING

As Chris Zarzana puts it, "It's unethical to know about the best practices and not use them." Much was known about the teaching of reading, but this knowledge had not been tapped for Skycrest students. The focus on reading instruction and assessment made sense for many reasons. Teaching reading brings great rewards for the students as new worlds open up for them. Teachers feel they are making a difference in the lives of children. Research provides clues about how to teach reading, reading success is measurable, and teachers can learn to be more effective. As progress is made, one can build on a series of small successes. Most important, reading is at the core of learning and understanding.

When Chris became Skycrest's principal in 1991, there were no California state reading standards. The school created its own standards and used them to drive reading instruction. The school's curriculum content and evaluation tools were aligned with the school's standards; content benchmarking enabled both students and teachers to measure individual progress. Skycrest was ahead of the curve.

When California finally created reading standards, the Skycrest staff welcomed them with open arms, because they knew how important standards were—and they had less to do; the school's reading program was aligned with the state standards.

The Skycrest staff began each year with a comprehensive look at each student in terms of reading (as well as writing and mathematics) skills, using both district- and school-based aligned assessments. These baseline data helped to place students in the school's Collaborative Reading Program, which, for a portion of the school day, divided students of the same grade into small groups. These small groups brought together children from different classrooms so they could meet and work with other students who were at the same reading level. As students developed their skills, each would be assigned to a different collaborative group, which matched the higher reading level.

The schoolwide reading program was predicated on research-based strategies and embraced a balanced literacy approach, built on the ideas of J. David Cooper. The kindergarten through second-grade students focused on phonemic awareness, phonics, reading fluency, and developing reading comprehension. In Grades 3 through 6, the emphasis shifted to developing strategic readers. Shefelbine's word syllabication strategies were used; vocabulary building became more important; and expository writing folded into the process. Skycrest's comprehensive reading program and the school's remarkable results became the talk of the San Juan Unified School District.

THE GENERAL

As Chris Zarzana looked back at the district's history, she described two previous superintendents who differed in style but not in results. One separated himself from the school administrators and teachers. He didn't understand schools and did not include principals on his core team. The second superintendent, considered by some to be a "healer," had better interpersonal skills but wanted to keep everyone happy. He did not make bold or controversial decisions. During the tenure of these two superintendents, academic performance remained low in many of the district's schools, including Skycrest.

In 1997, Dr. General Davies became the superintendent. Although his first name signified a military presence, General Davies had not served in the military. However, he personified precision, high expectations, and results. More important, he knew about classroom instruction, and he positioned the district office to support schools. Like Chris, when he assumed his new position, he asked others what was right and what was wrong. General Davies conducted focus group discussions built around one central question: "What is getting in the way of student achievement?"

Davies was not happy with what he heard. He expected more from his teachers and his students throughout the district. During his tenure, low expectations and poor results would not be tolerated, and within two years all but two schools were doing significantly better. Student success became a crusade. Caring about kids became the district's mission. A poster in Davies's office declared "Child, let me walk in the light of your faith in me." For Davies, Chris Zarzana embodied the poster's message.

In 2000, as Davies looked back at the astounding success of Skycrest, he credited five factors:

1. A strong vision articulated by the principal; Chris made the school's purpose and priorities clear to one and all.

2. Constant assessment of students with the identification of what was needed to reach each student; those discussions became the focus of many meetings held by the Skycrest staff.

3. Changing the culture of the school; new rituals, ceremonies, and routines shifted the attitudes and beliefs of the staff.

4. Consistency and celebration; on a regular basis the good work conducted by staff and completed by students was acknowledged.

5. Finally, and especially critical, leadership; Davies described Chris Zarzana as "maybe being a little more autocratic than [I] wished, but being demanding was what was called for at Skycrest."

Davies was an experienced superintendent, with 30 years in education, when he came to the San Juan Unified School District. Davies made it clear he was focused on instruction and used a transition team to identify cultural and structural impediments. He quickly reorganized his central office staff and required them to think about specific things the district office could do to support principals. As he put it, the goal was to "have the district office staff see the principals as their boss."

Davies combined his actions with a deep understanding of change. As he put it, "This is painful stuff. I am asking people to let go of their security blankets." Davies appreciated what change involved and why transitions were difficult for many people. For Davies, change was a normal part of life but was often misunderstood. Frequently, people did not realize what they were changing or how hard it would be to do it. Change involves loss, and leaders needed to realize that. Nonetheless, schools could be transformed, and Skycrest became an example of significant school change.

EVERY STUDENT, EVERY DAY

The Skycrest weekly teacher bulletin closed with this simple yet significant pledge: "Every student, every day, in every class, will learn something that is worth remembering." This was a powerful message, because it committed the staff to shaping instruction that had meaning, relevancy, and utility for the students.

Skycrest Elementary became a school based on collaboration and celebration. Teachers who previously had worked in isolation learned together, planned together, and taught together. The Skycrest staff became a family.

The dreary staff room was converted into an inviting teachers' work space. Cubicles set against one wall contained a host of supplies, virtually anything an elementary teacher could wish for. Three copy machines were available. There was a Coke machine and a microwave. A professional library, dominated with books and articles about reading, sat in one corner. One wall was covered with a six-foot-long banner divided into two. The top portion was labeled "What we are doing well" and the bottom portion declared "What we need to do better." Both lists were updated biweekly.

On Fridays, the teachers' room hosted a food festival, with two staff members providing a hot and cold food buffet. Teachers wandered in during their free periods to sample the food and socialize with their colleagues. The following Friday, another pair of teachers provided the food. A new climate and culture evolved. Informal conversations about students, teaching, and the school's progress created a positive tone and symbolized a shift in values. Staff who could not buy into this shift in the school's culture left the school through transfer or retirement. Chris hand-picked their replacements, and in the eyes of her staff she did an extraordinary job in discovering new talent. Skycrest had become a new school.

By 2000, Carolyn Troyan had lived in the area forty-seven years and had been employed by the San Juan Unified School District as an instructional assistant for twenty-two years. Carolyn had a son in the sixth grade at Skycrest, a boy whose seven years in the school matched Chris's tenure as principal. Carolyn was able to view Skycrest from multiple perspectives. For Carolyn, the emphasis on student achievement was central to the school's newfound success. In her view, the staff committed themselves to helping each child reach her or his academic goals, with a range of intervention programs to help at-risk students. Ceremonies bestowed awards on students; recognition of growth and achievement, no matter how large or small, became part of school life. The teachers were constantly learning. Carolyn noted with pride that Skycrest was now receiving visitors from all over the United States who wanted to know how reading could be taught and how student achievement could be dramatically improved.

EXPLAINING WHAT HAPPENED

Chris told a story of how the district administrators transformed one of the mundane monthly principals meetings into a debate session. First, they had each principal decide whether he or she favored a constructivist approach to student learning, whereby students discovered answers and constructed their knowledge. Principals marched onto the stage to declare their position on this debatable perspective on learning. Then they met in small groups and argued with each other about their positions. Finally, the principals were asked to create a plan for staff development for their teachers that would open their minds to the value (and cautions) about the constructivist approach.

This was a new way to conduct business in the San Juan Unified School District. General Davies modeled teaching. He forced his principals to reflect on student learning and the achievement gap. He made it clear that student learning and student achievement were the district's most important concerns. He emphasized that meeting state standards did not mean that the creative engagement of students had to be sacrificed. He made the development of teachers important. He made change important. Davies sent out a clear and powerful message and created the context for a shift in attitudes and priorities.

Chris Zarzana could not have asked for a better alignment with her philosophy, purpose, and goals. Her actions reflected Davies's message. Although the superintendent did not directly intervene in the Skycrest rebirth, he created a districtwide reform agenda; provided advice to individual principals, such as Chris; and rewarded progress. Davies applied insights and knowledge acquired through a long and distinguished career. Chris Zarzana would do the same.

Chris brought vast experience as a reading specialist and principal to her challenge at Skycrest. Simply speaking, she knew what she was doing. She used data, would not accept substandard work, and demanded results. Chris provided leadership. She blended consistency with compassion, discipline with demands, standards with support. Chris used informal and formal conversations to give meaning to her agenda. She revived a school leadership team that regularly met to review school progress.

Timing mattered. California was quickly moving to rigorous state standards. The San Juan Unified School District was ahead of the curve. The district office generated its own set of standards, and principals were told they were going to be held accountable for their schools' success (or failure). Data do not lie.

"For the first time, teachers and principal were looking at the same students and were working together," is how one Skycrest veteran described the new environment at Citrus Heights. Chris Zarzana challenged the staff to think about why they were doing what they did. Conversations about what happened in classrooms became routine; a new sense of sharing became the norm. As one teacher put it, "The thing I love about this school is how we look at information about achievement."

The students were assessed regularly, not in a punitive way but as an effort to generate formative data. The idea was to identify the signals indicating progress (or the lack of progress). Waiting for year-end test scores made no sense; this may have been the way of the old Skycrest, but it was not part of the ethos of the new Skycrest.

Asked to visually portray the variables central to the Skycrest story, several individuals drew overlapping or connected circles that contained phrases such as "new programs," "whole school behavior," "high expectations," "a more organized and supportive district," "a belief that every child could learn," "trained teachers," and "leadership."

One person drew a formula indicating that shared leadership (administrators, teachers, and nonteaching staff) *plus* dedicated teachers (who collaborated and conducted meaningful assessments) *plus* parents (who were seen as active participants in education) *equals* happy and successful students who were "citizens of character."

As depicted in Figure 6.2, one teacher drew a series of boxes that were vertically connected to each other. The bottom box said "a clean modernized campus," "a place promoting pride." The box above used the words "clear expectation across grade levels." Moving up the line were boxes that mentioned individual intervention; focus on students; curriculum leaders in reading, writing, and math; and finally, at the top, the words "Chris Zarzana" and "Consistent leadership." Hanging over this set of connected boxes was an umbrella labeled "character education." The sidebar comment reads "I think that our emphasis on good character is an 'umbrella' over all our programs. It is helping our students to *want* a great school."

California's lure has been celebrated in song dozens of times, from "California, Here I Come," popularized by Al Jolson in 1924, to "California Dreaming," recorded by the Mamas and the Papas in 1968. In other words, in California one could dream and one could overcome obstacles to make those dreams come true. Skycrest Elementary in Citrus Heights exemplified that struggle and, ultimately, that success.

Figure 6.1   Demographics for Skycrest Elementary School, 2000

Grades: K–6	No. staff: 50
No. students: 723	Size of district: 48,000 students;
White: 72.2% African American: 10.2% Hispanic: 12.4% Asian: 2.9% Other: 2.3%	86 schools Elementary schools: 52 Middle schools: 10 High schools: 9 Other schools: 15

Figure 6.2   One teacher's interpretation of the school change process at Skycrest
Elementary School

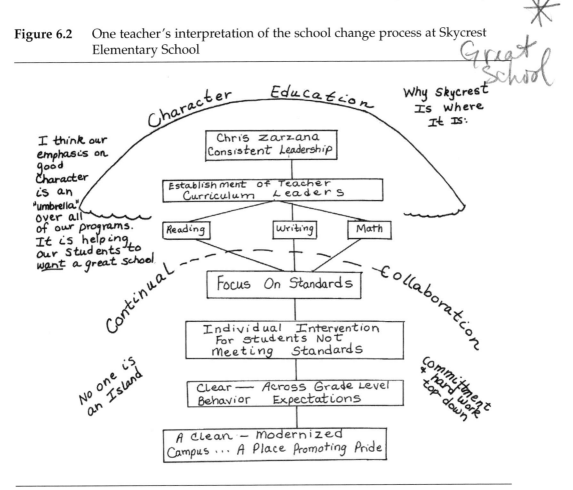

Drawing done by Pauline Spangenberg

7

"We Succeed. No Exceptions. No Excuses."

South Heights Elementary

Henderson, Kentucky

Rob Carroll, Principal

One does not usually associate hockey with the state of Kentucky. Perhaps Illinois, Michigan, or Massachusetts. But Kentucky, in a small rural town named Henderson? Yet hockey was the metaphor used by South Heights Elementary School to propel itself from being a school deemed failing by the state to one of the best. Kentucky has 1,200 public schools; in 2000, only twenty ranked lower than South Heights. Four years later, the school's achievement scores were above the national average. Kentucky's academic index scale used 140 as the maximum score; South Heights nearly doubled its score, going from 41.4 to 81.4.

MIRACLES DO HAPPEN

The Disney film *Miracle*, which portrays the astounding victory of the American hockey team at the 1980 Olympics, stimulated South Heights Elementary's focus on the sport. The film depicts how a self-centered, undisciplined, and underperforming collection of college hockey players was transformed into a tightly knit, skilled, and determined American team. It is a story of how a dedicated coach, hard work, and focus can work miracles.

Rob Carroll, in his seventh year as principal of South Heights, saw the film with his family and knew it would help sustain the remarkable strides the school was making. On February 12, 2004, he called a special four-hour staff meeting, allegedly to engage everyone in a review of the latest data and to start intensive planning. When the staff convened in the library, a three-minute trailer of *Miracle* greeted them. Rob announced that everyone would carpool to nearby Evansville, Indiana, to watch the entire film. Off they went, and for days afterward the staff could not stop talking about the film. Soon the students wanted to see it as well.

The annual round of state tests was imminent, and the staff decided the film could be used as a motivational device for the students. Rob called the theater to arrange for a discount for the entire school, students and staff. He was told it was impossible because the film was being shipped back. Rob persuaded the theater owner to intercede with Disney on the school's behalf. He did, and on Friday, March 19, buses took South Heights' third-, fourth-, and fifth-graders to the theater.

During the following week, students were asked to write an essay describing the similarities between the U.S. hockey team and the students of South *Miracle* Heights. A fifth-grader saw it this way: "We both have people who motivate us so we will do good on whatever they give us." Another said, "The similarities between the USA hockey team are that we were both the underdogs." A fourth-grader noted, "In the movie *Miracle* it was like our school. We are family and nothing can change that." A third-grader wrote, "We like school and they liked hockey. They were trying to win the medal and we are trying to win our goal of 78. Seventy-eight will be great!"

"YOU DO NOT WANT TO SEND YOUR CHILD TO SOUTH HEIGHTS"

In the past, South Heights Elementary had a poor reputation. Parents were told by their friends that the children at South Heights were not learning. They were not getting what they needed; the school was not student focused. One parent, frustrated with her son being sent out of class on errands because he was bored, wanted to know what was happening. The South Heights teacher told her that she didn't know what to do. Another parent, who needed to purchase a bigger home for her family, seriously considered moving out of the area so her children would not attend South Heights Elementary.

Everyone knew South Heights was a dumping ground for teachers who were not successful in other schools. Teachers knew it. Parents knew it. Community residents knew it. It was not unusual to find teachers in the hallways socializing while teacher aides were with the children. More than one child had his or her head down on a desk, sleeping. Many teachers would defend the poor student achievement results by saying it was not the teachers' fault. In their eyes, the problem lay with the children, and what could one expect? It was impossible to "build them up," said a teacher.

Teachers worked in isolation. One new teacher was eager to collaborate with her peers to discuss her students' progress. She was told by a veteran teacher to go back to her room and work by herself. New ideas would mean more work. Some teachers did come together—to form cliques, which competed for power and influence.

South Heights was neither welcoming nor joyful. Parents, on arrival at the school, would be greeted by a demand to know what they wanted. Even the drab brown walls reflected a negative attitude and low expectations. One teacher cried when she was told she was going to be transferred to South Heights. In the words of another staff member, "The culture was so pitiful." An editor of the local newspaper described the school's standing and status by noting how academic achievement data about Henderson's schools are published each year and "we always have the usual suspects at the bottom of the list. You could bet South Heights would be there."

[handwritten margin note: "new ideas = more work!!"]

KEEP PUSHING THAT FLYWHEEL

In his number-one bestseller about corporate success, *Good to Great,* Jim Collins (2001) used the metaphor of a flywheel, which he described as "a massive metal disk mounted horizontally on an axle" (p. 164). Your job is to get this 5,000-pound disk to rotate on the axle as fast and long as possible. It takes hours for you to move the flywheel one rotation. You keep pushing and the flywheel gradually picks up speed. Eventually, there is enough momentum created to enable the flywheel to move on its own. Collins argued that it is not one big push that makes the difference; instead, it is steady effort that does it. There is no one magic moment.

Achieving school success is also a continuous and committed endeavor. The South Heights story can be described in three overlapping phases: (1) laying the groundwork, (2) responding to the shock, and (3) knowing no bounds.

LAYING THE GROUNDWORK

The first three years, 1997 to 2000, of Rob Carroll's principalship were devoted to laying the groundwork. Rob was a new principal. He had to learn what it meant to be a principal, who the key people were, and how to influence the South Heights culture. As he began, each new idea met strong resistance; arguments were waged at staff meetings. Staff members would say "We did this before, and it didn't work" or "Can you guarantee this will work?" Only a small core of staff, perhaps a half-dozen, understood and accepted Rob's vision for the school. The rest fought to keep the status quo or stood on the sidelines watching the opposing sides slug it out.

Nonetheless, there were small but significant victories. Parents loved the way Rob greeted each student at the start of the school day. To deal with what seemed to be staff indifference, Ron modeled hugs and encouraging words. He came to know every student. He gave incredible amounts of time to students who were acting out. Staff meetings were soon devoted to talk about the students and how to motivate them and meet their needs.

It was a very tense first year, and there were some who thought Rob would not make it. Tom Hurt was an elementary school principal at that time, and he later became deputy superintendent. In his view, Rob had to move the school away from a "you do your own thing" attitude. There had been no sense of togetherness or success, and that had to change. Rob saw it the same way. He called a meeting and candidly told the South Heights staff that if they did not want to change, then perhaps South Heights was not the place for them. Many on staff were not happy with this message, and some were quite angry. When Rob returned to school the next morning he found a fist-driven hole in the wall above his office chair. He left it there to show he was determined and would not be intimidated or deterred.

At the end of Rob's first year, six of the thirty teachers decided to retire or transfer, giving Rob the chance to build his own team. His criteria for new hires? They had to love kids. When the six new teachers arrived in the summer, the first thing they asked was whether they could paint their rooms with bright colors and decorate them with motivational posters. Rob told them to do it. At the end of the second year, three more new teachers arrived, and Rob's original core team joined in the painting. As a result, half of the school had a dramatic new look.

However, it was not how classrooms looked that was important, it was the instruction that unfolded in those classrooms. In 1998, the school district became involved with a program called Different Ways of Knowing (DWOK), which uses an interdisciplinary approach, an emphasis on the arts, and considerable teacher training. The program failed at South Heights. Why? It was a district top-down mandate, not something that the South Heights teachers discovered and desired. It was confusing. It had to be implemented on top of everything else already in place. Although DWOK had been successful in numerous schools in other districts, including many in Kentucky, it did not work at South Heights. There had to be a better way to improve teaching and learning.

Rob Carroll learned a great deal about facilitating change from the DWOK episode. He took a team to a technology conference in Orlando, Florida. Once there, Rob and his three staff members divided the workshops among themselves. The sessions were interesting but not relevant to what South Heights needed. During the only slot for which the team had not planned who would attend which session, all four unexpectedly went to the same workshop. Attending that session laid the foundation that radically changed South Heights Elementary.

The workshop focused on a program called Project CHILD (Changing How Instruction for Learning is Delivered), developed by Dr. Sally Butzin at Florida State University and successfully launched in south Florida. Project CHILD is a research-based instructional model that brings together three teachers across grades. For example, a cluster of three teachers—one from the third, fourth, and fifth grades—is assigned three classes, students whom they, as a team, follow for three years. One teacher serves as the math specialist, the second focuses on reading, and the third focuses on writing. The team plans together and shares information about each student. Additionally, the Project CHILD materials are coordinated across the subject areas (including science and social studies) and across grade levels; the materials are aligned with state standards, and they are updated annually. Computers are fully integrated into classroom instruction. There is an emphasis on active learning, reflective engagement, and students learning how to work collaboratively. Project CHILD learning stations in each classroom enable students to use a variety of learning modalities.

Two of the South Heights teachers on the Florida trip immediately committed themselves to the program, and they recruited a third. This team went through the required training, and in September 1999 they implemented a pilot with an intermediate cluster (Grades 3–5). The program was successful at South Heights, with the Project CHILD cluster students outperforming their peers in terms of attendance, behavior, and academic achievement. It ultimately became the instructional model for all South Heights students.

Rob Carroll and his core team were not satisfied with their progress, and there were rumors that the state also was not happy. To prove that student achievement could be increased at South Heights, Rob searched on the Internet to find an elementary school with similar demographics. He found Englehard Elementary in Louisville, Kentucky, a school that had experienced spectacular student success. In October 2000, Rob took a volunteer team to Louisville. They were amazed at what they saw, and they had the opportunity to speak with the teachers who made it happen. If this school, with similar students, could score in the top 25% in the state (instead of South Heights, which was in the bottom 25%), then why could they not propel their students to those heights?

RESPONDING TO THE SHOCK

However, it was too little, too late. The Kentucky State Department of Education provided the blow that moved the school to Phase 2, "responding to the shock." The state of Kentucky had become one of the national leaders in school improvement with the passage of the Kentucky Education Reform Act of 1990. Under that law, the Commonwealth Assessment Testing System assigns specific academic goals to each school, which must be met in two years or else required state assistance sets in. Although South Heights had made some minimal progress in Rob's first four years, moving from 41.4 to 52 (in a scoring system that established 140 as the top score), the school remained in the bottom quartile.

The state became involved. First, in November 2000, a state team conducted a very comprehensive audit, asking questions about every aspect of school organization, governance, and teaching and learning. They looked at all the school's records. They wanted evidence about every program. They were

data driven, and they expected South Heights to be data driven as well. Despite praising Rob's initiative, energy, and passion, the state audit report was critical of the school's culture and performance. Much had to be done, and the Kentucky State Department of Education assigned a highly skilled educator to make sure it happened. Susan Higdon was that educator, and she "lived" in South Heights for two years, working closely with Rob Carroll to bring about change.

The audit required South Heights to respond to eight standards that looked at (1) curriculum and instruction; (2) evaluation and assessment; (3) school culture; (4) organizational structure and resources; (5) comprehensive and effective planning; (6) student, family, and community support; (7) professional growth; and (8) leadership. Committees were formed to discuss each of these, and the chairs and cochairs of those committees formed a Guiding Coalition. This coalition in turn presented recommendations to the school's Site-Based Decision Making Council (SBDM). The first task the coalition took on was changing the lengthy, formal, and politically correct mission statement and rewriting it with six simple words: "We Succeed. No Exceptions. No Excuses." The SBDM approved. A six-foot banner with that declaration was displayed at the school's entrance.

Data collection took on new meaning for the South Heights staff. It led to decision making. Susan Higdon played a major role in teaching Rob and his leadership team how to collect and use data, make contacts, and secure grants.

For example, student, parent, and staff surveys showed the need for a comprehensive, proactive, and instruction-oriented discipline program. Tapping Susan Higdon's expertise and experience within the state education department, the school submitted a grant proposal and was accepted into the Kentucky Instructional Discipline and Support project. The program was based on the idea that classroom organization affects students' behavior; students must deliberately be taught to behave responsibly; teachers needed to focus more attention and energy on acknowledging responsible behavior; and, to be consistent, teachers must preplan their response to possible misbehavior.

The program required writing and implementing new schoolwide rules and procedures that focused on guidelines for success, referral procedures, and classroom management. A teacher from each cluster received training, which was then turned key with the other teachers in the cluster. A school portfolio was created to track behavioral data, looking at the degree the new rules and procedures were working. These data, in turn, helped the staff make needed adjustments.

The program worked on two levels. Schoolwide, there were guidelines for success that made the school's expectations clear to both the students and the adults. At South Heights, the guidelines became a school pledge, recited each morning along with the pledge of allegiance: "Strive for success; accept responsibility; interact respectfully; and learn to cooperate."

At the classroom level was CHAMPS of the WEEK, a classroom management model that offers rewards for positive behavior and consequences for inappropriate behavior. In the words of one teacher, "Students began to respect us more because we respected them more."

More decisions were made. The SBDM approved the use of Title I funds to hire one full-time and one part-time teacher so the kindergarten program could be lengthened from a half-day to a full day. The SBDM also decided to apply for a Comprehensive School Improvement and Demonstration grant, funds they secured to expand Project CHILD throughout the school.

Rob reorganized his funding so he could create a triangulated leadership team. A Title I accountability grant was secured to create the position of Instructional Specialist, a post filled by Bridget Lutz, one of the original Project CHILD teachers. The guidance counselor, Cara Jameson, became the Behavioral Specialist, who trained the staff on universal behavior strategies, helped teachers monitor targeted behavior strategies, and provided service to students with special needs.

In the fall of 2001, the South Heights staff decided to set a schoolwide testing goal. Each staff member anonymously wrote down a number of a slip of paper; Rob averaged the projections. The staff's goal score of sixty-two greatly exceeded the state's expectation of 53.7. The motto became "We will do 62!" Students chanted it; staff repeated it; parents joined in. Signs were posted everywhere. The words became a mantra, repeated aloud as part of the morning ritual with daily announcements and acknowledgments, the pledge of allegiance, the guidelines for success, and the school's mission statement, "We Succeed. No Exceptions. No Excuses."

KNOWING NO BOUNDS

The effort picked up speed. In the words of one teacher, "This was now a staff that saw they were in this together." The 2001–02 academic year brought a further expansion of Project CHILD into the remaining classrooms. CHAMPS became the tool for classroom management in everyone's room. The three-person leadership team of Rob and his two specialists, Bridget Lutz and Cara Jameson, worked well together. Susan Higdon, in Rob's words, "was accessible, supportive and down to earth."

The school year ended with a sense of hope, with everyone still anxious about the state test scores. The state department called on September 11, 2002, to announce that the South Heights' academic index was not 53.7 or 62; it was 65.7! Many tears of joy and celebration flowed that day.

But it was not enough. Why not strive for a higher state score and more success for more students? In 2003–04, the new slogan became "78 will be great!" The South Heights staff started to set six-week assessments to gauge how well students were doing. The data were reviewed, with the findings driving classroom instruction and the after-school tutoring program. More focused planning took place at cluster and content area meetings. These agendas and discussions helped Rob and his team plan for the appropriate professional development and support.

"Right here, right now" is the dominant lyric in a popular song with the same name. The words rang out as students gathered for an academic pep rally in the spring of 2004. They had seen the film *Miracle*. They believed in themselves. They had made it happen. They surpassed their goal of 78, with 79.3. In 2004–05 the goal rose to "84, we will soar." Evidently, the South Heights' students, parents, and staff knew no bounds.

Be Uncommon

AN UNCOMMON PRINCIPAL

Here is a multiple-choice test: As principal, Rob Carroll led the cheerleading and celebrating at South Heights by (a) dressing up like Donald Trump, (b) allowing the students to throw water balloons at him, (c) being duct-taped to the wall (two feet off the floor), (d) taking his staff and their families to a University of Kentucky basketball game so they could see a great team in action. The answer is (e), all of the above.

"Be uncommon" became the newest slogan to be displayed throughout the school; Rob already was. The local media ran the unusual story about the duct tape incident. So did national Fox 5, which posted the story about elementary school principal Rob Carroll standing on a chair while students used pieces of duct tape to attach him to the wall. Eventually there was enough tape so the chair could be moved, leaving Rob "hanging in the air."

For Rob Carroll, uncommon meant drawing inspiration from unusual places. He was a regular reader of *Fast Company*, a magazine that centers on innovation and leadership in the corporate world. As Rob noted, "If these creative approaches could work for them, why not for us in the education world?" Uncommon for Rob meant collecting music from Disney films so it could be used to inspire students. Uncommon for Rob meant keeping an air hockey game in the principal's office for students who had greatly improved to use at the end of each week.

Rob Carroll became known for inspiring the staff, setting the bar higher, and giving children the attention they wanted and needed. He acknowledged people all the time. Every day, when he read the morning announcements with a student who served as his current assistant, individual staff members and students were saluted for their accomplishments.

For Rob Carroll, the focus was on high expectations, persistent effort, and results. For him, walking through the halls and into classrooms meant "high-fives" and hugs connecting the pupils with their principal. Of course, all the students knew Mr. Carroll; more amazing was Rob knew the first names of all 450 students. Support was extended to staff as well. Rob defined his job as providing the resources and help his teachers needed. He provided comfort and warm settings. No meeting was conducted without light refreshments. As one staff member mentioned, "Rob does feed us well."

Rob knew himself. He recognized that he was not the most talented instructional leader, so he selected his best teacher and created an instructional specialist's position for her so that strong support could be given to the teachers. In a similar fashion, he redefined the role of the school's guidance counselor. He made her a behavioral specialist, who would troubleshoot student behavior problems and provide both individual and group counseling.

Both moves flew in the face of district procedures and policies. Rob was attacked and undermined by people in the central office and by malcontents in the school. He outlasted the opposition and justified the redefined positions with new data about higher academic achievement and fewer disciplinary incidents. Rob was data driven and research based. He encouraged new ideas but wanted to know about the evidence that made the decision a wise one. He also wanted to know whether an idea was adult centered or would benefit the students. He encouraged change, but not for change's sake; he asked for the reasons behind someone's proposal. He thought about how the change would be introduced and its potential impact.

Rob had learned about change as he grew up. His dad worked for the National Weather Service and had to frequently uproot the family. Before going off to college, Rob lived in a small town near Seattle, Washington; in Minneapolis, Minnesota; in Key West, Florida; in northern Maine; and, finally, in Henderson. Growing up in locations and cultures that were quite diverse, Rob learned how to respect and work with a wide range of people. As Rob remembers it, everyone was poor. But no matter where he was, "we were just kids having fun." He watched his dad look for the unique talents in people, no matter who they were.

Rob had to work his way through college as a preschool assistant and later as a worker in a mental health hospice. As he described it, this combination of experiences taught him that without successful interventions at an early age, "dreams could die and lives could be lost." His fraternity life taught Rob how a group could bond in a common mission. His coursework prepared him to work with the most difficult students as a special education teacher. Rob came to understand a great deal about behavior modification and individual growth. As one teacher stated, "Rob wants you to be unique and he wants you to be yourself."

AT SOUTH HEIGHTS, THEY DO SUCCEED

One parent told the story of the day she cried in the principal's office. She had just moved back into the community and enrolled her child in South Heights. After one week, she was summoned to school and told that her second-grader had significant learning problems. She had not been told this in the former school district. As she described it, the South Heights team "had everything laid out for me." They were prepared with comments about her child's work, their observations, and team findings. "I was heartbroken, but I knew there was help." At South Heights she found the support she and her child needed.

At South Heights, there were probably more slogans, award announcements, and inspirational posters per square inch than in any sports locker room, school, or corporate setting anywhere. Successories is a company that produces striking

posters around dramatic words such as *challenge, commitment, courage, perseverance,* or *possibilities*. More than two dozen of these framed posters were on the South Heights walls, each one with a 2-in. × 3-in. brass plate telling who among staff, parents, alumni, or community members had donated that specific poster. Homemade signs were also displayed, such as "Kids don't care how much you know until they know how much you care" and "To play it safe is not to play."

Student work was celebrated, and samples were displayed next to the academic standard to which the work responded. On one hallway wall the standard specified, "Students are to know about a land food chain." The third-grade students had pasted together colorful collages displaying the sequence of flowers–worm–bird–cat. Classrooms were rich in color and the display of student work. Learning centers in each room allowed students to apply their knowledge through drawings, writing, construction of models, use of manipulatives, and so on. In one room, a chart reminded everyone about "evidence of understanding" with words like *define, prove, summarize, compare, describe, classify,* and *explain*.

The all-purpose room, usually used as a gymnasium, was converted twice a month into the Hard Work Café, modeled after the well-known Hard Rock Café. Students wrote answers to open-ended questions related to their portfolio work. Those who earned three or more points (out of a total of five) won a lunch period in the café, which was filled with games and other fun activities. Decorations and food were related to the theme of the day, which might be Space Jam, A Salute to the 50s, or The Rainforest. A set of banners hung from the ceiling, all declaring "Strive for excellence." Each individual banner offered a specific recognition the school had received: State Demonstration Site for the KY KIDS Project, National School of Merit, National School Change Award, and National Demonstration Site for Project CHILD, among others. Individual achievements were also recognized: a Kentucky teacher of the year as well as an outstanding school media librarian of the year.

The community surrounding South Heights was low in terms of socioeconomic status. The majority of the families were poor. In that setting, there was little optimism for great change. However, what had changed was their school. In the words of one staff member, "Our school culture has changed because we have changed. We know we have created something special and none of us take it for granted. We are changing the lives of the students we serve. We are making a difference."

EXPLAINING WHAT HAPPENED

When asked how South Heights was able to significantly change, the most common words and phrases suggested by staff and parents were new vision, professional development, teamwork, hands-on instruction, heightened student self-esteem, rewards for students, parental engagement, encouragement of the entire staff (not just the teachers), and the setting of specific testing goals. Rob's role was emphasized, especially in terms of data-driven decision making, cheerleading, inspirational slogans, his total dedication to students, and creating a sense of being able to achieve the impossible.

Angie Hawkins, the media specialist, was one of the original six staff members who bought into Rob's vision. She drew a diagram using the metaphor of a road carefully traveled. The journey began with the impetus of the state audit due to the poor test scores. The initial signposts along the way included the piloting of Project CHILD, the staff visit to Louisville, the new mission statement, the state appointment of a "distinguished educator," and the mandate to gather evidence of change. This caused some of the resisters to leave, something Angie called the "exodus of negativity." The trip continued with the CHAMPS project; curriculum alignment; and the wider adoption of Project CHILD, which was labeled "productive planning." Angie added a set of side comments: strive for excellence, accept responsibility, interact respectfully and learn to cooperate. A celebratory arrow pointing skyward declared, "Test scores are up!" A smiling face said "Make it fun!" The final set of words declared "scores are up more," "awards and recognition," and "we are a school that other schools visit" (see Figure 7.2).

The change process at South Heights was certainly a journey; however, it must be seen in the context of a larger landscape. Both directly and indirectly, the Kentucky educational reforms played a major role, serving as an external force. The rating of each school made denial impossible; newspapers across the state prominently summarized school performance. Specific school academic goals left no doubt about state expectations. The warnings about possible state intervention was followed by the state taking action. This signaled state policies could not be ignored.

At the same time, state resources were made available in the form of technical assistance and funding. In the case of South Heights, the school sought and secured money to conduct staff development, reorganize its administration and staff, and launch new instructional and discipline programs.

Rob Carroll's attitude toward the state's intervention and the role of the "distinguished educator" Susan Higdon cannot be underestimated. At the time of the state audit, Rob was quoted in *The Gleaner*, the Henderson, Kentucky, daily newspaper, as saying "We really welcome [the state audit] here. If there's anything we're doing wrong, we need to know it. If there's an area we need to improve, we'll attack it." It is significant that in the article Rob conceded that school reform was a slow process, one that would take years. It would require a great deal of patience. It would require becoming uncommon.

Herb Brooks was the uncommon hockey coach who announced to the American Olympic officials in 1980 that he was going to create a team that would beat the Soviet Union, the legendary Olympic powerhouse. Months of grueling practice built on severe discipline transformed the players into Olympic champions. In *Miracle*, the actor playing Herb Brooks declares that, to become winners, "We need to change the way we play the game." Twenty years later, that story was repeated at South Heights.

Figure 7.1   Demographics for South Heights Elementary School, 2004

Grades: K–5	No. staff: 70
No. students: 550	Size of district: 6,896 students;
White: 83% African American: 16% Hispanic: 1%	12 schools Elementary schools: 9 Middle schools: 2 High schools: 1

Figure 7.2   One teacher's interpretation of the school change process at South Heights Elementary School

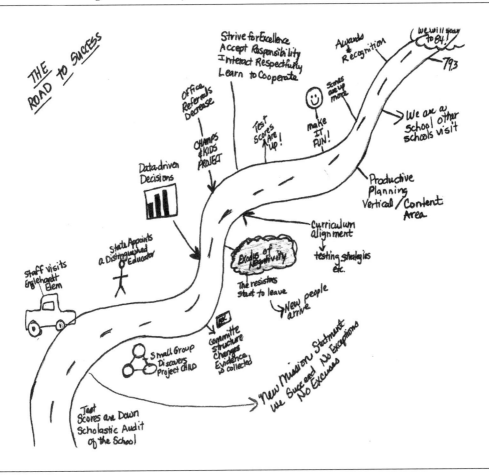

Drawing done by Angie Hawkins

PART III

The Secondary Schools

Adolescence is one of the most fascinating and complex transitions in the life span: a time of accelerated growth and change second only to infancy; a time of self discovery, and emerging independence; a time of metamorphosis from childhood to adulthood . . . The events of this crucially formative phase can shape an individual's life course and thus the future of the whole society.

—Great Transitions, Concluding Report of the
Carnegie Council on Adolescent Development

Making changes means making waves, and it's inevitable that some people become nervous when change happens. It's particularly true in bureaucratic, tradition-bound organizations like our public schools.

—Lorraine Monroe

Imagine a group of students who are willing to leave the familiar and take the risk of participating in a new and better kind of education. Imagine a group of parents who are willing to drive their kids to school, and then stay to help. Imagine curriculum that is designed with student engagement as its greatest priority, its surest route to real understanding . . . Imagine all this, dream, and then work to make it happen.

—Nancy Sizer

Adolescence involves rites of passage, celebrated in many other societies by tests of physical strength, rituals, and ceremonies. Beginning in the preteen years (ages 10–12, Grades 6–8), a push and pull reigns supreme. As we all know from our own development and from our roles as parents, adolescents want to belong, yet be independent; be secure, yet be adventurous; have routines, yet be rebellious. In the past, the secondary schools in this book didn't understand who their students were, what they needed, and how they could be engaged. In effect, the students had few reasons to attend school. Fortunately, that changed.

Important questions include the following:

- Many reformers contend that secondary schools are more difficult to change than elementary schools. Is that true? Why?
- It has been said elementary school teachers teach children, while secondary school teachers teach subjects. If this is true, does it matter?
- In looking at the portraits of four secondary schools that dramatically changed, what common descriptors might we use?

8

"If the System Doesn't Work, Go Around It"

Gustav Fritsche Middle School

Milwaukee, Wisconsin

Bill Andrekopoulos, Principal

Bill Andrekopoulos is a maverick. Known as "Mr. A," he asks "Why?" and does not accept the traditional answers. As an educator in Milwaukee, long a hotbed of educational reform, Bill became the principal of Gustav Fritsche Middle School, a school that had experienced a steep decline. The challenge of turning around the school became linked with challenging and converting "the system." It was not easy, and it took a long time.

OUT OF CONTROL

Gustav Fritsche Middle School had been one of the better schools in the 1970s, but in the 1980s it fell to the bottom. In the eyes of the Milwaukee school community, Fritsche was not a place where you wanted to be. As one teacher described it, "It was the school no one would choose to go [to]." There were dozens of students in the halls, which were filled with litter. There was no principal in sight; the principal's office door was always closed, and students did not know him. There were neither rules nor anyone willing to enforce any rules that might be suggested.

Students ran wild, doing what they pleased. Fights between students were common, and Fritsche had a reputation as a "gang school." As one assistant principal recalled, "The fighting among the students was all about the students not seeing any other way to resolve their issues." The school was not safe, yet the school administrators were reluctant to call the police when things got out of control.

It was every staff member for her- or himself. Teachers did not work together; in fact, many did not even like each other. Most belonged to one clique or another and, as one teacher remembered, if you were in the "right group, you were favored, while others got nothing." Staff meetings were few and far between, and they did not allow for meaningful conversation and the exchange of ideas. Instead, teachers took the opportunity to share horror stories.

With safety and survival such a great priority, student achievement was not a primary concern. Teacher-centered instruction, using lectures, served as the main instructional method. As one teacher looked back, "The seats were fixed in straight rows and it was not an environment for student exploration." Additionally, Fritsche was a segregated school. The gifted program was almost exclusively filled with White kids; the regular classes, which were considerably larger, were filled with students of color.

In short, Gustav Fritsche Middle School had terrible conditions and a well-deserved poor reputation. The dirty windows told it all. The sunlight could not even get into the classrooms.

Despite this bleak picture, in April 1988 Bill Andrekopoulos applied for the principalship of Gustav Fritsche Middle School. Two months earlier, Bill had applied for the principal's position in another middle school and finished second in that selection process. This time, Bill got his chance and was selected as the principal of Gustav Fritsche Middle School. However, there was a problem. Bill only knew of Fritsche's poor reputation and he had to call a friend for some basic advice: How do I get there?

MR. A, HE ASKS WHY

Bill Andrekopoulos has always wondered how to get there, literally and figuratively. Bill cannot sit still. He is a 5-foot 8-inch whirlwind of energy that cannot pack in enough in his fourteen-hour workdays. He often asks why things are the way they are. He challenges others to grapple with this same question. When he arrived at Gustav Fritsche Middle School, teachers, students, and parents quickly realized that their school would soon change, dramatically change. Bill told a staff who didn't believe they could make a difference that, despite a negative image, Fritsche would climb to the top.

From where did this energy, determination, and goal-setting come?

Bill Andrekopoulos was born and raised in Milwaukee, a product of the city's public schools. Coming from a conservative and religious family, he followed a traditional regimen: Go to school, listen to your parents, do the work that had to be done. As Bill remembers, "When I went to high school, I was the penny-loafer type; I was a conformist." Bill thought he was going to live out the typical American dream: Go to college, get a job, get married, and have kids. Nothing special. He was not encouraged in high school. In fact, one of his counselors told him he shouldn't go to college.

But something was lurking inside that shy exterior. Everyone, including Bill, had underestimated his drive and determination. He would make a difference, and he would make his mark. And he did. Bill Andrekopoulos now says, with satisfaction, "My friends are very proud of me."

Bill describes himself as "not one of those guys who can stay with the status quo." He goes on to say that perhaps it is a personality flaw, but "No matter where I am, I am viewed as someone who is different, a rabble rouser, as someone who challenges and pushes the envelope . . . I see things differently than other people. I see things upside down." Bill sees change as part of the natural rhythm of life: "I have a hard time doing things the same way. I even change the route I take to go home . . . Change is normal, change is fun."

Bill is described by the Fritsche teachers as a go-getter; very driven; a constant learner; and a good listener, open to suggestions. As one teacher put it, Bill "makes people feel their opinions are valued." He is viewed as creative and crafty; creative in his thinking and crafty at getting people to try new things. He is not afraid to push things through; another teacher said, "Bill won't be pushed aside."

Bill credits his personal development to a disparate array of role models and experiences. His first sergeant in the National Guard, Bill Krucek, taught him that it is people who make a difference in an organization. He modeled for Bill how people could be motivated. His sergeant also pointed out that rules and regulations are important, but there was a way, in Bill's words, "to get to the other side of the rules." One did not have to do things the way they were always done. One could ask why.

Dr. Howard Fuller, the superintendent who appointed Bill as Fritsche's principal, reinforced that message. Fuller was a maverick, and he recognized similar qualities in Bill Andrekopoulos. Fuller, for example, completely overhauled how school budgeting was done in the district, changing the system to a more efficient per-pupil allocation. Consequently, when Bill came to him with a different approach to budgeting or staffing or school evaluations, Fuller was supportive.

Fuller encouraged Bill to read, read, and read some more—not books about schools, but books about leadership. He took Fuller's advice. From Jim Collins's *Built to Last* Bill learned organizations make a difference when they build a structure, which will enable new initiatives to be sustained. From *The Leadership Challenge*, by James Kouzes and Barry Posner (1995), Bill learned it was important for a leader to understand what he or she stands for.

BUYING ALARM CLOCKS

Bill Andrekopoulos did not need an alarm clock; he was wired to go. During the two weeks before the start of his first year as Fritsche's principal, Bill focused on four things. He made lists. He contacted one of Fritsche's former principals to gain some background. He made more lists. Bill gathered data about the school from as many sources as he could. He revised his lists. As Bill remembers, the most consuming and challenging task was crafting his opening day speech.

When Bill addressed the Fritsche staff on September 2, 1988, he announced that in five years, Fritsche was going to be recognized as a National Blue Ribbon school. He told the staff he was serious about making a difference and that they would be part of the school's renewal. Furthermore, he pointed out that if any of them badmouthed their school, they were really badmouthing themselves. Bill set the bar high; Fritsche's staff looked at him with wary and wondering eyes. Becoming one of the best was a tall order if you currently were among the worst.

There were eighteen middle schools in Milwaukee. Three of them had open enrollment, and families from across the city sent their children to those schools because of their superior image and top academic results. Teachers competed to work at these three "optional" schools, and these three were generally better funded. As Bill looks back, he remembers being determined that "Fritsche would prove that a neighborhood middle school could be as good as the three highly lauded, open enrollment middle schools."

The staff heard the "we can do it" message again when Bill, as Fritsche's new principal, addressed the students. Bill told the students that Fritsche was *their school* and that it would be as good as they were. Fritsche would not be the same as it was before. They could and would take pride in their school. Additionally, every student could come to see him; his door would always be open.

Bill wanted to make sure no one would be intimidated by his hard-to-pronounce last name; he asked everyone, students, parents, and staff to call him "Mr. A." This gesture did more than eliminate a pronunciation problem: It conveyed the message that this new principal wanted to make himself accessible to one and all. Bill walked around and informally chatted with virtually everyone. He took it all in and began to expand his already lengthy to-do lists.

"I was responsible for school climate," Bill noted. He shaped that climate by never staying in his office and remembering that he had once been a young adolescent. He knew these students needed and wanted rules, and he and his staff would need to set these rules and make sure they were being followed. The discipline system was strengthened. The dean went from shuffling a mile-high stack of referrals on his desk to working with individual teachers. The staff were taught how to prevent discipline issues and how to be proactive rather than reactive. The chaos among students in the school ended, and the students who were not in school were brought back.

"Why aren't you at school?" is a question frequently sidestepped by truants and dropouts. The answers—when one gets a response—range from not caring; having other family responsibilities; feeling unable to do the schoolwork; being bored; and much of the mundane: lost my books, cannot afford school supplies, oversleeping. Some solutions to these problems demand intensive intervention; other strategies are simpler, such as giving a student an alarm clock. That response is both practical and symbolic; the message is clear: "We care about you."

Bill gave dozens of students an alarm clock.

NOT MAKING THE MARK

Bill's rallying cry was that Gustav Fritsche would win a National Blue Ribbon award after five years of his leadership. As promised, in 1993, the school applied for the blue ribbon recognition. Although Fritsche was praised by the state of Wisconsin, the school fell short of securing the national award. The Fritsche staff joined Bill in asking why. As Bill remembers, "We were very disappointed in not getting the National Blue Ribbon. We needed to do something different, but at first, we didn't know what."

There were three areas that needed to be addressed. First, although the building was orderly, safe, and welcoming, much more needed to be done in classrooms; the quality of teaching was not "blue ribbon." Second, academic achievement was flat; Fritsche lagged behind many Milwaukee middle schools. Third, there was the question of leadership. Mr. A was certainly a dynamic leader, but not enough had been done to develop other leaders.

Mr. A transformed himself into Mr. C, as he became intrigued with the stories of corporate leaders who turned around failing companies. Bill, like other educational reformers, believed these "out-of-education" ideas could be applied to the school world. For example, Bill followed the story of Midwest Airlines, a small company that captured a specific piece of the market (in Milwaukee and other Midwest destinations) by emphasizing passenger comfort, generating employee loyalty, and using attractive airfares. The airline served their customers well. Couldn't schools also search for new ways and be accountable for results? Couldn't school staffs develop a sense of ownership and loyalty? Couldn't schools do a better job of serving their customers?

Bill's feelings about corporate models deepened after he read *Flight of the Buffalo* by James A. Belasco and Ralph Stayer (1993). In it, Belasco and Stayer promoted a new leadership paradigm. As they put it:

> Then one day I got it. What I really wanted in the organization was a group of responsible, interdependent workers similar to a flock of geese . . .
> I could see the geese flying in their "V" formation, the leadership changing frequently, with different geese taking the lead. I saw every goose being responsible to wherever the gaggle was going. (p. 18)

Bill appreciated the idea; everyone could have a leadership role. He reshaped Fritsche into a learning organization, encouraging teachers to take a lead and experiment with new approaches.

LET'S TRY IT

The great debate in American education during the 1990s and beyond has pitted one side, advocating stronger student achievement, versus the other side, pushing for engaging and student-centered instruction. According to these opposing debaters, one has to choose between raising test scores or creating motivating and meaningful instruction.

Some of us believe the debaters have led us astray, because academic achievement and stimulating instruction are not mutually exclusive. Gustav Fritsche Middle School is an example of a school that dramatically improved scores (e.g., with math results becoming three times as great as those of other Milwaukee middle schools) while implementing exemplary middle school practices, such as advisories, integrated curricula, block scheduling, peer mediation, and looping. How did this happen?

The move toward block scheduling, for example, demonstrated the importance of process. Bill Andrekopoulos was quite intrigued with time: how time was used in schools, how school time could be configured differently. He read a great deal about the exemplary middle school practice of *block scheduling*, which rejected the typical eight-period day of forty-minute classes. In the spring of 1995, Bill put an article about block scheduling in all the staff's mailboxes and waited to see who would take the bait. A team of teachers came forward and said they wanted to try block scheduling.

This launched an action research project. Fifteen students were selected to have a different schedule with longer teaching blocks in mathematics, science, social studies, and English. Data were collected as this pilot group was compared with a control group that had the traditional school schedule. The results were dramatic: The students in the pilot group scored higher on all internal and external assessments.

Moreover, the students in the pilot group had exciting things to say about how they were learning. Bill remembers one of his class visits, when a student pulled at his sport jacket and pointed to the pyramid he was constructing and told his principal that he was "really getting into Egypt." Bill ran to the main office to grab his secretary, assistant principal, and counselor (the people he could find the quickest). He said to them, "You've got to see this!" as he dragged them down the hallway to the class, which was learning more deeply about Egypt because they had longer blocks of time to work on innovative projects. It was proof that academic achievement and engaging instruction were not mutually exclusive.

Bill had the teachers in the pilot project give testimony to the rest of the staff. The enthusiasm was contagious: Nineteen teachers came forward to adopt a block schedule for the following year. In his words, Bill learned that "Collecting data and doing research can make a difference in a school." Fritsche had a process for change: Learn something new, gather research about its effectiveness, pilot it, assess the results and impact, and make adjustments as needed.

Year by year, the changes moved forward. In March 1996, Fritsche's teachers voted for a schoolwide block-scheduling model, which was implemented the following fall. Additionally, during the 1996–97 school year, ten classrooms replaced the existing desks with round tables, the inclusion of special education students began, and staff development focused on cooperative learning and curriculum integration. After a thorough review of the expanded block scheduling, the teachers voted to continue it for three more years.

The 1997–98 school year brought more change: Another ten classrooms replaced desks with round tables; staff development focused on problem-based learning, cooperative learning, and Socratic seminar; and the inclusion program was evaluated.

The cycle of change continued. For example, some teachers came to Mr. A and told him they had read about *looping*, a practice whereby students stay with the same teachers for two years. Bill told them find out more. The Fritsche process unfolded: Looping was investigated in 1997, piloted in 1998, and adopted for the entire sixth and seventh grades in 1999.

By 2000, Fritsche's organizational structure and strategies for learning were firmly in place. Each of the three grades—sixth, seventh, and eighth—was organized into grade-level houses. Each grade-level house was in turn organized into four teams of eighty-five students, with three teachers in each house, which created small learning communities and a personalized approach. Each and every house was organized heterogeneously, including gifted students as well as at-risk and special education students. The school day was divided into four 88-minute blocks, allowing for extended class periods, integrated curriculum, thematic units, and problem-based learning.

This new school structure mirrored many of the exemplary middle school practices advocated by reformers nationwide. Fritsche became a model middle school. But that was not enough.

BUCKING THE SYSTEM

Built into the fabric of most school principals is the role of advocate, fighting for the resources you need and want for your school. Bill Andrekopoulos took on those battles and did not retreat. In response to the inevitable resistance of the central office bureaucracy, Bill suggested new ways budgets could be constructed, different ways allocations to schools could be determined, better procedures that would be both cost effective and more in tune with school needs. The bureaucracy dug in and Bill was, for the most part, stymied. That did not stop him. It became a matter of wills. Who would persevere? Who would retreat? Bill won most of the battles, but he was weary. Why did it have to be that way? Perhaps becoming an autonomous charter school was the answer.

The four Fritsche assistant principals were in agreement with Bill on the need to "go charter." As one of them put it, "We wanted complete local control; the system took forever to respond." Another summarized, "We wanted the freedom to break some of the rules. We wanted the ability to take the steps to meet our school's needs, instead of always asking for permission. In our school's development, it was the next logical step."

In 1997, the Wisconsin state legislature passed innovative but confusing charter school legislation. The law allowed public schools to become public charter schools, giving them the benefits of public funding combined with autonomy. However, the legislation had many problems. For example, the law said teachers who worked in charter schools would lose their benefits; that clearly was unacceptable to teachers unions across the state.

Bill Andrekopolous was intrigued with the idea of Fritsche becoming one of the first public charter schools, and he made serious inquiries to that effect. He quickly spotted the flaws in the legislation and, taking his own initiative, volunteered to work with several legislators to improve the law and help them figure out a solution to the teacher unions' opposition.

In 1999, a new and better version of the law was passed, and Bill was ready to submit Fritsche's application to become a charter school. However, another major roadblock had to be cleared: the approval of the Milwaukee school board, which at the time had absolutely no policy about charter schools. Undeterred, Bill moved ahead. The state required 50% of a school's staff to present a petition declaring their desire to become a public charter school; 75% of the Fritsche staff signed on.

But the district still did not know what to do; these were uncharted waters. Bill challenged the school board and told them he was locking the school's petition in his school's safe for two months. After two months, if the school board still did not have a policy, Bill and his staff were going directly to the state. Fritsche and the school board were locked in intractable positions. Fortunately, the roadblock cleared with a new school board election. Of the nine school board members, five were newly selected, and these five were reformers.

Still, no one knew how to proceed. Using research he gathered, Bill wrote a position paper about charter schools and presented it to the new board. The board reacted favorably, and much of Bill's position paper evolved into the district's charter school policy. Fritsche's charter school application was approved by the school hoard and the state. Fritsche officially became a charter school on July 1, 2000.

This chapter in the Fritsche story is important for three reasons. First, charter status gave the school incredible latitude in its program development, staffing, and budget. Second, Fritsche was able to access additional funding directly from the state. Third, and probably most important, it united school administration, staff, parents, and community members in a common cause. As Bill remembers, "it accelerated a sense of community up a notch. It became clearer this was our school." Additionally, the charter chapter created a sequel.

"YOU DO NOT HAVE A QUALITY CLASSROOM"

One part of Fritsche's charter school application committed the school to total quality management. This focus had evolved from corporate change models and accountability systems that had captured Bill's attention. After attending a National Quality in Education conference in Atlantic City, New Jersey, in 1999, Bill took eight of the Fritsche staff to visit a school in Pensacola, Florida, that was successfully implementing the quality management process.

Once there, Bill could not believe what he saw. He remembered "feeling like a kid who has unlimited access to everything in a candy store." The Florida school was doing everything possible to raise the bar for their students and to measure student progress. Core practices, which all students had to master, were clearly posted, as were reports of individual student progress. Data were displayed everywhere, with charts noting the class's attendance, grade-point average, math scores on the state assessment examination, and so on. Individual student folders contained data about that student's performance, as compared with the class' performance. Students were asked to discuss what would drive their class to higher levels of learning and what was getting in the way.

Upon returning to Fritsche, Bill visited the classroom of Roseanne Clancy, the best mathematics teacher in the school, and perhaps in the district, who had recently been recognized as a National Science Foundation mathematics winner. Bill looked around Roseanne's classroom and told her she did not have a high-performing class, but someday she would have one. Roseanne, with wide-open eyes, looked at Bill in amazement. Bill went on to explain what he had seen in the Florida math classrooms and told Roseanne they were going on a journey.

Roseanne took on the challenge. She added to her repertoire of teaching methods. She concentrated on constant assessment of student progress. Every day, she took digital photographs of her class. Bill became a frequent visitor, and the two of them discussed what was unfolding with her students. Two years later, Bill walked in Roseanne's class, looked around, and went up to her to give her a hug. He told her, "You have a high-performing class." Both had tears in their eyes.

FROM PRIVATE SCHOOL TO FRITSCHE

In 2000, after enrolling her daughter in Fritsche's seventh grade, a mother went to speak with Mr. A. She told him that until that moment her daughter had attended only private schools. The Fritsche program, profile, and promise brought her back to public schools. From all perspectives, there was much to draw people to the new Fritsche.

Teachers felt they had a new school. In their eyes, Fritsche had become a learning community, a place where change was encouraged and supported. Moreover, the staff felt they were respected. There was a new sense of unity, a common purpose. As one teacher put it, "You felt good to be a member of the Fritsche team." No longer were there favored and disfavored groups. As another staff member put it, "No one at the school holds a title. A staff member is a staff member."

Parents were happy with their increased involvement and with the higher levels of student achievement. In 1996, only 39% of the eighth-graders read at or above grade level. For math, the figure was 38%; for science, 34%; and for social studies, 36%. Four years later, in 2000, the percentages had consistently climbed at least ten points in each subject: Reading rose to 51%, math to 63%, science to 48%, and social studies to 49%. The Fritsche eighth-grade math results were three times the district's average. The sixth-graders outperformed district students by two times in the writing assessment average and four times in the district's math assessment average.

When asked in the spring of 2001, a group of eighth-graders described their school by noting the following: "This school is unique; it's a different kind of school because the teachers make it fun"; "All the teachers are understanding; they speak to you all the time, not just when you're having a problem"; "You know why you're doing the class assignments"; "The teachers are always thinking of new things for us to do."

When these same students were asked what advice they would give to a new principal, they suggested that the new principal would have to be both tough and nice, have patience, be interested in the kids, always walk around, know the students' names, and never yell at anyone. As one student summarized, "Be just like Mr. A."

SPEAKING WITH GRADUATES

In his initial months as Fritsche's principal, Bill did everything he could to learn about his new school. Why not, he thought, ask Fritsche alumni about the school they had attended? He did. Bill visited several high schools attended by Fritsche graduates, and he sat with them individually and in small groups. One significant finding concerned Program Academic Talented (PAT), the district's gifted and talented program. Fritsche's highest-scoring students were the only ones in the PAT classes, which incorporated enrichment experiences such as participation in the district's science fair. Bill was taken aback one afternoon when several Fritsche graduates, who had not been in the PAT program, asked why weren't they allowed to enter the science fair. Because PAT students were the only ones allowed to participate in the fair, they wanted to know whether the Fritsche teachers had low expectations and didn't think they could do the science projects.

Bill went back to Fritsche, convened the staff, shared his conversations with the Fritsche graduates, and told them the school had to get rid of PAT. End the PAT program? The staff was shocked and overwhelmed. Bill changed tactics and instead declared that *all* students would have the PAT program, with "the gifted" students being part of heterogeneous grouping in each classroom. As expected, he faced much resistance from parents of the students in the PAT program. They were concerned whether their children would continue to have enrichment experiences. Bill said yes, they would! The changes were made.

The PAT controversy revealed three things about what happened at Fritsche. First, Bill Andrekopoulos was a constant learner and sought a wide range of avenues by which to gather new knowledge and data, including logical yet generally untapped sources. Speaking to graduates seemed like an obvious strategy, yet it was infrequently used. Second, the Fritsche school community, once approached with a mixture of decisiveness and diplomacy, was capable of change. Finally, change involved courage, courage embraced by both the leader and his followers.

EXPLAINING WHAT HAPPENED

Change at Fritsche did not come easily or quickly. As one Fritsche teacher summed up, "People don't mind change. They just don't want to be changed." Consequently, the critical question is: How do we bring about change? How can significant change, affecting values and practices, be initiated, implemented, and sustained without causing great discomfort and a feeling that "we are being changed"? At Fritsche, significant change unfolded because there was a combination of unusual leadership; extended periods of time; the desire to pilot, test, and evaluate; and a deliberate and sweeping—yet gradual—process.

Three of the Milwaukee central office supervisors described "the Fritsche phenomenon" in these ways: First, "Bill and his Fritsche team understood and knew the system very well. They used the system instead of following it." Second, "The Fritsche team was eager to change, push the envelope and take risks." Third, "They wanted to be a laboratory school, [were] willing to pilot things, and then disseminate[d] what they learned and achieved."

Bill Andrekopoulos was very intrigued with data, and this attitude became infectious among the Fritsche staff. One teacher explained the Fritsche motto: "If it moves, we survey it. If it doesn't move, we analyze it." Nothing escaped the extensive school data portfolio, which chronicled school progress over time and documented incremental successes. Feedback to staff about student performance became a ritual and routine. It became part of the school culture. In 1998, U.S. Secretary of Education Richard Riley recognized Fritsche for school improvement efforts through data-based decision making. The following year, Fritsche was invited by the University of Wisconsin–Madison to pilot a new data management software program.

In the Fritsche story we find a tricky tension between the power of the leader and the need to empower others. There is no question Bill Andrekopoulos provided the vision, the drive, and the creativity to move Fritsche onto a higher level and do it again and again. The force of Bill's personality was impossible to resist. The pace, the energy, and the challenges could be overwhelming, but Bill developed a loyal set of followers because it was clear he was going to get the job done.

Bill Andrekopoulos saw himself as one of his favorite literary and film characters, Captain Kirk of Star Trek. Kirk treated his crew and ship as his family and his home. There was no question that Kirk cared about his mission and the people who joined him. That image described the Bill–Fritsche staff relationship, one built on caring, confidence, and trust.

The rebirth of Fritsche took time, a lot of time. Bill Andrekopoulos arrived at Fritsche in 1988. During the first phase of his principalship, 1988–93, the school was stabilized, made safe, and grounded in better attitudes toward students. Some attention had been paid to classroom instruction, but much more needed to be done. The second phase began with the 1993–94 school year. Pilot projects looked at how students learned. Student achievement became the first priority. However, it took another five to seven years to reach national recognition. Two phases, taking twelve years, represents a considerable amount of time—more than 4,380 days.

During those twelve years, a new culture was created, one that celebrated learning for both the students and staff. Bill Andrekopoulos's question of "why?" took on new meaning. He encouraged his staff to ask themselves why certain things worked and others did not. On what basis were they deciding something did work? What kind of data could be collected, and how might they interpret that data? Fritsche became more than a school; it became an educational laboratory. A new and rather unusual routine set in: Imagine, learn, pilot, review data, and adjust.

From the first day Bill Andrekopoulos received his assignment as principal of Gustav Fritsche Middle School, he began composing lists. However, these lists kept changing. Bill and his staff constantly found new ways to "do school," and they consistently had to consider how others could be brought on board. Bill understood he needed to develop a critical mass of support if the school were to move forward. He spent much time building that critical mass.

Bill Andrekopoulos walked the thin line between being the main figure, in the center of the action, and standing aside, serving as a coach and cheerleader. On one hand, as one teacher put it, "You always know where Mr. A stands, where he is coming from." On the other hand, Bill drew from his reading, school visits, conference attendance, and personal experiences. Slowly, he grasped the importance of building a legacy of leaders and moved more and more toward empowering others. As another teacher put it, "Mr. A empowered us in the sense [that] he got us to do what he knew we could do."

Two striking examples involved personnel decisions. In 1996, Bill shocked the entire Milwaukee school system because he turned over the evaluation of himself, as principal, to the staff. They were going to determine how well he was performing. In April 1999, he turned over the prospective teacher interview process to a committee of staff and parents. That committee conducted the screening, interviewing, reference checking, and all other steps they needed to recommend individuals to be hired as new Fritsche teachers. Both personnel moves exemplified Bill Andrekopoulos as a renegade and revolutionary. These steps were quite radical, but they worked.

One drawing depicting the school change process at Fritsche used the image of a dragon that needed to be slain. Accomplishing that impressive feat were a series of arrows labeled "Baldridge management," "increased parent involvement," "peer mediation," "block scheduling," and "looping grades." Playing a prominent role was a sword held high by Mr. A, which was titled "knowledge builds peace." Floating above the battle scene were shields, which read, in turn, "charter school," "blue ribbon award," and "change award."

Another teacher described the school by stating, "Leadership at Fritsche is no longer a defined position; it is the function of the entire learning community." This belief developed as a result of time, the personal growth of the principal, and risk-taking on the part of the staff. Two of the points made in Bill's favorite book, *Flight of the Buffalo* (Belasco & Stayer, 1993) are "Leaders transform ownership for work to those who execute the work" and "Leaders learn fast themselves and encourage others also to learn quickly." That was the Fritsche story.

Figure 8.1   Demographics for Gustav Fritsche Middle School, 2001

Grades: 6–8	No. staff: 127
No. students: 1,041	Size of district: 99,990 students; 156 schools
White: 39.5% African American: 36.8% Hispanic: 16.3% Asian: 4.1% Other: 3.3%	Elementary schools: 115 Middle schools: 23 High schools: 18

Figure 8.2   One teacher's interpretation of the school change process at Gustav Fritsche Middle School

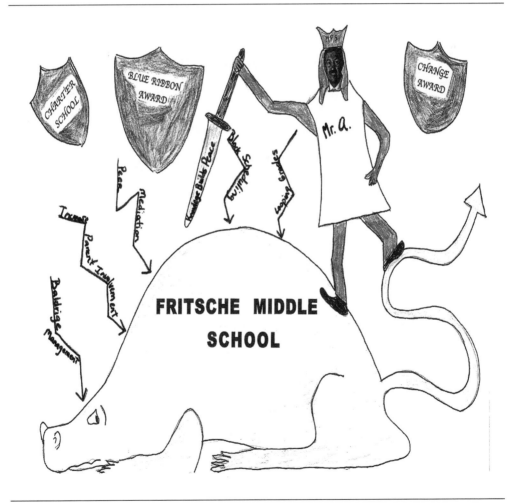

Drawing done by Dorothy Schuller

9

"Desegregation or Else"

George Washington Carver Academy

Waco, Texas

Molly Maloy, Principal

Federal court orders cannot be postponed forever. They can be ignored or resisted for a time, but eventually they demand compliance. For close to a half-century, the Waco, Texas, school system faced such an order, in the form of a mandate to desegregate its schools. Finally, the George Washington Carver Academy, once a source of great Black pride in the city, was selected to serve as the solution. However, the first two desegregation strategies involving Carver didn't work. Success came later. Ultimately, partial school desegregation was put in place in the district, and quality middle school education was created at Carver.

WHEN YOU THINK OF WACO . . .

Two associations are quickly made with Waco, Texas. The first is tragic. In 1993, Elk, Texas, 10 miles from Waco, was the site of a fifty-one-day standoff between the Branch Davidian religious cult and the FBI. Four agents from the Bureau of Alcohol, Tobacco, and Firearms and five Davidians had already been killed. David Koresh, the cult leader, had a huge arsenal of assault weapons he was prepared to use. Finally, on April 18, the FBI was authorized to raid the compound and, in the words of then-President Bill Clinton, "The raid [went] terribly wrong. After the FBI fired tear gas into the buildings where the people were held, the Davidians started a fire" (W. J. Clinton, 2004, p. 497). More than eighty people died, including twenty-five children. International press swarmed on the scene, and Waco's name was tarnished.

The second association with Waco is in the neighboring town of Crawford, twenty miles away, where President George W. Bush spends a great deal of time at his ranch. Foreign dignitaries frequently visit the President at the ranch, which serves as a second White House as well as a presidential retreat. Presidential guests stay in Waco, and so does the press corp. Military helicopters are frequently overhead; Secret Service agents are a common sight. These activities are routine for Waco residents.

THE PRESSURE TO DESEGREGATE THE SCHOOLS

History is no stranger to Waco. Its desegregation issues of the 1990s stretched back to the landmark 1954 U.S. Supreme Court decision, *Brown v. Board of Education of Topeka*. In 1955, the Supreme Court declared that the federal district courts would have jurisdiction over lawsuits to enforce the desegregation decision and asked that the desegregation proceed "with all deliberate speed." However, neither a sense of urgency nor speed characterized school desegregation in Texas.

In 1956, after a lawsuit by the National Association for the Advancement of Colored People supporting three Black high school students, the Mansfield, Texas school district was ordered by a federal court to desegregate its schools. It was the first district in the state to receive this mandate. White citizens did not take this well. Mobs of 300 to 400 White citizens prevented the three Black students from enrolling in the school.

Schools across Texas remained segregated. In November 1970, the chief judge of the U.S. District Court for the Eastern District of Texas ordered the Texas Education Agency (TEA) to assume responsibility for desegregating Texas public schools. The TEA was to conduct annual reviews of school districts with one or more campuses having a 66% or greater minority enrollment to determine compliance with federal desegregation laws. If violations were found, the TEA was to impose sanctions, including denial of accreditation.

Meanwhile, in Waco, resistance to desegregation remained strong. Although in 1955 the Waco school board said they had a plan to proceed with desegregating one grade per year, the plan was constantly stalled—and never implemented. In September 1962, seventeen Black students went to five White Waco schools to enroll. The principals refused to admit them, and the National Association for the Advancement of Colored People sued the district in federal court on the students' behalf. This led to the Waco school board setting a schedule in 1963 to desegregate its schools between 1964 and 1968. It still didn't happen.

In 1970, the federal courts and the TEA pushed the Waco school board again, and the school board turned to George Washington Carver as a way to satisfy the pressure to desegregate Waco's schools.

PRIDE IN THE PAST, PROBLEMS IN THE PRESENT

The neighborhood around Carver was predominantly Black, and it had been this way for many years. George Washington Carver, of course, was a legendary figure in African American history. He had earned worldwide respect as one of most talented scientists of his time because of his groundbreaking work in crop rotation. His work, which was concerned with the loss of nutrients in the soil, led southern planters to shift from sole reliance on cotton to planting peanuts. George Washington Carver, as a scientist and educator, symbolized progress and achievement. His namesake, The George Washington Carver High School, with its many successful graduates attending college, its state-recognized band, and state championship athletic teams, mirrored that reputation. One was proud to be a Carver alumnus. Until 1970.

The federal desegregation orders forced the transfer of Carver High School and its neighboring elementary school from an adjacent school district to the Waco school system. The plan involved vacating the high school and transferring its Black students to the two Waco high schools so those schools could be integrated. The Carver building was emptied of its students, its windows were boarded, and some of its space was converted into Waco district administrative offices. Carver High School was no more. For people who had graduated from and knew Carver as a prestigious high school, it was "like a knife in the back," as one alumnus lamented.

In 1988, desegregation pressure re-emerged. The federal government and the Texas state education officials were not accepting Waco's solution. The Waco board of education came up with a new plan: Create one sixth-grade school and one ninth-grade school in the district. These two schools would be integrated, because there would be no other choices. It seemed logical. This plan, too, was doomed to failure.

George Washington Carver was designated as the one sixth-grade school. As one teacher at Carver summarized, "It just wasn't working. The students had no interest in what was being taught; the staff had to spend 15–20 minutes getting the kids into their classes." Another teacher remembered, "The kids were constantly in the hallway, waiting for someone to take action in regard to their lateness or cutting of classes." Action seldom came. A third teacher noted in hindsight, "The kids were not buying into school. We were doing something wrong."

No one at that time faced the fact the school needed to be overhauled or closed. Each school year unfolded as it did the previous year: ringing bells the students ignored, a building that was physically deteriorating (a metaphor for the instructional program), routines for the sake of routines, outdated textbooks, class worksheets and drill, low expectations, and terrible results. In 1992, fewer than 40% of the students read at grade level.

Teachers never came together to discuss issues. As one veteran remembered, "I was on my own." Another cited, "We didn't know how to improve and change." Parents remembered the school as overcrowded and full of discipline problems. As one put it, "It was a disgrace to the district." Another called it "a disaster." One teacher stated, "The school was depressing, with negative teacher attitudes and poor morale. It felt like a prison; having bars on the windows did not help." Test scores plummeted, ironically, at a time when external pressure for increased academic achievement intensified.

PASS THE TAAS, LATER THE TEKS

The story is told of the Texas state legislator who supported and voted for the rigorous testing program for elementary and secondary students. However, his perspective changed when the testing was brought down to third-graders. In an effort to make sure all the third-graders would do well on their state-mandated tests, the second-grade curriculum was changed so it concentrated only on mathematical and literacy skills. Other subjects, such as social studies, science, physical education, art, and music, were drastically cut back or eliminated. What did this mean? With no social studies instruction, the legislator's seven-year-old daughter would not be able to learn about how the state government worked and what her father did for a living.

The national standards movement, born in the 1980s, was a response to high school graduates' inability to function successfully in the most basic lines of work or in college. Many graduates simply could not read, write, or compute, much less be critical thinkers, problem solvers, and team players. At the same time, embarrassing comparisons were being made between what American students could do academically compared with their peers in other countries. The business world was demanding school improvement, and state legislators jumped on the bandwagon. Texas took the lead as one of the first states to mandate statewide testing. The annual testing was first called *TAAS* (Texas Assessment of Academic Skills) and later *TAKS* (Texas Assessment of Knowledge and Skills). The testing began with fourth-graders and expanded over the years to its current testing of virtually all grades.

Perhaps the Texas testing had gone too far, but in the 1980s and 1990s it served as a major push toward school improvement in the state. By 1992, testing was firmly in place. Data about academic achievement could not be ignored; George Washington Carver Academy's test scores ranked at the bottom in Waco. Something needed to be done, and that challenge fell to Molly Maloy, newly assigned as Carver's principal.

MOLLY'S MISSION

From childhood, Molly Maloy had been a fighter. The two fundamental lessons that shaped Molly's development were about determination and social justice.

Both of Molly's parents had not finished college but insisted their children would get degrees. As Molly remembered, "It was a given from day one, we were going to college; it was never even a question." All six Maloy kids earned bachelor's degrees, three went on to earn a master's, and one got her doctorate. The message was clear: You can be whatever you want to be.

At the same time, Molly was taught that all of us have to give back something to others. Molly's mom was a role model; she had started the Meals on Wheels program in Waco. All the Maloy kids were expected to do something to help others. Consequently, Molly and her siblings helped with the Meals on Wheels program, tutored elementary school students, served as hospital volunteers, and taught Sunday school.

As a "baby boomer," Molly finished high school and started college during the 1960s. Molly got caught up in the passion of the times: The world was a mess, it had to be changed, and Molly and her generation could do the job. The era was filled with heroes and heroines. She centered her admiration on powerful women such as Texas congresswoman Barbara Jordan; the state's governor, Anne Richards; poet Maya Angelou; and social activist Mother Teresa. As Molly said, "I was influenced by their ways of thinking, messages, charisma, and actions."

Born and raised in Waco, Molly attended Catholic schools, where "the right answers" were given to her and questioning was discouraged. Things were done the way they were because they had always been done that way. This mind set did not sit well with Molly, and when she went off to college at Sam Houston State University, in Huntsville, a whole new world opened for her. Molly gained new friends and new perspectives. She could live again in Waco, which she did, but, as Molly put it, "I could not go back." Molly was not the same person; she saw the world in very different ways.

A refusal to accept the status quo fueled Molly's personal and professional lives. For Molly, it was important to "look at things, question them, see how they fit into my world, reject them, accept them, modify them." This outlook grounded Molly's approach to school leadership.

THE FIX THAT FAILED

Young adolescents, twelve to fourteen years old, are complex: dependent, yet rebellious; shy, yet rambunctious; self-centered, yet concerned with larger ethical issues. "Beset with raging hormones" joins the descriptors, as do *unpredictable*, *curious*, and *confused*. Sixth-graders move from the relative calm of childhood into this challenging world of young adolescence simultaneously charming and challenging their parents and teachers. It is not an easy age.

The Waco school board underestimated young adolescent power when it decided to put all the district's sixth-graders in the same school. Because some of these students were White and others were people of color, mostly African American, the school would inevitably be integrated. The pressure of the federal desegregation court order would be relieved. Regrettably, the plan, from the start, was an educational disaster.

Several problems and naïve assumptions doomed the strategy. First, Carver had a terrible reputation and would not be appealing, even in a supposed new configuration. Second, the surrounding neighborhood was considered unsafe. Third, many parents of White children simply would not send their children to Carver; they opted for private or parochial schools. Fourth, the plan called for busing, an inconvenient and expensive practice, one associated with conflict over desegregation in other communities. Finally, placing all the sixth-graders in one building produced a "hormonal hurricane." As one teacher remembered, "It was crazy. So many sixth graders." It was not simply the numbers. There were no older children to serve as role models and no younger children whose presence might have kept the middle school students in check.

When Molly Maloy came to Carver, in 1988, the sixth-grade school had operated for five years. The school was not working. Molly's first task was to deal with safety issues, cited by everyone as the major problem. Molly and her team implemented a stricter discipline system. They cleared the halls. Visitors had to sign in. However, the school had an unwieldy number of overage students; some 17-year-olds were still repeating the sixth grade. Molly had some of the oldest and most troublesome students transferred to an alternative school. Knowing something different had to be done with the others, Molly and her staff created an innovative accelerated program. These overage students were able to complete two years in one. The teachers used *USA Today* and other relevant materials to help students master essential skills. These students were organized as their own learning community and given more intense attention. These steps, although not completely successful, provided important lessons for the staff, experiences they would later use when Carver became a magnet school.

Many of the ideas influencing Molly Maloy and her Carver staff came from William Glasser, M.D., a proponent of reality therapy. As summarized in his book, *Building a Quality School*, Glasser's philosophy is based on five interlocking ideas. First, the success of an endeavor is dependent on how well people get along. Second, a system of rewards, punishments, bribes, and threats is a form of control and, as such, is "a plague on mankind." Third, there is an alternative to stimulus–response psychology: choice theory. This means teachers help students identify what they want and help them make a plan. Fourth, in a quality school, the child is responsible for his or her work and the teacher is responsible for developing a caring and supportive relationship with each child. Finally, learning is dependent on opportunities for students to use what they have learned and their ability to self-assess their performance and progress. In effect, the Glasser approach sensitized the Carver staff to the needs of young adolescents.

The Glasser strategy was focused, which was a good thing but it was also limited. Classroom instruction didn't change very much, and student achievement stayed flat. Just when Carver needed to be especially attractive and appealing, the school remained second rate. It became clear that radical surgery was required and, finally, in 1992, the school board gave up on the "one sixth-grade school" experiment and told Molly to create a magnet school.

DO-OVER, DO-OVER

In effect, Molly Maloy got a chance to have a "do-over." As kids, many of us would plead for a do-over when our baseball went astray or our basketball bounced off the rim in the wrong direction. As adults, we might ask for a do-over after an out-of-bounds tennis ball or an errant golf ball. (Golfers call the free shot a *mulligan*.). For Molly, the do-over had more serious implications. She had presided over the "Carver as the solitary sixth-grade school" solution, which was largely a failure. She was anxious to have another chance to remake Carver Academy. In 1992, she got it.

Molly Maloy did not accept failure, so the initial Carver setback was devastating for her. It had a great impact. As one teacher put it, "Molly likes to be an innovator. She wants to change things and see them work for the kids." When Molly got her second chance to change Carver, she also changed. The determination stayed, but the style shifted.

The "old Molly" was unapproachable, was inflexible, would not admit mistakes, and liked challenging others. Many perceived her leadership style as "It's my way or the highway." She was tough. The "new Molly" softened; she became more flexible, approachable, and team centered. Molly admitted people tended to be scared of her because she "lays it out there." In her words, "I don't have time to play games." But, Molly went on to say, "What I learned is together we could do this better."

Molly also credited the Glasser training for her change. Glasser contrasts a *boss* with a *leader*. The boss is the undisputed authority, creates fear, and drives others. The leader creates confidence, shows how, and breeds enthusiasm. A boss orders you; a leader is out front, and you follow the leader because it is to your benefit.

Both the old and new Mollys pushed the envelope, relentless in the quest to make new things happen. Molly did not just think out of the box; she created a new box, with a very different shape, size, and set of materials. Molly was an impatient risk-taker and therefore had to learn to give others the freedom to be creative. She stopped micromanaging. She learned how to trust others to get the work done.

In an early stage of the Carver change process, Molly took the staff to an overnight outdoor team-building camp where there was a ropes course. She walked the ropes as if they were circus tightropes. That was how she approached her job, walking the fine line between challenging the status quo and watching how far she could change others. The team-building experiences for the Carver staff included an exercise where you fall backward, hoping others will catch you before you hit the ground. Molly took the risk, and the others did catch her. As Molly remembered the experience, "I was hesitant. But I knew they would catch me. After all, who else would be the leader?"

ON THE BEACH IN FLORIDA

As soon as the sixth-grade Carver experiment was pronounced dead, Molly asked the superintendent to declare all the school's staff positions open so she could form a new staff. He agreed. Molly organized a planning team, the "Magnificent Seven," by bringing together two district office administrators and five members of the Waco staff, including herself. The septet developed a preliminary outline for a magnet school, which the Waco Board of Education enthusiastically approved.

Molly then turned to her team and asked "OK; now what do we do?" The team took to the road; there was much to be learned. The first middle school conference they attended was in Phoenix, Arizona. While learning about strategies presented at conference sessions, Molly met one of her education heroes, Jim Beane, considered a curriculum guru. Shy as she was, Molly asked Beane to autograph the book she was carrying, *A Middle School Curriculum—From Rhetoric to Reality*, which he had written. The subsequent conversation and the team's participation at targeted conference sessions gave the Carver school planners the conceptual framework for creating a theme-based integrated curriculum. But they still needed more.

Three weeks later, while attending an integrated-learning conference in Fort Lauderdale, Florida, the team found themselves on the beach, trying to create a school plan. What would capture the interest of their students? How could state mandates be woven into a curriculum that was authentic and exciting? Did this integrated-curriculum approach actually work?

Beane had suggested visiting Brown Barge, a middle school in Pensacola, Florida, that was successfully doing integrated-curriculum work. After reading and discussing Beane's book, the Magnificent Seven made two trips to Brown Barge. They observed classes, talked to students, and grilled the teachers about what they were doing and why. A bond was formed between the two staffs, and Brown Barge teachers traveled to Waco to help the Carver teachers implement their newly created theme-based integrated-curriculum units.

This was a critical phase in four ways. First, Molly's personal involvement with the national middle school movement became a team endeavor. This meant looking at exemplary middle school practices and deciding how they could be adapted for Carver's students. An integrated curriculum became the first and most fundamental of these strategies; a strong cocurricular program, service learning, and advisories soon followed.

Second, the Magnificent Seven reflected a very strong district commitment to Carver's renewal. Not one, but two key district people were actively involved during the entire planning process: (1) Vivian Baker, the assistant superintendent for curriculum, and (2) Hazel Rowe, the director of secondary education. The district duo contributed an outside perspective as well as practical advice. Moreover, they kept the superintendent informed and strengthened school board support for the new Carver.

Third, the Brown Barge visits enabled the Waco team to connect theory with reality. It was not enough to read Beane's book. It was not enough to see other teachers do things differently. They needed to both understand the concepts behind interdisciplinary instruction and see how those concepts were translated into everyday classroom practices. The Waco staff became eager to develop its own innovative curriculum. The staff's capacity had been strengthened, and they believed they could get the job done.

Fourth, the importance of teams became very clear. The integrated-curriculum approach involved grade-level teams, with each team having an English, social studies, science, math, and special education teacher. If team members did not work well with each other, then the curriculum and instruction would fail. Consequently, much of Carver's work went into team building. A consultant was hired to administer the Meyers–Briggs Type Indicator, which reveals personality styles. According to this instrument, individuals are introverted or extroverted, feeling or thinking, sensing or intuitive, judging or perceiving. The Waco staff was organized into diverse teams whose members had a range of work styles. The strategy worked.

EXPERIENCING LEARNING AS AN ADVENTURE

The new interdisciplinary odysseys had limitless possibilities. Would the theme be space exploration or justice? The 1960s or pollution? Would the students create a model for a space colony or debate a controversial issue? Could they plan a 1960s fest, with heroes, fashions, and songs of the times, or is a community beautification project on their agenda? No matter the choice, Carver students plunged into activities they would never forget.

Calling these theme-based interdisciplinary units *odysseys* made sense. They were more than a curricular scope and sequence; they were magical journeys. The odysseys worked because they operated on two levels. First, they were imaginative, promoted creative expression, and made kids think in new ways. At the same time, they provided a venue for skill development, fundamental skills students would use throughout their lives: interpreting what they read, making mathematical calculations, looking at data, operating as a team, and making decisions they could explain and defend.

The odysseys became a powerful experience for parents, who were invited to visit whenever they wanted, and for teachers, who looked at curriculum development as an opportunity, not a burden. As one teacher noted, "We're all learning and that is what gives us a feeling of excitement." Grade-level teacher teams spent several weeks each summer creating new odyssey choices and revising ones conducted in the past. They created several options; each quarter, the students chose one for the next nine weeks. In all cases, connections were made to state academic standards and to the social and emotional development of young adolescents.

For example, in the Energy Odyssey, students created a scale drawing for an energy-efficient house, which incorporated the math skills of multiplication, division, and proportion. In the Animals Odyssey, students developed a wildlife park, taking into account the compatibility of various animals, types of habitats and biomes, animal needs, and budgetary constraints.

Carver's Secret Garden was an odyssey project. A very neglected and unwelcoming inner courtyard on the campus was transformed into a peaceful garden. Students completed the Pollution Odyssey by transforming the inner courtyard into a space with an outdoor classroom and greenhouse. The project won a "Keep Waco Beautiful" environmental award.

According to much research, young adolescents have a strong need to face ethical dilemmas. They want to do the right thing and make a difference. In the Connections Odyssey, they worked with senior citizens. In the Justice Odyssey, they interviewed criminal justice officials and conducted a mock trial, using their new knowledge of the judicial system, forensics, and pathology.

The Carver odysseys responded to one of the strongest recommendations advanced by the landmark middle school reform report "Turning Points," which called for teaching young adolescents to think critically; develop healthful lifestyles; be active citizens; and to learn well, not just test successfully. The odyssey format drew from significant middle school research, such as Beane's (1992) findings: "When we are confronted with a problem or puzzling situation in life, we hardly stop to think about which part is science, which mathematics, which language arts, and so on. Instead, we bring to bear any knowledge or skill that is pertinent to the situation" (p. 46).

Odysseys were the driving force at Carver and, as an eighth-grader described it, "We do fun stuff every odyssey." In the words of Carver teachers, "I like that I don't have to just teach English"; "We make something relevant and exciting"; "I love the teamwork we have."

EXPLAINING WHAT HAPPENED

The Carver success story was multilayered, building on several external forces: access to a major reform movement; strong district office support and involvement; leadership that transformed itself; and, eventually, an unwavering focus on how students learn.

The external pressure came from the federal government, the state of Texas, and the Waco community. The federal mandate to desegregate was a thorn in the side of the Waco community, a problem long resisted and avoided. For most Waco residents, school integration was a second thought at best and anathema at worst. Besides, the concept of federal "interference" didn't sit well in most communities. But the federal court order would not go away, forcing the Waco school board to look for a solution to satisfy the courts but not disrupt its deeply rooted ways of doing things. Families, both Black and White, expected their children to walk to their neighborhood school. Consequently, it was essential that disruption to this long-expected and accepted practice be minimized. The 1988 Waco school board response impacted only sixth- and ninth-graders.

Fortunately, or unfortunately, depending on your point of view, the Waco school desegregation plan failed. Creating one sixth-grade school and one ninth-grade school for the entire school district made no sense, educationally or logistically. It was token compliance with the spirit and substance of the court order. Thirty-five schools in Waco were left as they were; only two schools became integrated. Desegregation failed: White families, for the most part, did not send their children to Carver. Improving school quality failed: The Carver Black community still did not have a school they could look to with pride. Meaningful school reform failed: It was the same old thing in a new package.

The state pressure focused on test scores. The academic achievement of Waco students was being compared to students from across the state. Within Waco, schools were being compared to each other, and Carver's bottom-level rankings could not be ignored. The Waco school board had to fight off state intervention, satisfy angry parents, and demonstrate that they were capable of fixing the problem.

Parent dissatisfaction was the third piece of external pressure. The Black community surrounding Carver remembered how their neighborhood school once had been a symbol of achievement and a source of pride. They wanted that back. Most important, no one was happy with the one-sixth-grade-school solution. Families who had to bus their children hated it; the Carver students acted out against it; the teachers were demoralized by it. There had to be a better path to take.

During the 1980s and 1990s, schools in America educating sixth- through ninth-graders had an important decision to make. They could stay in their traditional ways, calling themselves junior high schools and assuming their students were merely younger versions of high school students, or these schools could accept the fact that young adolescents have their own set of needs, priorities, and concerns. This new emphasis on the distinctive nature of young adolescents drove the middle school reform movement, an outlook attractive to educators like Molly Maloy. Creating an integrated curriculum and emphasizing teamwork were borrowed from this reform movement; they became essential elements of the new Carver.

School reform stories typically include a wide cast of characters playing different roles, inherently supportive, neutral, or oppositional. The Waco story was unique because of the active engagement of important district office leaders during the entire reform process. Vivian Baker and Hazel Rowe brought the district office to the school in the form of ongoing advice, needed resources, and unwavering advocacy. Vivian and Hazel did not monitor or supervise the creation of the new Carver Academy; they sat as equals and peers on a very bonded team, the Magnificent Seven, that created this new school.

Teams, however, did not just spring to life. The bonding, drive, and commitment to getting things done required a leader. In the Carver scenario, this leader was the first Molly Maloy; later, it was another Molly Maloy. As previously discussed, the first Molly Maloy was strong, tough, unwavering, and intimidating. The second Molly Maloy was softened in style but not in determination and drive. The newer Molly Maloy stepped back a bit and let others take the reins.

Molly looked back at the end of the magnet school's second year as a critical moment. It was the first year the Carver Academy had had sixth-, seventh-, *and* eighth-graders. The staff and the students felt good about the year. The eighth-graders were the first graduating class, ready to move on to high school. However, one cloud hung overhead. It was the first year Texas was testing all eighth-graders, and the Carver community wondered how well their eighth-graders scored.

When the examination results came back, there was cause to celebrate the strong language arts scores, but the math scores were terrible; Carver's students were deficient in many math skills. It looked like the innovative interdisciplinary approach had failed. What was to be done?

It was the last week of school, and Molly called the staff together. The mood was somber. The staff and students had worked very hard, and they were deeply disappointed with the math examination results. Molly presented three options: (1) They could do away with the odysseys, (2) they could teach math separately instead of integrating it with the other subjects that focused on a specific odyssey theme, or (3) they could keep their commitment to integrate all subjects into the odysseys and do a better job with math in that context.

The Carver team chose the third option; they were not going to give up. It was the first time they were teaching eighth-graders and the first time an eighth-grade state assessment in mathematics had been administered. They were in a learning mode, and they wanted a "do-over." Consequently, the staff reviewed every page of their curriculum documents and identified where every state-mandated math skill was taught (or could be taught). Adjustments were made to the odysseys. Unnecessary repetition of math skills was eliminated; other de-emphasized or missing skills were inserted. As Molly remembered, "The curricula was tweaked with every required math skill given the depth and complexity needed. We believed we could succeed and we did." Math scores soared the following year.

In portraying the Carver success story, one teacher focused on both the past and the present. Her drawing depicted five boxes, all pointing to "G. W. Carver Academy Science & Technology School." At the same time, another set of arrows led from one box to the next. The first box, sixth-grade center, had four elements: (1) "desegregation order," (2) "community dissatisfaction," (3) "student disinterest," and (4) "dissent." This box led to "teachers & administrators brainstormed new ideas," which then led to "presented idea & plan of tech magnet school to school board." The arrows continued as the school board presentation was followed by implementation. The implementation box provided details: staff development, recruitment, curriculum writing, and mission statement. The fifth and final box on the horizontal line was "faculty retreats & team building" (see Figure 9.2).

Carver succeeded because the focus was on teaching and learning. Carver succeeded because the staff changed their strategies, as needed. Carver succeeded because they kept their eyes on the prize.

Figure 9.1   Demographics for George Washington Carver Academy, 2000

Grades: 6–8	No. staff: 43
No. students: 511	Size of district: 15,000 students;
White: 9.2% African American: 41.3% Hispanic: 48.7% Other: 0.8%	33 schools Elementary schools: 21 Middle schools: 7 High schools: 5

Figure 9.2   One teacher's interpretation of the school change process at George Washington Carver Academy

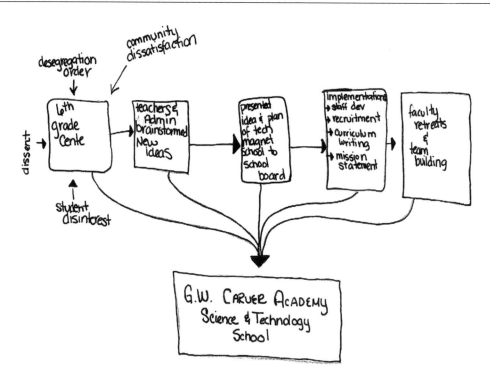

Drawing done by Jeanne Kuchera

10

"*Surrender Was Not an Option*"

Louis W. Fox Academic and Technical High School

San Antonio, Texas

Joanne Cockrell, Principal

On the early morning of March 6, 1836, thirteen days of skirmish and stalemate ended with 3,000 Mexican troops storming the Alamo, a fortress in San Antonio, in the Mexican province of Bexar. Mexico was determined to restore control over its territory and put an end to the Texan rebellion. The battle was fierce, with both sides displaying "remarkable courage, one in bitter defense against overwhelming odds and the other in open assault against fortified sharpshooters and about twenty artillery pieces" (Chambers, 1999, p. 718). Despite casualties numbering close to 600, General Santa Ana's Mexican army took the fortress, killing all 187 of the defenders.

THE BATTLE SITE

The battles in San Antonio have not ended. One hundred sixty years later, they took the form of a war against poverty, failure, and hopelessness. Just a few miles from the Alamo, the forces of defeat and despair had to be addressed at Louis W. Fox Academic and Technical High School (Fox Tech). Serving a largely Latino student body, the school had become a symbol of all that was wrong with American education. Like the Alamo, Fox Tech represented a lost battle. In 1995, the school was designated as low performing for the third year in a row by the state of Texas and became known as "the worst high school in the state."

The high school ranked last in San Antonio in terms of academic achievement. In math, 22% of the Fox Tech students were at the bottom; in reading, 47% were at the lowest level; and in writing, 71% were barely at the minimal standard. Additionally, enrollment was in a downward spiral, going from 1,500 students in 1990 to 900 students in 1995. Only 153 students were in the June 1995 graduating class.

Fox Tech is located in a section of the city that has no true local community. Surrounded by failing businesses and empty lots, it is a dangerous area known for its crime, violence, and drugs. The school was run down and had a terrible reputation. Teachers did not want to be assigned there, parents did not want to enroll their children, students did not want to come. At least twice a month, Fox Tech was in the news—for a stabbing, neighborhood trouble, or gang activities. Some Fox Tech teachers were afraid of the students and did not venture from their classrooms; the students were aware of this. Many Fox Tech teachers did not believe their students could make it; the students knew this as well.

Many students ate in their classrooms, and many more gathered in the halls. The carpet in the lobby was filthy; the walls were bare or, worse, scarred with graffiti. The classrooms were focused on teacher comfort. Many had couches, refrigerators, and coffeepots. They served as a refuge from the chaos of the hallways. However, despite a "home away from home" sense of safety for the teachers, the school's parking lot was emptied within ten minutes after the end of the school day.

Things were no better outside. A Sears store was located across the street from the school. It lost its customers because dozens of Fox Tech truants would gather in front of the store. In 1994, the store closed.

The absentee rate for students—and faculty—was high. District office administrators described Fox Tech as unwelcoming and bleak, limping along with obsolete programs. As one administrator remarked, "It was a school in real trouble." Fox Tech, it seemed, was doomed to failure, caught in a downward spiral.

DISESTABLISHMENT

It was a Friday afternoon in May 1995, the last day of the school year. The Assistant Superintendent of Human Resources, a surprise visitor, was at the closing faculty meeting at Fox Tech. Rumors had been rampant for weeks that Fox Tech was going to be closed, but such rumors had been a consistent piece of gossip for several years. The assistant superintendent came to address the rumors. Surprisingly, she told the staff the rumors were true, that Fox Tech was to be "disestablished." Every staff member, from principal to teacher to secretary to custodian, was to leave. Although staff members had the option to reapply for employment, there was no guarantee any of them would be rehired at Fox Tech. The school was to start anew.

Although the Texas Education Association had issued warnings over the previous four years, those warnings had been ignored. The Fox Tech staff felt the state would never take such a drastic step; they had never done this before. Many of the 102 Fox Tech teachers thought this latest announcement was a scare tactic and that they would continue to work at the school. Instead, they were told to report to the district's job fair or submit their resignations from the school system.

What the Fox Tech staff failed to realize or accept was that they were the last holdout. Just a year before, there were only two San Antonio high schools designated as low performing: Fox Tech and Lanier. Fox Tech got worse while Lanier had heeded the warning, addressed their problems, and boosted their academic achievement. Lanier was removed from the low-performing list; Fox Tech remained. The high school was referred to Dr. Diana Lam, who was finishing her first year as superintendent. Diana was given a choice: Have the state come in and disestablish the school or have the district take the drastic step. She decided to have the district assume the responsibility.

Disestablishment was not a new concept, but it had rarely been used across the United States, and never in the state of Texas for low-performing schools. However, in New York City, in the early 1980s, a failing high school that had defied numerous reform efforts and renewal plans was deemed too broken to fix. The school's culture was dysfunctional. The school had to be completely closed, with its students and staff phased out. In its place, a new school, with a new name, staff, and set of students, came into the building. Benjamin Franklin High School died; the Manhattan Center for Mathematics and Science was born.

The Texas legislature began to consider this concept in 1992. These lawmakers knew disestablishment would be a drastic step, but Texas, with its strong accountability system, had to take severe actions with schools that did not improve. The legislators moved cautiously and gave the Fox Tech staff a chance to work with district officials in developing a school improvement plan. Together, they would have to identify the problems and develop a set of strategies. They would have to reach a consensus about the steps to be taken. However, in the words of one of the participating teachers, "Our consensus was we could not come to consensus."

Some at Fox Tech welcomed disestablishment. They knew the school was going nowhere. As one teacher put it, "We were at the point we needed focus, leadership, and a definite direction." Fox Tech got what they needed.

THE NEW LEADER ARRIVES

To lead this battle, a successful middle school principal, Joanne Cockrell, was assigned as Fox Tech's new principal. A tall, imposing woman, Joanne had won the admiration of her San Antonio colleagues as an excellent high school mathematics teacher and a winning coach of girls' track and basketball teams. Joanne cared about kids and was relentless in fighting on their behalf. Joanne was tough and suffered no fools. She was ready for a huge challenge, and she got it.

Joanne received the call on the Monday following the disestablishment announcement, telling her of her new assignment as principal of Fox Tech. The next morning, Joanne and Elsa Catala, her assistant principal from Connell Middle School, were at the district's job fair. Within days, Joanne had organized an interview committee of teachers who had worked for her or whom she knew. Groups of potential staff were assembled, twenty to twenty-five at a time, so they could hear Joanne's educational philosophy. She told them, "I expect you to be here [every day]. I expect you to do your job. I expect you to do what's best for kids, not for teachers." The interview committee then screened those who were still interested.

Finally, Joanne personally met with each candidate and posed two central questions. Joanne wanted to know whether the teacher liked kids. It was that simple. Second, she wanted to know whether the potential staff member watched the clock. She was not interested in the staff parking lot emptying immediately after the end of the official school day. Bringing pride and success to Fox Tech would take a tremendous effort and a commitment that defied typical school schedules. As Joanne declared, "If you're not willing to do extra, you should not waste your time thinking about being here at Fox Tech."

Not everyone wanted to take on the challenge. Ten of Fox Tech's teachers did not even apply to return. Joanne hired back one third of the Fox Tech staff. She recruited another one third from other district schools; these were educators she knew and worked with over the years. The last one third were new to her and to the school. All signed on with a clear sense of what needed to be done and what their new principal demanded. Joanne Cockrell's message was direct, dramatic, and evidently clear. As one teacher put it, "Joanne was not subtle."

During the summer of 1995, the school building was cleaned, the lobby was painted, new school rules were posted, and a new dress code was set. Joanne Cockrell and her team were ready.

THE STUDENTS LOOKED DOWN AT THE FLOOR

In August 1995, when the new school year officially started, three things struck Joanne Cockrell. First, the Fox Tech students were polite and respectful, but they did not look you in the face. They stared down at the floor. Joanne understood the deference to authority figures was part of the Hispanic culture and tradition. Nonetheless, Joanne sensed sadness, as if these students had repeatedly been told they were doomed to failure. Furthermore, they knew their school ranked last and that many adults said the students were to blame.

As Joanne walked around the building, several students stopped her to ask "Who are you?" After she told them she was the new principal, the students reacted in amazement. They had never seen the previous principal, and many students did not even know her name.

During the second week of school, Joanne was visited by the police, who asked her what in the world she was doing. Joanne did not know how to respond.

The police officers went on to explain there had not been any calls for assistance from the police during those past two weeks; that had never happened before. The police were accustomed to being part of the landscape, and they were amazed at the change in atmosphere and climate. Joanne explained the school had adopted a policy of zero tolerance for inappropriate behavior. There were school rules, and they would be enforced. The police officers became Joanne's partners.

THE COACH AS CHANGE AGENT

You cannot ignore or forget Joanne Cockrell. She is large in terms of physical appearance, voice, and presence. In many ways, Joanne exemplifies the old John Wayne style of leadership. She rides in on her horse, ready to save the troubled town (in this case, the school). She is compassionate with the less fortunate and ferocious with the villains. She cuts an imposing figure and can come across as intimidating. She emanates power and authority.

Joanne took her discipline and disposition as a coach and brought it to her leadership at Fox Tech. Athletic coaches walk a fine line. On one hand, they need to develop a sense of team, fusing together a group of self-centered individuals into a cohesive unit. The welfare and success of the team must be paramount. The coach's role is to facilitate and nurture that development and to develop a team leader who will motivate and manage her or his teammates. Great coaches empower players.

Tapping her coaching instincts and talents, Joanne also knew that a team needs a series of small successes, a cheering and supportive environment, and the opportunity to celebrate. Joanne created these conditions at Fox Tech, securing a series of small victories in both the academic and athletic arenas.

On the other hand, coaches tend to be dominant figures. The first person you typically will see on a basketball court is the coach, running up and down, shouting instructions from the sidelines. Everyone knows the coach is in charge. The coach develops the game plan, monitors the players, and is the final arbiter.

Coaches insist on discipline and focus. They will not tolerate a lack of effort, apathy, or continued poor performance. They will be direct. They will not be shy. They will tell it like it is. Coaching never stopped for Joanne Cockrell when she became a high school principal; she brought those instincts into a larger arena. As a trio of Fox Tech teachers put it, "Joanne will tell you when she's happy and when she's not"; "She shoots from the hip and with two guns"; "When Joanne speaks, we listen." Joanne was determined to win, and for her it was not a game.

How did Joanne Cockrell become who she is? Joanne was born in Smithville, Texas, forty miles east of Austin. Her dad was a postal worker for forty-three years, and her mom stayed at home raising four children. Joanne was the eldest, and her parents insisted she break out of the traditional family mode. They wanted her to go to college and move from Smithville to places with more opportunities. Joanne did it, becoming only the second member of her large extended family to finish college. She moved to San Antonio to attend Our Lady of the Lake College and, except for one summer of graduate work at the University of Texas at Austin, she never left.

As soon as Joanne entered the San Antonio school system as a mathematics teacher, she met her future role model, mentor, and greatest supporter: Frank Clark. At that time, Frank was the school district's director of personnel; he was the one who hired Joanne. Eight years later, Joanne transferred as a math teacher to Sam Houston High School because Frank Clark had become the principal and wanted her to work at his school. Three years later, Frank moved to the central office and urged Joanne to complete her master's degree in administration. She did.

In 1977, Joanne earned her M.A. at the University of Texas at San Antonio, finishing at the same time Frank Clark was assigned as the principal of Highlands High School. Once again, Joanne joined Frank, who continued to guide and develop her.

Joanne learned a great deal about leadership from Frank Clark, who was the "single greatest influence," outside of her mother, in her life. In Joanne's words, "I could have followed that man anywhere." As she remembers, Frank Clark treated everyone with respect; brought competing groups together; and told it "how it was, whether it was good news or bad, whether he was praising you or chewing you out."

Joanne also credits her master's program at the University of Texas at San Antonio. The program was unusual because it was a middle management program, designed to develop leaders in many fields. There was a core of courses for everyone and specialty courses in specific disciplines such as government, public service, and education. The professors were leaders in their respective fields; San Antonio's mayor taught one course, others were taught by CEOs.

Joanne threw herself into her work. Her math classes were places where you did your work, no questions asked. They were alive with activity and punctuated by Joanne's sharp wit. Not satisfied with only academic contact with her students, Joanne took on high school athletic coaching. The new Title IX legislation required schools to provide equal access to girls for athletic programs; Joanne became the first girls' basketball coach in San Antonio.

Her determination to win was infectious, and she inspired her teams. Joanne saw the tight connection between reaching kids in the classrooms and on the athletic field. In her words, "Coaches are good teachers; I never saw a bad teacher become a good coach." Joanne worked as a high school math teacher and coach for seven years. Her students won in both arenas. Academically, they surpassed the basic math requirements (even before there were state standards), and many went on to higher mathematics, including calculus. At the same time, her basketball teams won, moving from one victory a year to consistently being one of the top three teams in their division. Coaching expanded Joanne's understanding about teamwork, something she had first learned as captain of her high school basketball team.

Joanne took the lessons, the ideas, and the wisdom shared by others and put pen to paper. Her notebooks filled as she thought about what she would do when she became a high school principal. Her first principalship generated many of the journal entries. In 1993, Joanne was assigned as the principal of

Connell Middle School, a low-performing school with a good staff. At the end of Joanne's first year, the school was removed from the low-performing list. At the end of Joanne's second year, she was tapped to turn around Fox Tech. Joanne learned much about "schools within schools" while she was at Connell; she brought the concept of dividing a large school into smaller units to Fox Tech.

Joanne continued to write in her notebook when she went to Fox Tech. Many comments were inspired by what students told her and by her observations. The themes reflected Joanne's philosophy: Unleash the potential that rested inside, perhaps deeply inside, each and every student. Find every way to do that and enlist others in the campaign. As Joanne put it, " All these kids wanted was someone who cared."

SCHOOLS WITHIN SCHOOLS

By 2005, the small-school movement was considered the magic bullet of high school reform. The strategy makes sense, for several reasons. Large urban high schools have no chance of reaching every student. Their massive size makes student anonymity inevitable. High schools become buildings, not centers of learning. Dividing a school with, for example, 1,800 students into four academies of 450 students places about 100 students in a particular grade team. This is a manageable number; every student can be reached, motivated, and helped. Organizing teachers into teams that serve each of the grades enables teachers to know students as individuals and create a sense of family. By giving teacher teams time during the school day to meet, they can discuss student progress, share ideas about teaching and learning, and take the time to assess their progress as a small school. Finally, a sense of ownership and pride develops. Students take responsibility for themselves and for each other, and teachers become invested in the success of their students.

In August 1995, Joanne Cockrell and her team were ahead of the curve as they immediately reorganized Fox Tech into four theme-based academies. As their plan stated, "This concept visualizes and makes concrete efforts to create small, caring communities within the framework of the large school building." Each new academy was assigned teachers for the core subjects—English, social studies, math, science, and foreign language. Each academy was given an assistant principal, counselor, instructional guide, and core magnet teachers who were related to the theme. It was up to each of these new academy teams to create the climate, make the instruction relevant to the theme, and enforce the school rules. Academies were organized for college-bound students (Pre-Law and Humanities Academy or the Health Academy), vocational students (Tech Prep Academy), and for other students with no expressed goals (Universal Global Studies Academy). All the academies had a heterogeneous mix of students.

Not all students responded to the school's new organization. Many continued to fail and fall behind. This time, however, it was easier for the staff to identify students at risk of failing, and they were able to intervene earlier. The Texas Assessment of Academic Skills (TAAS) examinations in mathematics, reading, and writing were given each October to high school sophomores. Fox Tech freshmen took practice examinations, and the staff looked at the data to identify who needed help. These results were used to place students, when they became sophomores, into homogeneous groups that met thirty minutes a day from the start of school year until the examinations.

For students who did not pass the actual examinations in their sophomore year, the data were examined again, and students were prepped in their weakest subjects before they retook the examination in the summer or in the following fall.

The academy concept at Fox Tech yielded results. In May 1996, at the end of the first year, Fox Tech enrollment rose by 305 students; the dropout rate was cut in half, to 7.6%, and the math scores, for the first time in many years, exceeded state minimal standards. Perhaps most important, there were a new climate and culture. As Joanne described it, "I saw a real change especially in the attitudes of teachers. No longer was it *those* kids or *their* kids. It became, 'These are *our* students.' "

However, the academy concept was no magic solution, and adjustments had to be made over the next two years. Each academy had to face issues common to small theme–based high schools: constantly creating new courses as students moved onto their next grade; infusing the theme, such as law, into the core classes; building in career and college exploration; and developing a sense of family. To facilitate this process, a director was assigned to each academy; student, parent, and teacher surveys provided important feedback; and the curricula development became the responsibility of each academy's teachers.

Expectations continued to rise, and so did results. In June 1998, at the end of the third year, Fox Tech was the talk of the district and state. TAAS math results rose to 66% of the students meeting minimal standards (first in the district), writing jumped to 84% (second in the district), and reading climbed 13 percentage points to 73% (fifth in the district). Fox Tech won second place in attendance (up to 92.9%) and dropout rate (down to 1.2%). Discipline referrals were reduced, as were in-school and out-of-school suspensions. More special education students successfully completed regular education classes, and a few took and passed the TAAS, even though they were exempt. The good news about Fox Tech quickly spread through the district; 600 new students enrolled, bringing school enrollment to 1,500.

Fox Tech became a new school. As Fox Tech teachers described it: "The focus here is on how we are going to improve the students"; "Everybody here—from top to bottom—works hard"; "We have set of goals and we work as a team."

"LET'S HIT THE STREETS"

On one of my visits to Fox Tech, I was in Joanne's office when three students rushed in to tell their principal some important news. Joanne told me to come with her to her car. I asked why. Joanne replied that she had just been told a gang dispute was about to take place. She knew the kids and was determined to stop the fight. I watched from the car as Joanne found one of the gang leaders, took him aside to defuse the situation, and then searched out his adversary. Peace was restored, violence was avoided—this time. The area surrounding Fox Tech is rough, and adolescent conflicts are constantly brewing. But Joanne Cockrell had won the respect of her students, and usually they would listen to what she had to say.

Joanne had a unique relationship with her students. On the one hand, it was formal. Everyone knew Ms. Cockrell was the principal; she had the authority and, more important, she had the respect of both the students and the staff. On the other hand, her relationship with her students (and she did see them as *her* students) was informal, with students sharing information that typically would not be shared with an authority figure. Joanne's car rides were a ritual. She hunted down truants, warned away dropouts who stayed near the school to not bother students, and responded to local shopkeepers who complained about some of the students. As one teacher observed, "Joanne loves the kids, and they love her."

Joanne brought together student representatives to serve as the Principal's Advisory Council, which was more than a cosmetic feature of the school. The students made decisions, and the students' feedback was taken seriously. These student leaders cared about their school because the school cared about them. As one student put it, "You feel the love and sense of family here." These student leaders felt that teachers stayed after school to help if a student was not doing well. However, as another student put it, "Teachers say they will help us but only if we understand that we have to first help ourselves."

The students serving on the Principal's Advisory Council in the spring of 2001 became concerned when I reminded them Joanne Cockrell could, one day, leave. They offered this advice to anyone who became the new principal: First, be patient, don't become discouraged, and never give up; second, be involved with the students; third, don't smile too much or look weak; fourth, show you are in charge; finally, make sure your staff loves your students. These Fox Tech students believed in their principal because she was strong and decisive and because she believed in them.

WALLS AND WORDS WITH POWERFUL MESSAGES

The best-kept secrets for the Fox Tech students were the stories of the school's alumni. Joanne Cockrell and her team knew that had to change, and consequently the Wall of Fame was created on a scarred set of balcony walls overlooking the school's lobby. Photographs and biographies of prominent Fox Tech alumni were posted because Fox Tech students needed to know that the school's graduates were among San Antonio's leaders. These alumni were successful doctors, lawyers, business owners, educators, union officials, artists, poets, activists, and entrepreneurs. H. D. Zachery made millions in the construction field. Evangelina Vigil-Pinon won recognition as a widely published poet. Oliver Garza served as the U.S. ambassador to Nicaragua. Charlie Munoz dropped out of Fox Tech and then returned; he became one of San Antonio's high school principals. Dr. Ricardo Romo went from being a Fox Tech track star to become the president of the University of Texas at San Antonio. Veronica Zamora-Campos became the head of pediatrics at General Hospital.

Joanne contacted many of these alumni and recruited them as motivational speakers and mentors. Individuals were selected as the "Fox Tech Leader of the Year" and invited to a special school ceremony. In Joanne's words, "These alumni felt honored and our students developed great pride in their heritage and their school. They understood they had a promising future."

The wall symbolized the new Fox Tech. The school was committed to success. A new belief statement was put on paper and posted throughout the building. It affirmed the following:

- Institutions, not students, are at risk.
- Educators build the foundations of future success for their students and support them every day, not just during class time.
- Education is the key to breaking the bonds of poverty.
- Lack of family support does not negate our support; it only increases it.
- There is no special education world; therefore every child must be serviced in a regular education setting.
- It is our responsibility to provide a safe, friendly learning environment and provide opportunities for the growth of all students, academically, emotionally, physically, and socially.
- All students can and will learn when their interests are addressed.

EXPLAINING WHAT HAPPENED

Recognition for Fox Tech's accomplishments started in 2000, when the school received a National Blue Ribbon of Excellence Award. The acclaim intensified in 2001, when the school won the National School Change Award and simultaneously was honored in *Time* magazine as one of six "Schools That Stretch." The article noted that "Great schools ask everyone to stretch. They give kids the tools they need to reach their goals" (Schools That Stretch, 2001, p. 71). In summarizing Fox Tech's remarkable rise from worst to first, *Time* mentioned that "Failure [at Fox Tech] had become routine, expected, and excused." This pattern of failure might have continued if the school district had not "unleashed the neutron bomb of school reform, disestablishment" (Goldstein, 2001, ¶ 2–3).

There is no question external forces, such as the disestablishment action, were a central piece of the Fox Tech story. But there was more. In 2001, when the Fox Tech staff looked back at their dramatic journey, they used the metaphor of the buffalo. As they explained, at the end of the nineteenth century the buffalo was close to extinction until a new breed was developed and endangered species laws were passed. At the same time, in 1879, a new school opened in San Antonio, then the largest city in Texas. The school was called San Antonio High School; it later was renamed the Louis W. Fox Academic and Technical High School. Its mascot, "in deference to the strong, noble, and vanishing beast," was the buffalo. One hundred years later, the high school stood on the brink of extinction. It was saved, and Joanne Cockrell symbolically awarded buffalo pins to staff members who participated in school events and activities.

Joanne Cockrell understood a new Fox Tech needed a culture that was very different from the old Fox Tech. She built that new culture through symbols (the buffalo), rewards (the buffalo pins), rituals (morning announcements acknowledging student achievements), celebrations (student recognition for passing the TAAS), and heroes (Fox Tech alumni). Cultures influence, and are influenced by, everyday practices and larger priorities. Joanne brought Fox Tech from chaos and confusion to academics and achievement. Her executive team announced that there would be zero tolerance for serious infractions, and they kept their word.

Joanne started with what she did best: relate to students. She wandered the halls and walked the streets. She counseled, cajoled, and cautioned. The students quickly understood that their new principal cared. Story after story about Joanne Cockrell spread among the student body. You could talk with Principal Cockrell. You didn't have to make an appointment (although you could, and the principal would keep it). If Ms. Cockrell was in her office and not busy, you could speak with her. You could tell her things in confidence. You could talk about yourself or tell her about a friend who was having problems. As one teacher stated, "I think [the students] feel they can trust us."

Trust, however, was slow in coming. As one teacher explained, "The kids don't trust the adults because of what has happened to them and to their families in the past." For the most part, the Fox Tech students lived in impoverished neighborhoods and took two buses (or more) to school. They might count on some of their peers, but few, if any adults, offered to help. In the students' eyes, the adults were indifferent, uncaring, or afraid. They could not be trusted.

Fox Tech teachers also had lacked trust—of each other and of the school administration. As the culture and climate changed, so did the trust level. Teachers began to trust more fully the students. These teachers came to understand their students could achieve, that they could go beyond the minimum standards. They could be prepared for college, get accepted, and succeed. They needed the opportunity and support.

Simultaneously, the teachers began to trust each other. Teachers no longer took refuge in their own classrooms. The academy structure broke down teacher isolation. They had to learn how to work with others. Meanwhile, as principal, Joanne earned the trust of her staff. As one teacher stated, "Everyone knows where she's coming from. Her word is her bond."

Trust unfolded on another level. The superintendency changed a year before Joanne took over Fox Tech. The previous superintendent retired after 17 years on the job, and Deputy Superintendent Diana Lam moved up to the position. Although Diana was barely selected by a 4–3 vote by the school board, she launched a school reform agenda. She was bright and energetic, very familiar with the latest research on teaching and learning, and a risk-taker. She also knew she could impact her schools only if she developed her principals. She nurtured the newer principals, such as Joanne Cockrell, shaping them as change agents. Diana's message was clear, forthright, and passionate: It was about kids, not politics. As superintendent, she taught her staff and the district's principals to look at data and to use those data to drive change.

As Joanne recaps, "When [Diana Lam] spoke, we listened. She communicated through stories and reached people's hearts." As Fox Tech teachers remember, Joanne Cockrell led in the same way. "[Joanne Cockrell] was the change. She willed it to happen," is how one teacher described it. Another added, "She expected things would get better and would accept nothing less." Joanne could be tough, very tough. For example, Joanne reduced Fox Tech's dropout rate from 13% to 0.5% by taking 250 students and their families to truancy court.

Joanne was also an instructional leader. As she clarified, "I learned a little about a lot of things. I couldn't help science teachers if I didn't know some science and the same for the other subjects." Joanne would not accept inferior instruction, low expectations, or blaming others. Some of her math teachers claimed that entering freshmen were too ill prepared to master algebra. Joanne disagreed. In her view, these students could be reached, and she proved so by teaching one semester of Algebra I.

One teacher's artistic version of the Fox Tech story, obviously influenced by Joanne's presence, was divided into three parts. The first section listed "Strong leadership, pride, unity, hard work, students first, and change." The second section was a drawing of the state of Texas, with a buffalo inside. The sidebar read "Buffalo busting through the map of Texas—represents busting through barriers. Going from a rich history to a new beginning." The third section was headed "advice" and included "Don't forget who the change is for: the student"; "hard work, hard work, hard work"; and "Don't be timid in your leadership. If it is good for the student, push hard for the change" (see Figure 10.2).

When several other teachers were asked what could symbolize the Fox Tech story, the siege of the Alamo was the most prevalent suggestion. One teacher said "We're both still standing after a fierce battle. Fox Tech was not expected to succeed, and some still want to believe we will fail." Another offered, "The odds were against us." A third teacher compared Fox Tech's struggle with the Texas fight for independence by noting that both had sad beginnings. The massacre at the Alamo was a horrible start of that war; the disestablishment of Fox Tech was a horrendous way to fight for school improvement. Finally someone simply said, "Surrender was not an option."

Figure 10.1 Demographics for Louis W. Fox Academic and
Technical High School, 2001

Grades: 9–12	No. staff: 149
No. students: 1,521	Size of district: 54,399 students;
White: 2% African American: 9% Hispanic: 89%	74 schools Elementary schools: 51 Middle schools: 15 High schools: 8

Figure 10.2 One teacher's interpretation of the school change process at
Louis W. Fox Academic and Technical High School

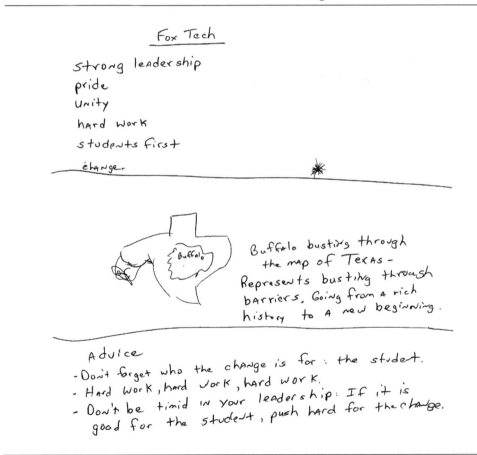

Drawing done by Joe Kethan

11

"Why Are We Here?"

Niles High School

Niles, Michigan

Doug Law, Principal

Muhammad Ali briskly entered Niles High School and headed for the offices of Betty Perkins, the newly appointed principal, and Molly Brawley, Betty's assistant. After a bear hug, he asked these two school administrators how they were adjusting to their promotions. They were old friends. Ali's son played for the local Little League club coached by Brawley's husband. Perkins, meanwhile, ordered the mounting of one of Ali's quotes. The handsome and huge poster plaque was the class gift from the graduating class of 2000. It was prominently displayed and autographed by Ali.

It read, "Champions aren't made in gyms. Champions are made from something they have deep inside them; a desire, a dream, a vision. They have to have the skills and the will. But the will must be stronger than the skill." The symbolism was powerful. Ali, who broke new ground as a boxer and civil rights leader and was selected as "the athlete of the twentieth century," stood out as a change agent. He lived out his dream, desire, and vision. Living in nearby Berrien Springs, Michigan, he was a supporter of Niles High School, nationally recognized for its ability to change, for exercising its will.

WE'RE IN MICHIANA

The strangest thing about the Michiana region is that it has two time zones for half the year. Because it is located on the fringes of the two states, Michigan and Indiana, one frequently, in the same day, moves from one state to the other. However, Indiana refuses to adopt Daylight Savings Time, so in the spring, summer, and early fall one has to be certain about meeting times, asking, for example, whether the appointment is set for 7:00 Michigan time or 7:00 Indiana time.

Located in Michiana, the town of Niles is also part of the "Four Flags" territory, which the Niles Chamber of Commerce booklet describes by noting:

> Our history dates back more than 300 years. Since then four nations— France, England, Spain, and the United States—have fought over what one explorer called "paradise on earth" . . . four flags have flown over this land at different times in its history.

Michiana is best known for the University of Notre Dame, on the Indiana side, in South Bend. Chicago is 90 minutes away by train and attracts some of the locals for work. People like living in Niles, Michigan. For many of them, it is paradise, blending the best of an urban center and rural life. Lake Michigan is a half-hour away; the area is scenic and peaceful. The Niles Chamber of Commerce booklet further notes that although Niles has been an industrialized city, it hasn't "lost our small town feel and leafy tree lined environment [while] many innovations and products have been developed right here in our small town . . . things that influenced the quality of life around the world."

In the 1960s and 1970s, Niles, like much of Michigan and the industrial centers of the Midwest, suffered an economic setback when the automobile and other major industries were being outpaced by foreign competitors. Manufacturers in what was called the "Rust Belt" needed to change the way they did business. Many communities did not adjust or recover, but Niles slowly moved its economic base into the 21st century. As noted in the Chamber of Commerce booklet, "In a sense the bends of the river running through our community [the oldest in Michigan] represent the flow . . . constant and forward of our citizens and local government."

By the start of 2000, more than 100 manufacturers—four of which located their international corporate headquarters in Niles—and 4,200 employees were in the area, turning out high-quality, high-tech products. The community changed with the times. Niles High School did not.

JUST MUDDLING ALONG, AS USUAL

Doug Law, a school district administrator who became the high school's principal, called Niles High School an "ordinary and typical American high school." It was not in crisis, but neither did it win awards. Teachers came to work, students reported to class. At the end of the day, most left to return the next day for the same drill. For students, as one put it, "I do my time, and I'm out."

Academic achievement was mixed. There was an honors group of students, small in number, who were college bound. A middle group, the largest, got average grades; most of those students got jobs after graduation or entered the armed forces. Some went on to college. Students from the lowest-performing group were channeled into vocational courses and expected to secure blue collar jobs. For the most part, Niles students were homogeneously grouped: The more academically skilled students were placed together in classes, the middle group of students programmed with each other, and so on. The school culture honored only the best and the brightest; other students were allowed to slip by or slip through.

Students had a six-period day, with fifty-five-minute classes, characterized mostly by lectures, day in and day out. Those in the vocational track took most of their classes in the vocational wing of the building. Those in the academic track never took a job-related course and never ventured past the swinging door that led to the vocational wing. That was foreign and unknown territory, a different world.

The school year unfolded in a manner similar to how most high schools conducted their business. School opened; students settled into their course schedules; teachers took out their tried-and-true lesson plans; and classes began with their typical curriculum, which usually was boring and irrelevant. The football season opened the school year with its pep rallies, cheerleaders, homecoming, school rivalries, and tales of athletic heroics. The Thanksgiving and Christmas holidays arrived, and the basketball season geared up. The winter doldrums—interrupted, it was hoped, with an unexpected basketball triumph—led to spring, and a final sprint toward the end-of-year examinations. Graduation and the prom signaled the close of a typical and traditional academic year. Nothing terrible, nothing special.

As Doug Law described the school, "It was exactly the high school the staff had gone to; nothing had changed. No one thought about why we were doing what we were doing."

THINGS CHANGED, FOR THE WORSE

By the early 1990s, there was a sense that things needed to improve. There was commotion in the halls; the traditional emphasis on order and control was being ignored. Fights became more frequent. The school was acquiring a bad name in the community. The school board wrestled with the question of what to do about the high school.

Students, even the 30% who were headed to college, lacked focus. Students did not know what lay ahead. They left Niles High School unprepared for college and, if they were entering the world of work, without marketable skills. Students felt disorganized and unmotivated. They did what they were told. They didn't see the value of what they were studying. As one student explained why he had taken his courses: "They told me I had to take them."

Teachers were trapped in typical isolation, which is common to many schools, and did not have a clue about what other teachers were doing. As one teacher put it, "I went into my room, closed my door, and did my thing."

The staff had become increasingly rigid, conservative, and distant from the students. As a district administrator commented, "They [at the high school] were definitely not student centered."

The watchword was *maintenance*, not change. One teacher noted, "We were doing the same things we had been doing for thirty years, while the times had changed." If things were not going as expected, teachers did not point to themselves for the problems or disappointments. Instead, teachers felt that "It was the system's fault." Or they blamed the students. As one teacher remembered, many on the staff explained the school's decline by contending that "Half the kids were from the trailer park." The reference to the poorer section of the town implied lower expectations for those students and no need for the staff to work very hard.

The school administration emphasized diligent supervision, seeing that people were in the right places, doing the right things. It was an autocratic and inspectorial view of school life, which remained constant even though the high school experienced a revolving door of principals, five in seven years. There was little trust between teachers and administration, a situation that worsened in 1986 with acrimony over teacher contract negotiations and, finally, a teachers' strike. A difficult settlement ended the strike, but not the bitterness, which lingered for many years. As one teacher remembered, "There was a huge *us versus them* mentality."

Among the high school staff there was a feeling of discontent, which boiled to the surface when student behavior worsened. Teachers would peek beyond their isolated doors and complain to each other about the overall school tone. Why wasn't anyone doing something about the disruptive students, the unacceptable behavior, the chaos in the halls? Some teachers stepped forward and demanded action. Others, more discreetly, spoke with school board members. Some complained to the principal (who was about to retire); others went to the superintendent. Virtually everyone believed something had to be done.

GOOD NEWS! LOTS OF COMPLAINTS

Two watershed events made it clear that change was not only desirable; it was essential.

The first event resulted from a school board decision, which in hindsight could be seen as fearless. Or foolish. It was 1990, and the state of Michigan edged toward legislating school choice. Proposals in the state legislature were suggesting families could choose their schools; the nature of zoned, neighborhood schools (with their captive populations) was to be turned on its head. Student decisions about where to attend school would greatly impact enrollment figures, budgets, and jobs.

Most residents knew a state policy on school choice was coming. The Niles school board voted to pilot a school choice program, working with two neighboring school districts, Brandywine and Edwardsburg. According to this plan, families could select one of the three high schools. The Niles families were not required to send their children to Niles High School. At the same time, the families in Brandywine and Edwardsburg could send their students to Niles

High School. The results were quite disappointing for Niles, because few students from outside Niles decided to attend Niles High School and, worse, many Niles families chose one of the other two options. Niles High School enrollment went down by more than 100. The message was clear; something had to be done, and the Niles school board did not know what to do.

The second watershed moment involved Niles High School alumni. They came back—not to celebrate, but to complain. Dozens of Niles graduates who had gone on to college told their former teachers they had not been prepared for the more rigorous college work. Some had flunked out. Meanwhile, dozens of graduates who entered the work world could not find or keep a decent job, a job with a good salary, career advancement, and the promise of a bright future. These graduates lacked marketable skills, the experience of working in teams, and the ability to think critically. These were not the Niles dropouts, another disenfranchised and underserved group; these were graduates. They didn't fail; their high school did.

THE JOHN AND DOUG SHOW

John Huffman, the Niles schools superintendent, had mixed reactions to the growing complaints about the high school. In one sense, he was pleased that discontent at and with the high school had reached a breaking point. It would be easier now to do something about the school. John turned to Doug Law, an elementary reading consultant, whom he had recruited seven years before to come to the district office. Doug had served as an assistant to the superintendent, tending to a variety of instructional and curricular issues; later, he became assistant superintendent, serving more formally as John's confidante and partner.

John and Doug were well prepared for the Niles High School challenge, philosophically and tactically. Their personal experiences and their professional training made them natural change agents.

Superintendent John Huffman was the son in a family that had moved frequently because of his father's high-level corporate job; John attended twelve different schools in his twelve years of elementary, junior high, and high school. He knew how to adjust; he lived change. John understood why people have difficulty with change and what steps needed to be put carefully into place to effect change. John served as a perfect coach for Doug Law, who was going to lead the change at the high school.

Doug Law was uniquely prepared for the assignment. He understood change and, like John Huffman, his background had developed his instincts about what people could accomplish. For Doug, it started in the fifth grade when he, as a "middle of the road student," was placed in Mrs. Clute's "top kids" class. In Doug's words, "She helped me not to act like a middle kid. She convinced me I could do the top-level work." The lesson was repeated in the seventh grade, when Doug's math teacher showed him how he could master the "new math." Doug's heroes reinforced a message about vision, determination, and tenacity. Doug saw Walt Disney as a visionary, whose dream would not be denied, even though it took him several years to sell the idea of Mickey Mouse. Doug pointed to Benjamin Franklin, "a truly unique character, who as an inventor, intellectual, and diplomat had more influence than anyone in his generation."

Perhaps the greatest influence on Doug Law was the twenty summers he served as an assistant director of a YMCA camp, where he polished a variety of skills that were very helpful in his professional assignments. Doug designed, practiced, and refined a range of team building exercises. He learned about group process. He helped run a camp premised on empowering others. Doug identified the YMCA camp director, Dr. Patrick Rode, as his mentor. In Doug's words, "Rode was one of those folks who had a strong optimistic view of youth." Rode took pleasure in watching the campers and the college-age staff members develop. Consequently, as Doug put it, "Rode taught me the rewards of helping people grow." This became a lesson that enabled Doug to transform Niles High School.

TRUST, CREDIBILITY, AND RISK-TAKING

John Huffman and Doug Law jointly developed a plan for change. As assistant superintendent, one of Doug's responsibilities was school improvement, which, among other things, meant working with site-based teams at each school. In the fall of 1992, John sent Doug to the high school to be his eyes and ears and to work with the struggling and disempowered School Improvement Team (SIT).

Starting with his first meeting with a newly formed team, Doug asked one question: "Why are we here?" He pushed for answers as he pressed the team members to think about what they were currently doing and what they might be doing. In effect, Doug asked whether the students at Niles High School were receiving the education and preparation for life they needed and deserved. Throughout the coming months, the SIT members became more outspoken. As the team dealt with the school's faults and failures, the question "Why are we here?" became a mantra.

Doug Law had a unique opportunity. He had a very strong, close, and trusting relationship with his boss. He had a mission. He had a chance to pursue it the way his instincts told him would be best.

Although there was still a principal in the high school, Doug Law became heir apparent, as he revived a Parents Advisory Council and continued to strengthen the SIT.

In the spring of 1993, Doug asked John Huffman for four afternoons of release time so he and the SIT could facilitate discussions with the staff. The first of these sessions set the tone. Everyone sat in a circle of chairs (without desks to hide behind), and the SIT asked, "Why are we here?" The comfort zone had been breached; some real risk-taking had been initiated. As Doug recalled, looking back, "We had to go beyond going through the motions. Although the staff didn't want to experience the pain associated with change, something had to be done."

The pace slowly picked up in the 1993–94 school year. Doug Law was assigned half-time at the high school to continue to work with the SIT. The discussions continued, and both the SIT and Doug Law grew in stature. The team knew the high school had to change. What they could not determine was "change to what?"

In September 1994, Doug Law was named the high school principal. He again asked John Huffman for release time for the teachers. The faculty spent four afternoons writing a guiding statement. It stated the school's purpose, which was "to prepare our students to be responsible, productive adults." The guiding statement's words included "mastery of basic academic skills, being self-disciplined and self-motivated, being a problem solver in academic and social arenas, and developing positive attitudes and habits." Writing a guiding statement had multiple purposes. First, it forced the staff to think about their beliefs. Second, it gave the staff experience in building consensus. Finally, it committed the school to a new direction.

As Doug saw it, a new direction was imperative. In his view, the Niles students were making decisions about their futures without a knowledge base. "[The students] just didn't know what was out there." For example, a student might decide to become an engineer because her uncle had a large house on a lake due to all the money he made as an engineer. Another student might choose engineering because her skills in math and science made engineering seem like a logical choice. Or, as Doug described it, "Mom and Dad could be convinced to send her away to Purdue, known for its engineering program and its great social life."

Whether engineering matched the student's talents and interests was not considered. Whether there were engineering job opportunities was ignored. Whether the student understood what engineering involved and required was not explored. The Niles staff recognized this made no sense, and consequently their guiding statement committed them to "implement a curriculum that focuses students in a career/educational direction." The school world was going to relate to the work world.

THE SCHOOL-TO-CAREERS MOVEMENT

In the late 1980s, a school-to-work movement, later called *school-to-careers*, became a force in thinking about what American high schools should do. Simply put, many high school graduates in America were not prepared to succeed at jobs, be they blue collar or white collar. Kids graduated high school with no marketable skills. Furthermore, these graduates did not know how to work in teams or solve problems. There was no path from high school to employment. Niles High School was not alone; all across America, many high school graduates knew little about life after high school.

The federal government responded to the problem by disseminating research findings and providing funding for school-to-careers programs. These funds typically were awarded to state or regional departments of education. In Michiana, this meant the Berrien County Intermediate School District (ISD), an educational service agency serving sixteen public school districts and thirty parochial/private schools. Paul C. Bergan, the ISD Regional Director for Career

Technical Education and Career Pathways, and Becky Meier, the ISD Director of School Development/Career Pathways, were watching the events at Niles with keen interest. They were intrigued by the Niles staff's effort to create a school guiding statement. At the same time, Paul and Becky were writing proposals for a new wave of school-to-careers federal funding. They received the funds; now they had to decide what to do with them.

In the fall of 1994, Doug Law and his SIT team were invited, along with teams from the other high schools in the area, to hear Steve Olzcak, an experienced high school educator, make a presentation at an ISD dinner. Olzcak made an impassioned plea for school-to-careers programs. Doug's team was impressed. They wanted to visit schools using these career pathways programs.

Teams of Niles teachers traveled far and wide, to Seattle, Washington; Annapolis, Maryland; and Charleston, South Carolina. They came back excited and motivated to plan a more relevant way to prepare their students for the future. Those who went on the trips made formal and informal presentations to their colleagues. Momentum built. Niles High School became the first school in the area to apply for a Career Pathways grant. They got it.

The Niles High School staff also began to look at block scheduling. Small discussion groups, sometimes by department, sometimes by interest, began debating the virtues of a career-focused instructional program and a new student schedule. By June, a commitment was made to move in that direction.

Deepened understanding came in the summer or 1995. Most of the staff participated in a workplace program, which included field trips to local employers such as Tyler Refrigeration, the South Bend *Tribune*, and Memorial Hospital. These trips gave teachers an awareness of how work was conducted at these sites. It also heightened their understanding of the knowledge and skills high school graduates needed to be successful at these jobs. Most important, new partnerships were developed. These employers helped shape curriculum, provided internship experiences, and served as guest lecturers.

ISD staff, meanwhile, played an ongoing support role. They did more than provide funds. They helped to make trip arrangements to other schools in other states; they provided advice; they served as cheerleaders; they assumed the role of external change agent, catalyst, and coach.

When listening to Paul Bergan or Becky Meier at ISD or John Huffman or Doug Law at Niles, one is taken by their acute sensitivity to the change process. Each of them understood change and played complementary roles. Doug was the public leader, John was the behind-the-scenes advisor, Becky and Paul took on consultant roles. They provide incentives and assistance but left center stage for the Niles school actors.

GO OR NO-GO?

By September 1995, activities were in high gear, and Doug Law accelerated the process. He asked John Huffman for fourteen "late starts." This meant students would report two hours late to school on fourteen Wednesday mornings. This provided time for the faculty to divide into work teams to plan the details of the proposed changes. The trust and confidence established between and among Doug, John, and the school board brought approval. Everyone understood the stakes were high. Some concrete plans had to be produced by the end of these sessions. As Doug candidly pointed out to his staff, it was his job that was on the line.

The staff went to it. Groups planned the details of the Freshman Connection, an approach that would help new students make the transition to high school. Others looked more deeply at block scheduling. Some planned details of the Career Pathways program. Others developed interdisciplinary curriculum units. Things seemed to be moving along well—or were they?

By late fall, there had been considerable talk but no firm consensus, no definitive decisions. The process stalled. As one SIT member confessed, "We knew something had to be changed about the way the meetings were heading." Consequently, at a SIT planning session, which always preceded the late starts (so those sessions could be well planned), Doug turned to the teachers and asked, "Would it help if the school administrators were not there?" A long pause settled in. Finally, someone spoke up and agreed that was a good idea.

Doug Law and his assistant principals were in the meeting room when the staff arrived for their Wednesday late-start session. Molly Brawley, as SIT chairwoman, was nervous; she knew in a few moments she would have to take charge. This was to be a defining moment for her and the SIT. As Molly recalled, "I was fed up being accused of being Doug Law's puppet."

Five chairs were in the front of the room, facing the rest of the staff. As Doug and his fellow administrators left the room, Molly and her SIT colleagues sat down in those chairs. Brian Pyles, a marketing teacher, was the first to speak; Molly quickly joined in. They told the staff the planning sessions were not working because compromises were not being reached and decisions were not being made. Molly and Brian acted out a typical argument that had transpired among SIT members in regard to a detail of block scheduling. They shared with the staff how the five SIT members were in disagreement but had found a way to reach a consensus. They learned how to move ahead and not stay stalled.

Finally, the SIT team confronted the staff. They had to move ahead with their plans and do Career Pathways, or postpone action for another year of study, or just "bag it." The staff reacted passionately; voices rose in disagreement. Finally, Bud Magrane, the varsity basketball coach and a physical education teacher, got up. Bud had originally been a negative voice but had slowly shifted his views as a result of his visits to other schools and what he learned about career-focused programs. When Bud spoke, people listened; he was held in high esteem. Bud rose and quietly said, "What the heck, we can do this. It will really help our kids." Molly whispered under her breath, "Thank you, Bud." This was another watershed moment. A voice vote was taken. Overwhelmingly, the staff decided to move forward.

THE *NILES DAILY STAR* GOES TO NEW YORK CITY

By the end of the 1995–96 school year, the new Niles was ready to be launched. A Freshman Connection program, which included advisers for each new student to assist with the difficult transition to high school, was launched. Freshman had an additional class each day, which focused on topics such as managing conflict, the art of learning, career choices, morals and manners, an introduction to the career pathways, and a series called "Where Are You Going and How Are You Going to Get There?"

By the end of the freshman year, each student had selected a career pathway. These career clusters—Business, Fine Arts and Communication, Health and Human Services, and Engineering and Industrial—included many courses related to the specific field, which were to be completed in the sophomore, junior, and senior years. The total number of required graduation credits increased from twenty-four credits to thirty-two, with an additional required credit in math, science, and English, and five credits in the career core.

Block scheduling was adopted, with four 85-minute blocks each day. Teachers worked with each other in developing interdisciplinary approaches. Business partners agreed to provide out-of-school career-related experiences for the Niles students. These took on different formats, including apprenticeships (learning a trade), internships (on-the-job work experience), job shadowing, and mentorships (being "adopted" by a specific skilled worker).

Niles High School became a school that rejected top-down, heavy-handed management and embraced a commitment to teacher ownership. The school culture honored the achievements and career choices of all students. Everyone, from Chamber of Commerce members to new students, felt pride in the school. The business community became engaged. Parents were recognized and involved. The SIT continued to set direction.

The Career Pathways program enabled students to think about life after high school. They developed portfolios demonstrating mastery of and interest in specific fields. The school decreased its dropout rate, raised its academic indicators, and became a showcase for other educators. As one district administrator put it, "At Niles High School, they now believe they have something to say."

In 2000, Niles's achievement and accomplishments were recognized in two important ways. The Milken Family Foundation honored Doug Law with a $25,000 check as a way to "celebrate, elevate, and activate outstanding educators." Niles High School was one of the first six schools to win the National School Change Award (then called the *Chase School Change Award*), the only high school in America to receive that honor. This was very big news in Niles and was prominently covered by the local television station and by the *Niles Daily Star*.

The full banner headline across the front page of the paper proudly announced "Niles High program one of six honored nationally." Dave Perozek, the reporter, later accompanied the Niles contingent, which included John

Huffman, Doug Law, Betty Perkins, and Molly Brawley, to New York City for the national awards presentation and the National Principals Leadership Institute. Each day, Dave electronically sent a story back to Niles. At the end of the week, a sixteen-page souvenir section of the newspaper, called "A Diary of Change," was printed. It included stories about the broad and deep changes in Niles, the change process, and the win–win situation benefiting both students and local businesses in Niles.

EXPLAINING WHAT HAPPENED

Niles High School moved from being ordinary to extraordinary, from a place of concern to a site for conversation about what high schools could be. The Niles staff had searched for answers, visiting other schools around the country. By 1999, they were hosting educators from across America who wanted to find out how Niles had converted itself into a school that prepared its students for college and the work world.

Because of the frequency of visits, the Niles team prepared a presentation packet, called "A Career-Focused High School," that offered advice on how to get started. The guide provided the following suggestions: "Think big, identify a representative group to lead the change process, schedule time to support change, and make sure there is central administration and Board of Education support." Doug Law, as a supportive central office person and, later as principal, modeled that advice. He encouraged the Niles staff to think big as they wrestled with the "Why are we here?" question. Doug empowered the SIT to be the representative group leading the change. At three different stages, he asked for—and received—significant time for the staff to identify problems and create solutions. He worked closely with his change compatriot, superintendent John Huffman, and the school board's support was secured and maintained.

As Doug commented, "I knew when I became a principal, I wanted to set a tone." Doug also wanted to make things happen. He described the Niles staff as a typical group of educators who "perfected the technique of assigning everything to committees," which meet endlessly without solving any problems. Although the Niles staff, under Doug's leadership, did work in committees, these groups met with a focus and a charge to produce specific programs within a set time frame. The Niles guide described this as "Take initiative . . . you can talk forever."

A number of concurrent and overlapping factors came into play with Niles High School. There was much discontent at the school, while at the same time the external perceptions of the high school continued to worsen. The fact that a series of principals could not take hold of the situation made it feel like fixing the high school was an unsolvable problem.

John Huffman, as superintendent, came under increased pressure from his board. His credibility with the school board would mean nothing if the high school problem were not fixed. The problems with the high school were confirmed when the pilot school choice plan demonstrated that, given other options, some Niles families would elect to send their children to other high schools. The pressure was intense; something had to be done to make Niles High School a place to which residents would want to send their children, a school that generated pride.

Fortunately for John Huffman, he had the leader available to do the job. Not only was Doug Law skilled, but also a long history of close collaboration had created a strong bond of trust and a common philosophical base between him and John. Both men were doers and knew how each other felt. Their thinking patterns and views of the world meshed. They both understood, instinctively, what a change process would entail. For example, a new principal at Niles High School could not just go in like gangbusters and impose heavy-handed mandates. The experienced and cynical high school staff would rebel; nothing more than cosmetic changes would be made.

Instead, John and Doug practiced what many of the books on change preached. They moved in discrete, carefully orchestrated, incremental steps. They created a mechanism for the high school staff to buy in and develop a sense of ownership. They found a way to create time for discussion, exploration, and reflection. With the ISD funding, they used the grant requirements to channel staff discussion.

As John and Doug have summarized the effort,

> In some ways, it did not matter what we were exploring and discussing. We might have selected another way to change the way our students learned. What was important was the fact that the staff was empowered to make this journey and make those decisions. It had to be their quest since they were the ones who would have to do it.

Both John Huffman and Doug Law and, later, the SIT, were willing to take risks. They were willing to push people to see things in a new way; the trips to other schools were not initially greeted with joy. John and Doug took careful steps to build their credibility. With Doug's formal inauguration as high school principal, the process accelerated, and more empowerment unfolded. The revival of a Parents Advisory Council enabled new and important voices to be heard; this added to the pressure to get something done at the high school.

The role of the external partner was quite important. The ISD provided a sense of credibility because they knew about nationally recognized programs. They gave Niles High School a sense of recognition by awarding them the first school-to-careers grant. They sponsored field trips, which created a knowledge base for the Niles teachers and a chance for them to debate what could or could not be adapted to their own school setting.

What is especially remarkable about the Niles story was the awareness that the culture at the high school had to be dramatically shifted. This could not be done by fiat or by massive teacher transfers (there was no other high school to send them to!). A definitive process was required. Doug Law described that process as first building trust and relationships and then developing a felt need for change. That was followed by the development of a guiding statement, a tool for building consensus among the staff. Then, and only then, could the staff move ahead with making specific plans.

The planning stage had critical characteristics. It looked at real problems, such as the inability of many new students to adjust to high school. It was staff driven; teachers planned and led discussions. Time was provided during the school day with no students or conflicting demands. Although the discussion looked at many things, it was primarily focused on how students were learning. It was student centered.

The change journey was supported, in many ways, by the district administration. Besides the time that was granted, trips were endorsed. Materials were provided. Guidance and advice were available. The school board backed the superintendent, who backed his new high school principal. The level of trust and cooperation among the "power brokers" was unusually high. Requests for specific professional development came from the bottom up. The typical mandated staff training ("This is the year the district says we need to learn . . . ") was replaced by teacher requests for learning more about a block schedule or how to create interdisciplinary thematic units.

The Niles High School graduating class of 2000 was the first group of students to go through the four-year Career Pathways program. After working with both elementary and junior high students, one Niles graduate decided to go into secondary education. He noted, "[Career Pathways is] a good program because it helps you choose what you want to do and what you don't want to do." Another graduate declared,

> Up until I was a freshman, I wanted to be a doctor but then I changed my mind because of the classes I took in the program. When my junior year came around, I changed to a business career pathway.

A third graduate, headed into a university plastics engineering program, commented, "It's a good idea because it gives kids an idea about what they will be doing for a career. I would have gone to college undecided without the program; now I know what I'm going to be doing."

When staff members were asked to graphically portray the change process at Niles, one person drew a circle in the middle, labeled *Niles High*, with eleven arrows emanating from it. Some arrows led to practical factors: money available, connection and partnerships, time. Another group of arrows identified process factors: changes in leadership style, integration of responsibility and respect, up-front process, teacher and student involvement. A third set of arrows addressed the larger issues: wake-up call to change; development of trust; purpose, focus, whys (see Figure 11.2).

Niles High School became a school that knew what it wanted to do. The Niles High School presentation packet ended with the quote, "Change requires the willingness to take risks and even to fail on occasion." Muhammad Ali could not have said it better.

Figure 11.1   Demographics for Niles High School, 2000

Grades: 9–12	No. staff: 70
No. students: 1,000	Size of district: 4,000 students;
White: 82% African American: 15% Hispanic: 2% Asian: 0.01% Other: 1%	6 schools Elementary schools: 4 Middle school: 1 High schools: 1

Figure 11.2   One teacher's interpretation of the school change process at Niles High School

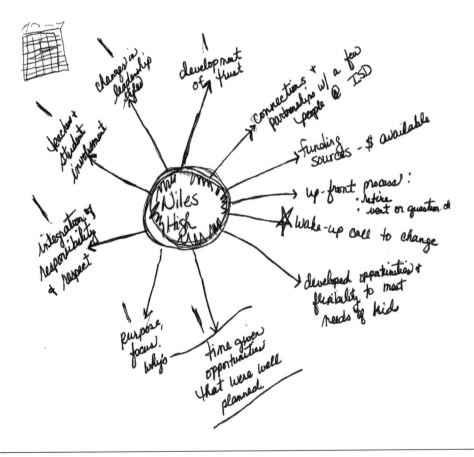

Drawing done by Becky Meier

PART IV

Bringing About Significant School Change

The Essential Elements

We can, whenever and wherever we choose, successfully teach all children whose schooling is of interest to us. We already know more than we need in order to do this. Whether we do it must finally depend on how we feel about the fact that we haven't so far.

—Ronald Edmonds

Taken collectively, human societies have gone a long way toward exploring the full range of human excellences. But a particular society at a given moment in history is apt to honor only a portion of the full range. And wise indeed is the society that is not afraid to face hard questions about its own practices on this point.

—John. W. Gardner

Excellence demands the pursuit of seemingly unattainable goals. Those teachers and schools that truly succeed are those which inspire their students to move beyond the expectation of conventional wisdom.

—James D. Watson, Nobel Prize winner
and codiscoverer of DNA

C learly, every school exists within a context, has a certain degree of capacity, and is filled with a range of conversations. In terms of this book, these elements can be viewed as essential, because understanding them and deliberately changing them were indeed essential for significantly changing each of the eight schools. Each of the three essential elements—context, capacity, and conversations—is a system onto itself, with interactive elements. At the same time, the three elements are linked to each other. They serve as givers and receivers. They impact each other and feel the impact of the other two.

Think about the following:

- What are the specific ways context will affect capacity and conversations; how does capacity affect context and conversations, and how do conversations affect context and capacity?
- Can you make the case that one of the three elements is especially important?
- What specific things can a school leader do to significantly change each of the three essential elements?

12

The Essential Elements

Context

WE NEED TO UNDERSTAND
CHANGES IN THEIR CONTEXT

When you visit a specialist for the diagnosis of a persistent and problematic medical condition, you are asked to describe the context: the conditions at your home and work site, current allergies, personal and family medical histories, frequency of symptoms, food recently eaten, outdoor exposure, stress-producing events, your attitude about regularly seeing a doctor, and so on.

When you report an automobile accident to your insurance company, you also are asked to describe the context: the car's reliability, your driving history, weather and road conditions, traffic signals, the number of passengers, possible distractions, the number of recent driving violations, your attitude about road rage, and so on.

We live within a definable and describable context.

DEFINING CONTEXT

Webster's *Third New International Dictionary* (2000) defines *context* as a "connection, or coherence." It further states that it means "to weave, to join together" (p. 270). The dictionary goes on to suggest that *context* implies an intimate association of words that throws light on the meaning of something. It is the interrelated conditions in which something exists or occurs. It enables people to gain an understanding of themselves or of things around them. It provides coherence.

In this study, I use *context* in a similar manner to look at change efforts. School systems and school leaders can create a context for a proposed change. This means they can signify its importance, reward those who are leading the change, and provide resources. Leaders can talk about the coherence of a proposed change, that is, how it makes sense for their particular school. Echoing the dictionary definition, context can be established by weaving together the various component pieces.

In 1997, Max DePree synthesized decades of experience in the corporate and nonprofit worlds into a thin volume called *Leading Without Power*, in which he argued for "places of realized potential." He defined these places as organizations that have opened themselves to change, that support individuals in their growth, offer the gift of challenging work, shed their obsolete baggage, encourage people to decide what needs to be measured, help them do the work, heal people with trust, create social environments, and celebrate (DePree, 1997, pp. 9–18).

DePree (1997) argued that organizations can become places of realized potential if we "become much more skilled in affecting the context in which we're going to be working" (p. 83).

Fullan (2003) devoted the first chapter of his book, *The Moral Imperative of School Leadership*, to "Changing the Context." He argued that "the leader's job is to help change context—to introduce new elements into a situation that are bound to influence behavior for the better" (Fullan, 2003, p. 1).

THE FOUR FACETS OF CONTEXT

In this discussion of schools and their ability to significantly change, we will look at context in four ways:

1. First, in terms of *culture*, meaning what people believe, value, and prioritize. Some things are more important than other things for individuals, groups, and organizations as a whole. We need to understand what these things are in a particular school.

2. Second, in terms of climate, which means the tone, the feelings one senses upon walking through a school. Are people friendly? Is there a welcoming feeling? Are things orderly? Busy? Chaotic? Is there a sense of joy and excitement? Does one want to be there?

3. Third is the physical environment. Is it bright and colorful? Is it drab, pedestrian, and stifling? Is the building well maintained? Are there areas that are designed or decorated by the students? Are there plants, posters, and photographs?

4. Fourth, what are the dominant messages being conveyed? Are there displays of books the staff has read and discussed? Does a banner proudly

proclaim an accomplishment or goal? What is being conveyed through newsletters and announcements? What do the superintendent and principal say, and how do they deliver those messages?

My research has shown that significant change unfolds when the current context is understood and deliberate efforts are made to change it.

THE INTERLINKING OF THE FOUR FACETS OF CONTEXT

As you can see in Figure 12.1, there is a symbiotic relationship among culture, climate, environment, and messages. Imagine a four-sided spinner; if one of the four facets moves, then the spinner will shift and create a different context. The more dramatic the movement (faster, longer, deeper), the greater the impact on context.

Let me cite an example drawn from one of our eight portraits. At John Williams School No. 5, Michele Hancock started her new principalship with three strategies. The first, painting the major public areas of the school, was a dramatic change in how things looked. That shift in the physical environment sent a message ("We can make dramatic improvements") and created a new climate ("This school feels welcoming"). The second strategy sought to change belief systems—culture—through Michele's individual meetings with staff members ("I value what you have to say, and your voice will be heard"). Third, the staff read and discussed *Who Moved My Cheese?* by Spencer Johnson (1998). This strategy allowed Michele to shift the culture from fear of change to a revised belief system ("Although change is fearful, we can embrace it").

Figure 12.1   The links among culture, climate, environment, and messages

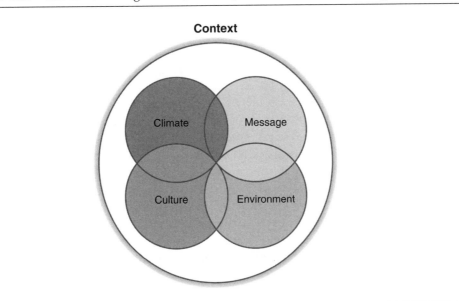

UNDERSTANDING CONTEXT IS ESSENTIAL

I am not the first to suggest the interdependence of influences shaping schools. My conceptual framework models the research findings of Metz, whose 1980s landmark study of three magnet schools was republished in 2003. As she summarized,

> Influences from outside each school set conditions which interacted with internal processes to form the context of the school's life. The influences which operated within the school generally had their effects in a highly interactive way, so that circles of causation were more common than chains of causation. (Metz, 2003, p. 221)

According to Fink (2005), contextual knowledge is essential for change agents. As he put it, "Successful leaders make connections by developing firm knowledge and understanding of their contexts. Context relates to the particular situation, background, or environment in which something is happening" (p. 104).

Change agents must appreciate the concept of context in each of its four facets of culture, climate, environment, and messages. In addition, they must understand the power of context in the school being changed. Finally, school leaders need to take these two understandings and use them as a springboard to create a new school context.

INDIVIDUAL SCHOOLS IN THE LARGER CONTEXT

We, of course, need to consider the larger context beyond the school and even beyond the school district and local community. To return to the automobile accident example given at the beginning of this chapter, it would be important to know the federal regulations concerning highway construction, the recent changes in state motor vehicle policies and practices, the shifting financial health of car insurance companies, the political influence of car manufacturers, the advocacy work of environmental groups concerning car emissions, global oil production, and so on.

Understanding schools in a larger context involves looking at federal legislation such as *NCLB* the state's response to such legislation as well as its own education initiatives; the funding sources (e.g., the local tax base, which affects the resources allocated to individual schools); the power held by school board members, mayors, state legislators, and others; the demands made by advocates supporting the interests of special needs students; and so on.

In looking at the larger context, Tony Wagner (2002) referred to the rapid pace of change in our society. However, he warned that "just saying that everything has changed except schools doesn't get us very far in deepening our understanding of what must be done to improve them" (p. 15).

Wagner sees changes in our society unfolding in four arenas: (1) work, (2) learning, (3) citizenship, and (4) motivation for learning. The move into a technological, information-oriented, and service economy requires new skills; the commitment to rigorously teach all children demands a new look at what we teach and how we teach it; the quest to shape students as inventors, creators, problem solvers, and critical thinkers forces us to remember "real learning happens at every age through a dynamic interaction between the student, his or her prior experiences and understandings and new experience or information" (Wagner, 2002, p. 21). These demands on schools are part of the larger context.

Richard Boyatzis and Annie McKee (2005) used the framework of organizational behavior, psychology, and multidisciplinary research to comment, "Think about it: virtually everything we have taken for granted for hundreds, if not thousands, of years is in the midst of profound transformation" (p. 1). As examples, they cited climate change, the increase in natural disasters, new diseases, unstable social systems, global conflicts, the transformation of the business world, and so on. These far-reaching changes are part of the larger context.

Pedro Noguera, sociologist, activist, and researcher, urged us to understand our schools in terms of their social context. For example, Noguera (2003) contended, "Politicians who often lead the chorus of criticisms have largely failed to devise policies to address the deplorable conditions present in many inner-city schools and communities" (p. 6). These societal factors and conditions are part of the larger context.

I believe we must pay attention to this larger arena. Although this book does not look at how and why policies are made (e.g., the crafting of state standards), it does look at the encompassing changes in the world and in our society from the perspective of individual schools. In a sense, this is an inside-out point of view. For example, new and more rigorous state academic achievement standards forced one of our award-winning schools to no longer accept its terrible state rankings; the threat of a state takeover became a wake-up call for another school; the failure of a high school to produce graduates who could meet the new demands of the work world prompted the question of "Why are we here?"

In effect, schools do not exist in a world by themselves.

CULTURE AS CONTEXT

> By the time I go to Tau I will have made a fairly comprehensive survey of the life of the Samoan girl, ceremonies and observances surrounding birth and marriage, her theoretical functioning in the community and the code of conduct which governs her activity. (Mead, 2001, p. 32)

In this manner, in 1925, Margaret Mead wrote to her family about her fieldwork in Samoa. As an anthropologist, she was trying to destroy the existing stereotypes about the native Samoans by explaining their culture.

In H. Gardner's (1995) view, Mead was a leader because she was "a person who affects the thoughts, behaviors, and feelings of a significant number of individuals" (p. 84). She caused scientists and social scientists, as well as the general public, to appreciate the distinctiveness of specific cultures and to recognize how important it is to study them.

In the business world, there has for more than a half-century been a strong emphasis on the concept of culture. For example, when Jody Hoffer Gittell explained the huge success of Southwest Airlines in the 1990s, she credited CEO Herb Kelleher, "because he helped to shape a truly unique culture for this organization [Southwest], unlike that of any other major U.S. airline" (Gittell, 2003, p. 13). The Southwest success has been built on its "relationship focus, its commitment and passion for shared goals, shared knowledge, and mutual respect" (Gittell, 2003, pp. 16–17).

Although Edgar Schein (1999) emphasized the importance of organizational culture in the business world, he also cautioned us against thinking that cultures can easily be changed. In his view, they need to be studied until we understand them. Then, over time, leaders "can propose new values, introduce new ways and articulate new governing ideas" (Schein, 1999, p. 334). In this way, the stage is set for new behaviors, which, if adopted successfully, can cause the organization to embody a new set of assumptions.

Although anthropologists devote their lives to discovering and describing cultures, and corporate leaders build their reputations and records by changing cultures, many educators have lagged behind in understanding what culture means and how hard it is to change.

WHAT DO WE MEAN BY *CULTURE*?

Seymour Sarason's many books, monographs, and articles center themselves around the concept of culture. This is how he sees it:

> There is a sense of individual and group identity derived from the past that gives structure and meaning to the present and future . . . The concept of the school culture refers to those aspects of the setting that are viewed by school personnel as "given" or essential features, which they would strenuously defend against elimination or marked change, and to which to them reflect psychological concepts and value judgments. (quoted in Fried, 2003, pp. 80–81)

Additionally, school culture has been defined as conveying "a sense of what is and is not valued as well as expectations regarding appropriate behavior and beliefs" (Duke, 2004, p. 133); "a pattern of shared basic assumptions that a group learned as it solved its problems" (Schein, 1992, p. 12); and "the complex pattern of norms, attitudes, beliefs, behaviors, values, ceremonies, traditions, and myths that are deeply ingrained" (Barth, 2001, p. 8). Perhaps the most succinct description was offered by Deal and Kennedy (1982), who wrote, "Culture is the way we do things around here" (p. 4).

DIMENSIONS OF SCHOOL CULTURE

Sarason (quoted in Fried, 2003) contended:

> One of the ways to get at aspects of the school culture is to focus initially on activities that characterize the setting. The next, and most important and difficult, step is to determine how each activity is justified, and its centrality to the individual's conception of a school and sense of identity with it. (p. 82)

Culture is the way individuals and organizations, such as schools, define, describe, and drive themselves. It is the manner in which individuals see themselves and how others see them. It involves what is accepted and what is not.

There are several ways cultures reveal themselves. I call these the *dimensions* of culture: artifacts, beliefs, celebrations, ceremonies, heroes, history, priorities, rewards, and rituals. For agents of change, these dimensions of culture are important for two reasons: They help us identify and describe a culture as it exists and they provide opportunities for impacting an existing culture.

In *Shaping School Culture: The Heart of Leadership*, Deal and Peterson (1999) argued that "Changes cannot be successful without cultural support. School cultures, in short, are key to school achievement and student learning" (p. xii). More important, from my perspective, is the argument that cultures are *not* static, stable, and set firmly in place; they *can* be shifted and shaped.

Deal and Peterson (1999) believed that leaders (both administrators and teachers) can be proactive in shaping a school's culture by taking on eight major symbolic roles: (1) historian seeking to understand the past; (2) anthropological sleuth probing the current set of norms, values, and beliefs; (3) visionary defining a picture of the future; (4) leader affirming values through behaviors and routines; (5) potter using heroes and rituals to touch core values; (6) poet using language to sustain the school's best image; (7) actor improvising in the school's dramas; and (8) healer overseeing the transitions in the school's life (pp. 87–88).

NOT APPRECIATING THE POWER OF CULTURE

The FDR Drive, a six-lane highway built during the presidency of Franklin Delano Roosevelt and named after him, is on the east side of Manhattan. It stretches from Harlem in the north to the financial center in the southernmost tip of Manhattan. Overlooking a northern stretch of the road sits an imposing school building that for decades had been called Benjamin Franklin High School.

During the 1960s and 1970s, it became obvious that Benjamin Franklin High School was failing its students. The dropout rate was one of the highest in New York City, the skill level of its few graduates was abysmal, the staff commitment had eroded, and the school was unsafe. No one wanted to go to Ben Franklin.

Like storming the beaches at Normandy, the generals—the superintendents—sent waves of reformers and redesign plans into the school. Unlike the D-Day assault, no beachhead was established and maintained. No victory was in sight. The school's negative and dysfunctional culture could not be changed.

There was only one solution: The school had to be closed, its staff dispersed to the winds and the students phased out. For three years, no new entering classes were enrolled. A young, energetic, and idealistic new principal, Colman Genn, started a new school in the building, deliberately creating a new culture very different from the one that had existed. Today, people who travel the FDR Drive see a new sign on the building: the Manhattan Center for Science and Mathematics. The building houses a school that wins awards and graduates students who win college scholarships.

Hargreaves et al. (2001) urged us, as change agents, to appreciate the role of culture. As they put it:

> The cultural perspective is concerned with the meanings and interpretations teachers assign to change, how changes affect and even confront teachers' beliefs as well as their practices, how teachers (alone or together) understand the changes that face them, and the impact of change on teachers' ideas, beliefs, emotions, experiences, and lives. (Hargreaves et al., 2001, p. 117)

CHANGING THE CULTURE IN SCHOOLS THAT HAVE DRAMATICALLY IMPROVED

School cultures *can* be changed, and they *must* be changed if significant school improvement is to be implemented. Fullan (2001) noted most school reform efforts are based on "restructuring." He argued that instead what we need is "reculturing":

> Most strategies for reform focus on structures, formal requirements, and event-based activities, for example, professional development sessions. They do not struggle directly with existing culture and which new values and practices may be required. (Fullan, 2001, p. 34)

In the school portraits presented in this book we see examples of deliberate culture change. In the most extreme cases, removing the staff was the only way to change the existing culture. Louis W. Fox Academic and Technical High School was considered to be the worst high school in Texas, and the state moved to disestablish it. Joanne Cockrell, appointed as the new principal of this San Antonio high school, was given a free reign to hire new staff and create a new culture, one that was unwavering in seeing the students' welfare as the highest priority.

Molly Maloy at George Washington Carver Academy led change at a school whose culture was extremely entrenched in the belief that all children could *not* learn. When the school was designated as a magnet school, a strategy that required a new way to look at how students learn, the Carver staff did not understand what had to be done—and, more significantly, they did not understand why it had to be done and how it could be done. Organizing students into teams to work on interdisciplinary projects was not something they could believe in. It was not the way they had learned; it was not the way they taught. Like Joanne Cockrell, Molly had to hire new staff and immerse them in activities that would shape a new and very different culture.

At Niles High School, the change-the-culture plan was slower and more subtle. The high school staff believed they were doing a good job. They believed that it was not their responsibility to change what the school was doing; that was the principal's job. They believed that it was natural for students to drop out of high school; not everyone was capable or motivated enough to make it. Principal-designee (and, later, principal) Doug Law had to change attitudes. He channeled alumni complaints into a discussion that centered on the school's shortcomings. He challenged the teachers' practices and the rationale for what they did. He changed the locus of responsibility. At Niles High School, teachers did not value looking at statistics—that, too, was the principal's job. Nonetheless, Doug gave data to the staff, and once they had examined the dismal dropout rates they could no longer believe they were doing a good job. He revived a school leadership team. Given the power to make schoolwide decisions caused the teachers to believe they could shape what the school did or did not do. The culture changed.

CLIMATE AS CONTEXT

Robert Coles, a professor of psychiatry at Harvard University, wrote a groundbreaking and Pulitzer Prize-winning series entitled *Children of Crisis* that captured the voices of children across America. Inevitably, Coles visited a large number of schools. As he put it:

> Throughout, I hoped to learn whether something was actually happening in schools said to be places of improvement, of reform, of uplift. I looked at everything in the school . . . its past history; its present policies; its architecture; its facilities; its curriculum; its personnel . . . and most intangible but very real, "its tone." (Coles, 2003, pp. 436–437)

Many educators, parents, and visitors to schools will say they can tell what a school is about within fifteen minutes of being in the school. They talk about "picking up the vibes" or "sensing a tone." These first impressions and surface characteristics are an exposure to a school's climate. What did the visitors see, hear, and feel? It could be any combination of the following: orderly hallways, displays of student work, noisy students, a sense of things being out of control or under control, classroom desks in straight rows or in circles, activity centers in classrooms, teachers speaking with each other, minimal socializing in the teachers cafeteria, a welcoming school office staff (or the opposite), a parents' room filled with eager parents, a bellicose custodian, a dean's office filled with students who have been referred, and so on.

As previously mentioned, there is an interactive and interconnecting relationship between culture and climate. The climate is an extension of the school's culture. A school's climate is driven or preordained by its culture. If a school staff does not value rewarding and recognizing student achievement, there will be few, if any, displays of outstanding student work. If a school holds sports success in high esteem, one will find trophy cases filled with athletic awards. If order is a top priority, hallways will be clear and unacceptable behavior will bring serious consequences.

On the other hand, changing the climate, through small yet significant steps, can impact the culture. Climate is easier to change, and the principals in our stories started with climate—initially. Then they changed the tone and feel of their schools.

John Williams School No. 5 is an imposing, intimidating building. Situated in a dangerous neighborhood, its doors are locked, and it appears to be an armed fortress. This did not fit how Michele Hancock viewed school. By placing a friendly yet diligent security person (not in uniform) at the entrance, the tone became welcoming. This new feeling continued when the front office staff were told to ask visitors how they could help them, instead of the more typical "What do you want?" Posting student work created a tone of accomplishment. A sense of student success replaced a feeling of defeat.

Bill Andrekopoulos, at Gustav Fritsche Middle School, Wisconsin, talked incessantly about the books he was reading. He became a walking reference library. As the principal, Bill did not mandate that others read those books, but many did. Offering all-expenses-paid travel to visit other schools (some out of state) and attend conferences created a different climate, which in turn created a new set of values. Bill stimulated a sense of curiosity and promoted the practice of inquiry. He encouraged teachers to come forward with new ides that could be piloted. Bill was shaping a learning organization.

Rituals first impact the climate and, later, the culture. In South Heights Elementary, a rural school that undervalued student and staff achievement and lacked a commitment to success, Rob Carroll turned morning announcements into a daily affirmation. Students and staff were asked to recite the pledge of allegiance, the school's mission ("We succeed. No excuses. No exceptions."), and its most recent state test goal (e.g., "78 will be great!"). Also, every day Bill would publicly acknowledge the achievement of a particular student and staff member.

ENVIRONMENT AS CONTEXT

The physical environment is what one sees in a school. This involves the condition (good or bad) of the façade, doors, walls, floors, bulletin boards, offices, classrooms, and public areas. Is garbage strewn about? Is there graffiti? Does the school look like a prison, with bars on windows? Has the building been neglected?

The environment may be the easiest thing to change, and by changing it one can create a new climate, convey important messages, and be able to shape a new culture. Although Cuban warned us about superficial, or first-order changes, the change in environment may have important symbolic and practical implications. Cuban's distinction about levels of change is built around the idea that schools frequently stay stuck with first-order changes, which attempt only to make their current conditions more efficient. Second-order changes, in Cuban's view, attempt to influence the values, beliefs, and attitudes of individuals in an organization; Cuban wants us to change cultures. If environmental changes stand alone, then we have failed in our efforts to significantly change schools. If, however, these changes in the physical environment are a part of a larger and deeper strategy, they can be a very powerful step.

Anthony Bryk and his research teams have studied in detail the campaigns to reform the more than 500 schools in Chicago. For example, field research conducted in 1993 looked at "six schools that had taken especially good advantage of the opportunities provided by reform to initiate fundamental change." The research team's goal was to identify "the common ingredients and processes in these promising school development efforts" (Bryk, Sebring, Kerbow, Rollow, & Easton, 1998, p. 37).

One common theme that emerged involved school environment. As Bryk et al. (1998) pointed out, "At the start of reform, many schools felt they had to take greater control of their physical and social environments before they could attend to improving their educational programs" (p. 120). In a new governance structure that depended on strong parent and community involvement in each school, the image of the school became quite important. Buildings had to look inviting and welcoming if meaningful educational discussions—at the school—could take place.

Rob Carroll's enthusiasm was contagious. He understood the depressed expectations, even despair, that seized South Heights Elementary, and he changed the environment. Inspirational posters and banners took over the space. At Fox Tech, Joanne Cockrell created a Wall of Fame, with photographs of successful alumni. The message was clear: You, too, can make it. Chris Zarzana converted one of the buildings on the campus of Skycrest Elementary into a well-equipped and well-supplied teachers' workroom.

MESSAGES AS CONTEXT

Conveying messages, through the environment, climate, and culture, shapes context. Messages also can be transmitted as a distinct, deliberate, and direct strategy. Leaders tell stories and consciously appeal to the needs of their followers.

In *Leading Minds,* Howard Gardner (1995) contended, "The ultimate impact of the leader depends most significantly on the particular story he or she relates or embodies and the receptions to that story on the part of audiences [or collaborators or followers]" (p. 14). Gardner built his leadership theory through deep profiles of twentieth-century leaders, such as Margaret Mead, George C. Marshall, Pope John XXIII, Eleanor Roosevelt, Martin Luther King Jr., and Margaret Thatcher. These leaders were quite different from one another in terms of profession, background, mentors, critical experiences, and degrees of success; however, all of them knew what was important to their audience.

These leaders told stories about themselves and their groups, about where they were coming from and where they were headed, about hopes and fears. They connected with their followers. In the same way, the principals of our award-winning schools delivered strong messages through their actions; their behaviors; their countenance; and, most significantly, through their words. None of them was shy about speaking about what needed to be done.

Sandy Stephens inherited an elementary school in Anchorage, Alaska, that was about to be closed. The staff did not believe the majority of the remaining students, who did not have the option to leave, could succeed. English was not their first language, and so, in the eyes of many teachers, their learning potential was limited. Sandy strengthened a dual-language program that both attracted middle-class families and proved all the children could learn at high levels. This was a new and very important message.

When the staff of John Williams School No. 5 arrived back at school to start their new school year and meet their new principal, Michele Hancock was ready for them. She did not mince words: The students had not failed; the teachers had failed. They had let the students down. They had let their school building rot. They could do better and had to do better. School No. 5 was to be a sanctuary and a place where students learned and achieved. If Michele and her family and friends could work fourteen-hour days in the hot summer to symbolically renew their school, imagine what all of them could accomplish.

In a tone that was soft, but delivered in a voice that was strong, Chris Zarzana delivered her message at Skycrest Elementary. Students needed a sense of discipline and order. Chris provided that for her elementary school students and teachers at Skycrest. Once that was established, the larger mission—reading, reading, and reading—had to be attended to. Chris told and taught. She made it clear to the staff that the disappointing data had to be confronted, and she taught them how to analyze those data. The staff could no longer ignore the poor reading scores or place the blame on external conditions. This was their school. These were their students.

CONTEXT: THE LESSONS TO BE LEARNED

One of today's influential leaders of American education is Ted Sizer, who served as a high school principal, dean of the Harvard Graduate School of Education, and founder of the Coalition of Essential Schools. In a memoir titled *The Red Pencil: Convictions From Experience in Education,* Sizer (2004) wrote of the

"American paradox," in which actions in education contradict espoused beliefs. As he put it,

> The fact that we shy away from school reform's hard realities is fascinating. It is not that we do not talk about them, research them, and exhort "leaders" to address them. It is that we largely fail to marshal the honesty and intensity that reform requires. (Sizer, 2004, p. xiii)

In my view, therein lie the fundamental lessons to be learned through examining context. We shy away from realities because we don't understand and appreciate them. We contradict ourselves because we talk in generalities, not in the specific realities of a particular school in a specific place at a precise time. We are not honest about what needs to be done, how we move a school from Point A (where it is) to Point B (where it could and should be), because we do not appreciate the school's current condition.

Examining the context of a school will help us understand its starting point and its desired destination. Only with these two understandings can we heed Sizer's (2004) words and "marshal the honesty and intensity."

To start, we need to debunk the myths surrounding context.

The first myth is that *all schools are alike*. This is a dangerous myth because it leads to thinking there is one miraculous strategy for improving all schools. Every school has its own personality, evidenced by its culture, climate, environment, and messages. These four components of context are interrelated. They affect each other and, in turn, are affected by the others.

The second myth is that *culture and climate are the same*. Although the terms *culture* and *climate* are frequently used interchangeably, they are not the same. *Culture* refers to underlying values and beliefs; *climate*, which is certainly impacted by the school's culture (and vice versa), is the tone and "feel" of a school.

The third myth is that *changing a school's environment is merely a cosmetic step, a classic superficial change*. That could be the case if a change in the environment were the only strategy. Instead, school leaders must also communicate clear and powerful messages and take deliberate and sustained steps to change the school's climate.

The fourth myth is that *schools "live" in a larger context, which makes it impossible to facilitate significant school change*. Surely, some things are virtually out of our control. For example, an individual school cannot impact the rapid growth of technology or the changes in demographics or the new demands of work in society. However, understanding that larger context gives us the power to turn those conditions into assets, for example, revitalizing an irrelevant curriculum. There are other things out of our immediate domain (the school) but still within our ability to impact, usually with the help of others. For example, we could lobby for additional resources for our school. We could request more support from the district office. We could ask to use the district's professional developers in a new way. Finally, there are many other things directly in our control, such as painting the lobby area (environment), developing a more effective discipline system (climate), or publishing a dual-language parent newsletter (messages).

The fifth myth is that *changing the school's context is a pipe dream*. This is simply not true. As demonstrated by the portraits of the eight schools presented in this book, a school's context can be changed, even its most difficult aspect, the school's culture. As Sarason and many other educational reformers have cautioned, the task will not be easy, fast, or simple. It will evoke resistance, mis-understandings, and swings in degrees of success (or failure). However, it can be done.

A critical element to creating the schools we want for our children and ado-lescents involves addressing the concept of context and its four components: (1) culture, (2) climate, (3) environment, and (4) messages. Similar to the other essential conditions (capacity and conversations), which are discussed in upcoming chapters, we need to understand the concept of context on three levels, by asking ourselves these questions: What does the concept of context mean? How can the concept of context be described at the school being studied and/or changed? Finally, as agents of change, how can we impact the school's current context?

13

The Essential Elements

Capacity

My good friend Stacy Allison was the first American woman to climb Mount Everest. As she remembers her decision,

> I wasn't about to spend the rest of my life following. I had a restless itch in the deep core of my spine. I was ready to push for freedom, for the liberation that would come when I could climb either side of the rope. Eventually, I had to try for myself. (Allison, 1999, p. 4)

Imagine Stacy appearing at your door and asking you if you would like to join a group of climbers who will be making an Everest expedition. Although you have never even rock-climbed, you pause to think about it. Stacy goes on to say the expedition will depart in a week and that there will be training sessions before the group leaves. Do you join the Everest expedition?

I don't think so. You have no idea what is really involved. You have no experience. You do not have enough time to prepare or practice. You do not possess the capacity to take on this challenge.

Although this is a logical conclusion to reach, educators often disregard the concept of capacity. A change is mandated, and then compliance is expected. A new way to teach is introduced, and then mastery is expected. A different viewpoint about a practice, such as heterogeneous grouping, is encouraged, and then understanding, acceptance, and implementation are expected.

DEFINING *CAPACITY-BUILDING*

In arenas outside education, we assume capacity-building will take place. Indeed, we expect and often demand scientific, political, military, and sports leaders to build effective teams, make critical decisions, and equip themselves to achieve victory. For example, in the award-winning film *Apollo 13*, Gene Kranz (played by Ed Harris) calls together his team at the National Aeronautics and Space Administration to solve an urgent problem: The three astronauts headed toward the moon are stranded in space. What was to be done? The subsequent dynamic between and among the team members ranged from anger to concern to reflection. Not one team member was hesitant in making or reacting to suggestions. Team members had their colleagues consider other perspectives. The discussion was free, open, and passionate. The team assessed the situation with the pros and cons of various options. Kranz, the flight commander, listened and eventually synthesized the competing notions into a concise and clear plan. Ultimately, despite tremendous risks and several unknowns, the team was successful; the astronauts were brought home.

FIVE INTERLOCKING CAPACITIES

The Apollo 13 story illustrates how capacity was built in five arenas. The space experts needed to *plan* a solution, *teach* their colleagues various options, and continually *assess* the state of the emergency and the effectiveness of their strategies. They worked as a *team* and, in doing so, they *learned* from each other.

Successful teams, with enhanced capacities, are lauded in our society, as symbolized by American films. In *Hoosiers*, an undersized, undermanned—and underestimated—high school basketball team achieves the impossible: They win the Indiana state basketball tournament.

The coach, played by Gene Hackman, needed a fresh plan if his team was to win the championship game. He taught his players to put aside their individual egos and play together as a team. He assessed his team's execution of the game plan and made adjustments accordingly. Building a sense of team had been his underlying goal, and the coach created a culture that enabled the players to learn how to be a cohesive unit.

In the film *Thirteen Days*, President John F. Kennedy taps into the advice and counsel of his cabinet as he struggles with the threat of Soviet nuclear-armed missiles in Cuba. Kennedy created a learning environment and included veteran military leaders and experienced policymakers, who had lessons to teach. The Cuban Missile Crisis required the President to assess the latest military intelligence, discover whom he could trust, and develop his own decision-making capacity. As the world stood by in a heightened state of anxiety, the Kennedy-led plan for a blockade and diplomatic concessions worked, and Russia's missiles were removed from Cuba. The threat of nuclear war between the Soviets and America had been resolved and removed.

CAPACITY-BUILDING IN SCHOOLS THAT SIGNIFICANTLY CHANGE

Anthony Bryk et al. (1998) commented on capacity-building by comparing the demand for school improvement with the challenges athletes face:

> Simply raising the bar in the high jump to world class standards does little to help an ordinary athlete achieve a much higher level. Absent strong and sustained support for individual and collective improvement, the more likely consequence would just be increased public frustration about continued failure. (p. 15)

My school research has highlighted the idea of building capacity. Superintendents, principals, teachers, and parents realized, consciously or subconsciously, that change would be difficult and that new ways of schooling required time and preparation. People needed to do things that were unknown, unfamiliar, or uncomfortable.

Our look at building school capacity will be organized into the three arenas previously mentioned: (1) the capacity to *plan* (including the ability to make data-driven decisions), (2) the capacity to *teach* (in new and more effective ways), and (3) the capacity to *assess* (decide on how success would be measured). The award-winning schools profiled in this book built those three capacities as the staff worked in teams (instead of working in isolation or depending on one leader). Each of these three capacities, in turn, was built on a fourth: the capacity to *learn*.

As illustrated in Figure 13.1, the three capacities to plan, teach, and assess are interrelated and connected. Effective planning leads to dynamic teaching,

Figure 13.1   Capacity-building

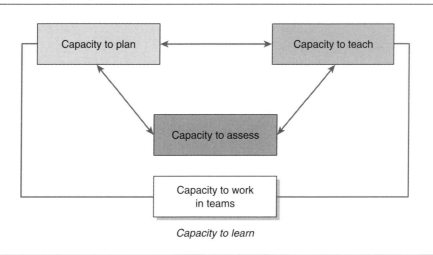

Capacity to learn

Figure 13.2   Capacity-building at Skycrest Elementary

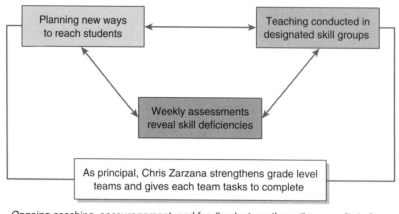

Ongoing coaching, encouragement, and feedback strengthens the capacity to learn

which in turn is subject to assessment, which provides data about how to plan for future teaching, and so on. All three of these capacities—to plan, teach, and assess—are enhanced when a fourth capacity, to work in teams, is strengthened. Furthermore, these four capacities will never substantially improve without a context that supports both student and adult learning. In essence, adults and students must learn how to learn.

The story of Skycrest Elementary's dramatic improvement in Citrus Heights, California, illustrates the interplay of these capacity-building arenas (see Figure 13.2).

BUILDING THE CAPACITY TO PLAN

The 100th anniversary of the 1906 San Francisco earthquake generated scores of articles, commentaries, monographs, and books. One of them, Philip Fradkin's (2005) book, *The Great Earthquake and Firestorms of 1906: How San Francisco Nearly Destroyed Itself*, contends:

> San Franciscans, not the inanimate forces of nature, were primarily responsible for the extensive chaos, damage, injuries, and deaths ... Despite earlier devastating earthquakes and fires that should have served as warnings, they were dismissive of the past and failed to prepare for the future. During the earthquake and fire, military and civilian officials reacted foolishly under great duress. (p. xvii)

Unfortunately, the terrorist attacks on September 11, 2001, and Hurricane Katrina in August 2005 yielded similar commentary. For our purposes, the ideas of being unprepared and overwhelmed, of lacking foresight, and suffering from poor—or nonexistent—planning are themes that often surface in the school world.

In schools, it is easy to forgo or forget the idea of planning. Schools are complicated, complex institutions with idiosyncratic climates and cultures, moving at a fast pace, usually following the same routines (whether they work or not), draining energy from those who work in them. Consequently, many educators feel there is little, if any, time to assess data, respond to that assessment, plan new ways to teach, and teach differently.

There are instances, however, of when planning plays a critical role in a school's daily life. In the 1990s, during her extensive studies of two exceptionally successful schools, International High School and Central Park East Elementary School in New York City, Linda Darling-Hammond noted the importance of building the capacity to plan: "Shared time for planning, professional development, and governance is much more extensive in the restructured schools" (Darling-Hammond, 1997a, p. 185). Cluster teachers at International High School had six hours of planning time each week, organized as seventy minutes of planning time daily and a half day each week for collective work. At Central Park East Elementary School, teachers had seven and a half hours weekly for joint planning in addition to five hours weekly of personal planning time.

In the eight award-winning schools profiled in this book, planning was pivotal. For example, planning at South Heights Elementary had unfolded as it does in most schools: Some time was provided during the school day; during that time, individual teachers prepared for their classes or graded student work; team meetings, if there were any, proceeded without agendas or measurable outcomes. After three years of flat data and no increase in student achievement, Rob Carroll knew a different planning model was required.

Three planning modalities were created at South Heights. Sometimes, the entire Grade K–5 faculty met together to discuss data implications, alignment of curriculum, proposed teaching methodologies, new programs being implemented, and so on.

Vertical planning brought together a triad of kindergarten, first-, and second-grade teachers who would teach the same students over a three-year period. This provided the opportunity to articulate clear expectations for each grade, discuss student progress, and create a logical sequence of learning activities for the three-year period. Two additional triads of K–2 teachers did the same thing.

Horizontal planning also took place. A new specialization in literacy and mathematics replaced the typical pattern of one teacher teaching the children in her class all their grade-level subjects. The three literacy teachers for the primary grades (kindergarten, first grade, and second grade) met together, as did the three literacy teachers for the intermediate students—Grades 3, 4, and 5. The two sets of mathematics teachers (K–2 and 3–5) organized their planning in the same manner.

Rob Carroll reinforced and rewarded the planning process by encouraging the teams to set specific goals; generate updated plans; and request help, if needed. In turn, Rob assisted by purchasing materials and books, providing staff training in the school, and sending teachers to appropriate conferences.

BUILDING THE CAPACITY TO TEACH

Before becoming the award-winning author of *Angela's Ashes* and *'Tis*, Frank McCourt taught for thirty years in a New York City high school. He recounted those experiences in *Teacher Man*, and as the book comes to a close, McCourt commented,

> The classroom is a place of high drama. You'll never know what you've done to, or for, the hundreds coming and going. You see them leaving the classroom: dreamy, flat, sneering, admiring, smiling, puzzled. After a few years you develop antennae. You can tell when you've reached them or alienated them. It's chemistry. It's psychology. It's animal instinct. You are with the kids and as long as you want to be a teacher, there's no escape. (2005, p. 255)

For Frank McCourt, teaching was more than a profession, more than an art, more than a craft—it was a calling and an opportunity to creatively involve students and to impact their lives. In how many classrooms do we have a Frank McCourt—not necessarily his quirks or personality, his methods or madness, his wit or wisdom, but his energy and enthusiasm for teaching and learning? Schools characterized by pedestrian teaching, irrelevant topics, and inconsequential activities are schools that need to dramatically improve in much the same way our eight portrait schools changed.

McCourt's story raises critical questions. Does a school know its teaching and learning need to be changed? Does the school understand how that can be done? Has the capacity of the teachers to teach, and the capacity of school leaders to help them, been strengthened?

Sarason (cited in Fried, 2003) got right to the point: "If contexts for productive learning do not exist for teachers, those teachers cannot create and sustain those contexts for students" (p. 218). Loewenberg Ball and Cohen (1999) acknowledged the heightened expectations of teachers who were being asked "to help diverse learners become competent and skilled, understand what they are doing and communicate effectively" (p. 3). But, they warned, "if plans are to move in any significant way beyond rhetoric to permeate practice, significant professional development will be crucial" (p. 3). Teachers will have to become better at what they do. Elmore (1999–2000) warned that new, innovative, and successful teaching practices cannot be installed from the outside. His research shows that instead, good practice "has to be learned, and learning is a vastly more complex and conscious process than instigation" (p. 98).

For the principals of our award-winning schools, everything revolved around building the teachers' capacity to teach. For example, the driving school improvement strategy for Sandy Stephens at Government Hill Elementary centered on effectively launching a dual-language program. However, there was a problem: The elementary school staff did not understand how to teach a dual-language program. They needed professional development, and Sandy planned and led that effort.

The Government Hill faculty were organized into teams of two classes on the same grade level and, for the first time, viewed curriculum development and teaching collaboratively. Sandy summarized her strategy in the proposal for a federal grant, which the school secured, by noting the teachers would develop thematic, integrated units and, in so doing, "will closely examine and take apart the curriculum, then decide who will teach, what will be taught, and how it will be taught." In looking at individual teacher strengths, one person might teach a unit integrating science with literature to both classes, whereas the other teacher might be better prepared to teach the social studies/language arts unit. With Sandy's advice and assistance, teachers taught and coached each other. In the rhythm of daily school life, teachers built their capacity to teach.

Joanne Cockrell had an unusual opportunity to build the capacity to teach in Louis W. Fox Academic and Technical High School because she selected a new faculty for the high school. During that hiring process, Joanne stated that her main requirement for her teachers was they like students and invest extra time with them. In effect, she set the foundation for good teaching: care and prepare. She looked for and hired good teachers and acted to make them better in four ways.

First, she created a new zero-tolerance discipline system enforced by the assistant principals and principal. With that change, teachers could attend to their teaching and not be overwhelmed by disruptive behavior, because others were tending to that concern.

Second, she created four positions called *instructional guides*, who were specialists in English, social studies, mathematics, and science. These "teaching experts" had dual assignments. Each one was attached to one of the "schools within the school," serving as a generalist with all the teachers within that small school. At the same time, the instructional guides provided their content and pedagogical expertise to, for example, all the mathematics teachers throughout the entire school.

Third, Joanne tapped into her own attitude about coaching and defined the instructional guides as coaches, not supervisors. Their job was to work *with* teachers instead of trying to catch them doing something wrong or mandating them to do what the instructional guide thought was right.

Fourth, Joanne believed in ongoing professional development. At first, the school's budget allotment did not have sufficient funds to send teachers to conferences. Consequently, Joanne strategically sent the four instructional guides to additional training. Once they returned, the instructional guides were able to turn-key what they had learned with their teachers.

BUILDING THE CAPACITY TO ASSESS

Few leaders had a more pressing need to assess than Franklin Delano Roosevelt (FDR) when he assumed the presidency in March 1933, in the midst of

America's Great Depression. As columnist and historian Jonathan Alter noted, "Anyone who wasn't alive at the depths of the Great Depression is at an empathetic disadvantage when considering it, like a mentally healthy person trying to imagine what it must feel like to be clinically depressed" (2006, p. 75).

Alter continued:

> Americans were flat on their backs, hit with something worse than job loss or poverty . . . Fifteen percent fewer children were born in 1933 than in 1929 . . . Suicide rates tripled . . . the job losses were unfathomable by today's standards. By 1932, unemployment had tripled in three years. More than 16 million Americans—25 percent of the workforce—found themselves without jobs, many with three or more dependents. (2006, p. 75)

For FDR, assessment had two sides. First, what were the current conditions—in terms of depth, extent, impact, and implications? What did the numbers really mean? What did the data reveal about what to do? On the second, and perhaps more important, level, FDR had to assess how well his New Deal strategies were working. Alter (2006) quoted Roosevelt as saying,

> The country needs, and unless I mistake its temper, the country demands bold, persistent experimentation . . . It is common sense to take a method and try it: If it fails, admit it frankly and try another. But above all, try something. (p. 93)

The principals of our award-winning schools tried many strategies and determined the degree to which those strategies were effective. They built their school's capacity to assess.

The school improvement and reform literature emphasizes the need for individual student and overall school assessment. For example, in the 1990s, Giancola and Hutchison (2005) documented and assessed the school reform efforts at Theodore Roosevelt High School in Kent, Ohio. They credited the school's improvement on what they call a "journey of self reflection" (Giancola & Hutchison, 2005, p. 5). Their discussion centered on the ideal Roosevelt High School graduate and was premised on *"human systems grow toward what they persistently ask questions about"* (Cooperrider & Whitney, 1999, p. 10).

Chris Zarzana used assessment to drive her teachers and serve the students at Skycrest Elementary. However, she quickly discovered that her staff had little experience in analyzing test scores. She taught them. At the beginning of the school year, Skycrest conducted comprehensive testing to provide baseline data to be used throughout the year to measure student growth and achievement. This information was shared with the students and their parents. In monitoring the progress of students, their growth was measured, and information was gathered about the strengths and weaknesses of each instructional program.

Chris sat with each grade-level team to help them practice disaggregating the students' reading, writing, and mathematics scores. Once the team had identified the specific weaknesses of every student, they grouped the students in two ways. During most of the school day, each teacher had her or his own heterogeneous class, which learned the same material together. However, forty minutes were set aside every day to bring together all the teachers and their students on a particular grade level so resources and teaching strategies could be targeted to individual student needs. For example, all the students from the fourth-grade classes were assigned, by skill deficiency, into activity corners that focused on the students' needs. When a child mastered those skills, he or she moved onto another skill-based corner.

At John Williams School No. 5, the walls were filled with data. Some of the data tracked how the school was progressing toward meeting school goals and state standards, and much of it involved the display of student work that centered on the state standards.

In the lobby, a 20-foot by 5-foot long roll of paper prominently displayed the school's annual improvement plan. Parts I and II were devoted to School No. 5's vision and mission. Part III listed the school's customs and partners, and Part IV focused on the school's beliefs and practices.

Part V looked at relevant information for the year: a summary of the baseline data, the causes of and reasons for the results, the required support and development, the preliminary strategies, and the planning template. Posted nearby was a quote from Helen Keller: "Alone we can do so little, together we can do so much."

BUILDING THE CAPACITY TO WORK IN TEAMS

Perhaps one of the most unusual teams ever assembled was the cabinet forged by Abraham Lincoln when he assumed the presidency in 1861. Not only were the personalities, experiences, and temperaments of these cabinet members very different from each other, but also three major players—William Henry Seward, Edward Bates, and Salmon Chase—had been Lincoln's rivals for the Republican presidential nomination. Moreover, each of the three had little regard for Lincoln and dismissed his chances of victory. When asked why he put together a team of rivals, Lincoln responded, "We needed to hold our own people together. I had looked the party over and concluded that these were the very strongest men" (Goodwin, 2005, p. 319).

Turning to today, what do firefighters, emergency room doctors and nurses, jazz musicians, and championship basketball teams have in common? Magic. Each team member instinctually seems to know exactly where to be and what to do. The individual contributions mesh together without verbal cues; the resulting synergy saves lives, creates music, choreographs the ballet of basketball. Basketball Hall of Famer Bill Russell describes it:

By design and by talent, we were a team of specialists, and like a team of specialists in any field, our performances depended both on individual excellence and on how well we worked together . . . we all tried to figure out ways to make our combination more effective . . . [it] would be magical. The feeling is difficult to describe and I certainly never talked about it when I was playing. When it happened I could feel my play rise to a new level. (Senge, 2006, pp. 216–217)

In the research about successful companies, the value of teams is a consistent theme. Senge (2006) contended, "Team learning is vital because teams, not individuals, are the fundamental learning unit in modern organizations" (p. 10). In the same manner, Kotter (1996), in *Leading Change*, called for a "guiding coalition" that has "the composition, level of trust, and shared objectives" (p. 52), and Collins (2001), in *Good to Great*, advocated a "Level 5+ Management Team," which gets "the right people in right seats on the bus" (p. 41).

Steve Wadsworth, President of the Walt Disney Internet Group, described it this way:

I believe there is inherent leadership in the strength of a well-organized, focused team . . . I rely on the wisdom of a team to set a clear vision, I rely on the intellectual capital of a team to develop creative ideas, and I rely on the resources of a team to execute. (Yaverbaum, 2006, p. 237)

Molly Maloy and her core team fondly remember "the beach breakthrough." At a technology conference in Florida, the seven of them, as a close and trusting team, struggled for days in shaping a plan for a new George Washington Carver Academy. They understood fifth-grade students from throughout the city of Waco were no longer required to attend George Washington Carver; previously, Carver was the only sixth-grade school in the school district. As a newly designed magnet school, Carver would have to attract its students, both Black and White. The team knew both a nurturing and motivating learning environment were essential. However, the challenge to redo Carver did not rest only on Molly's shoulders; a team had bonded, and all team members, not just the principal, were invested in shaping the solution. They developed a plan that worked.

However, learning to work as a Carver team had not been easy. Individuals fought for power and control. At times, team members listened to each other; at other times, an individual's enthusiasm for an answer overshadowed her instinct to listen to her colleagues or accept their criticism. They disagreed with each other and later agreed to disagree. There were frustrating moments and moments of joyful breakthroughs.

Perhaps it was the sun or the sand that triggered their insights. They decided if the seven of them could work closely and effectively together, why couldn't their school's structure, organization, and learning modality be built around teams? As one teacher stated, "they adopted the team approach to education . . . [they would have] teams of teachers teach teams of students in a caring and fostering atmosphere."

In the months that followed, functional teams did not magically appear at Carver. Careful thought was paid to the formation of the academic teams, with personality profiles, expertise, surveys, and experience providing clues. Once formed, team members connected with each other on staff retreats, daily team meetings were built into the school schedule, and teams were given the responsibility for the teaching (through interdisciplinary Odysseys) and assessment of their students. The staff as a whole became a team; the Odyssey teams of students and teachers bonded; and teams were formed for specific responsibilities, such as teacher hiring. The ability to work in teams made a critical difference. As one Carver teacher declared, *"We* invented the school."

At Niles High School the challenges for the newly formed SIT were different for several reasons: Larger groups are more difficult to mold into teams, inexperienced staff functioning as teams is problematic, leaderless teams fail. Furthermore, recognizing and accepting a new team's authority and advice is very different in an existing school compared with newly formed teams creating new schools.

Doug Law started the team building process at Niles before he was officially designated as the high school principal. Like many schools, there had been a school leadership team—on paper. In creating a new team, Doug needed to bring together a cross-section of the staff: experienced and new staff members, teachers of all the subject areas, and reform-minded and enthusiastic individuals as well as those who were more traditional and cautious. Consensus building took a great deal of time and effort.

As in many schools, Niles teachers generally worked in isolation; it was not in their value system or practice to collaborate, much less solve problems outside the domain of their individual classrooms. Furthermore, both Doug Law and John Huffman, the superintendent, believed Doug's role had to be visible at the start and less visible later in the planning process. Although the new team initially needed Doug's challenging questions and strong facilitation, Doug had to get out of the way. It was important that the teachers stopped deferring to the wisdom and control of the school's administrators. They were the ones who worked with students, day in and day out; they had to be the ones shaping the new instructional programs.

Teachers emerged as team leaders, and they learned a great deal: how to bring key team members on board, allow for candid discussion, accept dissent, resolve conflicts, and promote consensus. Although it was fine for the team to slowly work through their concerns, the discussion could not go on endlessly. Decisions had to be made; deadlines needed to be met. For Doug Law and John Huffman, the final plan was important, yet secondary. In their eyes, the critical accomplishment was not a particular feature of a new freshmen transition program or the school-to-careers approach. The victory was the new ability of the staff to work together—as a team.

LEARNING HOW TO LEARN

Johnsonville Foods in Sheboygan, Wisconsin, acquired an international reputation for more than their outstanding line of sausage products. In 1994, Tom Peters, acclaimed business and management guru, traveled to the factory to research and report on an organization where workers were called members, members hired and fired their colleagues, supervisors acted more like coaches, anyone could suggest a new idea, and there were no automatic pay increases. Individuals earned more after they learned a new skill or served as a team leader; professional development was conducted on company time. Johnsonville Foods transformed itself from a very profitable business to something more—it became a learning organization.

Learning organizations, popularized by Peter Senge (2006) through his landmark book *The Fifth Discipline*, radically depart from the way corporations, nonprofits, and schools typically operate. Attention is paid to five disciplines: (1) personal mastery, (2) mental models, (3) shared vision, (4) team learning, and (5) systems thinking, all of which are crucial to facilitating substantial change.

Personal mastery involves setting personal goals, understanding the gap between those goals and one's current capacity, and making a commitment to lifelong learning. Furthermore, individual growth is intimately linked (as at Johnsonville Foods) with organizational growth. In the schools I have studied, a strong commitment was made to the growth of individual staff members, which in turn enabled each school to become more successful.

Everyone has *mental models*, images of the world as we assume it to be. Senge (2006) urged us to suspend those assumptions. If we do not, then we will have great difficulty seeing things in a new way and believing we can do things differently. For example, the principals of our award-winning schools encouraged their staffs to no longer assume certain students couldn't learn complex concepts.

Shared vision calls for an individual enrolling in a cause rather than being compelled to participate. It involves discovering what Senge (2006) called "shared pictures of the future." The staffs of the schools in this study could not avoid paying attention to the current (and discouraging) set of school conditions; however, their schools became more successful because most teachers moved out of that mind set and collectively created a new vision for what their school could be. Because this was a shared view, staff members voluntarily joined the venture.

Team learning is based on common experiences that propel individuals and the organization. It is premised on dialogue, people listening to each other in an effort to "discover insights not attainable individually" (Senge, 2006, p. 10). Each of the eight schools profiled in this book created teams, which learned together as they explored options and argued whether they could be adapted for their schools.

Each of the eight principals implicitly understood the four disciplines summarized above, as well as the fifth, *systems thinking*, which in Senge's (2006) view is the most important. Senge contended that "We can only understand a rainstorm by contemplating the whole, not any individual part of the pattern" (p. 7). In the same way, we must view businesses and schools—and all human endeavors—as systems. The eight principals knew that to significantly change their schools, they could not look only on how teachers were teaching. That "snapshot" would not be enough. Classroom instruction was affected by how the school organized its resources, how success was going to be measured, and so on. Each element was part of a larger, interconnected system.

As I see it, the concept of change is intimately and inevitably linked to the idea of learning. How could it not be? For us to change as individuals, and for us to lead change in organizations, we need to know more—and sometimes less—by unlearning what does not work. We need to learn new ideas. We need to see things a different way. We need to understand new perspectives. Senge's (2006) message is that *we need to learn how to learn*.

John Williams School No. 5, under Michele Hancock, became a community of adult learners. By posting signs outside classrooms, which announced that the teacher inside that room was an expert on a specific teaching strategy, such as direct instruction, cooperative learning, or phonics, Michele conveyed several messages. The teacher–expert in that classroom had learned a new teaching strategy; colleagues could—and would—learn from each other; and the principal would support and encourage learning by creating a system of classroom intervisitations.

Michele wanted her teachers to learn four things. First, she wanted them to learn how to implement different teaching strategies. This took place through soft encouragement and a hard mandate for teachers who *had* to change what they were doing. Because Michele would take over the class when a teacher left it to visit a colleague, she embodied her message.

The second learning goal merged with Michele's attitude about teams. She formed grade-level teams, and consequently teachers learned how to work as a team and share what each team member was doing with her students. These team meetings were important, and Michele required a brief summary of what was accomplished. This carrot ("Here is time for you")-and-stick ("I am monitoring what you are doing") approach worked.

The third learning activity involved leaving the confines of School No. 5. Teachers typically spend most of their careers working in one or two schools in the same school district. They only "know what they know," which is limited. However, School No. 5's teachers continually visited other schools, in district and out of the district.

The fourth learning experience involved the entire staff being exposed to the use of data; they "learned how to learn" through examining indicators, achievement results, student weaknesses, and individual student progress. As one teacher stated, "Michele showed us there was so much to learn and in doing so, we would be able to better serve our students."

On the other side of the Great Lakes, Bill Andrekopoulos was converting his Milwaukee middle school, Gustav Fritsche, into a learning organization. Unlike

Michele Hancock, who had embarked on her first principalship in an elementary school, Bill was a seasoned principal who was disappointed in his efforts to improve Fritsche. He knew his middle school could do better.

Bill attended numerous conferences and read many books about schools and leadership; he frequently and informally shared themes and insights with individual teachers. Like Michele Hancock, he arranged visits to other schools, usually schools with comparable student populations. If Bill had not already visited the particular school, he went with his teachers. Each visit was discussed with teachers who taught the same subject or taught on the same grade level, or with the entire staff.

Readings, school visits, and examination of data merged into opportunities for teachers to take risks. Groups of teachers were encouraged to try new teaching strategies. However, there were guidelines. The change had to be based on research, meaning it had been attempted elsewhere, and data could be provided about its effectiveness. Once launched, the change had to be monitored and assessed at Fritsche; if it worked, teachers were asked to consider how it could be further improved. If it did not work, teachers had to explain why, consider adjustments, and eventually decide whether the new practice should be modified or abandoned.

For example, a team of Fritsche teachers identified sixty students who were not doing homework and had low grade-point averages. For six weeks, half of those students were required to attend a forty-five-minute after-school homework and tutoring program. The other thirty students did not attend those after-school sessions but did have a private ten-minute meeting each week with a counselor. The motivational counseling made a difference—academic indicators went up for these students; the after-school program had little impact. As a result of this action research, Bill and his faculty implemented the counseling approach with the entire school.

School No. 5 and Fritsche—and the other six schools in this book—practiced what educational reformer Roland Barth (1990) preached when he wrote,

> The concept of schools as a place where all participants—teachers, principals, parents and students—engage in learning and teaching [is important]. School is not a place for important people who do not need to learn and unimportant people who do. Instead, school is a place where students discover and adults rediscover the joys, the difficulties, and the satisfaction of learning. (p. 43)

CAPACITY: THE LESSONS TO BE LEARNED

The powerful stories and dramatic lessons drawn from 9/11 will not disappear and will fill thousands of volumes. Tom Peters dedicated his 2003 book *Re-Imagine* to an examination of "the failure of organizations invented for another era" (p. 13). In Peters's words,

On September 11, 2001, a tiny band of Internet-savvy fundamentalists humbled the world's only superpower. It turned out that the FBI, the CIA, a kiloton of tanks, and an ocean of aircraft carriers and nuclear subs were no match for passionate focus, coordinated communication, and a few $3.19 box cutters. (p. 13)

The 9/11 Commission's report echoed the same sentiments in a section named "Capabilities":

Before 9/11, the United States tried to solve the al Qaeda problem with the same government institutions and capabilities it had used in the last stages of the Cold War and its immediate aftermath. These capabilities were inefficient, but little was done to expand or reform them. (9/11 Commission, 2002, pp. 350–351)

The 9/11 Commission's report also advocated "institutionalizing imagination," which the report admitted is an oxymoron in that "imagination is not a gift usually associated with bureaucracies" (9/11 Commission, 2002, p. 344).

Schools need to commit themselves to imagination as they learn to learn. The capacity of school stakeholders—teachers, students, administrators, parents, and community members—needs to be strengthened in terms of planning, teaching, assessing, working in teams, and learning how to learn. In a world that is dramatically different from the world in which we adults grew up, we cannot do less. Schools by their very nature ought to be dedicated to capacity-building. More than 100 years ago, John Dewey (1902) argued:

In the case of the educator, the demand for imaginative insight into possibilities is [essential] . . . while the educator must use results that have already been accomplished he cannot, if he is truly an educator, make them his final and complete standard. Like the artist he has the problem of creating something that is not the exact duplicate of anything that has been wrought and achieved previously. (p. 7)

14

The Essential Elements

Conversations

There is a story of a principal who accompanies one of her new teachers to his classroom and gives him the supplies he will need for the year. The principal points out where the books are stored, where the chalk is kept, and the way the windows work. Finally, the principal says to her new staff member, "Good luck. I'll see you in 20 years, at your retirement dinner." When a workshop of teachers and aspiring administrators is told this anecdote, they chuckle and nod in agreement. The anecdote might be an exaggeration, but it still holds several truths.

THE CONCEPT OF SCHOOL CONVERSATIONS

Teachers in American schools typically work in isolation. Their classroom is their castle. Colleagues do not enter. If the school district policy requires it, the principal arrives for an annual pro forma lesson observation. Teachers work their way through the school day, perhaps socializing for a period in the teacher's lounge or cafeteria. Some teachers do not venture outside their classrooms, eating lunch as they grade papers, prepare lessons, and take a break.

Few professional conversations unfold in many schools. New teachers are often left to find their own way, with no support. There is little collegial activity; lesson planning and student assessment are considered solo activities. When teachers do talk with each other, the conversations often focus on family news or planned vacations, sports, stocks, and social events. Little conversation focuses on the students or the art of teaching.

When Ogden and Germinaro (1995) divided American schools into three categories—conventional, congenial, and collaborative—the vast majority of schools fell into the conventional category. The principals and teachers were satisfied with the state of their schools and felt no need for collaboration and professional conversations. In congenial schools, teachers spoke with each other, but their conversations were adult centered, not focused on the students. The smallest category of schools was collaborative ones, where teacher isolation evaporated and teams of teachers worked together on a regular basis. Sharing became commonplace. Conversations about student progress and teaching and learning were woven into the school culture.

In the early 1990s, Tony Wagner completed extensive research on three Massachusetts schools and then revisited those schools ten years later. He used these studies, and much of his other research, to explore why it is so difficult to change schools. He concluded:

> there are three essential, interrelated components to a successful school improvement process: establishing clear academic goals . . . creating a caring community with explicit core values; and encouraging many forms of collaboration between teachers and with students, parents, and community members. When one or more of these parts is missing, change is thwarted. (Wagner, 2000, p. 235)

The eight schools profiled in this book dramatically changed from conventional to collaborative. The conversations in each school drove the reform process and addressed the essential elements suggested by Wagner (2000). As I look back on these discussions, dialogue, and debates, I place them into four categories: (1) conversations about students, (2) conversations about teaching and learning, (3) conversations about the school's vision, and (4) conversations about progress.

THE IMPORTANCE OF CONVERSATIONS

What we talk about tells much about ourselves, as do the frequency, intensity, and passion of those conversations. The subjects of our conversations reflect what we consciously or unconsciously consider important, what we believe in, what we value. Conversely, what we don't talk about has great significance.

In many schools, the typical conversations among teachers and administrators, parents and students do not focus on the children and adolescents, or on teaching and learning, much less the school's vision and progress toward actualizing that vision. However, in the eight schools in this book the conversations shifted from the mundane to the meaningful. For example, the focus changed from "There's nothing we can do about this" to "It's going to be a lot of work, but we can make a difference." Problems became challenges; obstacles became opportunities. The comfort of the adults was superseded by a concern for the students.

As depicted in Figure 14.1, the subjects of the new conversations in the eight schools in this book were linked. When the school staffs talked about students, it was natural to include an examination of instruction. Likewise, when teaching methods and materials were discussed, the readiness, interests, and achievement levels of the students became an important consideration.

Generating from the conversations about students, teaching, and learning were conversations about the school's vision. Where did the school want to be? What type of school did the stakeholders envision? What steps could be taken to address who the students were and who they could be in terms of their growth, development, and achievement?

Linked to a discussion of the school's vision, where the school wanted to be (Point B), was an assessment of where it was (Point A) and the progress of moving the school from Point A to Point B. In the award-winning schools, deliberate steps were taken to assess how far the school had moved, how close the school was to its vision.

Additionally, leaders in these schools, both administrators and teachers, were conscious of *how* to facilitate conversations. They developed a sense of trust, focused attention on what mattered, stimulated new thinking, and promoted honest and candid exchanges. Adults, and frequently students as well, were asked what they thought, how they felt. An ongoing conversation was promoted. Instead of being ignored, individuals were rewarded for speaking out.

Figure 14.1   How conversations connected with each other

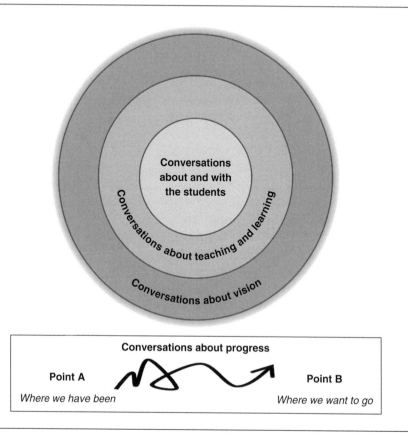

THE POWER OF CONVERSATIONS

As illustrated in Figure 14.2, the four arenas of conversations were clearly connected and interlocked at Niles High School. Niles alumni forced the conversation about students: Why had the high school failed to prepare them for college or the work world? The hard data about student success after graduation could not be ignored; neither could the disappointing statistics about the large number of freshmen who routinely dropped out. It was tempting to blame the students' abilities, the lack of parental involvement, or the quality of teaching in the middle school and elementary school. However, principal Doug Law would not let the discussion head in that direction.

The concern shifted to what and how students were learning. New curriculum and support programs were designed for the freshmen so they could better adjust to high school. The Niles staff visited schools with successful school-to-careers

Figure 14.2   How conversations connected with each other at Niles High School

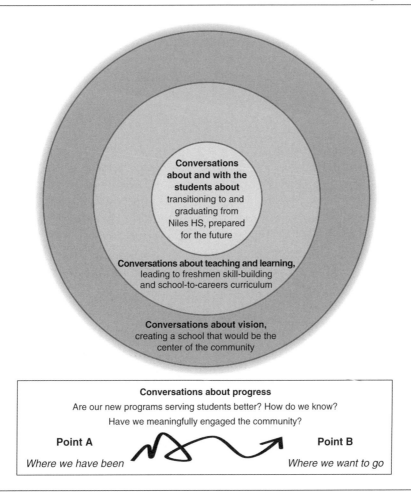

programs and developed a radically different curriculum for the sophomores, juniors, and seniors. For the first time, the staff talked about instruction being built on student needs, interests, and aspirations.

The Niles High School staff envisioned a school at the center of the community, important to students, their families, community residents, and local businesses. To gauge the school's progress toward that vision, the Niles staff would consider the school's dropout rate, the success patterns of their graduates, the degree of business partner involvement, the quality of internship experiences, and feedback from potential employers.

CONVERSATIONS ABOUT AND WITH STUDENTS

Veteran educator Herbert Kohl spent more than forty years working in New York City schools, authored ten books, and became recognized as an advocate of joyful teaching. For Kohl, talk about and with students was fundamental:

> Education has to be shaped so that the timbre of students' voices can emerge. This is essential if substantial learning is to develop. The teacher's voice must emerge as well, and students must have the opportunity to dialogue with their teachers. Students and teachers have to learn to speak to each other across culture, class, age, gender, and all the other divides that inhibit the development of intelligence and sensitivity. (Kohl, 1998, p. 44)

Meanwhile, Burrello, Hoffman, and Murray (2005) introduced three stories of school transformation by posing some essential questions, such as "Why do some schools transform? Why do some schools sustain their transformation? Why do some schools know their purpose and direction? Why do some schools succeed with all students?" (p. 1). To answer these questions, they provided three case studies of schools that experienced significant school change.

One of the important elements of achieving significant change, according to one of the principals, involved conversations about the students. In the principal's words,

> We started to develop what I would say would be a very common vision. We decided that we knew we couldn't hand pick our students and we didn't want to . . . but we knew the one thing that we could control would be the work we gave the students. (Burrello et al., 2005, p. 5)

As Burrello et al. (2005) added, this principal "argued that each student had to be successful each day and that the faculty's job was to figure out how to achieve this" (p. 13).

The elementary school staff at South Heights Elementary could not avoid talking about and with their students. The culture, nurtured by principal Rob Carroll, required it; conversations about students became a way of life at South Heights. In the past, teachers had complained about who the students were, wishing to have different students with better preparation, stronger skills, and more positive attitudes. Student failure was accepted; the students couldn't change, so why focus on them and why do anything different?

Rob Carroll made it clear to the entire staff they had to change, declaring "It's us changing for them." Rob made the students the focal point in five ways.

First, he centered his workday on the youngsters: talking with them; encouraging them; and, when necessary, giving individual attention to students. Rob served as a role model.

Second, he created routines that recognized and rewarded student progress and achievement. Daily announcements by different students included news of student (and staff) accomplishments. Weekly bulletins, banners, posters, and displays pointed to student success stories. Students talked with each other about their progress; student growth and improvement became natural topics of conversation among the staff.

Third, the school's motto was simplified to "We succeed. No exceptions. No excuses." It became a mantra, repeatedly chanted by students and staff. These six simple words placed the school's obligation to its students ahead of all else. The staff began to measure themselves—and their school—on the basis of meeting (and exceeding) state-mandated levels of achievement. The staff talked about students in general and focused on specific students who had to be targeted for additional help.

Fourth, Rob constantly asked the staff about particular students. To follow up, Rob adjusted the school's budget to create a new position of behavioral specialist, a person who would facilitate conversations about students with the appropriate teachers.

Fifth, the staff made visits to every student's home before the academic year started. This activity stirred pride in the students and their families, who felt they were important enough to receive this attention. Those families talked about the staff in a different way; the staff, with a new understanding of their students, discussed them in deeper and more meaningful ways.

CONVERSATIONS MADE A CRITICAL DIFFERENCE AT FOX TECH

When your school has won the notoriety of being called the "worst high school in the state of Texas," you know there is a great deal to talk about. In describing the journey from failure to success at Louis W. Fox Academic and Technical High School (Fox Tech), principal Joanne Cockrell credited the range of conversations at the school but noted, "Conversations take many different forms. It is what we say—and at Fox Tech that meant saying to the students they were important. But we needed to back up what we said with what we did."

Student success became the major topic at Fox Tech. Breaking up a large high school, which treated students as anonymous numbers, was the first step. The new smaller theme-based "schools within a school" allowed and encouraged teachers to talk about the students, especially in terms of their academic performance. These ongoing conversations intensified after the identification of students who did not pass the practice Texas Assessment of Academic Skills examination in the ninth grade. Success was the goal; failure was not tolerated. Expectations were set high, excuses were not accepted, and the talk shifted to "What can we do to help each student?"

Joanne rewarded both the talk and the actions. In her words, she "made a big deal about everyone saying and doing something positive." Joanne believed her students (and she called them *her* students) had had few positive experiences and the school could replace their feelings of failure. As she constantly reminded her staff, "We are going to do whatever it takes to move the students from where they are to where they need to be."

Joanne's words—and actions—modeled the way. She talked *about* the students, and she talked *with* the students. She conducted her meetings with the other school administrators with a focus on what teachers were teaching and what students were learning, which inevitably were linked to student achievement indicators. Nearly everyone bought into the school's new vision, which was built around increasing student self-esteem and success.

Monitoring progress was built into the fabric of school life. The teachers were not the only ones discussing the state of the school; students were invited into the conversation. Joanne formed a Principal's Advisory Committee, in which the students were asked what their peers thought about specific policies and practices. Joanne wanted to know what the students needed. Joanne believed if students brought something to the principal—at a formal meeting or through an informal conversation—then it had to be important, and it had to be discussed and acted on. Conversations about students mattered at Fox Tech.

CONVERSATIONS ABOUT TEACHING AND LEARNING

The staffs of the eight schools profiled in this book came to accept the idea that school success was primarily going to be measured by the success of individual students. Therefore, conversations centered on what happened in classrooms, because effective and engaging instruction was essential. The goal was to reach every student and help all of them reach the highest possible levels of achievement. To do that, the walls of teacher isolation had to come down. Teachers needed to come together, informally and formally, to talk about curriculum, standards, instruction, and assessment.

Linda Darling-Hammond (1997b) expressed it this way:

Behind the scenes in schools that have successfully restructured are new kinds of relationships and conversations among teachers, principals, and other staff, supported by new organizational structures that allow all these individuals to work together in ways very different from those they once used. (p. 148)

As Susan Moore Johnson (1990) noted,

In the ideal world of schooling teachers would be true colleagues working together, debating about goals and purposes, coordinating lessons, observing and critiquing each other's work, sharing successes and offering solace, with the triumphs of their collective efforts far exceeding the summed accomplishments of their solitary struggles. The real world of schools is usually depicted very differently, with teachers sequestered in classrooms, encountering peers only on entering or leaving the building. (p. 148)

It is ironic that Johnson's (1990) review of the research on teacher collegiality showed that when schools are characterized by conversations about teaching and learning, the work is more satisfying for the teachers and more effective for the students.

Thomas Sergiovanni (1996) connected the conversations among teachers about teaching to the intellectual development of students:

There is growing acceptance of the idea that general improvement in student performance will occur only when classrooms become learning communities, and teaching becomes more learner centered . . . Few axioms are more fundamental than the one which acknowledges the link between what happens to teachers and what happens to students. Inquiring classrooms, for example, are not likely to flourish in schools where inquiry among teachers is discouraged. (p. 139)

Debbie Meier, the cofounder of Central Part East in East Harlem, built that innovative school around conversations. For her, it was essential that teachers start thinking through the tasks before them, collectively and collaboratively. As she stated, "This continuing dialogue, face to face, over and over, is a powerful educative force . . . the school itself is an educator for the kids and staff; it's its own staff development project" (Meier, 1995, p. 109).

In looking at Chicago school reform in the early 1990s, Bryk et al. (1998) found that schools that created a culture of conversations about teaching and learning were more likely to maintain their school reforms.

From the very beginning, the teachers at the "new" George Washington Carver Academy learned to work together and also involved their middle school students in conversations about teaching and learning. During the summer months, the Carver teachers collaboratively planned new Odyssey interdisciplinary units, such as The Sixties, Space, The Environment, Careers, Oceans, Illusions, and so on. The final decision about which units to conduct during the school year was made by students, who also contributed ideas about how the instruction could be conducted. The Odysseys were living documents, not tied to a required textbook or mandated scope and sequence. Language arts, social studies, science, mathematics, and the arts were connected with each other as students completed culminating projects.

For example, the Sixties Odyssey culminated with a performance called "The 60s Fest." The program began with the national anthem sung by a student in costume as Jimi Hendrix; a student recitation of the poem "With God on Our Side," written by Bob Dylan; and a trio of students dressed as The Supremes singing their hit record "Stop in the Name of Love." Students playing the roles of Gen. Curtis LeMay, Cassius Clay, and César Chávez made special guest appearances; a debate was staged pitting the idea of peaceful nonviolence (Rosa Parks) against the Black Power movement (Angela Davis). There also was a fashion show. The performance concluded with Martin Luther King Jr.'s "I Have A Dream" speech, and everyone joining with Mahalia Jackson in the singing of "We Shall Overcome."

In effect, Molly Maloy empowered her teachers and students to drive instruction. As one teacher noted, "Carver gives you enormous latitude in how you shape the curriculum; you can reach out to different students in different ways." Because a sense of family, team, and learning community was created, the talk centered on how students were learning and how they were (or were not) mastering the customized curriculum. As one teacher put it, "We were given the power to shape our odyssey, encouraged to solve our own problems as it related to shaping the instruction, and motivated to tap our unlimited imagination." Another teacher noted, "We're all learning—that is what gives Carver that feeling of excitement."

It became clear to the Carver staff that they could not teach the way they had been taught when they had been middle school students. The instruction had to relate to the real world their students faced; the school had to meet the students' needs, interests, and concerns. At the same time, classroom activities were designed to make students think, work together, and problem-solve, learning skills that would prepare them for their future. As a parent noted, "Everything [for the students] is relevant; they tie it all together; and the curriculum encourages conversations between children and their families." One teacher summarized by saying, "We all changed in the way we do school."

After taking care of the basics (order, discipline, and rules) at Skycrest Elementary, Principal Chris Zarzana brought to bear her expertise as a reading specialist and her experience as a successful principal. Teaching and learning—especially reading instruction—became paramount. Conversations about student skill mastery, understanding, goals, and student progress were formally and informally conducted. Teachers talked with students, and students talked with each other. Students shared their reading scores, their strengths and weaknesses, and what they had to do to further improve.

These conversations did not accidentally unfold. Chris built into the school's School Improvement Plan and Title I budgets considerable funding for professional development. In response to teacher requests and needs, Chris planned school-based training, and at times those sessions deliberately overlapped with district staff development. Chris encouraged and supported teacher attendance at conferences and seminars. Teachers shared what they had learned with their colleagues, and frequently the proposed methods and materials were used with the students, with their impact measured and assessed. As Chris explained,

> At Skycrest, teachers are encouraged to gather data, become keen observers of student behavior, and draw conclusions based on their evidence. Research cadres are developed so that teachers can meet periodically throughout the year to discuss student progress and to support each other's growth.

The conversations about teaching and learning also involved parents, whom the school considered to be their partners. For example, as soon as parents enrolled their children in kindergarten, Skycrest staff encouraged them to develop basic skills, such as teaching their children to write their names. Parents were offered parent education workshops and invited to visit Skycrest classes and talk about the instruction and their child's progress.

Extensive data analysis was done before instructional decisions were made; teachers were asked to consider the following questions: What do I know (and not know) as a result of examining these data? What else do I want to know? How might these data help to improve instruction? Do we need other data? These questions were important, but more important was the commitment to both individual teacher reflection and teacher group discussion. In effect, Skycrest Elementary experienced ongoing and meaningful conversations about teaching and learning.

CONVERSATIONS ABOUT VISION

Senge and his colleagues stated that a vision statement

> shows where we want to go, and what we will be like when we get there. The word comes from the Latin *videre*, "to see." The link to seeing is significant, the more richly detailed and visual the image is, the more compelling it will be. (Senge, Kleiner, Roberts, Ross, & Smith, 1994, p. 302)

To encourage individuals and organizations to create a shared vision, Charlotte Roberts suggests an exercise built on one question: "It is five years from today's date and you have, marvelously enough, created the organization you most want to create. Now it is your job, as a team to describe it—as if you were able to see it, realistically, around you" (Senge et al., 1994, p. 337).

Kouzes and Posner (1995) noted, "Leadership is not a monologue, nor should the creation of a vision statement be done individually and without the active involvement of others who must attend to their operations" (p. 182). They buttressed their argument as they stated, "Because vision exists in the future, leaders have to get others in the present to imagine what that future will look like, feel like, sound like, even smell light" (Kouzes & Posner, 1995, p. 185). Roland Barth's (1990) *Improving Schools From Within* became a highly regarded work for educational reformers. In it, Barth lamented that the need for teachers to talk about vision was generally being ignored:

> The personal vision of school practitioners is a kind of moral imagina-
> tion that gives them the ability to see schools not as they are, but as
> they would like them to become . . . A personal vision, then, is one's
> overall conception of what the educator wants the organization to
> stand for; what its primary mission is; what its basic, core values are;
> a sense of how all the parts fit together; and, above all, how the vision
> maker fits into the grand plan . . . I can think of nothing so conspicu-
> ously missing in the effort to improve our schools as the continuous
> engagement of teachers and principals in constructing visions. (Barth,
> 1990, p. 147–148)

Vision-making characterized the work of the eight schools. For example, the challenge facing Sandy Stephens was to initiate, facilitate, and maintain conversations about two very different student populations at Government Hill Elementary. On one hand, she had a middle-class population that demanded special programs for their children. Without the enrollment of the children from these families, Government Hill would close. At the same time, Sandy needed to engage her staff regarding how to reach the families for whose first language was not English.

Sandy's vision was to serve both populations; to bring together this diverse set of families; and to provide meaningful, engaging, and motivating instruction for everyone. The school's standards would be high, and every student would achieve. Her dream was to make Government Hill the center of its multicultural community.

Sandy understood that conversations about a new vision for the school required several elements. First she had to be clear about the vision and unwavering in her emphasis that a new school, serving all students, could be created. Second, she needed to build trust with her staff, students, parents, and community members. Third, Sandy knew that conceptualizing a future was not enough; deliberate, effective, and strategic steps were essential to creating the new school. Fourth, she had to transform her vision for Government Hill into a shared vision to which the school's stakeholders would feel allegiance and adopt as their own. As Sandy put it, "You can't make change happen without having everyone involved."

Sandy Stephens had started her service as Government Hill's principal by asking members of her staff "If you could do anything [in our school], what would it be?" Creating a school that made a difference in the lives of all its students became the answer. As one teacher noted, "Before, didn't have our own identity." Another teacher, in comparing the "new" Government Hill to the "old" one, explained, "the level of conversation is so different."

At Niles High School, the level of conversation also became very different. Although 3,711 miles separated the two schools, and one was elementary and the other secondary, there were many parallels in the Government Hill and Niles stories.

Neither school was effectively responding to the needs of their students. Significant numbers of Niles students never made it to graduation day. Both schools were ignoring the needs of the local community. Both schools had drifted along, without much thought to what they were and what they could be. Doug Law, who became the new Niles High School principal, challenged that comfort zone with his mantra of "Why are we doing what we are doing?" In Doug's words, he was trying to create a "discomfort zone," because Niles High School, like Government Hill, needed conversations about vision.

For principal Doug Law and superintendent John Huffman, it was clear their high school was out of step with both the aspirations of its students and the job demands of its community. Additionally, competing high schools were a threat, because families were deciding to send their adolescents to other high schools. Although Niles High School did not have as severe an enrollment crisis as Government Hill had faced, the handwriting was on the wall: Become relevant or become obsolete.

How to develop a new vision for the high school was the hard question. As Doug noted, the typical process whereby a committee of five disappeared for a half-day and wrote some flowery sentence, which would no doubt include the phrase "and we shall live happily ever after," would not serve the high school. Because the vision had to address how teachers taught and how students learned, Niles teachers had to drive the "vision conversation."

A teacher-led SIT visited other schools across America, read about various programs, and discussed what they discovered. The team struggled with a new vision for the school; faced much cynicism; and tackled several logistical issues, such as how to adjust the school schedule, program students for out-of-school experiences, and convert existing facilities.

Local business leaders, in turn, were not shy. They contributed ideas, provided internship experiences for the students, and shaped the curriculum. In effect, they helped the school staff develop a vision for the school. As the business involvement intensified, everyone in the community stopped referring to "that school" and began to call Niles High School "our school."

CONVERSATIONS ABOUT PROGRESS

Conversations about progress focus on four interrelated things: (1) the purpose of school, (2) the school's advancement toward its vision, (3) its fulfillment of projected outcomes for the student body as a whole, and (4) the achievement of individual students.

Many schools spend little, if any, time discussing their purpose. Ironically, this is the most basic discussion, and it drives, implicitly or explicitly, the measurements used to gauge how well a school is doing. For example, if a school defines its purpose as developing empowered and knowledgeable citizens, then it might engage its students in community service projects, with feedback from project supervisors and the students' reflective logs serving as measurements. In a similar fashion, a school's purpose might be to produce students who understand how to conduct research. Demonstrations, exhibitions, and team presentations might determine how well students (and staff) develop and test hypotheses.

In their study of school reform in Chicago, Bryk et al. (1998) documented

> how capable leadership in many Chicago schools used the institution of local governance to create opportunities for an extended discourse about school aims and the effectiveness of school organization. Over time, this discourse promoted a sense of shared purpose and fomented a moral force to advance improvement. (p. 265)

In other words, the conversations about school vision and school's progress became important and had impact.

Using his experience in the corporate and nonprofit worlds, Max DePree (1997) raised questions about outputs, as he contended, "What outputs does an organization need to measure? I think we begin with two things. How does our performance compare with our plan, and how does our performance compare with our potential?" (p. 54).

Furthermore, DePree (1997) warned,

> It's so easy to fall into the trap of measuring only what's easy to measure. Our real job is to figure out what's significant to the organization and to the people who actually do the work and find ways *together* of measuring what's significant. That's tough. That's essential. That's beginning to reach for potential. Only then can we be faithful to our mission and begin true transition. (p. 56)

Mike Schmoker (2001) was optimistic about schools looking at themselves, as he stated, "A rapidly growing number of schools have made a momentous discovery. When teachers regularly and collaboratively review assessment data for the purpose of improving practice to reach measurable achievement goals, something magical happens" (p. 1). Schmoker gave the example of three schools in Los Angeles that were cited, in 1999, as the most improved schools in what is the second largest school district in the United States. These three schools set academic achievement measurable goals that looked at academic achievement. Then a process unfolded, which Schmoker (2001) described thus:

> They worked in teams to reach their goals. Teachers talked to each other about their work, got together regularly to analyze successes and failures, shared materials, and refined their instruction. [Then they] made regular use of achievement data to identify and address areas of concern. (p. 2)

Moving Gustav Fritsche Middle School forward was paramount to principal Bill Andrekopoulos. The school's progress reports most intrigued Bill. He loved gathering data and teaching his staff how to analyze them. The questions came spilling out: What do we see? What does this mean? What do we know now that we didn't know before? What else do we need to know? Additionally, the Fritsche staff asked themselves: What are the implications? How do these data inform us about what works and what does not? What might we do differently?

Data were disaggregated about student achievement in every subject, at every grade level, and at various times in the school year. Data were collected about discipline referrals, student attendance and punctuality, class size, guidance interventions, and so on. Comparisons were made with similar schools in other school districts, with other Milwaukee middle schools, with previous data collected at Fritsche, with district requirements, and with state and national trends.

The staff looked at how each student progressed in terms of raw scores, mastery of specific standards, and comparisons with other students. Teachers learned about the concept of "value added." For example, although it was important seventh-graders would be able to read at the eighth-grade level by the end of their seventh-grade year, it also was important to celebrate the achievement of a seventh-grader who had started that year reading at the third-grade level and had improved to reading at the sixth-grade level, an increase of three years.

Transparency guided the Fritsche advance toward its vision. Nothing was hidden. Everyone knew what was working and what wasn't; everyone knew what progress was being made; everyone could examine test scores and other indicators. Starting in the 1992–93 school year, Bill Andrekopoulos's fifth as principal, Fritsche published an annual School Visionary Report, which set the goals for the year and reported on the progress made during the previous year. The first three-page issue, appearing in fall 1992, displayed a bar graph that showed the great increase in the number of students scoring above the 50th percentile in mathematics. However, reading and writing student progress lagged behind. Data showed that the decrease in the number of course failures had leveled off, while the lateness-to-class statistics continued to fall. A new

"At Risk" program piloted the previous year involved matching teaching methodologies with a student's learning style. The results? Dramatic increases in the students' grade-point average. The plan? Expand the program to 90 sixth-graders.

Eight years later, in the sixteen-page 2000–01 Vision Report, Bill's introductory letter noted that because of "our success with block scheduling, looping, Connected Math Projected (CMP) instruction and our newly granted charter status, we had many visitors who wanted to find out *How does Fritsche do it?*"

It would have been impossible to miss the ongoing concern with measuring progress at John Williams School No. 5. Charts, posters, banners, photographs, and displays surrounded you; questionnaires were constantly discussed, with their themes and trends used for planning; time was set aside for reflective exercises. Michele Hancock, as the school's new principal, regularly engaged staff members in conversations and encouraged them to share with each other.

At first, the staff had to be given the hard data, which Michele called "the facts." After the sense of denial was overcome, the staff looked at where the school was headed and how far along it had traveled. It was an essential discussion. John Williams School No. 5 had been the worst elementary school in Rochester in 1999; four years later, it was designated as one of twenty-four "most improved" schools out of 2,900 in the state. Discussions about progress drove the dramatic climb. As Michele wrote to Clifford Janey, the superintendent, "the focus on facts provided a sense of urgency in terms of again establishing a desired future state of the school."

Grade-level teams were created and given time during the school day to talk about both the academic and social/emotional growth of students, and achievement data were used for a discussion of best practices. Specific state standards for each subject were posted in classrooms and hallways. Alongside each one were samples of student work that revealed different levels of proficiency. Students talked with each other and with their teachers about the posted work and other work in their portfolios. Teachers talked with each other and with parents about the students' work.

A significant piece of a massive wall display was labeled *Data Analysis*. It focused on specific assessments. For example, under the column labeled "Academic Focus Area" were the baseline data indicating that the fourth-grade English language arts proficiency was 27.4%. The "Causes/Reasons" included "lack of familiarity with expository text and lack of understanding of content-based vocabulary." Among the items listed under "Areas Requiring Support and Development" was "content-based teaching." "Preliminary Strategies" mentioned "demonstration lessons and observations of model classrooms."

Like the other principals of the change-award-winning schools, Michele Hancock had a mantra, repeated so often it became an integral part of the school language: "What are we doing? Why are we doing it?" Michele wanted teachers to think about those questions. As one teacher put it, "Michele made us reflect more on our practices."

CONVERSATIONS: THE LESSONS TO BE LEARNED

Nobel Peace Prize winner Al Gore's 2006 award-winning film and book, *An Inconvenient Truth*, look at the "planetary emergency of global warming," an issue desperate for more attention and action yet generally not considered critical in the minds of most Americans. Through a set of powerful slides presenting indisputable data, clear explanations, and frightening photographs, Gore explained what global warming means and how its long-range impact will cause the demise of our planet. His arguments are powerful and persuasive.

The important question is: Will Gore's many presentations around the world make a difference? Like most reformers and change agents, he deeply believes it must and it will. In his words, "My hope is that [others] will begin to feel as I have for a long time, that global warming is not just about science and it is not just a political issue. It is really a moral issue" (Gore, 2006, p. 8).

Gore's environmental campaign illustrates the need for conversations and their crucial role in bringing about significant change. As he put it, "The truth about the climate crisis is an inconvenient one that means we are going to have to change the way we live our lives" (Gore, 2006, p. 10).

The global warming issue mirrors the work of educational reformers, who also have used hard data and somber forecasts. In both cases, the dangers are frequently ignored; it is a great effort to capture the ongoing attention and concern of Americans, who are often distracted by other things. In both cases, the ability to look years and perhaps decades ahead diminishes the attention paid to the issues. In both cases, people must talk about those affected (e.g., students); the learning that needs to take place (e.g., classroom instruction); the ultimate goal (e.g., a school's vision); and what is being done to reach that goal (e.g., progress toward the school's vision). Furthermore, as Michele Hancock, principal of John Williams School No. 5, pointed out, there is a need to project a sense of urgency, and as Joanne Cockrell, Fox Tech's principal, reminded us, conversations mean both talk and action.

If we don't talk about the dangers of global warming or the need for significant school change, then it means it is not a high priority, not an important concern, not something we value. It means that little, if anything, will happen. Fortunately, in the eight schools profiled in this book, conversations—many conversations—were used to bring about significant change.

PART V

Bringing About Significant School Change

The Catalytic Variables

Dear Mr. Einstein, I am writing to you to settle an argument another boy and I had in school today. We are both in the eighth grade. This is a rather unusual question, but it concerns you very much. . . . I said that you were a genius and you hadn't gone insane. My friend said that you would go crazy in a year or less. I said you wouldn't.

Admiringly yours, Sam

Education should be a source of nurturance for the spirit as well as a means of teaching understanding, though it can be, and too often is conducted in a way that deadens and demoralizes.

—Linda Darling-Hammond

I am only one, but still I am one. I cannot do everything, but still I can do something. And because I cannot do everything, I will not refuse to do the something I can do.

—Edward Everett Hale

S ome people have contended that trying to bring about significant change in schools is an act of insanity. Others would define insanity as doing the same exact thing and expecting different results. A parallel conundrum is whether it is easier to change oneself or instigate change in others. In addressing these contrasting interpretations and points of view we must grapple with how change efforts can be stimulated and accelerated, how catalysts within organizations and from outside can, with exceptional leadership, take schools to places they did not know or believe could be reached.

Among the questions to be raised in this section are the following:

- What meaning can be given to the term *dissonance*?
- How bad does a school have to get before its stakeholders say, "Enough is enough"?
- Can significant change in an organization happen without some push from outside?
- What roles do school leaders play in the effort to significantly change a school?

15

The Catalytic Variables

Internal Dissonance

One of the most memorable lines in American feature length films is in *Network*, when the main character, prominent television newscaster Howard Beale (played by Peter Finch), announces to millions of viewers:

> I don't have to tell you things are bad. Everyone knows things are bad ... No one seems to know what to do ... I want you to get mad. You've got to say, I'm a human being, goddamn it. My life has value ... I want you to get up now; I want all of you to get out of your chairs and go to the window, open it, and stick your head out and yell, *"I'm mad as hell and I'm not going to take it anymore."*

Surprisingly, thousands of audience members opened their windows and followed Beale's instructions. He had tapped into their anger and frustration about crime, inflation, unsafe food and air, unemployment, the oil crisis, and so on. Although deliberately overdramatic, the statement "I'm not going to take it anymore" symbolized the condition of internal dissonance.

THE IMPORTANCE OF INTERNAL DISSONANCE

It is not good news when the prefix *dis-* is added to a word. Look at the words *disillusioned, disappointed, dismayed, disturbed*. Consider *discomfort, discord, disdain*. Think about a state of *disarray* or *distress*.

How would you like to be *dismissed, disinherited, discredited, disrespected*? In extreme terms, you could be *discarded, dissolved, disgraced*.

Things could be a *disaster*. Even the prefix *dis* itself has taken on its own meaning in the popular vernacular; when you "dis" someone, you are putting him or her down.

The *American Heritage College Dictionary of the English Language, Fourth Edition* (2006) defines *dissonance* as "a harsh disagreeable combination of sounds, discord . . . a lack of agreement, consistency, or harmony; conflict." In music, the dictionary notes dissonance is a "combination of tones contextually considered to suggest unreliable tension and required resolution" (p. 523). However, as I am using it, dissonance also borrows from many of the "dis" words mentioned above. Dissonance signals something is wrong. Dissonance, sometimes quite overt and sometimes beneath the surface, is not a desirable condition. By *internal* dissonance I mean dissonance within a particular school.

ENOUGH IS ENOUGH

In each of the stories of the eight school-change award-winning schools, internal dissonance played an important role. The school staff, students, parents, and/or community members directly or indirectly signaled that "enough was enough." Like Howard Beale, their frustration and anger had reached a boiling point; their complaints, unhappiness, and distress could no longer be ignored.

In each of these schools, internal dissonance deprived or attacked the school's sense of security, order, support, professionalism, and pride.

In some cases, there was no sense of security; individuals were simply afraid. Unruly students roamed the hallways; teachers locked themselves in their classrooms; teachers, and often students, did not feel safe. The school became dangerous, as did the immediate environs, the neighborhood, or section, of the city. Incidents of violence and crime were common. As a result, the perception and reputation of the school suffered; school enrollment and daily attendance (of students and staff) plummeted. The ability to focus on academics disappeared.

Frequently, the school was without a sense of order. Although not overtly dangerous, the school was "out of control." Chaos ruled. Students, even elementary school students, did what they pleased. There was no coherent discipline system, no rules, no consequences. School leadership either pretended these chaotic conditions did not exist, or didn't know how to respond to them, or made attempts to bring order that were ineffective.

In some schools, teachers, and ultimately students and parents, did not feel supported. New teachers asked for help; it did not come. Veteran teachers knew those new teachers needed help, but they didn't have the initiative, time, or energy to assist others; they were worried about their own survival. Providing support was not a priority for school leadership, which was often overwhelmed by the school's problems.

A sense of professionalism suffered in many schools. Despite the school's failing status, some teachers would push ahead, trying to separate themselves and their students from the poor school conditions. Often, this had two negative effects. First, the individual teacher's heroic attempts to create classrooms filled with learning sometimes could not be sustained. The school's chaos and disorder invaded their space, frustrating them. Or, second, these successful teachers became increasingly angry in response to the unacceptable school conditions. If they could make things work in their classrooms, why couldn't the others? Where was the school leadership?

Sadly, there were instances when there was no sense of pride among the school's stakeholders, staff, students, parents, and community members. For example, when a reporter from a local newspaper predicts that, once again, your high school would continue to rank at the bottom of the list of all high schools in the state in terms of academic achievement, the cynicism hurt. When nearly all the district's middle schools showed impressive improvement, but your school did not, you were embarrassed. When parents told their neighbors to avoid, at all costs, sending their children to your elementary school, you felt humiliated.

As depicted in Figure 15.1, more than one field of dissonance can be present in a school at a time and, in fact, a particular field of dissonance may affect other fields. For example, dissonance in terms of chaos in the school (order) could be coupled with a feeling of danger (security). A sense that the school is underperforming (professionalism) may be connected with a sense of embarrassment (pride). In the most extreme cases, not uncommon to our eight award-winning schools, four or five of these fields of dissonance could be operating at the same time.

Figure 15.1   Fields of internal dissonance

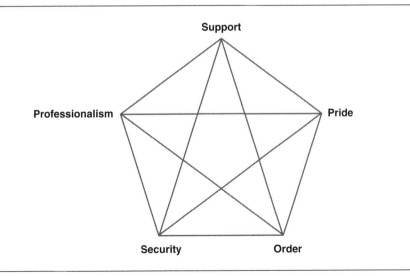

A SENSE OF SECURITY

The February 1, 1988, cover of *Time* magazine displayed an imposing Black man with a baseball bat in his hands. The story described how Joe Clark, a high school principal in Paterson, New Jersey, had to confront crime, drugs, and violence at "Eastside High," a school threatened with state takeover. The subsequent feature length film *Lean on Me* dramatically and graphically portrayed the school's conditions: walls filled with obscene graffiti; students, labeled by Clark as "miscreants," who resorted to hooliganism instead of attending to academics; drug dealers conducting their business on school grounds; and teachers immobilized by fear. In response, Clark, with a heavy hand, had the walls cleaned, expelled the miscreants, physically threw out a drug dealer, and screamed at his teachers to do better. Joe Clark cleaned up the school, and only then did he turn to raising the reading scores so the high school could avoid state takeover,

As a school change agent, Clark's concern about order was not unusual. In his studies of Chicago school reform, Anthony Bryk and his colleagues discovered that academic reform did not take place until students, parents, and teachers felt safe. As they put it, "Thus, the adults in each of these school communities made a commitment to making their school a safe, child-centered, and caring place—perhaps the only such environment their students and families might know" (Bryk et al., 1998, p. 120). My studies revealed the same thing.

When a new teacher was assigned to Gustav Fritsche Middle School, his friends asked him whether he was scared to go. The school's reputation was terrible; it was considered unsafe, out of control. One parent saw the school as a dumping ground for students who had behavior problems; in her words, "It was a zoo." As one teacher put it, "You did not walk the halls." Another noted, "You kept your doors closed." As they looked back, many teachers remembered their resentment because the school administrators would not call the police, even when things became dangerous. No one responded to the internal dissonance, the dismay, the disrespect, the disarray.

When high school students are afraid to come to school, you know there is a serious security problem. At Louis W. Fox Academic and Technical High School, scores of students did not enroll, transferred out, or dropped out. Many of those who stayed on the official rolls simply did not come to school, or they came only when they pleased. Gangs were ever present; the police were constantly on call; shopkeepers locked their doors—and, in some cases, moved away. One teacher remembered at the end of the school day "being afraid to walk back to [her] car." The time was ripe for a new leader to convert that dissonance into a positive force.

A SENSE OF ORDER

Joyner et al. (2004) wrote about mobilizing schools for instructional excellence:

> Education and psychosocial growth are best facilitated in an orderly environment characterized by fairness, justice, and clear standards of

behavior that are supported and enforced by all stakeholder groups. Harmony and synergy are inherent in order, as is the sense that things are well organized and working together for the common good. On the other hand, disorder threatens the potential for the common good. Consequently, the first order of business is to build structures, processes, and helpful mechanisms that move schools and school organizations from chaos to order. (p. 94)

Richard Elmore (2004) observed:

Educational reformers are gradually, unavoidably, and reluctantly approaching the inevitable conclusion [that], asking teachers and administrators to increase academic performance for students without fundamentally altering the conditions under which led to produce student learning in the first place is a dead end . . . If schools are not meeting expectations for student learning, it is largely because *they do not know what to do*. (p. 217)

In the schools I studied, not knowing what to do frequently started with not effectively responding to chaos.

When asked to talk about the school they used to have, Government Hill teachers described the students as noisy, disrespectful, and disruptive. One teacher told herself, "This is too much. I'm going back into my room." Another noted, "No one had a handle on discipline."

Things were so bad; the school had a very high rate of turnover—with students, staff, and even principals. As one teacher described it, "You put in your two years and then you would go somewhere else."

Skycrest Elementary teachers complained there was no schoolwide discipline system. One teacher would have one set of rules; another teacher would have a different set of rules. As one teacher remembered, "There were no guidelines; everything was so loose." The school was not known for its academics; it was the place where there was a lot of fighting and kids didn't get along.

As principal Chris Zarzana remembered, there was a felt need "to take back the school from the kids." As the school's new principal, she had to first restore order, and then she could turn to academics.

"It took 15–20 minutes to get the kids into the room," was how one teacher at George Washington Carver Academy remembered things. As Waco's only sixth-grade school, chaos was virtually inevitable.

One parent recalled Carver as "the worst of the worst." Despite the fact that the building felt like a prison, with its locked doors and barred windows, there was no order or discipline.

A SENSE OF SUPPORT

Whitaker and Moses (1994) contended that significant change cannot occur without people deviating from their norms, being shaken from their complacency, and moving from turf issues to a concern for the entire organization. In schools, this means principals, who are serving as change agents, must ask teachers to be courageous and take risks. As Whitaker and Moses put it, "the best way to combat entrenched norms is to highly support teachers who want to try new and innovative techniques" (p. 42). However, imagine a case when teachers feel no support for what they currently do, feel no support for them as individuals. Is it reasonable to think they will move into uncharted waters?

As Mink et al. (1993) put it,

> The individuals in the organization are the key to successful achievement of its transformation . . . To succeed, we must put the individual first and the change second . . . Fundamentally, to help another person learn, change facilitators must develop the capacity to approach that person with patience, friendly persuasion, and unconditional positive regard. Philosophically speaking, all human beings deserve this level of respect. (p. 114)

In short, the absence of support is a form of internal dissonance, and until it is resolved, there will be no significant school change.

At Government Hill, everyone was out for him- or herself. One teacher said, "Everyone did their own thing. Teachers simply did not get along with each other." Another one noted, "I learned to stay to myself and not make waves. Nobody would deal with [the problems]." Teachers felt isolated. No one seemed to care. No one asked how you were doing or said, "Yes, you did a great job."

A familiar refrain at John Williams School No. 5 was "I felt that I didn't have the support of the administration" and "There was very little teacher backup." These elementary school teachers felt they had to go it alone. As a result, they became angry at the school administration and filed grievance after grievance with the teachers union representative, a sure sign of discontented people.

The "change agent principals" walked through their schools, spoke with adults and students, and generally made them accessible, but many of their predecessors had done the opposite. They stayed holed up in their offices; frequently, the principal's secretary's main job was to serve as a gatekeeper. One principal was noted for his very long lunches—outside the school building. Another was characterized as "knowing what to say, using the buzz words, but not really understanding [the school reform]." Still another spent almost all of his time at the district office.

A SENSE OF PROFESSIONALISM

Both Matt Miller (2003) and Mike Schmoker (2006) have observed that good teachers are frequently upset about the work of some of their colleagues. As one teacher put it, the "incompetence of [my] colleagues is appalling" (Miller, 2003,

p. 116). No one less than Sandra Feldman, the former president of the American Federation of Teachers, told Miller that "There are an alarming number of incompetent teachers being allowed to teach" (Schmoker, 2006, p. 28). And, of course there are those committed teachers who do want to teach.

Susan Moore Johnson's (1990) study of the school as a workplace sheds much light on the idea of dissonance. In her view, teachers want to be valued, they want to be professionals, and they want to be treated as professionals. As Johnson (1990) observed,

> The features of the workplace that mattered most to these teachers proved to be the ones that enabled or inhibited them in the classroom. If school buildings were dysfunctional or decrepit, if materials and equipment were out of date or out of order, instruction suffered . . . they became discouraged about the possibility of doing a good job. (p. 323)

With some dismay, South Heights' teachers remembered that their school was not considered a good school in the community—quite the opposite, it was seen as the school where teachers were transferred to because they had problems at other schools. As one teacher said, South Heights was "the last one on the totem pole." Another noted, "The culture was so pitiful."

Parents of Government Hill students also saw their school serving as a dumping ground, the place where ineffective teachers were sent. One parent described the policy as "[The ineffective teachers] were here because no one was paying attention to them."

The San Juan Unified District Assistant Superintendent remembered Skycrest Elementary as a place where no one asked "What is being taught? Are the kids learning?" Some teachers knew those questions had to be posed and, consequently, those teachers were discouraged about their school's direction. One teacher regretfully remembered teachers not having a curriculum background and just "doing their own thing" in their classrooms. A parent remembered Chris Zarzana, as the new principal, having fertile ground to work with because teachers, frustrated with the poor performance of the school, were willing to change.

A SENSE OF PRIDE

In 1994, Jerome Freiberg brought twenty-five years of working in schools to producing an update of Carl Rogers's landmark study, *Freedom to Learn* (C. Rogers & Freiberg, 1994). In it, he shared stories of dissonance felt by teachers, as evidenced by a teacher's diary entry:

> Teaching frustrates me so much. There is always more to do, never enough time . . . Teaching no longer offers the chance to be creative and stimulating. Its frustrating not to be able to try something different.

How can you be a teacher without being creative? I feel angry when I feel stifled, not able to use everything I learned. (C. Rogers & Freiberg, 1994, p. 33)

Ted Sizer's (1984) classic *Horace's Compromise* also speaks to the issue of pride. His fictional character, Horace Smith, is a hard-working, dedicated, and well-liked high school English teacher. However, the conditions under which Horace works frustrate him. He has hundreds of papers to mark and cannot give them the attention they deserve. His classes are quiet and orderly but without the energy and passion generated by dialogue and debate. He will lecture, even though he knows that he ought to be coaching (i.e., facilitating discussion), "which is at the heart of high school teaching" (Sizer, 1984, p. 20). Although he keeps plugging away and plodding along, Horace is not proud of what he is able to accomplish with his students. As Sizer noted, through his character, Horace,

No one blames the system: everyone blames him. Relax, the consultants advise. Here are some exercises to get some perspective. Morphine, Horace thinks. It dulls my pain . . . Come now, he mutters to himself. Don't get cynical . . . Don't keep insisting that these "experts" should try my job for a week . . . they assure me that they *understand* me, only they say, "We hear you, Horace." I wonder who their English teachers were. (Sizer, 1984, p. 21)

Horace is angry and can't take it anymore. However, he is constrained and feels powerless to do much about his high school teaching. Imagine, if you will, a school filled with Horaces, teachers whose pride has been eroded, teachers who are consciously or subconsciously embarrassed by what they do or don't do.

It was quite dramatic for Niles High School when groups of graduates came back to complain that they had been unprepared for their college work or were unable to get a decent job. These angry alumni had not failed high school; they had graduated. The high school had failed them. As one teacher remembered the school at that time, "We had a traditional culture of honoring just 'the best and the brightest'." Ironically, however, the best students were the ones flunking out of college. Pride suffered even further when local employers complained the high school was not producing the type of graduate the workforce needed.

Pride was an issue for Bill Andrekopoulos. As a new principal, he assumed leadership of a school that lacked pride; teachers, students, and parents accepted their school's second-rate status. Bill had a radically different view. As he put it, "I wanted to prove that a Gustav Fritsche, a neighborhood school, could rise to the same level of the specialty middle schools." The first day he met with his staff, he set that lofty goal and talked about pride and high expectations. Furthermore, he emphasized that everyone had to develop pride. If they, as a staff, put down their school, then what could they expect from students, parents, and the community?

In many ways, George Washington Carver Academy resembled Gustav Fritsche Middle School. In both cases, the schools were serving young adolescents. In both cases, the principal's pride was hurt. Both school leaders, Bill Andrekopoulos, Fritsche's principal and Molly Maloy, Carver's principal were strong-willed, determined, and proud leaders. Unmet goals and setbacks were hard for both of them to bear. Additionally, at Carver, the school's decline hurt leaders in the surrounding Black community because, as alumni, they remembered Carver when it was the most prestigious school in Waco.

Humiliating physical environments worked to dissolve pride. Fritsche's windows were so dirty you could not see out. Carver's windows had bars on them. Garbage was strewn all across the Skycrest campus. John Williams's student cafeteria reeked of melted (and spoiled) ice cream. And on and on. Teachers either ignored the neglected and disgraceful buildings in which they worked or thought it was someone else's job to clean it, repair it, and improve it. They lacked pride.

THE POWER AND POTENTIAL OF INTERNAL DISSONANCE

Our principals handled their school's internal dissonance in one (or more) of three ways. They effectively *responded* to it, *converted* it, or *organized* with it.

At Skycrest Elementary, Chris Zarzana, as a seasoned principal, knew a focus on academics would not happen until she had first restored order, established discipline, and enforced rules. This is what teachers wanted; Chris very effectively responded to their needs and requests and, in so doing, she established her credibility.

At Niles High School, the school board knew the district's high school was underperforming; however, superintendent John Huffman and his assistant, Doug Law, understood this ever-present yet elusive sense of discomfort could be tapped, especially after negative comments from students, graduates, parents, and community members intensified. Upon becoming principal, Doug converted that dissonance into a reform agenda by challenging everyone to do something about the school's disappointing data.

At Government Hill Elementary School, new principal Sandy Stephens understood the school's staff and parents were embarrassed and upset that their school was designated for closing. Consequently, she organized a solution that responded to the internal dissonance. By strengthening and expanding the new dual-language program, Sandy built on the complaints from middle-class parents who were disappointed in the inadequate dual-language program and non-English-language-speaking families who knew they were underserved.

As Frank Smith, retired chair of educational leadership at Teachers College, Columbia University contended, "You cannot get people to change unless they see the current situation [they are in] as a negative. Successful school principals generally do not create internal dissonance, but they use it, as they *create an awareness* of it" (personal communication, September 2006).

Through their studies of Chicago school reform, Bryk et al. (1998) concluded there were two major phases of institutional change. The second phase involved the reshaping of individual roles, rules, and responsibilities; however, leading to that phase is what Bryk et al. called "an initiating or catalyst phase where a dysfunctional status quo is seriously challenged" (p. 31).

Smith and Bryk et al. are saying the same thing. In their personal lives, people may not feel well but do not understand why or what can be done about it. In a similar way, schools may be ill, but immobile, until they are asked to get an examination, look at test results, be willing to take medication, and change their daily lives. In both the personal and professional arenas, internal dissonance can lead to change.

INTERNAL DISSONANCE: LESSONS TO BE LEARNED

Revolutions and watershed events throughout history have been precipitated by internal dissonance. Societies have been turned upside down as a result of internal dissonance. Startling changes in how people lived and were ruled have come about through internal dissonance.

French citizens stormed the Bastille because they had had enough. Nat Turner led a slave rebellion because he and fellow slaves were "mad as hell" and were not going to take it anymore. A group of Jews "imprisoned" in the Warsaw ghetto rose up against their Nazi oppressors because they were pushed to their limits.

Mahatma Gandhi touched the hearts and minds of millions of people in India because they resented and would no longer accept arbitrary British rule. (In turn, the British officials underestimated the degree of dissonance in India and consequently they lost their control and power.) Vladimir Lenin galvanized the discontent of the Russian masses; the Communist revolution turned Russia's economic, political, and social systems upside down.

Internal dissonance is like a time bomb waiting to be set off. When its fuse is lit, internal dissonance may cause an individual, group, organization, or society at large to seek, even embrace, change. Revolutionary leaders, through various strategies, ranging from Gandhi's nonviolence to Lenin's coup d'etat, capitalize on internal dissonance.

Failing schools have internal dissonance. The discomfort and discontent may be pervasive because there is no sense of security, order, or support. A sense of professionalism and pride may have been undermined. Regardless of the field of dissonance, people do not like being ignored, uncared for, or neglected. Consequently, the state of dissonance calls for, even demands, a response. Effective school leaders understand that condition and act on it.

While shaping and sharing a new vision for a school, principals need to first change what school stakeholders feel needs to be changed. Only then can new dreams be pursued. As Ron Edmonds, the father of the "effective schools" movement, put it, "When you insist that a school staff carry out an instruction-ally effective program without dealing with the underlying feelings attitudes, or relationships, you get destructive reactions" (National Center for Effective Schools, 1989, p. 5).

The principals of our eight change-award-winning schools were revolutionaries in their own right. They captured and channeled the internal dissonance in each of their schools and ultimately were able to bring about significant—dramatic, radical, even revolutionary—change.

16

The Catalytic Variables

External Forces

A lbert Einstein was quite intrigued with change and the forces of nature. He was the leading physicist and mathematician of his day, and he transformed the way we see the world. He proposed new ideas about the nature and transformation of light (quantum theory), the speed of light (special theory of relativity), and the relation of mass and energy ($E = mc^2$), among other groundbreaking concepts.

With the arrival of the new millennium, many recognized Einstein as one of the greatest figures of the twentieth century. Despite his fame, Einstein credited his famous predecessors, Galileo Galilei and Isaac Newton, for their groundbreaking discoveries. In a letter published by the *Manchester Guardian* in 1942, Einstein pointed to Galileo's discovery that "a body upon which no external force is acting permanently maintains its own velocity [and direction]; if it alters its velocity [or the direction of its movement] the change must be referred to an external cause" (Einstein, 2006, p. 202). Newton took the idea further by hypothesizing that acceleration "both in magnitude and direction was proportional to the force directed upon it" (Einstein, 2006 [1942], p. 202).

These laws of physics serve as a powerful metaphor for looking at change in schools. The schools profiled in this book probably would have remained stuck in their cycle of disappointment and disarray if there were no external forces acting upon them. There would have been neither a new direction nor the acceleration of a change process. These underperforming schools would have remained at rest, in a state of inertia.

THE PHYSICS OF SCHOOL CHANGE

The science of physics helps us understand how the universe operates; how things change (or do not) and what can influence a state of stasis or a state of movement. Schools, by their nature, are bound by their routines and desire for order. They will continue to do the same things year after year. Their path, their speed, and their rate of adaptation stay within prescribed parameters. They do what they do because it is what they know. Generally, schools will not move out of their regular cycle unless one or more external forces compel them to do so.

Indeed, external forces play a critical role in the school change process. Although they are outside the school, external forces are intimately linked to how a school defines itself, what it does, and how it measures its success. Individual schools do not create external forces. Schools react to them, sometimes out of choice and at other times because they must.

There are two aspects to comprehend about external forces: (1) what each means and (2) how each is generated. These are illustrated in Figure 16.1.

Two types of external forces are depicted in Figure 16.1: "push-in" forces and "reach-out" forces. The push-in forces are completely out of a school's control; school districts and individual schools react to them. The push-in category includes outside reactions to the school's condition, school choice and enrollment, state warnings and interventions, and legal issues and court orders.

The reach-out forces do not directly push at a school. These forces exist by themselves, and it is possible none of them will touch an individual school, as compared with push-in forces, which must touch the school undergoing significant school change. In a sense, reach-out forces are opportunities. Consequently, an individual school *may* (but is not required to) pursue a grant, compete for an award, create or strengthen a partnership, and/or seek charter school status.

Another thing to note is *who* is exerting or presenting the external force. As depicted in Figure 16.1, the source could emanate from the federal government; from the state government; from the school district; and, finally, from an individual school. However, the external forces could go directly to the school (often with the district office merely serving as a conduit). Consider the roles played by the community, the district office itself, and the state.

The common characteristic among all external forces is their ability to move an object, the school, which seems to be immovable. As summarized in Figure 16.2, the external force may be experienced as a form of pressure (the push-in variety) or as an opportunity, a type of magnet (the reach-out variety). As the laws of physics dictate, the quantity and velocity of the external force matter, as does the state of the object being moved. For example, mild warnings by the state to a failing school may have little effect; the arrival of state monitors with precise mandates to be completed within strict timelines is a stronger and potentially more effective push-in external force.

Figure 16.1   External forces

Figure 16.2   A comparison of push-in and reach-out external forces

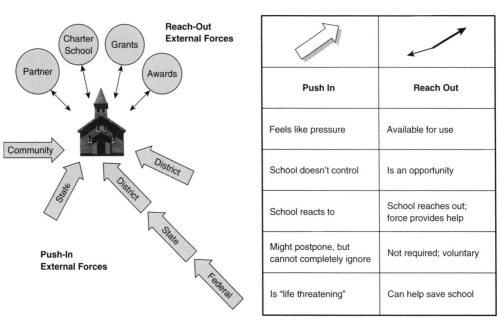

Push In	**Reach Out**
Feels like pressure	Available for use
School doesn't control	Is an opportunity
School reacts to	School reaches out; force provides help
Might postpone, but cannot completely ignore	Not required; voluntary
Is "life threatening"	Can help save school

THE RELATIONSHIP BETWEEN INTERNAL DISSONANCE AND EXTERNAL FORCES

Pushing someone to the ground could be quite daunting. However, if the individual is weak as a result of hunger and fatigue, the pushing may be easier. Additionally, if the person wants to be pushed, the task will be simpler. In our school change conceptual framework, both internal dissonance (weakened state or felt need for change) and external forces are required. Frequently, there is a symbiotic relationship between the two, as depicted in Figure 16.3.

Figure 16.3   The relationship between internal dissonance and external forces

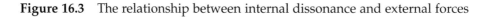

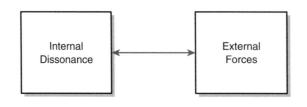

Figure 16.4   Case study of Skycrest: External force exacerbating internal dissonance

Figure 16.5   Case study of Fox Tech: Internal dissonance exacerbating external forces

On the one hand, external forces may create or exacerbate internal dissonance (see Figure 16.4). For example, at Skycrest Elementary, California's new academic achievement benchmarks were an externally imposed way to measure school success. Skycrest was ranked at the bottom, and the discouraged and disillusioned staff felt their pride further evaporate; they finally accepted that something needed to be done. An external force worsened internal dissonance.

Looking at it the other way, internal dissonance (and ineffective responses to it) can cause or accelerate an external force (see Figure 16.5). At Louis W. Fox Academic and Technical High School (Fox Tech), the staff's fear for their safety, lack of professionalism, and disregard for the worsening student achievement data could no longer be ignored. The internal dissonance had peaked; external forces had to be applied, and the school was disestablished.

As a result of his research, Conley (1993) noted that individuals in both the corporate and school worlds typically will react to a proposed change by saying, "I'm all for change—as long as I don't have to do anything differently." He goes on to emphasize that the idea of "readiness for change" is a condition that is very difficult to create. In his words, "It's hard for a company [or school] to look very closely at itself in the absence of some external challenge or threat, which precipitates an internal crisis" (Conley, 1993, p. 10).

Sarason also weighed in on this topic: "Changes in any traditional, complicated type of organization do not derive from one source. Changes always have internal and external sources that are not always compatible with each other" (cited in Fried, 2003, p. 33).

EXTERNAL FORCES IN THE AWARD-WINNING SCHOOLS

External forces, both the push-in and reach-out varieties, affected each of the eight schools in this book. As summarized in Figure 16.6, there are some patterns to discuss. First, the very nature of these schools being part of a research project looking at significant school change meant there was a set of poor and unacceptable conditions in each school.

In each case, there were strong reactions to that condition. Sometimes, the community exercised the pressure; other times, school district officials acted on their own accord or were pushed by the state to take some action. Starting in 2001, the federal government's role strengthened with the *NCLB* legislation. This external push-in force filtered down to schools by requiring the state and school district to take some action.

In half the cases (John Williams School No. 5, South Heights, Carver, and Fox Tech), the state's concern about the school's performance reached alarming levels. New York State had created a list of Schools Under Registration Review for schools that needed to be seriously restructured or lose their state accreditation and therefore their ability to stay open. John Williams was given its last warning before being placed on the Schools Under Registration Review list.

In Kentucky, the state education department set numerical goals, reflecting student achievement, for every school in the state. If a school did not meet those goals for several years, the state intervened, with a "school expert" being sent to work with the school's principal. South Heights Elementary had that experience.

Texas also had its own school rating system, based on academic achievement, dropout and graduation rates, and so on. Failing schools were given warnings and, in turn, the designated schools had to develop and implement school improvement plans. Sometimes, this went on for several years. The lack of a serious response by Fox Tech led to the state's most extreme measure: disestablishment.

The state of Texas was under its own pressure from the federal government in regard to the enforcement of school desegregation orders. The Texas Education Authority, the state education department, was assigned the responsibility of enforcing the desegregation orders. This meant strong state pressure on the San Antonio school district to change the school's conditions.

Half the schools (Fox Tech, Carver, Government Hill, and Niles) had suffered enrollment declines because a school choice program allowed families to select their schools. In southwest Michigan, there was a pilot endeavor among three high schools in adjoining school districts. One of them was Niles High School, which suffered an enrollment decrease during the pilot. In Anchorage, Alaska, the enrollment slide was so severe at Government Hill that this elementary school was slated to be closed. The failure of Fox Tech and its later revival was measured, to some degree, by school enrollment, which experienced a swing of 600 students. The enrollment issues at Carver were related to the attempts to integrate the school. When the school was perceived to be of low quality, few White families enrolled. When the school established itself as a very successful middle school in Waco, White student enrollment increased.

Carver was an idiosyncratic case, with legal issues serving as an external push-in force. The Carver case, as explained earlier, related to court school desegregation orders.

Figure 16.6 External forces that influenced the eight award-winning schools

		Govt. Hill Anchorage	John Williams Rochester	Skycrest Citrus Heights	South Hts. Henderson	Fritsche Milwaukee	Carver Waco	Fox Tech San Antonio	Niles Niles
Push-In Forces	Reactions to school conditions	X	X	X	X	X	X	X	X
	School choice/enrollment	X				X	X	X	X
	State warning/intervention		X		X		X	X	
	Legal issue/count order						X		
Reach-Out Forces	Award competition	X	X	X	X	X	X	X	X
	Grant proposal	X	X	X	X	X	X	X	X
	Partnership development	X	X				X	X	X
	Charter school application					X			

Govt. = Government; Hts. = Heights

In terms of reach-out external forces, each school took great advantage of the available opportunities to advance their change agendas. All of them applied for a grant and competed for an award. In most cases, the school also developed a partnership. Additionally, there was Fritsche's effort to become a charter school.

As for the number of external forces (combined total of push-in and reach-out) for each school, the two schools with the greatest number of forces were Fox Tech and Carver, arguably the two schools in the worst shape, with the state of Texas giving special attention to each situation.

EXTERNAL PUSH-IN FORCE: REACTIONS TO SCHOOL CONDITIONS

For the eight schools profiled in this book, external push-in forces were inevitable. When the change process was initiated in each of the eight schools, there were many reasons to push each school to change, not least of which was the abysmal record of academic achievement.

Consider the proficiency levels in the four elementary schools. In 1997, only 60% of the fourth-grade students in Government Hill could read at grade level. In 1998, at John Williams School No. 5, only 24% of the fourth-graders passed the English language arts examination. In 1995, Skycrest Elementary registered 44% who passed the SAT-9 reading examination; and, with 59% of fourth-graders passing the required reading examination in 2000, the situation at South Heights Elementary was not much better.

As for the secondary schools, in 1997, the rate of students who were reading on the sixth-grade level was 64% at George Washington Carver Academy. In 1995, 39% of eighth-graders at Gustav Fritsche Middle School were reading at grade level, whereas 28% of eleventh-graders at Niles High School and 50% of tenth-graders at Fox Tech were proficient.

When asked to describe their school before the change, administrators, teachers, and parents did not hesitate to share their views. Although there were specific conditions relevant to a particular school, some common themes emerged, which are summarized in Figure 16.7. These eight schools are in this book because they had been disappointing, dangerous, and dispirited schools. They had failed, dramatically. They had let down their students and their families. Sooner or later, reaction was inevitable.

The reactions to the negative conditions took several forms and, collectively, once aroused, these reactions built up tremendous momentum. Returning to our physics metaphor, the new external forces became strong enough to move the seemingly immovable object, the failing school. These reactions were potent, for a number of reasons.

- First, as explained earlier, the reactions fed one or more signs of internal dissonance: support, security, order, professionalism, and pride.

Figure 16.7   Sample conditions in the eight schools before the change

Category	Descriptors prevalent in the eight schools	Sample comment	Comment made at
Curriculum	Not relevant or tied to real world; no meaning; obsolete	"The kids were not buying it; we were doing something wrong."	Carver
Teaching	Boring; students listless; do what we did last year	"Students had their heads down on their desks, sleeping."	South Heights
School organization	Bright kids had different classes than other kids	"How are you going to teach those kids anything?"	South Heights
The students	Kids wanted to get out; kids just come & go as they please	"No one asked me if the kids were learning."	Skycrest
The staff	Complacent: just tell us what to do; didn't care	"You do your thing; I'll do my thing."	Fox Tech
Safety	Gang problems; lots of fights; afraid to leave classroom	"It was the school no one wanted to go to; it was out of control."	Fritsche
Physical environment	Bleak; not cared for; bars on windows; rats and roaches	"You could see the school deteriorate before your very eyes."	Skycrest
Climate	Stagnant; uninviting	"Didn't know who the principal was."	Fritsche
Culture	Students could not succeed; focus on teachers' concerns	"You had to put in your two years and then you could leave."	Government Hill
Attitudes	Negative; change will never happen; same old stuff	"It wasn't working, but who knew why? Who cared?"	Niles
School image	Always the worst; in real trouble; bad things happen; at all costs don't send your kid	"Students, teachers, parents & others viewed [Niles High School] as an unhappy, unproductive place."	Niles
Direction	No sense of vision; not goal driven; not going anywhere	"I felt everything was a façade."	John Williams

- Second, it became virtually impossible to ignore the worsening conditions.
- Third, as detailed in our discussion of state intervention, responsible parties, such as school boards and state education officials, were forced to take action.
- Fourth, the public became increasingly upset and vocal about their local schools. Where were their school taxes going? What will happen to housing values if people will not move into their neighborhoods because they are concerned about the quality of the schools? Why have promised innovative programs not been implemented?

- Fifth, school leaders were given an opportunity to raise their own hard questions. "Why must we do it this way?" (Fritsche); "Why are we here?" (Niles); "Do you like kids?" (Fox Tech, South Heights); "Can you interpret what these data mean?" (Skycrest, Fritsche, John Williams); "Are we teaching in effective ways?" (Government Hill, Carver); and so on.

EXTERNAL PUSH-IN FORCE: STATE WARNINGS AND INTERVENTIONS

A dramatic example of change leadership took place in Philadelphia in 1789, when the U.S. Constitution was written. During those proceedings, great tension and passionate arguments divided the Founding Fathers over the extent of federal power versus states' rights. A compromise was struck; some responsibilities would stay with the states, other powers would go to the new federal government. The authority to govern education fell to the individual states and, in the spirit of localism, much educational policy, procedure, and practice were left to individual school districts and their boards of education.

As depicted in Figure 16.1, external forces influencing an individual school emanate from several sources. These forces can come to the school directly from the community, school district, or state. Forces from the federal government, on the other hand, are channeled though the state because it is the state that has the responsibility for education. It is the state that ultimately decides whether an individual school should be left alone, warned about its unacceptable record and condition, or be a target for direct state action. State warnings and interventions are the ultimate push-in external force.

The state's role was particularly important in three of our eight schools. One of them, John Williams, was warned, and corrective action enabled the school to avoid state intervention. The second school, South Heights Elementary, received warnings, made serious attempts at progress, fell short, and experienced state intervention. The third school, Fox Tech, ignored warnings and, with great shock, received the ultimate form of state intervention, disestablishment, meaning all administrators and staff members were removed so the school could have a fresh start.

EXTERNAL PUSH-IN FORCE: SCHOOL CHOICE/ENROLLMENT

School choice was designed to be the means for school improvement.

In 1973, Community School District 4 in East Harlem, an economically depressed neighborhood, was considered the worst of thirty-two school districts in New York City. Only 16% of the enrolled students were reading at grade level. Truancy, dropout rates, discipline incidents, and teacher absenteeism were incredibly high. By 1987, the school conditions had been stabilized.

There was a new confidence in the district's schools. Academic achievement had soared. For example, four times as many students (64%) were reading at grade level (Fliegel, 1993, p. 3).

The decision to adopt a system of school choice had been the answer. In Sy Fliegel's (1993) words, "The decision . . . would transform a few scattered innovations into a system for innovative education, a rebellion into a permanent revolution" (p. 5).

School choice is lauded for four reasons. First, it empowers parents by giving a family a choice of where to send their children to school. Parents are no longer at the mercy of a school system limiting their educational options. The situation is quite the opposite: Parents are telling school systems the schools they will accept or reject.

Second, free market forces lead to inferior producers going out of business. Weaker schools experience declining enrollment, losing "customers" to stronger schools.

Third, a school choice system forces weaker schools to strengthen themselves. Fear of losing status and, eventually, existence (i.e., funding and jobs), motivates educators to overcome their fear of change.

Finally, the competitive atmosphere stimulates innovation. Schools re-create themselves to attract customers. Like parents, educators are empowered. They have an unusual opportunity to unleash their energies and imagination in reculturing and renewing existing schools or designing and launching new ones.

School choice drove significant school change in our eight schools in several ways. As mentioned in the last chapter, there was pride. Middle school enrollment in Milwaukee gave families a choice between their geographically zoned middle school and admission to one of three "specialty schools." For Gustav Fritsche Principal Bill Andrekopoulos, it was not declining enrollment but his school's perceived appeal and status that motivated him to push change at Fritsche. He was a proud principal who wanted his school to draw more students than the specialty schools.

In some of our eight schools the issue of declining enrollment was salient. The most dramatic case was at Government Hill Elementary, which was slated to close. Newly appointed principal Sandy Stephens used this very real threat to mobilize both school staff and parents in a drive to radically re-create their school.

In Niles, Michigan, the board of education, through wisdom or folly, volunteered to be part of a high school choice system that involved three school districts. The high school's enrollment dropped; the external pressure to change deepened. It hurt pride (internal dissonance) in the school district. It would be embarrassing enough for a school to lose students to a rival in the same district. Losing students to another school district was a hard blow.

Finally, enrollment figures served as a powerful metaphor. The San Antonio school district had fourteen high schools. As Fox Tech experienced its deep decline to become "the worst high school" in not only the district but in the state, one of the indicators was the steep drop in enrollment. The school had sunk so low in terms of safety, student achievement, and staff morale that students did everything they could to register in another of the district's high schools. On the other hand, with the upward climb of Fox Tech, enrollment increased, a sure sign the school was experiencing significant improvement. As some Fox Tech students explained, they selected Fox Tech because "it was safe, teachers helped you, and test scores were a lot better." But the students did admit that, not long before, Fox Tech had had a terrible reputation.

My research identifies school choice as an external push-in force, creating pressure on failing schools. In the case of the schools I studied, school choice systems negatively affected enrollment, which helped to accelerate a school change process. However, school choice is not a panacea. We cannot assume that, on its own, it will make a difference.

EXTERNAL PUSH-IN FORCE: LEGAL ISSUES/COURT ORDERS

> At 12:52 on May 17, [1954, Chief Justice] Warren . . . began without fanfare to read the decision of *Brown v. the Board of Education of Topeka, Kansas.* "We conclude, unanimously, that in the field of public education the doctrine of separate but equal has no place" went the Court's verdict on segregation. "Separate educational facilities are inherently unequal." (McWhorter, 2001, p. 87)

The *Brown v. Board of Education* suit had been argued before the Supreme Court by a team of Black lawyers headed by Thurgood Marshall. At the time of the Brown decision, Marshall was optimistic:

> As sure as I am sitting here . . . governmentally forced segregation . . . government discrimination because of race, creed, or color . . . will be off the books within the foreseeable future . . . Once the whole problem is laid bare and clear then democracy will take over. (Boyd, 2004, pp. 40–41)

But as Taylor Branch, Pulitzer Prize-winning historian described it, when the court

> had struck down school segregation as unconstitutional by a vote of 8–0 . . . the earth shook and then again it did not. There were no street celebrations in Negro communities . . . Southern politicians first announced that they would obey the Court and then changed their minds. (Branch, 1988, pp. 112–113)

School desegregation struck hard at the way both Blacks and Whites would view, interact, and live with each other. These changes were fought. Violent confrontations dominated the news reports of the time, with photographs of snarling police dogs, terrifying high-pressure water hoses, screaming public officials, and swinging baseball bats signaling ferocious resistance.

The history of school desegregation is a case study focusing on change. The resistance was born out of fear. It called for moving people far from their comfort zones. It involved new ways of thinking. It shook hard the perceptions and perspectives of everyone, both Black and White. It disrupted routines and challenged assumptions. It was clearly an emotional issue.

Fifteen years after the Supreme Court ruled in 1955 (in a decision since referred to as *Brown II*) that school desegregation must move with all deliberate speed, school segregation was still the norm in Texas. In 1970, the responsibility for enforcing desegregation was passed onto state education officials at the TEA.

In Waco, resistance to desegregation was incredibly strong—too strong, it seemed, to overcome. Despite the school board's announced intentions in 1955, 1962, and 1964 to end school segregation, it didn't happen. In 1970, the federal courts and the TEA pushed the Waco school board again. This time, the school board turned to George Washington Carver Academy as a means to satisfy the pressure to desegregate Waco's schools. Three plans for Carver were launched over the next twenty-five years. The three plans failed due to a lack of will, a series of ploys, or entrenched resistance. It took a magnet school plan, with an exciting and appealing program at Carver, to successfully create an integrated school.

In the history of American education, schools have been ordered by courts to change the way they educate students with disabilities and those for whom English is not the first language. Educational programs were required to be free of discrimination by race, color, or country of origin. Laws have enabled girls to enjoy the academic and athletic programs previously reserved for boys. Most recently, the *NCLB* legislation has mandated states to secure academic achievement for all students, especially those who would typically be left behind.

In many ways, laws and court decisions are the ultimate push-in external force. The story of George Washington Carver Academy is an excellent example of legislation's power *and* powerful resistance. Change eventually happened in Waco, specifically, at Carver, because an external force, a controversial court decision, kept pushing, pushing, and pushing.

On the other hand, the enforcement of court orders, as shown in the Waco case, can be endlessly delayed. In fact, some have argued that even with the fiftieth anniversary of the *Brown* decision in 2004, school segregation still exists.

Jonathan Kozol titled his 2005 bestseller *The Shame of the Nation: The Restoration of Apartheid Schooling In America*. In its first chapter, he shares an anecdote involving a teacher in Kansas City, Missouri, who taught in a school named after Thurgood Marshall. A poster in the school proclaimed "The dream is alive." However, 96% of the students were people of color; school segregation was still a reality. In this teacher's view, "Thurgood Marshall must be turning over in his grave" (Kozol, 2005, pp. 23–24). In Kozol's final chapter, he quotes civil rights leader Roy Wilkins:

Sometimes, you have to ask for something that you know you may not get. And still you have to ask for it . . . even if you don't believe that you will see it in your lifetime . . . [the] generation that comes next will . . . see it as a goal worth fighting for again . . . a segregated education in America is unacceptable. (p. 316)

EXTERNAL REACH-OUT FORCE: PARTNERSHIPS

Schools and school districts, over the last twenty-five years, have increasingly turned to external partners for advice and assistance, financial and otherwise. At the same time, the private sector, in particular, has made a greater commitment to public education. Partners have included corporations, small businesses, and chambers of commerce, as well as universities, nonprofit organizations, foundations, community-based groups, and individuals. Partnerships have centered on one specific program or project or evolved into a whole-school adoption. Sometimes, the school initiated the partnership; other times, the partner approached the school, directly or through an intermediary.

In the schools featured in this book, partnerships served as an external reach-out force for most of the schools. Probably the school that gained the most from partnerships was Niles High School. It needed to replace an outdated, ineffective, and irrelevant curriculum with an approach that would enable its graduates to pursue careers, not just secure dead-end jobs. In this pursuit, the school developed a comprehensive partnership with the Berrien County ISD, which provided funds and invaluable assistance with developing a school-to-careers program. Other partnerships involved local businesses, such as Tyler Refrigerator, the South Bend *Tribune*, and Memorial Hospital, that oriented teachers, helped develop curriculum, and provided student internships.

Like the three other reach-out external forces—awards, charter school status, and grants—no one required or mandated any of the eight schools to enter a partnership. The potential partnerships were or could become available. They were opportunities. The principals of our award-winning schools were entrepreneurial and understood how a partnership could be valuable in several ways; they seized the opportunities.

- First, partners provided funds and/or services that would not otherwise be available.
- Second, the school achieved a status it did not have before, especially if there was a competitive process. Significant school change involves winning and celebrating small victories; forging a new partnership was frequently more than a small victory.
- Third, a mutual commitment was made; the school had to meet expectations, and the partner had to fulfill its pledge. Reputations were at stake.

- Fourth, individuals outside the school invested themselves in the school; they cared about where the school was headed.
- Fifth, the school gained an external pair of eyes and one or more coaches. Partners became critical friends, able to provide a new perspective and constructive criticism. Schools were given invaluable advice; many times, the principal received informal individual coaching.
- Sixth, partners, especially partners who provided funds, wanted to see hard data and measurable outcomes, such as increases in reading scores, a higher number of students accepted by prestigious colleges, better job retention, and so on. In effect, schools had to learn how to gather, analyze, and present data.
- Finally, initiative and creativity were encouraged and rewarded. Potential partners looked for something new or different. They appreciated out-of-the box thinking, alternative approaches, and innovation.

EXTERNAL REACH-OUT FORCE: GRANTS

In our look at what helps schools to significantly change, the pursuit of grants was strategic for many of the same reasons partnerships played an important role. Funds were secured, small victories were won, advice became available, and individuals outside the school became invested in the school's success.

Seeking grants had its own special impact. To win a grant, one had to apply. This meant reviewing and describing current programs, establishing the credibility of the school and its leadership, and understanding what the grant would support and how the funds would fit into the school's agenda. Grant-makers would ask: Did the grant make sense for this particular school? What school needs would be met? What tangible gain could be measured and documented?

The Niles High School story demonstrates how the experience of applying for a grant was valuable in terms of both process and product. Both Niles superintendent John Huffman and high school principal Doug Law recognized how securing funds would serve as a victory for a school that needed to celebrate. However, more important to them was the process of creating a new program. In many ways, they didn't care about the program's details; the effect of the staff working together toward a solution would have more lasting benefits for the high school.

EXTERNAL REACH-OUT
FORCE: CHARTER SCHOOLS

Charter schools provide an option for families within a school district; they may choose a charter school instead of going to a regular school in the district. As Bierlein (1997) explained, "A charter school is a public institution that is conceptualized, organized, and eventually operated by any public or private person or organization" (p. 38).

As McMullan (1994) saw it,

> The most critical objective for advancing restructuring through charters is that it provide a clear opportunity to transform teaching practice by providing teachers with an opportunity to experiment with different approaches and with the control over time, resources, and policies. (p. 65)

There are two ways charters are formed. One is when a new school is created by a group of educators and parents or an organization, such as a nonprofit group, a for-profit organization, a government agency, a public university, and so on (McMullan, 1994, p. 65). The second way to create a charter school is to convert an existing public school; that became Bill Andrekopoulos's mission. Bill was tired of fighting Milwaukee's school district bureaucracy. He was exhausted from years of going around that bureaucracy to secure what Gustav Fritsche Middle School needed. Bill and his staff were committed to learning, piloting, and innovating, but it seemed that the Milwaukee school system, directly and indirectly, discouraged that creativity.

For Fritsche, the battle to secure charter status played a key role, because it bonded the staff, gave the school a new identity, and forced Fritsche's teachers to document and explain their current and planned innovations (and how the Milwaukee school system was blocking that effort). Perhaps most important, Fritsche's fight to become a charter demonstrated Bill's drive, determination, and leadership as well as the staff's willingness to be held accountable. In Bill's words, "The campaign to become a charter accelerated a sense of community."

When Fritsche was officially declared a charter school, Milwaukee school board member John Gardner commented, "Have you seen the Fritsche charter? It's rather rigorous in terms of what it expects from the school. I'm impressed by teachers and principals who will commit to that" (Williams, 1999, p. 1). Fritsche was not required to become a charter; it was not a push-in external force. The school, led by an extraordinarily energetic principal (who subsequently became Milwaukee's superintendent), elected to seek charter status. This reach-out external force accelerated the school's ability to significantly change.

EXTERNAL REACH-OUT FORCE: AWARDS COMPETITION

Frequently, a school does not care to or know how to look at itself; ignores "the brutal facts" (to use management researcher Jim Collins's term) when such an examination takes place; or thinks all is well, even when it is not. Consequently,

Mike Schmoker finds it quite ironic when such schools compete for and even win awards. He contends precious time is diverted from instructional improvement to completing award applications, "time that could be spent on allowing teachers to collaboratively improve lessons and assessments—which would have direct and immediate impact on student learning" (Schmoker, 2006, p. 32). Schmoker is right—and then again, he is wrong.

The National School Change Award, which the eight schools in this book won, requires valuable self-examination, using sixteen specific criteria. This activity helps schools overcome what both Elmore (2004) and Wagner (2002) call "the buffer." When schools buffer themselves, they build walls, as if their school were protecting itself from external forces that attack what the schools do. In these cases, schools proceed as usual and defend themselves from serious change. However, my research indicates that the awards nomination process helped schools to advance their change agenda.

The principals of these eight schools used award applications in several ways. The awards served as a goal, a rallying cry. The awards process was used to strengthen the staff's ability to use data, a skill that had been introduced and stressed. Frequently, awards, such as the National School Change Award, recognized the school's improvement in academic achievement and teaching and learning, validating what the school had accomplished. If an award was won, the school took the time to celebrate and recognize those who had made a difference. Meanwhile, if a school did not win the award, energy was placed in figuring out what was deficient and how it could be corrected.

As Chris Zarzana remembered,

> Skycrest had already begun receiving California Achieving School Awards when General Davies took the helm [as the new superintendent] . . . Luckily for me we started to win those awards . . . lucky for me because the staff could then see all the hard work and extra learning was getting results and they would not run me out on a rail . . . They were feeling successful and I was winning credibility.

EXTERNAL FORCES: LESSONS TO BE LEARNED

Jalilah Dobson is the granddaughter of Elijah Muhammad, the founder of the Nation of Islam, known for its militant actions in the 1960s. Arun Gandhi is the grandson of Mahatma Gandhi, the international figure who advanced the notion of passive resistance and who greatly influenced American civil rights leader Martin Luther King Jr., also active in the 1960s.

I had the unusual opportunity to bring together Jalilah and Arun in July 2006. As the two commented on the styles, perspectives, and goals of their grandfathers, stark differences were evident. Mahatma Gandhi believed in the rights and equality of all people, and in that vein he worked for India's independence and for the elimination of the caste system in India. As Arun put it, self-respect was fundamental "in a society that brought people together" (A. Gandhi, personal communication, July 12, 2006). His grandfather believed the control of India by the British had to end and that passive resistance was the only way to reach that goal. Passive resistance did not mean standing still; it was designed to provoke a reaction.

On the other hand, Elijah Muhammad, a much more controversial leader, urged separation of the races. His greatest concern centered on Black pride. In his view, African Americans were being put down and marginalized by the majority population in the United States As Jalilah put it, her grandfather believed that Black people had "to be proud and not accept the dominant, oppressive American society. They had to stand on their own" (J. Muhammad, personal communication, July 12, 2006). According to Elijah Muhammad, Americans understood only the power of violence, and ultimately African Americans had to separate from our toxic society. If attacked by Whites—physically, emotionally, or economically—Elijah Muhammad urged his followers to fight back.

Meanwhile, as Arun noted, "Grandfather would not accept violence in any form, at any time." Mahatma Gandhi believed violence was caused by anger and that anger festered due to a lack of self-discipline. Injustice, according to Mahatma, should not ignite violence. As he saw it, an eye for an eye would make the world go blind. Arun vividly remembers his grandfather's philosophy, because he spent three formative years of his adolescence living with his grandfather, who was assassinated by a known enemy who had previously attempted to kill him.

Despite the fact that Elijah Muhammad and Mahatma Gandhi were at polar opposites in many ways, they shared a common goal: to put pressure on the existing powers and change the existing conditions. Additionally, some of their tactics aligned. For example, as Jalilah and Arun agreed, both their grandfathers manipulated the media. In the 1930s, newsreels of the day captured the British beating down thousands of unarmed Indian protesters. More than twenty-five years later, television news broadcasts presented the violent, threatening, and fear-provoking reactions of Black Muslims to the injustices they faced.

Both historically important leaders used external forces to affect social change. A similar dynamic unfolded in our eight schools. As we have seen, although the principals did not initiate the external push-in forces, they used their power to their advantage and to the improvement of their schools.

17

The Catalytic Variables

Leadership

In the fall of 2005, Presidential Scholar David Gergen revisited the age-old question "Does leadership matter?" For him, the answer was obvious, as he noted:

> The 20th century taught us that progress is not inevitable. Each generation has to struggle and sacrifice to secure a better future for its children. When it fails, the world slips backward. Whether America moves forward will hinge in a significant degree upon the quality and number of those who lead. (p. 91)

THE NEED FOR SCHOOL LEADERSHIP

School reformers echo Gergen's call for leadership, if we are to "secure a better future for [our] children." As Barth (1990) pointed out, "There seems to be agreement that with strong leadership by the principal, a school is likely to be effective; without capable leadership, it is not" (p. 64). The research supports this premise. "Research findings from diverse countries and different school contexts have revealed the powerful impact of leadership on processes related to school effectiveness and improvement" (Day et al., 2000, p. 160). To be sure, although the research findings about school change vary, the leadership theme consistently emerges. "Whatever else is disputed about this complex area of activity, the centrality of leadership in the achievement of school effectiveness and school improvement remains unequivocal" (Day et al., 2000, p. 60).

REDEFINING SCHOOL LEADERSHIP

For years, school leadership was described in management terms—keep order, get the buses to run on time, clear the hallways—or in terms of the heroic figure. Times are different now. Effective school leaders, who serve as successful change facilitators, cannot afford to be just managers or to look for silver bullet solutions. They must resist modeling themselves after figures, real or imagined, who may temporarily provide dynamic, exciting, and even inspirational leadership. Today, school leadership is more demanding and dynamic. It requires a principal with a different profile.

During the 1990s, Louis and Miles completed a study of high schools in an attempt to document "not *what* is to be done, but *how* it can be done" (Louis & Miles, 1990, p. 5). They made a distinction between management and leadership by contending, "Leaders set the course; managers make sure the course is followed . . . Leaders stimulate and inspire; managers . . . translate that energy into productive work" (Louis & Miles, 1999, pp. 5–6).

For Spady (2001), leadership and change are intertwined:

> Leaders lead change—because there's nothing else to lead. If you're not leading change—moving beyond current conditions and taking your people where they wouldn't go on their own—you're administering or managing the status quo. Moreover, purposeful and lasting change doesn't happen by accident. It requires significant leadership initiative, skill, and persistence. (p. 99)

In his book *The Human Factor in Change*, Zimbalist (2005) noted that "Research indicates that change involves more than one charismatic leader charging up the hill to victory. The change process represents a complex combination of factors that, when assembled in the proper order can make reform possible" (p. 3). Consequently, if we are looking for more than a capable manager and less than a heroic figure, what do we want? In effect, what kind of leaders do we need to significantly change schools?

THE FINDINGS ABOUT LEADERSHIP

This chapter summarizes the findings about the leadership of the principals of the eight award-winning schools. These eight school leaders broke from the principal's traditional role. Their primary focus was on teaching and learning and student success. They did not accept the failure of their schools, and they created a new vision for what their schools could be. They understood change and the change process. They created a research-based learning community, were strategic, knew how to build relationships, could communicate powerful messages, empowered others, and had the courage to do what had to be done.

As Figure 17.1 suggests, at the core of a principal's work is an undeterred and unwavering concern that students are learning, teachers are teaching, and

Figure 17.1   Characteristics of successful principals

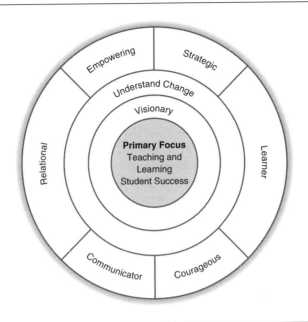

Copyright © 2008 by Corwin Press. All rights reserved. Reprinted from *Schools That Change*, by Lew Smith. Thousand Oaks, CA: Corwin Press, www.corwinpress.com. Reproduction authorized only for the local school site or nonprofit organization that has purchased this book.

there is a high level of success for *all* students. *Student success* is a richer term than *student academic achievement*, because the eight principals I studied believed the purpose of school is deeper than improved student achievement. Social and emotional growth; an awareness and understanding of social justice; and an ability to work in teams, solve problems, and think critically became important parts of the way these eight principals looked at student success.

Meanwhile, management responsibilities were not ignored, because safety, facility oversight, supervision of nonpedagogical personnel, and many other practical matters provide a foundation for schools. As our school portraits have shown, changes in instructional practices could not be addressed before discipline was restored, safety was ensured, the physical environment was improved, and so on. In the spirit of Maslow's hierarchy of needs, basic needs had to be satisfied before higher level needs could be addressed.

Wrapping around the core—the focus on teaching and learning and student success—were *vision* and an *understanding of change*. Each of the eight principals shaped and articulated a clear vision of what their schools should and could be (the product). They also had an uncanny sense of the change process, how to move their schools from where they were (Point A) to where they could be (Point B).

Drawing from and leading to the three core elements, the eight principals possessed six connected characteristics. They had a sense of when to take specific actions (*strategic*); conveyed a sense of caring and concern about other people, both children and adults (*relational*); communicated exceptionally well with individuals and groups (*communicator*); felt comfortable sharing and giving power to others (*empowering*); modeled lifelong learning and created an environment that encouraged and supported learning (*learner*); and did not waver despite opposition and obstacles (*courageous*). Although the eight principals were quite idiosyncratic in both style and personality, these six common themes emerged. Furthermore, each of these six characteristics is supported by the extensive research on organizational (e.g., school) change.

For example, Marzano, Waters, and McNulty (2005) looked at Cotton's research results, which reviewed fifty-six reports issued between 1985 and 2003 that dealt with the influence of principals on student achievement and another twenty-five reports that looked at related matters, such as student and teacher attitudes and behaviors, as well as dropout rates. Cotton used a narrative approach (similar to what I used), which looked for patterns and trends. In all, Cotton identified twenty-six categories of principal behavior that had a positive effect (Marzano et al., 2005, p. 24). The Marzano team used a quantitative study to look at sixty-nine studies completed from 1978 to 2001. Their meta-analysis involved 2,802 schools and an estimated 14,000 teachers and 1,400,000 students (Marzano et al., 2005, p. 29). They identified essential responsibilities of principals.

As summarized in Figure 17.2, there is a striking alignment between Cotton's (2003) twenty-six practices, Marzano's (2005) responsibilities, and my nine leadership characteristics.

Focus on Teaching and Learning

Conversations about teaching and the professional development of teachers are the linchpin to student success (Darling-Hammond, 1997a). If we do not focus on how students learn, then what is the point of our efforts to change schools (Elmore, 2004)? Harris et al. (2003) reminded us that the origin of the word *principal* was "master teacher," and he noted that "during the last three decades, there has been a call . . . for principals to 'return to their roots' and be more involved with the instructional program of the school" (p. 2).

On the basis of a study of 1,200 principals completed in the 1980s, W. F. Smith and Andrews (1989) contended "the direct responsibility for improving instruction and learning rests in the hands of the school principal" (p. 1). Of all the variables impacting effective schools, the role of the principal as an instructional leader was paramount. A principal who displays strong instructional leadership "places priority on curriculum and instruction issues" (W. F. Smith & Andrews, 1989, p. 8) and, in so doing, mobilizes resources, creates a supportive climate, stresses professional development, continually monitors student achievement, and models a commitment to high expectations. There is no doubt the focus is on teaching and student success as principals make their decisions about school goals, organization, use of time, ordering of supplies, and personal involvement in staff development. Even the emphasis on creating order and discipline is motivated by "minimizing factors that may disrupt the learning process" (W. F. Smith & Andrews, 1989, p. 9)

Figure 17.2   Comparing descriptions of effective principals

L. Smith's leadership characteristics	Cotton's (2003) practices	Marzano et al.'s (2005) responsibilities
Focus on instruction	• High expectations for student learning; instructional leadership • Use of student progress data • Norm of continuous improvement	• Focus • Knowledge of and involvement in curriculum, instruction, and assessment • Monitoring/evaluating • Focus, intellectual stimulation
Vision	• Vision and goals focused on high levels of student learning	• Focus, optimizer
Understand change	• Safe and orderly school environment • Protecting instructional time • Support of risk taking • Rituals, ceremonies, and symbols	• Order • Discipline • Change agent • Contingent rewards, affirmation
Strategic	• Community outreach/involvement	• Outreach
Empowering	• Shared leadership, decision making, and staff empowerment • Support of teacher autonomy • Sharing findings about student progress	• Input, communication • Flexibility • Monitoring/evaluating; focus
Communicator	• Communication and interaction • Visibility and accessibility • Role modeling	• Communication; relationship • Input and visibility • Knowledge of and involvement in curriculum, instruction, assessment
Relational	• Positive and supportive climate • Emotional/interpersonal support • Self-confidence, perseverance • Communication and interaction	• Culture • Relationship; visibility • Ideals/beliefs; optimizer • Communication; relationship
Learner	• Discussion of instructional issues • Classroom observation and feedback • Professional development • Opportunities and resources • Norm of continuous improvement • Collaboration	• Intellectual stimulation • Monitoring/evaluation • Resources • Focus, intellectual stimulation • Culture
Courage	• Self-confidence, responsibility, and perseverance	• Ideals/beliefs; optimizer

In 2001, the National Association of Elementary School Principals (NAESP) published *Leading Learning Communities: NAESP Standards For What Principals Should Know and Be Able to Do*. It noted:

> The idea of principal as instructional leader isn't new. Nor is it new to think of supporting principals in their lead teaching role. However, school leaders are thinking anew about how to define "quality" in schools and how to create and manage the environments that support it. (NAESP, 2001, p. v)

The book sets standards for principals that include formulating indicators of quality, centered on academic achievement; defining instructional leadership; setting high expectations and standards; demanding content and instruction that ensure student achievement; and creating a culture of adult learning.

Quite simply, as Hopkins (2003) noted, "the prime function of leadership for authentic school improvement is to enhance the quality of teaching and learning. 'Instructional leadership' as this approach has been termed, is about creating learning opportunities for both students and teachers" (pp. 55–56).

However, too many schools get caught up with other concerns and lose sight of their primary mission: to produce students who achieve academically and develop as individuals and to create an environment that will support the growth of both students and staff. Perhaps one of the most important common characteristics of the eight principals in this book was their ability not to be distracted from that primary mission.

To relieve state pressure to integrate Waco's schools, the school board turned to Molly Maloy and counted on her to create a magnet school that would attract both White and Black students. Molly and her staff knew George Washington Carver Academy would be able to attract an integrated student body only if the school successfully served all of its students in terms of academic achievement, social–emotional growth, and citizenship development. Molly and a core team visited other schools around the country to learn the latest middle school instructional strategies and settled on interdisciplinary instruction, which the Carver team called *odysseys*.

When seasoned principal Chris Zarzana was assigned to lead Skycrest Elementary School, she first took what she called "the kindergarten steps" of being a principal. She restored order and won the confidence of her staff. Only then did she turn to the most important focus: "reading, reading, and reading." Teachers were taught how to assess student progress, use weekly grade-level meetings to discuss each and every student, and adapt their teaching strategies accordingly. All decisions about organizing students, deploying staff, using facilities, and conducting professional development were driven by the reading achievement of the Citrus Heights students. With its dramatic reading success, Citrus Heights became a National Title I award-winning school.

Because of declining enrollment, Government Hill Elementary School was scheduled to be closed. New principal Sandy Stephens knew the school could stay open if they did a better job of teaching the many poverty-stricken students while at the same time attracting middle-class families. During the previous year, a dual-language program had been initiated for kindergarten students and first-graders, but because of the previous principal's lack of interest and support, the program was failing. Sandy led her staff in learning about such programs; converted the model; and expanded it to all grades, with students alternating a week of learning in Spanish with a week of learning in English. The new program worked, and Government Hill became the school of choice in the district.

Visionary

In the movie *Patch Adams*, a rather wise elderly man, serving as Patch Adams's mentor, raises his right hand and asks Adams (played by Robin Williams) to tell how many fingers he is holding up. The old man does not accept Adams's obvious answer of four. Instead, he asks Adams to look beyond the problem and try to find the solution. Adams suggests "eight" as an answer, and his new friend agrees, saying that is a plausible possibility. He proceeds to challenge Adams to "see what others cannot see."

Great leaders have a vision for what the future might look like. They inspire us to make that vision ours and to expend the tremendous effort needed to translate that vision into reality. As George Bernard Shaw (and, later, Robert F. Kennedy) urged, "Some men see things as they are and say, why; I see things as they could be and say, why not?" (Kennedy, 1963; Shaw, 1949).

Kotter (1996) described vision as "a picture of the future with some implicit or explicit commentary on why people should strive to create that future" (p. 68).

As W. F. Smith and Andrews (1989) saw it, "the principal articulates a vision of the school that heads everyone in the same direction" (p. 15). Lieberman (2001), in her review of several school change endeavors, noted:

> Change agents, in order to gain commitment from their clients to par-
> ticipate in an improvement project, have to provide vision for the direc-
> tion the project should take. Participants must, at some level,
> understand why they would want to involve themselves in yet another
> project. (p. 158)

Our principals had clear visions, powerful images of what their schools could be.

For Chris Zarzana, the vision centered on each and every student being able to become skilled readers, no matter their background, previous experiences, and starting points. The teachers at Skycrest Elementary had not believed that before Chris arrived. However, she was relentless in articulating her vision and showing the Skycrest staff how that vision could be achieved. The staff adopted Chris's vision; they became believers.

Bill Andrekopoulos was determined to show that Gustav Fritsche, a neighborhood middle school, without any special admissions requirements for its students, could perform as well (if not better) than Milwaukee's optional middle schools, which admitted only the highest-performing youngsters. Bill's vision centered on creating a learning community for the staff, which in turn would lead to increased student achievement. The vision was too powerful to resist, and it became a shared vision of the entire Fritsche school community.

In telling the struggle of a failing elementary school in a very tough and very poor neighborhood in Rochester, New York, Michele Hancock referred to John Williams School No. 5 as the school "where they found a body in the Dumpster, the school where a teacher was shot and killed" (L. Smith, 2005). For Michele, when she became the school's principal, School No. 5 would become a place where students learned and achieved. However, more important, the school would become a sanctuary, a place where children would feel safe and cared for. That was Michele's vision.

Understand Change

As Sarason put it,

> Initiating a change process is not for the naïve or the faint of heart. Good intentions are not enough. One must also have a relatively well-formulated conception of the obstacles ahead, as well as a time perspective that realistically assesses the strength of those obstacles. (cited in Fried, 2003, pp. 98–99)

James and Connolly (2000) echoed that sentiment: "Change in schools *is* mostly difficult and complicated. It *is not* often easy and simple" (p. 3).

According to Zimbalist (2005):

> Change is more than rearranging the furniture and schedules or replacing signs on office doors. Rather than just implementing change for change's sake, [one needs to] analyze the current condition of an organization to provide data to validate a change effort. Leaders who successfully implement positive changes in their schools have a clear understanding of the guiding principles associated with organizational change. (p. 61)

Wagner and Kegan (2006) prefered the term *reinvention* rather that the traditional term *reform*, which has a punitive overtone and

> implies that, at some point in the past, things were okay in schools, and all that is needed to return to the former state is a set of improvements that are relatively minor in nature . . . the basic assumption embedded in this definition of the challenge of change is that we already know how

to teach all students new skills, and so the problem is primarily a technical one of improving the existing system. (p. 9)

As discussed in Chapter 1, there are some pivotal and important descriptions of the phenomenon of change that impact our ability to significantly change schools. These include a reluctance to embrace change and the overt resistance it can cause. Additionally, change is generally unpredictable, nonlinear, and chaotic. It involves routines being disrupted and assumptions being attacked; it can be stressful, and it operates in the emotional arena.

Implications of reluctance and resistance. Sarason (2002) contended that little attention is paid to why people are afraid of change, that is, why they would be reluctant or even resistant to a specific change impacting them. Barott and Raybould (1998) reminded us that *"Not* is at the center of all changes" (p. 31). Change agents are telling change subjects that what was being done before cannot or should not be continued. As F. Smith sees it, "individuals will lose continuity in their lives if they cannot bridge their past to the contemporary agenda" (personal communication, June 2006). How can we not expect reluctance and resistance?

Sarason's extensive research on change motivated him to write:

> If anything is incontrovertible in the literature on educational reform, it is how difficult it is to get teachers to change their accustomed beliefs and practices. Their resistance to change should occasion no surprise. None of us likes to change. All of us in the face of change find that we like our "symptoms," that the pain associated with change appears greater than the pain the symptoms engender. (cited in Fried, 2003, p. 42)

Implications of change being unpredictable, nonlinear, and chaotic. Wagner and his colleagues at the Change Leadership Group reminded us that

> Reinventing schools and districts is awkward, hard, and messy work. Because there are no road maps, this work requires tolerance for ambiguity. Working as a team, leaders must coordinate their diverse perspectives and see the big picture of the change process. (Wagner et al., 2006, p. 138)

Uncertainty affects everyone in the change process. For the change initiators, there may be some initial high hopes and a sense that things will work. However, moving from initiation to implementation will probably involve some unplanned and unpredictable elements, causing the initiators to question whether their efforts will work. Those impacted by the change will feel uncertainty in terms of what the change will mean and how it will affect their work and personal lives. Duke (2004) pointed out that "another source of uncertainty involves not knowing what the ultimate impact of change will be" (p. 161). Furthermore, Duke advised change facilitators to expect the unexpected . . . no plan can anticipate every pothole, curve, or detour in the road to reform. For those who have experienced the change process, perhaps the greatest surprise will be for the implementation to unfold exactly as planned! (p. 163)

James and Connolly (2000) reminded us that any change will set in motion other changes unforeseen at the start of the process. In simple terms, a school operates as a system of interrelated parts. When one part is changed, it ripples through the other parts of the system.

Implications of assumptions being attacked and routines disrupted. Moving people out of their comfort zone and asking them to redefine what they believe and what they do is incredibly hard, both for those initiating the change and for those who will have to live with it.

As Sarason noted:

First, those who attempt to introduce a change rarely, if ever, begin the process by being clear as to where the teachers *are;* that is, how and why they think as they do . . . Second, those who attempt to introduce a change seem unaware that they are asking teachers to unlearn and learn. (Fried, 2003, p. 67)

Sarason (cited in Fried, 2003) calls routines *regularities* (p. 67). He described assumptions as so "overlearned" that individuals no longer question or think about them. They become second nature. If change leaders are to be successful, they must remember that they are upsetting the very fabric of who people are. Unfortunately, in most efforts, change agents focus on the outward behavior they expect (and want) to see while ignoring the underlying assumptions that give meaning to that behavior.

Duke (2004) pointed out there are two sets of assumptions that must be examined: (1) those of the change designers and (2) those of the change implementers. As he put it, "Individuals involved in the educational change process need to examine their own beliefs and assumptions about change and schools" (2004, p. 113).

Implications of change being stressful and operating in the emotional arena. James and Connolly (2000) noted that change is complex because it is linked to our emotions. Leithwood, Steinbach, and Jantzi (2002) reminded us that entering the emotional arena is daunting and dangerous. Change efforts involve what they called *emotional arousal processes,* which will provoke both positive and negative emotions among teachers.

Positive emotions include feelings of happiness, satisfaction, and enjoyment; teachers feel appreciated for their hard work (Leithwood et al., 2002, p. 103). Creating this positive emotional climate calls for frequent positive feedback from colleagues, parents, and students about the change initiatives.

This is especially important when short-term results are disappointing; positive emotions help teachers to go beyond those setbacks and move toward their long-range goals. Positive emotions also help teachers persist in their efforts.

Negative emotions are also part of the change equation. These emotions include anger about not being consulted, anxiety caused by pressure and uncertainty, annoyance at having "to do this," insecurity about their capability to do "the new thing," feeling overloaded with the additional workload, fear because they might misunderstand the new innovation, and worry about the possible negative effects on students (Leithwood et al., 2002, pp. 109–110).

The principals of the eight schools profiled in this book had significant experiences that enabled them to appreciate and understand the dynamics of change. For example, in leading and molding a summer camp staff for ten years, Doug Law came to understand that individuals had varying degrees of difficulty functioning in teams. In adjusting to his family being moved from place to place across the country, Rob Carroll learned how difficult it was to adjust to new settings and demands. In serving in the Army, where change was not the norm, Michele Hancock saw how people could get caught up in their long-established routines.

Each of the eight principals built on their personal experiences and intuitively understood that "The change process actually becomes an evolution of human dynamics within an organization" (Zimbalist, 2005, p. 57). Each of these principals appreciated human dynamics in their specific setting. Each of them brought their understanding of change to the specific challenges of their schools. Each was successful.

Doug Law took three years to lay the groundwork for change at his high school in Niles, Michigan. He understood that in his school, change had to be incremental, owned by the teachers, measurable, and celebrated. He deliberately planned experiences for the staff that would force them to recognize the need for change, confront the difficult questions, search for alternatives, select peers as leaders, and learn how to reach a consensus. He had patience as the change process experienced its natural ups and downs. He played a public role and worked in the background, providing support and guidance as needed.

Rob Carroll assumed the principalship of a school that did not believe in itself. At South Heights Elementary, students had low self-esteem, teachers felt their efforts had no impact, parents were uninvolved. Still, there was denial; staff did not understand "where they were." Consequently, although there was a vague sense of the need to change, prior to Rob's arrival, little was done. Rob realized the school needed three things: (1) It had to accept and feel the need to change; (2) it had to believe it could change; and (3) it needed a vision, a sense of where it could be. Therefore, Rob had the staff review the data; they were embarrassed and finally felt the need to move forward. Rob arranged visits to other schools so the staff could see comparable schools that had greatly boosted their students' achievement. Rob served as chief cheerleader, with posters declaring "persistence," "teamwork," and "desire." Also, Rob had his staff set goals that were a stretch, but still achievable.

John Williams School No. 5, an elementary school located in one of Rochester's worst neighborhoods, had a reputation of being unsalvageable. No one believed it could be improved. Consequently, when Michele Hancock became its principal, she took three initial steps to lay the groundwork for change. First, during the summer before her official start as principal, Michele met with small groups of staff so she could hear (and respond to) their concerns. Second, she enlisted three of those staff and, with family members, they painted the public areas of the school so that when the rest of the staff reported for the new school year they could see what could be accomplished with dedicated effort and determination. Finally, Michele mailed copies of Spencer Johnson's (1998) *Who Moved My Cheese?* to every staff member so they could understand that change, although difficult, could be embraced and enjoyed.

Being Strategic

We tend to accept the concept of being strategic when we think of military generals, football coaches, politicians, or corporate CEOs making precise plans to "win the battle and achieve victory." However, when brought to the world of education, being strategic has meant preparing strategic plans, which typically involve meetings that go on endlessly and massive amounts of paper filled with carefully crafted goals and objectives and many intervening steps. Reeves (2002) pointed out the traditional strategic planning model takes on too much and is paralyzed with too many well-meaning components, including vision and mission statements, identification of multiple needs, multiple strategies for each need, and multiple action plans. Instead, Reeves (2002) urged us to be brief, wise, and passionate about what we want to accomplish in our schools.

Jack Welch (2005) told the story of two local shops in his Boston neighborhood. Upper Crust Pizza is noisy, unadorned, cramped; its workers are indifferent. Nonetheless, the neighborhood residents, investment bankers, artists, and police officers join a line that could be twenty deep because "the pizza is to die for; you would faint just describing the flavor of the sauce, and the crust puts you over the edge" (Welch, 2005, pp. 168–169). Meanwhile, Gary Drug competes with a nearby twenty-four-hour CVS pharmacy, yet it continues to draw its loyal customers, who are greeted by name and offered advice and assistance. Upper Crust Pizza's strategy was product; Gary's was service. Both succeeded without drawing up strategic plans. Welch contended that strategic planning has been oversold and strategy is not scientific. In his view, strategy is "an approximate course of action that you frequently revisit and redefine, according to shifting market conditions. It is an interactive process and not nearly as theoretical or life-and-death as some would have you believe" (p. 166).

Being strategic involves shifting gears, when necessary. Malcolm Gladwell (2000), in his bestseller, *The Tipping Point*, told the story of Gloria Sadler, a nurse who wanted to increase awareness of diabetes and breast cancer in San Diego's Black community. Her strategy involved organizing and conducting seminars in Black churches around the city. However, fewer than 10% of the parishioners stayed after church to hear the health message.

Undeterred, Sadler changed her strategy. As Gladwell (2000) noted, "She needed a place where women were relaxed, receptive to new ideas, and had the time and opportunity to hear something new" (p. 253), and so Sadler moved her campaign from Black churches to Black beauty salons. It was a brilliant strategy, and it worked. Sadler's target audience of women was faithful to their particular hairdressers, they were a captive audience for two to eight hours, and they trusted their hairdressers and confided in her or him. As Sadler put it, "The stylist is your friend . . . it's a long-term relationship . . . it's a trusting relationship. You literally and figuratively let your hair down . . . they [the stylists] are natural conversationalists . . . they love talking to you" (Gladwell, 2000, p. 255).

Sadler thought through her strategy. She evaluated what was being done and made the necessary adjustments. Her plan worked, as more and more women changed their attitudes and had mammograms and diabetes testing.

The word *strategy* is derived from the Greek *strategos*, defined as a set of maneuvers carried out to overcome an enemy during combat (Carlson, 1996, p. 182). Dramatic school improvement does not require strategic planning but does involve planning that is flexible, contextual, and smart. It also requires being strategic by taking decisive and deliberate actions.

None of the principals of the eight schools featured in this book developed elaborate strategic plans. Neither did they seize every opportunity to accept an offer of help. Instead, they stayed focused, built on their experiences, and trusted their instincts. They were quite strategic and were no less determined and crafty as chess players, basketball coaches, or advertising executives. In these school settings, the target was school failure, and the eight principals took deliberate steps to win their battles.

Being strategic involves knowing the first steps to take and how those initial measures can lead to subsequent actions. In this regard, two common themes run through the eight school portraits. First, in nearly every case, the first step was restoring order and a sense of discipline. That strategy made sense, because the staffs at these schools were unable to focus on anything else, and the new principals were able to show they could make things happen.

The second commonality involved dramatically improving the school's physical environment. This, too, showed that the new principal cared about the children, the staff, and the school. The public areas of John Williams School No. 5 were repainted; the garbage at Skycrest Elementary was carted away; the window bars at George Washington Carver Academy were taken down. In each case, a new tone was created; a sense of determination and commitment was communicated.

In addition to these common elements, each school existed in its own unique context, and the strategic decisions were customized.

Sandy Stephens took over an elementary school that had a new, but poorly implemented, dual-language program. She strategically used a Title VII grant opportunity to create a schoolwide Spanish–English two-way immersion program. Sandy built on professional relationships she had formed the previous year when she played a major role in writing the grant proposal. She joined the teachers who were learning how to better implement an immersion program.

Sandy made sure all the necessary resources were in place. In a sense, Sandy was capitalizing on her strengths: the ability to focus on a problem, develop consensus, and create a product that benefited all constituencies.

At the same time, Sandy strategically built alliances. She knew that the school's major problem rested in teachers who would not or could not do an acceptable job in their classrooms. The teachers union could be an obstacle, blocking Sandy's efforts to improve or remove these teachers. Consequently, Sandy proudly pointed to her past union activity, relied on her past strong union relationships, and went to the Anchorage teachers union before its leaders came to her. She asked the union for its help, and these two potential antagonists became partners.

Joanne Cockrell took the worst high school in Texas and divided that large, dysfunctional school into four smaller learning communities. She hired new teacher leaders (i.e., directors) to create theme-based academies and strategically deployed new assistant principals to work with each school director. In response to poor teaching in math classrooms and a prevailing belief students could not succeed in math, Joanne gave herself a math class to teach. She strategically chose the time to do this (not in her first year) and used the opportunity to serve as a role model. It became very difficult for math teachers—and the staff as a whole—to blame poor academic performance on the kids.

Bill Andrekopoulos struggled to create a balance in his strategic moves as he reformed Gustav Fritsche Middle School. At times, Bill used reason and persuasion to secure resources for his school; other times, he went around the bureaucracy to secure approvals for exceptions to the usual policies and procedures. He figured out when to play along and when to take risks and challenge.

For example, when seeking charter school status for Fritsche, Bill made sure he was included on a team that was drafting new state regulations. With this strategic move he was able to demonstrate his resolve and credentials. When state approval for Fritsche's charter school status was imminent, Bill strategically had his staff collect (and exceed) the necessary number of signatures on the required petition; he then used that petition as a negotiation tool.

The next step in the charter approval process required that the district have a charter school process. The Milwaukee school system did not, and therefore Fritsche's quest to become a charter school could be derailed. Here, once again, there was strategic tension. Bill asked himself how much he could push the Milwaukee school board to create such a policy. Was it time to move more slowly? Bill decided to take an aggressive, almost arrogant stance. He gave the school board an ultimatum: Develop a district charter school policy within two months or else he would go directly to the state for an exception to regular procedures. Bill's strategy worked. A new, reform-minded board was elected, and it supported the Fritsche charter application.

Relational

Kouzes and Posner (1995) brought us back to our grade school report cards, which frequently commented on how well we "work and play with others."

They cited a study by the Center for Creative Leadership in which the number-one success factor in effective leadership was identified as "relationships with subordinates." Numerous other studies have emphasized being able to get along with people or rated social skills over technical skills.

Anthropologist and biologist Robert Sapolsky (1994) argued that humans, like other primates, can effectively deal with stress caused by change by having social support networks. When baboons (and humans) are on their own, they experience great stress. Interestingly, if a person is not alone and instead is with people who are strangers, his or her stress level actually increases. However, if someone is with friends, the stress response is reduced. In other words, social support networks are very important (Sapolsky, 2004).

These relational implications are critical for leaders, especially leaders who are facilitating change. Goleman, Boyatzis, and McKee (2002) took their work on emotional intelligence and translated it into a primer for leaders, *Primal Leadership*, in which he argued that we need resonant (not dissonant) leadership. Goleman et al. (2002) argued that when leaders "fail to empathize with, or read the emotions of, a group accurately, they create dissonance, sending needless upsetting messages" (p. 19). In effect, leaders need to be relational, with a strong and accurate emotional self-awareness; emotional self-control; social awareness, involving empathy and the ability to read the currents of one's organization; and relationship management, that is, understanding how to inspire, influence, develop others, resolve conflicts, and encourage people to work in teams (Goleman et al., 2002, p. 39).

In the school world, Fullan (2000) argued,

> we rarely stop to think what change really means as we are experiencing it at the personal level. More important, we almost never stop to think about what it means for others around us who might be in change situations. (p. 29)

Additionally, Fullan (2001) wrote:

> We have found that the single factor common to every successful change initiative is that *relationships* improve. If relationships improve, things get better. If they remain the same or get worse, ground is lost. Thus leaders must be consummate relationship builders with diverse people and groups—especially with people different from themselves. (p. 5)

In their five-year study of Texas schools that had improved, Huffman and Hipp (2003) noted that all schools "were diligent in their efforts to increase trust and respect and provide emotional and tangible support" (p. 570). That transformation begins with trust is the argument presented by Evans (1996), who went on to say, "Trust is the essential link between leader and led . . . it is doubly important when organizations are seeking rapid improvement" (p. 185). Leaders must be authentic. Their followers have to feel their leaders are honest, real, credible, not secretive, false, or slippery (Schwahn & Spady, 1998).

Ranking in the lowest 10% of the elementary schools in a mid-sized school district reinforces low expectations, injures relationships, and causes stress. As the new principal of John Williams School No. 5, Michele Hancock knew that student achievement could not improve unless teachers collaborated with and trusted each other and her. Teachers needed to be recognized for what they were doing right and what they had recently mastered. Michele connected teachers with each other by posting signs outside each room that announced that the teacher inside was fluent in a particular teaching method (e.g., cooperative learning). Teachers were encouraged to visit each others' rooms; Michele covered their classes. New relationships were built; new trust was created.

Doug Law had an unusual amount of time to forge new relationships and demonstrate he cared about the welfare of both the Niles High School students and staff. By initially spending only half of his time at the high school as an in-district consultant, Doug was able to build a new leadership team, which needed to learn to trust each other and trust him. Doug rejected negativity on the part of everyone involved, including himself. He created outlets so team members could express, rather than internalize, their frustrations. At the same time, Doug had an extremely open and caring relationship with John Huffman the superintendent, who in turn had a trusting relationship with the school board members.

At Fox Tech, Joanne Cockrell demonstrated her relational skills in three arenas. First, and for Joanne probably the most important, she showed the students she cared. For the student body, which had largely been ignored in the past, this made an incredible difference. Students knew Joanne's door was always open, and although Joanne was very tough, she was also fair and would listen. This principal–student relationship served as a model for the staff, who were encouraged to assume positive and supportive attitudes toward the students. The second set of relationships involved the staff. Again, Joanne was tough and demanding but also concerned and caring. Third, Joanne reached out to Fox Tech alumni and built relationships with them. They came back to the high school and shared their success stories with the students, building another set of relationships.

Communicator

For Howard Gardner, a crucial element of leadership is "the story." As he explained in *Leading Minds: An Anatomy of Leadership* (1995), "Leaders achieve their effectiveness chiefly through the stories they relate" (p. 9). They do not just tell their stories through words; they *relate* their stories; they connect with their followers. Effective leaders understand their audience and appeal to their sensitivities, needs, and aspirations.

Furthermore, leaders embody their stories; they believe in them, live them, symbolize them. We associate Martin Luther King Jr. with "I have a dream" and Franklin Delano Roosevelt with "We have nothing to fear but fear itself." Consequently, we associate King with the fight for civil rights and Roosevelt for leading the United States out of the Great Depression. Gardner (1995) went on to contend that the key to leadership is the effective communication of a story. He maintained that

> the most fundamental stories fashioned by leaders concern issues of personal and group identity; those leaders who presume to bring about major alterations across a significant population must in some way help their audience members think through who they are. (H. Gardner, 1995, p. 62)

Meanwhile, John Gardner (1990) explained:

> Most leaders become aware of the symbolic aspects of their roles and make effective use of them. One of the twentieth-century leaders who did so most skillfully was Gandhi. In the issues he chose to do battle on, in the way he conducted his campaigns, in the jail terms and the fasting, in his manner of dress, he symbolized his people, their desperate need, and their struggle against oppression. (p. 19)

Effective leaders understand that they must be skilled at both sending *and* receiving messages. They must be good listeners. As John Gardner (1990) put it:

> One generalization that is supported both by research and experience is that effective two-way communication is essential to proper functioning of the leader–follower relationship . . . Leaders, to be effective, must pick up the signals coming to them from constituents. And the rule is: If the messages from below say you are doing a flawless job, send back for a more candid assessment. (p. 26)

Bryk et al. (1998) wrote that "Given their highly visible role, principals have unusual opportunities to create the symbols, to articulate the values, and to reshape the images that can come to define how the school sees itself" (p. 101). As W. F. Smith and Andrews (1989) contended, the effective principal knows how to communicate in several different ways; with different audiences, inside and outside the school; and on different levels: one on one, in small groups, and in large groups. In their words:

> The principal as communicator has mastered confrontation and active listening skills, can facilitate the work of leaderless groups, and understands how to communicate school direction to outside forces that would move the school away from the direction the staff and principal has chosen. (W. F. Smith & Andrews, 1989, p. 15)

The principals featured in this book were exceptional communicators. They used motivational posters and photographs of students in their offices and around their schools. With the help of students, they made daily announcements that repeated school mottos, pledges, or goals. They communicated through their attitudes and actions. They modeled the behaviors they expected from staff and students. They were clear about what they would not accept. There was no doubt about what these principals believed and planned to do.

In Texas, when a school is declared disestablished, it starts over with a new principal and staff. Therefore, Joanne Cockrell had the unusual opportunity to hire the entire Fox Tech staff. Joanne was a veteran of the San Antonio school district and knew Fox Tech's culture had to be quite different from what it had been before. The "old" Fox Tech was a disaster in terms of how teachers looked at students and how students looked at themselves. Under those conditions, poor student achievement was inevitable.

As the new Fox Tech staff was hired, Joanne asked two questions during the interview process: (1) "Do you like kids?" and (2) "Are you going to watch the clock?" As one teacher put it, "Joanne was not subtle." She communicated an essential, much-needed, and powerful message.

Rob Carroll was determined to make South Heights Elementary a place where kids would feel love and believe they could be somebody. Rob communicated that message in many ways. He told the staff the school was to be child centered and that if they could not embrace that point of view, they could leave. Rob hung signs on the walls and from the ceiling that prominently recognized staff and student accomplishments. He left each day with sore arms caused by dozens of hugs wrapped around students who needed some attention.

The first time I met Molly Maloy was on a May evening in 2001, when I arrived at the Waco airport. Over dinner, she was, quite naturally, proud of her school and the award it was receiving. However, because she did not know me, she had many questions and wanted to know who I was. Her demeanor and tone told me she was a no-nonsense leader. Molly was tough. This first impression was not wrong. The next day, at George Washington Carver Academy, it was evident Molly was in charge. Although the staff appreciated being empowered, they also talked about Molly's messages: The students came first, instruction had to be meaningful, school rules were to be followed, parents would be respected. Molly lets people know she is all business. In private, and over time, Molly's hard edge was modulated, but the messages never wavered.

Empowering

James O'Toole (1999) wrote that we tend to look at leadership using personality adjectives, as if we have had our unconsciousness indelibly inscribed with "the image of George Washington astride his powerful white steed." O'Toole contended that "we got it wrong" when we saw leadership in terms of the "Great Man" theory. He argued for "cascading leadership" in which "a strong leader at the top empowers other leaders down the line" (p. 160).

Tichy (1997) made the same point when he argued that

Winning companies win because they have good leaders who nurture the development of other leaders at all levels of the organization. The ultimate success for an organization is not whether it can win today, but whether it can keep winning tomorrow and the day after. (p. 5)

Among John Maxwell's (1998) *21 Irrefutable Laws of Leadership* is "the law of legacy." To illustrate the concept, Maxwell used the story of Roberto Goizueta, a Cuban immigrant who rose from working as a bilingual chemist to become the CEO of Coca-Cola. Under his leadership, Coca-Cola became the second most valuable corporation in America. When Goizueta died in 1997, some expected panic among the company's employees and stockholders. There wasn't any, because Goizueta had left a legacy in the form of a very strong organization and a new generation of leaders whom he had empowered during his stewardship.

Doug Law took a behind-the-scenes role as he moved his high school forward. He resurrected a school leadership team that previously had existed on paper only. He had the team look at the school's problems: a high ninth-grade dropout rate, the inability of graduates to get jobs, and graduates flunking out of college because they were unprepared. Doug did not solve the problems; the school leadership team was empowered to figure out the solutions. Doug eventually left the team discussions and emphasized that the leadership team had to "own" the solutions they would implement.

The history of George Washington Carver Academy was filled with hope and disappointment. At one time, it had been the pride of the Black community, then allowed to decline; it was the school district's response to a desegregation order; the flawed plan failed. As principal of this middle school, Molly Maloy was a leader who wanted to be (and was) in charge of the school's revival. However, she realized she could not do it alone; she had to empower others. Consequently, she "let go" in three ways. First, she formed a planning team, whose members had an equal voice in deciding the school's focus and curriculum design. Second, the team hired the new teachers. Third, once grade-level teams were formed, those teams assumed the responsibility for selecting and planning themes, lessons, and activities for the new interdisciplinary units. The George Washington Carver staff "owned" their new school.

At Skycrest Elementary, the staff did not have, and did not want, empowerment. The chaotic state of their school was something they complained about but did little to correct and improve. Although they were angry at the lack of power and authority demonstrated by the principal, they were not willing to assume responsibility for improving the climate and environment. They wanted someone else to take care of things; they wanted a strong, decisive, and effective leader. They got it with Chris Zarzana, who took charge and empowered the staff at the same time. Chris enforced the new rules formulated by the staff, creating a sense of order and discipline. Meanwhile, Chris empowered teachers in the most important way. She taught them how to assess their students' progress and to make decisions, based on their assessments, about what and how to teach. The teachers drove the instructional program.

Learner

Elmore (2004) argued that "The premise that educators know what to do and all they need are the correct incentives to do it is essentially wrong. *Some* educators know what to do; *most* don't" (p. 241). Whitaker and Moses (1994) argued that "We need to build school structures that ensure that continuous learning and development are integral parts of the culture" (p. 52).

Senge's (2006) learning organization concept is predicated on continual learning. Hargreaves, Earl, Moore, and Manning (2001) argued, "Strong collaborative cultures and collegial relations . . . provide essential supports for implementing effective and sustained changes" (p. 169).

The principals featured in this book modeled learning and created research-based learning communities.

Bill Andrekopoulos was a voracious reader, with an inquisitive and curious mind. He loved to ask questions and prod others to do the same. He distributed articles, led field trips to other schools, and encouraged new ideas. The staff of Gustav Fritsche Middle School engaged in action research, translating their findings into new or revamped policies, practices, and procedures.

At first, William Glasser's name meant nothing to Molly Maloy and her new core team at George Washington Carver Academy. They heard him speak and read his book on choice theory. They dug further, discovered related research, invited Glasser to their school, and used his research-based ideas. Discipline issues disappeared, and a new understanding of young adolescents helped to drive additional reforms.

For Rob Carroll, once he became the principal of South Heights Elementary, learning unfolded in four ways. First, he continued to read, books like *Leading Change* by John Kotter (1996) and *Shaking Up the Schoolhouse* by Philip Schlechty (2004). Second, he searched for films, quotes, and symbols he could use to convey messages of hope, determination, and persistence. Third, he learned on the job when to be subtle and when public actions were more appropriate. Finally, he learned from the state intervention in his school. Many principals would become defensive and reject outside help, especially if it were sent by the state and the person "lived" in the school. Rob Carroll was different. When the state intervention was announced, Rob was disappointed, but nonetheless anxious to learn from Susan Higdon, the "highly skilled educator" sent by the state.

Courageous

In 1956, while recovering from major back surgery, John F. Kennedy wrote *Profiles in Courage*, in which he argued that leadership is built on the courage to stay the course, no matter the obstacles and opposition. Kennedy recounted the stories of Daniel Webster, who sacrificed personal political ambition to forge a compromise that postponed the Civil War for a decade; Sam Houston, who lost power and popularity for his refusal to endorse Texas's entry into the Confederate States of America; and Edmond Ross, who did what he thought was right, as he resisted tremendous pressure and deadly threats in the battle for his vote to impeach President Andrew Johnson. Ross refused to buckle under (Kennedy, 1956).

Trevor Coleman, then a civil rights reporter for the Detroit *Free Press,* had the opportunity, in 1991, to meet Rosa Parks, whose brave actions in 1965 triggered the Montgomery bus boycott, a watershed moment in the civil rights movement. Parks told Coleman, "I was just tired of being humiliated . . . I didn't like the way we were always being pushed around and humiliated by segregation laws." Coleman noted, in his retrospective commentary shortly after Parks died in October 2005, that people forget that Parks not only defied the law but also risked her safety because she faced down two healthy men: the bus driver and the man to whom she refused to give a seat. Coleman noted, "She literally could have been killed for her act of courage" (*Albany Times Union,* October, 15, 2005, p. 5).

Tichy (1997), in *The Leadership Engine,* wrote about *edge* meaning the capacity to make tough decisions, to give people honest feedback, to be unpopular. In his words, "Essentially, edge is having the courage of one's convictions. It is the willingness of a leader to make a decision and to take principled actions when others would do nothing . . . Edge is the refusal . . . to let difficulty stand in the way of acting on one's deeply held ideas and values" (p. 187).

Heifetz and Linsky (2002), in *Leadership On the Line: Staying Alive Through the Dangers of Leading,* pointed out the risks of being strong and decisive. In their view, every day you put yourself on the line: "You disturb people when you take unpopular initiatives . . . put provocative new ideas on the table . . . question the gap between colleagues' values and behavior . . . face up to tough realities" (pp. 2–3). In effect, "exercising leadership can get you in a lot of trouble."

Courage becomes a critical element of leadership in the school world. Heckman titled his 1996 book about schools *The Courage to Change: Stories From Successful School Reform.* According to Heckman, in education, courage means setting a new priority in looking at every aspect of what anyone does or thinks in classrooms. This essential examination and inquiry "requires courage—courage to question and override the ambiguity that arises when one questions what has seemed so normal" (p. 12).

Wagner and Kegan (2006) called highly effective school leaders "creative noncompliers" (p. 15) because they do not let "the system" dictate what they do or limit the innate creative possibilities of schools. However, this is risky. The principals profiled in this book had the courage to face the brutal facts; tell others what they did not want to hear; stick to their principles; and overcome a vast array of attacks, barriers, and obstacles. They had the moral imperative and the strength to do what needed to be done. They put their jobs, reputations, and safety on the line.

At South Heights Elementary, Rob Carroll became tired of and frustrated with the negative staff members in his school. At a staff meeting, he announced that the school was all about change and that if anyone were uncomfortable with that commitment, he would find them an assignment at another school. The next day, Rob arrived at his office and discovered a punched-out hole in the wall above his desk. Rob ordered the hole to be left alone; he was not going to be deterred from turning around his school.

When Doug Law became the principal of Niles High School, he asked the superintendent for fourteen "late starts," which meant the students would miss three hours of school for fourteen consecutive Wednesday mornings so the staff could have the opportunity to develop new programs. The superintendent agreed. However, the staff's planning stalled, and it looked like the valuable and "expensive" planning time would be for naught. Doug told his staff that *his job* was at risk. If the staff did not create a more responsive and successful school, then it would be Doug Law who would go. The Niles staff respected Doug's candor and courage and reached agreement on a set of new programs. The school drastically changed, for the better.

Joanne Cockrell's "drives around the neighborhood" were risky, but student centered. Joanne rode the streets picking up truants, scaring away hoodlums, and calming neighborhood storekeepers and residents. She toured the neighborhood so she could protect her kids and defend her school's reputation. Joanne was determined no one was going to hurt her kids. No one was going to throw away his or her future because of some random act of violence. No one was going to bring the Fox Tech name back into the mud. None of those things would happen if Joanne Cockrell had anything to do about it.

The eight principals exercised leadership and, in so doing, they acted in the spirit of what John Gardner (1990), in his book *On Leadership*, stressed:

> Some define leadership as leaders making followers do what *followers* would not otherwise do, or as leaders making followers do what the *leaders* want them to do. I define leadership as leaders inducing followers to act for certain goals ... values ... motivations ... wants ... needs, ... aspirations, and expectations—*of both leaders and followers.* (p. 19)

I would add one element to John Gardner's equation. Our eight principals did make decisions reflecting *their* wants, needs, aspirations, and expectations— and those of their *followers*: teachers, students, and parents. However, the focus and the purpose were special: Creating schools that dedicated themselves to the growth and achievements of the students and adults, schools that unleashed the creative energies of all.

In a sense, the eight principals were heroic, but they were much more. They exercised leadership in ways that were a departure from the traditional interpretation of school leadership. They never lost sight of their goal: meaningful teaching and learning tied to student success. They articulated a vision, a firm sense of what their schools could be. They understood how to facilitate change. They were learners, strategic, empowering, relational, communicators, and courageous. They made a difference. They created successful schools.

PART VI

Creating Meaning

Have you ever seen a finished picture? A picture or anything else? Woe unto you the day it is said that you are finished! To finish a work? To finish a picture? What nonsense! To finish it means to be through with it, to kill it, to rid it of its soul, to give it its final blow: the most unfortunate one for the painter as well as for the picture.

true &
Sad

—Pablo Picasso

Have the nerve to go into unexplored territory. Be brave enough to live life creatively. The creative is the place where no one else has been. You have to leave the city of your comfort and go into the wilderness of your intuition. You can't get there by bus, only by hard work and risk and by not quite knowing what you're doing. What you'll discover will be wonderful. What you'll discover will be yourself.

—Alan Alda

"It was much pleasanter at home," thought poor Alice, "when one wasn't always growing larger and smaller, and being ordered about by mice and rabbits. I almost wished I hadn't gone down that rabbit hole—and yet—and yet—it's rather curious, you know this sort of life! I do wonder what can have happened to me!"

—Lewis Carroll, *Alice's Adventures in Wonderland* (1865/1998)

Change involves reflection. It calls for a time to consider where we have been, where we are, and where we want to be. Even more important, it requires thinking about how we will get there. The stories of the eight schools featured in this book embraced that level of thinking and that course of action. They refused to accept where they were and what they were. The four elementary schools in Anchorage, Alaska; Henderson, Kentucky; Rochester, New York; and Citrus Heights, California, worked hard to keep alive the sparkle in each child's eyes. The secondary schools in Waco and San Antonio, Texas; Niles, Michigan; and Milwaukee, Wisconsin, understood they needed to better align their schools with the needs of adolescents and prepare them for their future. They created relevant schools.

Points to ponder:

- As you see it, what are the five most important lessons about significant school change suggested by this book?
- What makes some people cynical about schools significantly changing?
- There have been recent research interest and practitioner concern about the sustainability of school change. In your opinion, what does it take to sustain significant school change?

18

The Lessons We Can Learn

In 1999, when my students and I created the National School Change Awards, we did not know what to expect. Would the word go out? Would schools effectively apply the sixteen criteria to evaluate whether they had significantly changed? Would they be able to use data and documentation to make a strong case? That first year, in the spring of 2000, we were very pleased to receive sixty-two nominations, from seventeen states. We screened those to twenty-four finalists and invited a national panel of judges to a daylong session at Fordham University.

During that first judging session, thirty judges sat in one large room, working diligently in triads and arguing about each nominee: Had the school thoroughly described the "before" and "after" stages? How long had the "after" stage been in existence, that is, was this improved school condition temporary? Was there sufficient data to support their case?

After two hours, one judge raised his hand to pose a question. I wondered what his question might be; perhaps he wanted to know what the winning schools were going to receive or whether he could attend the ceremony. Instead, he paused and said, "How do we know these schools are telling the truth?" I paused and quietly responded, "I suppose we will have to assume they are."

The second scene of this anecdote took place two weeks later. I was sitting on an airplane leaving New York City's LaGuardia airport, bound for Detroit, Michigan. Frank Melia, one of the doctoral students who created the award, and I were on our way to conduct the first award ceremony at Niles High School, in Niles, Michigan. As we were on the plane waiting for takeoff, I turned to Frank and said, "Frank, I'm afraid." He replied, "Lew, are you scared of flying?" I said, "No, but, what if we made a mistake in selecting one of the winning schools?"

We didn't. Not once.

IT CAN BE DONE!

Dr. Susan Sclafani, Assistant Secretary of Education, represented the U.S. Department of Education at the 2005 presentation of the National School Change Awards. In her remarks, she congratulated the six winning schools on their momentous achievement. She told them:

> You are not just doing this for the children you serve. But, you're doing this as an exemplar for schools across America. You will probably find lots of people coming to visit you and all you have to say is you can do this, too, and give your children the quality of education they deserve.

The schools nominated for the National School Change Award completed miraculous work. They converted themselves from unacceptable to adequate to exemplary. The culture in each school changed; the way adults viewed and treated students changed; the willingness to take risks and try new things changed. A new sense of trust was born. Questions were raised about how students were taught and assessed, how the school's schedule was designed, how discipline was handled. These schools became concerned with student achievement and the growth of staff members. They looked at outcomes and developed strategies to reach higher expectations. They reached out to parents and involved external partners. They became exemplars.

THE RESEARCH PROCESS

One basic question cried out for investigation: How were the change-award-winning schools able to significantly change when most school cannot or will not?

In the first eight years of the change awards, 2000–2007, 601 schools, from forty-four states, were nominated for the National School Change Awards. Twenty-four finalists were selected each year, for a total of 192; six winners were chosen each year, for a total of forty-eight. All 192 finalists were formally recognized; their nominations were impressive, and in the eyes of the national panels of judges, all 192 were winners. Each of the forty-eight winning schools was honored at both a national ceremony and a local ceremony at its school.

I conducted the local ceremonies and had the opportunity to visit each winning school, meeting students, teachers, support staff, school administrators, district administrators, parents, community supporters, school partners, and state education officials. I was able to experience the rhythm of the school, observe classes, review documents, get a sense of how the school operated each day, watch adults interact with other adults and with students, interview individuals, conduct focus group discussions, and so on. I selected eight of these schools for deep, intensive, and comprehensive portraits. In these cases, I made multiple visits to each school.

As the visits to school winners took place each year, and return visits to the eight schools of this book were conducted, I developed new ways to conduct focus groups, including the use of drawings. I probed deeper in the interviews; I built on the mutual trust established between the school stakeholders and me.

I had dinners with principals and their spouses. I shared a glass of wine with school leadership team members. I convened groups of parents after the school day. I asked students to tell me the best things about their school. In one case, I frightened a group of high school students by asking them to think about their principal leaving the school. They became upset until I explained that she was not leaving. I just wanted to know what qualities they wanted in a new principal (when, in the distant future, the current principal retired) and what advice they would give to this new principal.

THE CONCEPTUAL FRAMEWORK

Each school's story was idiosyncratic. No two schools were alike. The key players had different backgrounds; the local settings posed different challenges; the sequence of events was never the same. However, certain themes did emerge. I summarized those findings, and each year I presented them at national conferences. Researchers and practitioners around the country discussed them, as did graduate students in leadership courses.

Although the portraits of the eight schools profiled in this book illustrate the conceptual framework I developed (see Figure 18.1), the visits to all forty-eight schools validated my findings. All these schools were better understood through the lenses of context, capacity, and conversations. All were impacted by three catalytic variables: (1) internal dissonance, (2) external forces, and (3) leadership.

Figure 18.1   The conceptual framework

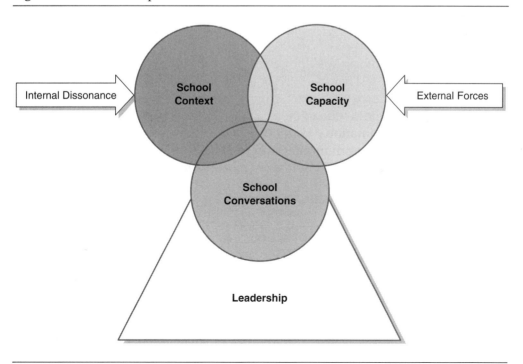

THE THREE ESSENTIAL ELEMENTS

Three essential elements—context, capacity, and conversations—emerged in every school portrait and exist in all organizations.

Context involves culture, climate, messages, and physical environment. It wraps around a school in terms of defining the setting and understanding how human actions and reactions are unfolding and impacting a particular school. The context could be healthy, or toxic, or somewhere in between. The context could be long standing or have a relatively new configuration. The context may need to change in very significant ways.

Changing the context takes time; we cannot merely announce that tomorrow we will adopt new beliefs, as wonderful as they may appear to be. Neither one person nor one single action changes the context. However, deliberate actions can reshape the context through reculturing, changing the climate, conveying new messages, and improving a school's physical environment.

Capacity refers to what individuals and organizations are capable of doing. For our purpose, there are five interrelated capacities: to (1) teach, (2) assess, and (3) plan, coupled with the capacity to (4) learn and (5) work in teams. Capacity is best seen as "degrees of capacity." For example, on a scale of one to ten (with ten being the strongest) one can ask, "What is the team building capacity of individuals in a particular school?" Additionally, we need to determine who is measuring the capacity; the tools with which each of the five capacities are being measured; and what will happen as a result of our new insights about a school's capabilities.

As for *conversations*, we need to appreciate what conversations currently take place in the school—and why. Then, we need to carefully think about how we initiate and sustain new conversations and how we align these conversations with the needs, desires, and dreams of school stakeholders. New and meaningful conversations will not take place because the leader wants them; those having the conversations must feel the conversations are relevant.

When we look at context, capacity, and conversations as a set of three essential elements, there are five lessons to be learned if one is to be successful at leading significant school change.

First, school and school district leaders need to fully understand the three overarching concepts. *What do we mean by each?* How do these three essential elements—context, capacity, and conversations—help define any school? How can we use all three to gain a better understanding of the past, current state, and possible future of a school?

Second, *how are these three elements functioning in a particular school?* What is the context—culture, climate, environment, and messages—in the school? At what level is the school's capacity, in terms of planning, teaching, assessing, and working in teams—and, most important, what is its capacity to learn? To what degree are conversations taking place about the students, teaching and learning, the school's vision, and school's progress?

Third, *what can be done* about each of these three essential elements? What aspects of the context can be the starting point for facilitating change? Which

Figure 18.2   The three essential elements of school change

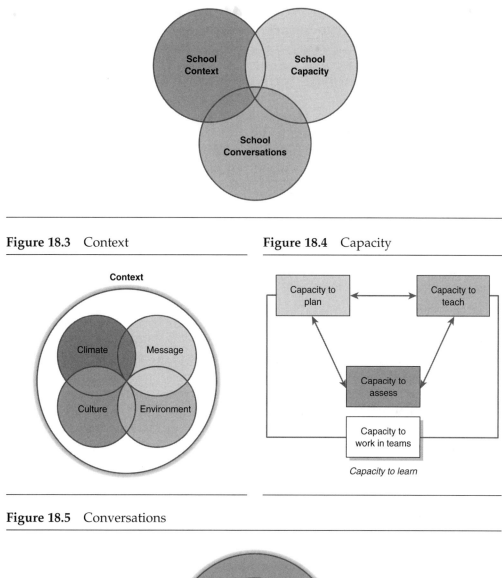

Figure 18.3   Context

Figure 18.4   Capacity

Figure 18.5   Conversations

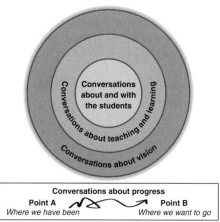

capacity needs the most strengthening? What are the first conversations to initiate, and how should they be initiated?

(4)   Fourth, *the three elements are interrelated,* supporting or negating, stimulating or denying, reinforcing or blocking each other.

(5)   Fifth, and most crucial, *all three essential elements must change.* Significant change in any organization (e.g., failing schools) will not take place unless we dramatically change the context, markedly improve the capacities, and widen and deepen the conversations.

THE THREE CATALYTIC VARIABLES

Three catalytic variables are at work: (1) internal dissonance, (2) external forces, and (3) leadership (see Figure 18.6). For schools to significantly change, all three of these variables need to be understood, appreciated, and leveraged.

Internal dissonance is already in place; it reflects the current conditions in a specific school (see Figure 18.7). It may be manifested as a concern about security, order, support, pride, and/or professionalism. We do not create internal dissonance; we inherit it. We observe it, understand it, and try to convert it into a positive force.

There are important questions to ask about internal dissonance. How important is the dissonance to school stakeholders? Is it painful to anyone and, if so, to what degree? What outcomes (i.e., benefits) can we expect if the dissonance is alleviated?

The change leader can use internal dissonance as a catalyst by addressing the concern in a number of ways: exacerbating the condition (within reasonable bounds); increasing awareness of the dissonance, both within and outside the school; providing a solution; and/or leading the staff in the collective development of a solution.

External forces exist (see Figure 18.8). Some of them, the push-in variety, are initially out of our control. For example, in every failing school the immediate push-in force are reactions to the unacceptable conditions. School stakeholders and authorities (state and district) no longer accept inferior outcomes. The second push-in force is school choice, which allows families to select their schools; the enrollment in failing schools drops. The third and fourth push-in forces come from beyond the local community. The state has the ultimate power over schools; its warnings and intervention have great impact, as do legal issues and court decisions.

In looking at the push-in variety of external forces, we need to consider the strength and breadth of the force. How powerful is it? Is it a force that had existed and been ignored, such as a state warning? Who is applying the force at this time, and why?

The reach-out external forces involve the school reaching out for resources and rewards, assistance and awards. Applying for a grant, competing for an award, developing a partnership, and applying for charter status will, for a number of reasons, support the school's quest to significantly change. The questions we need to ask include the following: Who is encouraging the school to take advantage of one of these opportunities? What benefits will be secured? Will there be any dangers caused by, for example, a repeated failure to secure a grant or award? Will seeking the opportunity drain time and energy better spent in other endeavors?

At the fulcrum of my conceptual framework sits leadership. Although the literature and research findings about organizational change, especially in the corporate and school worlds, is complicated and sometimes contradictory, one notion consistently emerges: Leaders make a difference. What this book offers is a new way to look at change agent leadership, leadership that enables a school to move from failure to success.

The principals of the eight schools possessed nine distinct qualities: (1) an unwavering focus on teaching and learning and student success, (2) an ability to develop and articulate a vision, and (3) an understanding of change. Additionally, these leaders were (4) strategic, (5) relational, (6) empowering, (7) learners, (8) communicators, and (9) courageous. As displayed in Figure 18.9, these qualities fit together like pieces of a puzzle and they work in tandem with each other.

For example, the creation of a learning community (learner) calls for sharing responsibility for learning among many people (empowering), and moving in that direction, despite opposition and resistance, takes a strong will and perseverance (courageous). In reflecting on the three catalytic variables, internal dissonance, external forces, and leadership, it is leadership that is most in our control. We can teach leadership, we can develop leaders, we can assign talented leaders to turn around failing schools as they bring about significant school change.

CONSTRUCTIVISM

Constructivists believe learners should construct their knowledge, discover and create it rather than having it force-fed to them. This is not to say that there isn't a body of knowledge that is valuable and serves as a foundation for learning. Constructivists take the position that, if properly guided and coached, learners can discover that knowledge and in the process, develop research, critical thinking, assessment, and decision-making skills. Furthermore, when working in teams, the search for answers and solutions builds the ability to review data, analyze findings, compare theories, communicate, persuade, reach consensus, and plan.

The three essential elements of my conceptual framework—context, capacity, and conversations—are built on constructivism as a learning modality. In the eight school portraits, although strong leadership was evident, individuals and teams were encouraged to discover the solutions. Operating in this manner promoted the idea of a learning community, enabled school stakeholders to

Figure 18.6   The three catalytic variables of school change

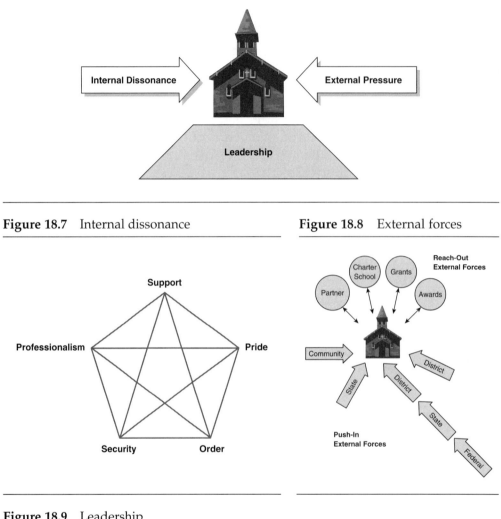

Figure 18.7   Internal dissonance

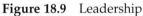

Figure 18.8   External forces

Figure 18.9   Leadership

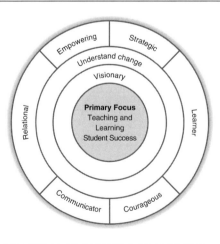

reach beyond what they already knew, created new synergy, developed more accomplished teachers and leaders, and stimulated a sense of ownership.

In reacting to the external push-in forces, new practices had to be developed, because the old ways had not worked. This was a constructivist approach involving reading, research, school visits, discussion, planning, and so on. Meanwhile, by their very nature, the reach-out external forces required the schools to construct something new—funded by a grant, recognized by an award, created in a charter school structure, or facilitated through a partnership.

TRAPS TO AVOID

Dangers lie ahead for those of us who choose to be agents of change; there are dozens of traps to avoid. I will review ten examples in the hope you will do three things. First, add to the list. Second, decide which traps are most likely to exist in your particular school's change journey. Third, think about what you will do to avoid them.

Trap No. 1: If you think this is a cookbook, go back to the bookstore.
Although I did not know what conclusions and recommendations I would eventually pose, I did understand one thing. I was not writing a cookbook. There would be no step-by-step, neat, and logical process. It would be more complicated than adding several ingredients together; four tablespoons of leadership, mixed with two cups of new teaching methods, baked in an oven for three years. There would not be one superior recipe perfected in test kitchens.

Trap No. 2: If you're arguing whether it's product or process, you lose.
Imagine two armies of school reformers facing each other on the battlefield of school change. The "Product Army" displays banners that attack their opponents; banners that say, "You're all talk, no action"; "Process yourselves to death"; "We will have to wait forever for a solution." Not to be outdone, the "Process Army" shouts out their slogans: "It's not what, but how!"; "Today's product will be history by tomorrow"; "The journey is the critical piece."

With their rallying cries, each army does not yield an inch. Finally, they charge at each other. After a fierce clash, the dust clears, and there is silence. Both armies of reformers lie exhausted on the ground. A third group appears, smiling at the fallen troops. It is this third contingent that has won. One of the felled reformers looks up and asks, "Who are you?" One of the strangers responds, "We are the status quo."

Trap No. 3: If you're future focused, you've got one third of it right.
Those who lead school change have three areas of concern that must be addressed. Only one will not do. Change, of course, implies getting to a new place. Therefore, we need to agree on a destination (Point B). However, there is an activity that must happen simultaneously, which is understanding where we are at the moment (Point A). In effect, we need to know where we are before we

can determine why the new destination is appropriate for us. The most important concern is the journey, how we will travel from Point A to Point B.

Trap No. 4: If it's quick and easy, consider it a failure.

Superficial change—clean the graffiti, post security guards at every entrance, install new computers, and so on—can be done quickly. These changes may be important and, if connected to a strategy for substantial changes, they can help the change process. However, significant change will take place only if the graffiti removal is part of a strategy to improve the climate; if the security guards fit a comprehensive plan to make people feel safer and more secure so they can pay more attention to teaching and learning; if teachers and students are taught how to use the new computers in meaningful ways. These substantial versions will take a great deal of time. In fact, researchers and reformers estimate that three to five years will be needed to significantly change a school, with high schools taking an additional two years.

Trap No. 5: If it's not broken, break it.

Dramatize what is wrong. Better still, have the school stakeholders discover what is broken. Make them face the brutal facts.

There is the story of a new principal, assigned to a failing school. She inherited a staff that did not face the unacceptable conditions; they pretended those conditions did not exist or felt it wasn't necessary to do anything.

At a staff meeting, the new principal distributed packets of data to each and every person. The data summarized their students' achievement in math and reading over several years and in comparison with schools with similar student populations. She included the state standards and the average scores of students across the state. The principal organized the staff into groups of six and asked them to do three things: (1) summarize what the data showed, (2) decide the implications, and (3) suggest what their school could do. She then said, "I'll be back in an hour." When she returned, it was clear a new conversation had begun.

Trap No. 6: If it appears one dimensional, it's not.

Some of us buy homes that need major renovation. It's more than fixing a leaky roof. If we're lucky, perhaps we do not need to build a new foundation, but only shore it up. However, in our house there are other important issues. The electrical and plumbing systems must be replaced. We do need a new roof, not just some patches. The appliances and fixtures are obsolete. The walls need painting but many of them need to be replaced and then painted. The previous owners had let the building slide into a state of such disrepair that some of our friends, colleagues, and housing experts suggest tearing it down and starting over.

So it is with schools. Fixing the leaky roof is not enough. Schools are not one dimensional. There are five dimensions that need to be understood and addressed: (1) instruction (teaching and learning), (2) organization, (3) governance, (4) accountability, and (5) culture.

Trap No. 7: If everyone likes it, you haven't changed it.

Few people welcome anger and conflict. Strong emotions are intimidating. Everyone likes to be liked. But real change, meaningful change, substantial change, requires disruption and discomfort. Routines will be broken and assumptions will be challenged.

Consequently, not everyone will support what change agents want to do. Some will resist as if their lives depended on it. And, in many ways their lives, both professional and personal, are being threatened. They are being told, in subtle or overt ways, that what they have been doing hasn't worked. If their school is being labeled a failure, what does that say about them?

Returning to the American Revolution metaphor presented in Chapter 1, about one third of the school's stakeholders will welcome a significant change, and about one third will not be sure but potentially could be won over. However, one third will oppose the proposed changes, either with passion, stubbornness, or apathy. Some of these individuals will never adjust and will be so uncomfortable with the new culture they will want to leave, either on their own accord or with encouragement. Let them go.

Trap No. 8: If you're taking the credit alone, the change won't last.

A new leadership model has come into vogue. We now hear about the law of legacy, school planning teams, distributive leadership, succession planning, and self-effacing CEOs. The theme is clear: Change led by one heroic figure will not last. Well-led teams generate more ideas and create a synergy. Leaders need to be judged not by what they do but what their successors are able to do. Their legacies lie in the future.

Trap No. 9: If you think you're finished, think again.

It may be quite frustrating to be told "You're not there yet." However, bringing a school from a state of distress and disappointment to an acceptable status is just the beginning. Bringing that school to exemplary levels becomes the next goal. Taking good schools and making them great is another venture. Furthermore, once significant change is achieved, the next challenge—sustaining the change—confronts us. Consequently, for agents of change, the journey never ends.

Trap No. 10: If you've plugged a breach in the levee, get ready for the flood.

Unfortunately, we have a Hurricane Katrina metaphor. Plugging a hole in the dike (the past metaphor) or a breach in the levee is, at best, providing temporary, often very temporary relief. It is a dangerous strategy—for levees and for schools—for several reasons.

First, the relief may delude us. As detailed in our discussion of superficial versus substantial change, cosmetic changes do not go to the heart of the matter. The important work is getting beyond the symptoms and quick fixes and addressing the roots of the problem.

Second, we may require a complete structural overhaul of what now exists.

Third, it may be necessary to dramatically change how we view levees (and schools). What purpose do they have? How well do they function? Are there better structures and systems? What do we do when they break and do not do the job they are expected to do?

Fourth, we must see the larger picture. Although we cannot immediately control weather systems, we can better understand the wide range of effects; the short-term and long-term consequences; how climate conditions are part of a larger system; and, in the eyes of global warming experts, how small steps now can lead to larger consequences later.

Fifth, the rebuilding of the levee calls for the involvement of many people with different skills, jobs, backgrounds, and experiences, such as engineers, meteorologists, city planners, and so on. The same is true for schools, which need to involve all school stakeholders, teachers, parents, students, and community members.

IT CAN BE DONE! (REPRISE)

The feature-length film *Dead Poets Society* offers some appropriate lessons for us.

The film stars Robin Williams, who plays the role of John Keating, a gifted high school English teacher. Mr. Keating is an unusual character, who asks his students to climb on a desk so they can see things in another way. He has his students change the way they walk so they are not stuck in doing things the way they have always been done.

The first time he meets his students, Keating beckons them to the hallway, where an impressive glass case displays photographs of former students. Keating asks his students to lean forward and study the faces of those students. Keating says, "these students were just like you," with adolescent interests and limitless dreams. They wanted to make a difference, but now they are pushing up daisies. Keating urges his students to lean forward some more. As they do, a soft voice declares, "Carpe Diem. Seize the day, boys. Make your lives extraordinary."

Seize the day. If not us, who? If not now, when?

References and Suggested Readings

Adams, D. (1991). Chapter 1: Planning model and paradigms. In R. V. Carlson & G. Awkerman (Eds.), *Educational planning: Concepts, strategies, practices.* New York: Longman.

Allison, S. (1999). *Many mountains to climb: Reflections on competence, courage, and commitment.* Seattle, WA: Milestone Books.

Alter, J. (2006). *The defining moment: FDR's hundred days and the triumph of hope.* New York: Simon & Schuster.

American Heritage Dictionary of the English Language. (2006). Boston: Houghton Mifflin.

Archer, J. (2006, April 12). Kinder and Gentler [Electronic version]. *Education Week, 25,* 34–36.

Barott, J. E., & Raybould, R. (1998). Changing schools into collaborative organizations. In D. G. Pounder (Ed.), *Restructuring schools for collaboration.* Albany: State University of New York Press.

Barth, R. S. (1990). *Improving schools from within; Teachers, parents, and principals can make the difference.* San Francisco: Jossey-Bass.

Barth, R. S. (2001). *Learning by heart.* San Francisco: Jossey-Bass.

Beane, J. A. (1992). Creating an integrative curriculum: Making the connections [Electronic version]. *NASSP Bulletin, 76,* 46–54.

Belasco, J. A., & Stayer, R. C. (1993). *Flight of the buffalo: Soaring to excellence, learning to let employees lead.* New York: Warner Books.

Bennett, R. S. (2004). *Year to success: When it comes to success, there are no shortcuts.* Sudbury, MA: Archieboy Holdings, LLC.

Bierlin, L. A. (1997). The charter school movement. In D. Ravitch & J. P. Viteritti (Eds.), *New schools for a new century: The redesign of public education.* New Haven, CT: Yale University Press.

Boorstin, D. (1972). *American civilization: A portrait from the twentieth century.* New York: McGraw-Hill.

Boyatzis, R., & McKee, A. (2005). *Resonant leadership.* Boston: Harvard Business School Press.

Boyd, H. (2004). *We shall overcome.* Napier, IL: Sourcebooks, Inc.

Branch, T. (1988). *Parting the waters: America in the King years, 1954–63.* New York: Simon & Schuster.

Brinkley, D. (2006). *The great deluge: Hurricane Katrina, New Orleans, and the Mississippi Gulf Coast.* New York: HarperCollins.

Brooke-Smith, R. (2003). *Leading learners, leading schools.* London: RoutledgeFalmer.

Bryk, A. S., Sebring, P. B., Kerbow, D., Rollow, S., & Easton, J. Q. (1998). *Charting Chicago school reform: Democratic localism as a lever for change.* Boulder, CO: Westview Press.

Burke, W. W. (2002). *Organization change: Theory and practice.* Thousand Oaks, CA: Sage.

Burrello, L. C., Hoffman, L. P., & Murray, L. E. (2005). *School leaders building capacity from within: Resolving competing agendas creatively.* Thousand Oaks, CA: Corwin Press.

Calaprice, A. (2002). *Dear Professor Einstein.* New York: Barnes & Noble Books.

Carlson, R. V. (1996). *Reframing & reform: Perspectives on organization, leadership and school change.* White Plains, NY: Longman.

Carlson, R. V., & Awkerman, G. (Eds.). (1991). *Educational planning: Concepts, strategies, and practices.* White Plains, NY: Longman.

Carnegie Corporation of New York. (1995). *Great transitions: Preparing adolescents for a new century. Concluding report of the Carnegie council on adolescent development.* New York: Author.

Carroll, L. (1998). *Alice's adventure in wonderland.* New York: Penguin Classics. (Original work published 1865)

Chambers, J. W. (Ed.). (1999). *The Oxford companion to American military history.* Oxford, UK: Oxford University Press.

Chopra, D. (2004). *Fire in the heart: A spiritual guide for teens.* New York: Simon & Schuster Children's Publishing.

Clandinin, J., & Connelly, M. (2000). *Narrative inquiry: Experience and story in qualitative research.* San Francisco: Jossey-Bass.

Clark, H. (Ed.). (1993). *Picasso in his words.* San Francisco: HarperCollins.

Clinton, H. (2003). *Living history.* New York: Scribner.

Clinton, W. J. (2004). *My life.* New York: Knopf.

Coles, R. (2000). *Lives of moral leadership.* New York: Random House.

Coles, R. (2003). *Children of crisis.* Boston: Back Bay Books.

Collier, V. P. (1995). *Promoting academic success for ESL students: Understanding second language acquisition for school.* Elizabeth, NJ: New Jersey Teachers of English to Speakers of Other Languages-Bilingual Educators.

Collins, J. (2001). *Good to great: Why some companies make the leap . . . and others don't.* New York: Harper Business.

Comer, J. P. (1997). *Waiting for a miracle: Why schools can't solve our problems and how we can.* New York: Plume.

Concise Oxford American Dictionary. (2006). New York: Oxford University Press.

Conley, D. (1993). *Roadmap to restructuring: Policies, practices and the emerging visions of schooling.* Portland: University of Oregon.

Conner, D. R. (1995). *Managing at the speed of change: How resilient managers succeed and prosper where others fail.* New York: Villard Books.

Cookson, P. W., Jr. (2006, December 13). The new, improved educational machine. *Education Week, 26,* 32.

Cooper, P. (1999). *Secrets of creative visualization.* Newburyport, MA: Weiser Books.

Cooperrider, D. L. & Whitney, D. L. (1999). *Appreciative inquiry: Collaborating for change.* San Francisco: Barrett-Koehler Communications.

Cotton, K. (2003). *Principals and student achievement: What the research says.* Alexandria, VA: Association for Supervision and Curriculum Development.

Croly, H. (1968/1909). The land of promise. In *The Annals of America* (Vol. 13, p. 214). Encyclopedia Britannica.

Cuban, L. (1988). A fundamental puzzle of school reform. *Phi Delta Kappan, 70*(5), 341–44.

Cuban, L. (2003). *Why is it so hard to get good schools?* New York: Teachers College Press.

Cuban, L., & Usdan, M. (Eds.). (2003). *Powerful reforms with shallow roots: Improving America's urban schools*. New York: Teachers College Press.

Darling-Hammond, L. (1997a). Reframing the school reform agenda: Developing capacity for school transformation. In E. Clinchy (Ed.), *Transforming public education: A new course for America's future*. New York: Teachers College Press.

Darling-Hammond, L. (1997b). *The right to learn: A blueprint for creating schools that work*. San Francisco: Jossey-Bass.

Davis, T. (1998). *Weary feet, rested souls: A guided history of the civil rights movement*. New York: Norton.

Day, C., Harris, A., Hadfield, M., Tolley, H., & Beresford, J. (2000). *Leading schools in times of change*. Buckingham, UK: Oxford University Press.

Deal, T. E. & Kennedy, A. (1982). *Corporate cultures*. Reading, MA: Addison-Wesley.

Deal, T. E., & Peterson, K. D. (1999). *Shaping school culture: The heart of leadership*. San Francisco: Jossey-Bass.

Department of Education. (2000, March 15). *Remarks as prepared for delivery by U.S. Secretary of Education Richard W. Riley*. Retrieved November 12, 2007, from http://www.ed.gov/Speeches/03-2000/000315.html

DePree, M. (1997). *Leading without power: Finding hope in serving community*. San Francisco: Jossey-Bass.

Deutschman, A. (2005). Change or die. *Fast Company*. Retrieved from http://www.fastcompany.com/magazine/94/open_change-or-die.html

Dewey, J. (1968/1897). My pedagogic creed. In *The Annals of America* (Vol. 12, p. 129). Encyclopedia Britannica.

Dewey, J. (1968/1900). The school and social progress. In *The Annals of America* (Vol. 12, p. 255). Encyclopedia Britannica.

Dewey, J. (1964/1902). *John Dewey on education: Selected writings*. Chicago: The University of Chicago Press.

Dickens, C. (1961). *Hard times*. New York: New American Library. (Original work published 1854)

Dougherty, C. J. (1996). *Back to reform: Values, markets and the health care system*. New York: Oxford University Press.

Doyle, D. P., & Pimentel, S. (1997). *Raising the standard: An eight-step action guide for schools and communities*. Thousand Oaks, CA: Corwin Press.

Duke, D. (2004). *The challenges of educational change*. Boston: Pearson Education.

Edmonds, R. (1979). Effective schools for the urban poor. *Educational Leadership, 37*(1), 15–24.

Einstein, A. (2002). *The Einstein reader*. New York: Citadel.

Einstein, A. (2006). *The Einstein reader*. New York: Citadel.

Elmore, R. F. (1999–2000, Winter). Building a new structure for school leadership. *American Educator*.

Elmore, R. F. (2004). *School reform from the inside out: Policy, practice, and performance*. Cambridge, MA: Harvard University Press.

Elmore, R. F., Peterson, P. L., & McCarthey, S. J. (1996). *Restructuring in the classroom: Teaching, learning & school organization*. San Francisco: Jossey-Bass.

Evans, R. (1996). *The human side of school change: Reform, resistance and the real-life problems of innovation*. San Francisco: Jossey-Bass.

Fabun, D. (1967). *The dynamics of change*. Englewood Cliffs, NJ: Prentice Hall.

Fink, D. (2005). *Leadership for mortals: Developing and sustaining leaders of learning*. London: Paul Chapman Publishing.

Fliegel, S., with MacGuire, J. (1993). *Miracle in East Harlem: The fight for choice in public education*. New York: Times Books.

Fradkin, P. L. (2005). *The great earthquake and firestorms of 1906: How San Francisco nearly destroyed itself*. Berkeley and Los Angeles: University of California Press.

Freiberg, H. J. (Ed.). (1999). *School climate: Measuring, improving and sustaining healthy learning environments*. London: Falmer Press.

Fried, R. L. (Ed.). (2003). *The skeptical visionary: A Seymour Sarason education reader*. Philadelphia: Temple University Press.

Friedman, T. L. (2005). *The world is flat: A brief history of the twenty-first century*. New York: Farrar, Straus and Giroux.

Fulghum, R. (1986). *All I really need to know I learned in kindergarten: Uncommon thoughts on common things*. New York: Villard Books.

Fullan, M. G. (1991). *The new meaning of educational change*. New York: Teachers College.

Fullan, M. G. (1993). *Change forces: Probing the depths of educational reform*. London: Falmer Press.

Fullan, M. G. (2000, April). The three stories of education reform. *Phi Delta Kappan*.

Fullan, M. G. (2001). *Leading in a culture of change*. San Francisco: Jossey-Bass.

Fullan, M. G. (2003). *The moral imperative of school leadership*. Thousand Oaks, CA: Corwin Press.

Fullan, M. G. (2005). *Leadership & sustainability: System thinkers in action*. Thousand Oaks, CA: Corwin Press.

Fullan, M. G. (2007). *The new meaning of educational change* (4th ed.). New York: Teachers College Press.

Gardner, H. (1991). *The unschooled mind: How children think and how schools should teach*. New York: Basic Books.

Gardner, H. (1995). *Leading minds: An anatomy of leadership*. New York: Basic Books.

Gardner, J. W. (1990). *On leadership*. New York: Free Press.

Genesee, F. (1999, January 1). *Program alternatives for linguistically diverse students*. Retrieved from Center for Research on Education, Diversity & Excellence, Educational Practice Reports Web site: http://repositories.cdlib.org/crede/edupractrpts/epr1

Gentiles, F., & Steinfeld, M. (1971). *Dream on America: A history of faith and practice, vol. 1*. New York: Harper & Row.

Gergen, D. (2005, October 31). Does leadership matter? *U.S. News and World Report, 139*(16), 91.

Giancola, J. M., & Hutchison, J. K. (2005). *Transforming the culture of school leadership: Humanizing our practice*. Thousand Oaks, CA: Corwin Press.

Gittell, J. H. (2003). *The Southwest airlines story: Using the power of relationships to achieve high performance*. New York: McGraw-Hill.

Gladwell, M. (2000). *The tipping point*. New York: Little, Brown.

Gladwell, M. (2005). *Blink: The power of thinking without thinking*. New York: Little, Brown.

Glasser, W. (1988). *Choice theory in the classroom*. New York: HarperCollins.

Goldstein, A. (2001, May 21). From Worst to First. *Time, 157*. Article retrieved November 13, 2007 from Newsbank Inc. database.

Goleman, D. (1995). *Emotional intelligence: Why it can matter more than IQ*. New York: Bantam Books.

Goleman, D., Boyatzis, R., & McKee, A. (2002). *Primal leadership: Realizing the power of emotional intelligence*. Boston: Harvard Business School Press.

Goodlad, J. I. (1984). *A place called school: Prospects for the future*. New York: McGraw-Hill.

Goodwin, D. K. (2005). *Team of rivals: The political genius of Abraham Lincoln*. New York: Simon & Schuster.

Gore, A. (2006). *An inconvenient truth: The planetary emergency of global warming and what we can do about it.* Emmaus, PA: Rodale.

Hall, G. E., & Hord, S. M. (2006). *Implementing change: Patterns, principles and potholes* (2nd ed.). Boston: Pearson.

Hamilton, D. N. (1991). An alternative to rational planning models. In R. V. Carlson & G. Awkerman (Eds.), *Educational planning: Concepts, strategies, and practices* (pp. 21–48). White Plains, NY: Longman.

Hargreaves, A., Earl, L., Moore, S., & Manning, S. (2001). *Learning to change: Teaching beyond subjects and standards.* San Francisco: Jossey-Bass.

Hargreaves, A., & Fink, D. (2006). *Sustainable leadership.* San Francisco: Jossey-Bass.

Harris, A., Day, C., Hadfield, M., Hopkins, D., Hargreaves, A., & Chapman, C. (2003). *Effective leadership or school improvement.* London: RoutledgeFalmer.

Hawley, W. D. & Valli, L. (1999). The essentials of effective professional development. In L. Darling-Hammond, & G. Sykes (Eds.), *Teaching as the learning profession: Handbook of policy and practice.* San Francisco: Jossey-Bass.

Heckman, P. E. (1996). *The courage to change: Stories from successful school reform.* Thousand Oaks, CA: Corwin Press.

Heifetz, R. A., & Linsky, M. (2002). *Leadership on the line: Staying alive through the dangers of leading.* Boston: Harvard Business School Press.

Herszenhorn, D. M. (2006, January 10). Toughening up for tests. *New York Times*, p. B1.

Hopkins, D. (2003). Instructional leadership and school improvement. In A. Harris, C. Day, M. Hadfield, D. Hopkins, A. Hargreaves, & C. Chapman (Eds.), *Effective leadership for school improvement.* London: RoutledgeFalmer.

Huffman, J. B., & Hipp, K. K. (2003). *Reculturing schools as professional learning communities.* Lanham, MD: ScarecrowEducation.

James, C., & Connolly, U. (2000). *Effective change in schools.* London: RoutledgeFalmer.

Johnson, S. M. (1990). *Teachers at work: Achieving success in our schools.* New York: Basic Books.

Johnson, S. (1998). *Who moved my cheese?* New York: G. P. Putnam's Sons.

Joyce, B., Wolf, J., & Calhoun, C. (1993). *The self-renewing school.* Alexandria, VA: Association for Supervision and Curriculum Development.

Joyner, E. T., Ben-Avie, M., & Comer, J. P. (2004). *Dynamic instructional leadership to support student learning and development.* Thousand Oaks, CA: Corwin Press.

Kennedy, J. F. (1956). *Profiles in courage.* New York: Harper & Brothers.

Kennedy, J. F. (1963). *Public papers of the presidents of the United States: John F. Kennedy, 1963.* Washington, DC: Office of the Federal Register.

Kennedy, J. F. (1999). A new frontier. In B. MacArthur (Ed.), *The Penguin book of twentieth-century speeches* (pp. 294–296). London: Penguin. (Original work published 1960)

King, M. L. (1999). I have a dream. In B. MacArthur (Ed.), *The Penguin book of twentieth-century speeches* (pp. 327–331). London: Penguin. (Original work published 1963)

Klarman, M. J. (2004). *From Jim Crow to civil rights: The Supreme Court and the struggle for racial equality.* Oxford, UK: Oxford University Press.

Kohl, H. (1998). *The discipline of hope: Learning from a lifetime of teaching.* New York: New Press.

Kohn, A. (1999). *The schools our children deserve: Moving beyond traditional classrooms and "tougher standards."* Boston: Houghton Mifflin.

Kotter, J. P. (1996). *Leading change.* Boston: Harvard Business School Press.

Kotter, J. P. (1999). *John Kotter on what leaders really do.* Boston: Harvard Business School Press.

Kouzes, J. M., & Posner, B. Z. (1995). *The leadership challenge: How to keep getting extraordinary things done in organizations.* San Francisco: Jossey-Bass.

Kozol, J. (2005). *The shame of the nation: The restoration of apartheid schooling in America.* New York: Crown.

Laham, N. (1998). *Why the United States lacks a national health insurance program.* Westport, CT: Praeger.

Lamperes, B. (2005). *Making change happen: Shared vision, no limits.* Lanham, MD: ScarecrowEducation.

Lawrence-Lightfoot, S. (1983). *The good high school: Portraits of character and culture.* New York: Basic Books.

Lawrence-Lightfoot, S., & Hoffman Davis, J. (1997). *The art & science of portraiture.* San Francisco: Jossey-Bass.

Leithwood, K. (1992). The move toward transformational leadership. *Educational Leadership, 49*(5), 8–12.

Leithwood, K., Steinbach, R., & Jantzi, D. (2002). School leadership and teachers' motivation to implement accountability policies. *Educational Administration Quarterly, 38,* 94–119.

Levitt, S. D., & Dubner, S. J. (2005). *Freakonomics: A rouge economist explores the hidden side of everything.* New York: Morrow.

Levy, A. (1986). Second-order planned change: Definition and conceptualization. *Organizational Dynamics, 15,* 5–20.

Lewis, M. (2005, December 4). Coach Leach goes deep, very deep. *New York Times Magazine,* p. 58.

Lewis, S. (1920). *Main Street.* New York: Harcourt, Brace & World.

Lieberman, A. (2001). The professional lives of change agents: What they do and what they know. In F. O. Rust & H. Freidus (Eds.), *Guiding school change: The role and work of change agents.* New York: Teachers College Press.

Lieberman, A., Saxl, E. A., & Miles, M. B. (1988). Teacher leadership: Ideology and practice. In A. Lieberman (Ed.), *Building a professional culture in schools.* New York: Teachers College Press.

Lindholm-Leary, K. (2000). *Bi-literacy for a global society: An idea book on dual language education.* Washington DC: National Clearinghouse for Bilingual Education.

Little, J. W. (1999). Organizing schools for teacher learning. In L. Darling-Hammond, & G. Sykes (Eds.), *Teaching as the learning profession: Handbook of policy and practice.* San Francisco: Jossey-Bass.

Louis, K. S., & King, J. A. (1993). Professional cultures and reforming schools: Does the myth of Sisyphus apply? In J. Murphy & P. Hallinger (Eds.), *Restructuring schooling: Learning from ongoing efforts* (pp. 216–250). Thousand Oaks, CA: Corwin Press.

Louis, K. S., & Miles, M. B. (1990). *Improving the urban high school: What works and why.* New York: Teachers College Press.

Louis, K. S., Toole, J., & Hargreaves, A. (1999). Rethinking school improvement. In J. Murphy & K. S. Louis (Eds.), *Handbook of research on educational administration.* San Francisco: Jossey-Bass.

Lowenberg Ball, D., & Cohen, D.K. (1999). Developing practice, developing practitioners: Toward a practice-based theory of professional education. In L. Darling-Hammond & G. Sykes (Eds.), *Teaching as the learning profession: Handbook of policy and practice.* San Francisco: Jossey-Bass.

Machiavelli, N. (1992). *The prince.* New York: Dover. (Original work published 1910)

Mann, H. (1968/1891). The pecuniary value of education. In *The Annals of America* (Vol. 7, p. 44). Encyclopedia Britannica.

Manzo, K. K. (2006, August 9). L. A. proceeds with plans to open `pilot schools' in Belmont area. *Education Week, 25,* 8.

Marzano, R. J., Waters, T., & McNulty, B. A. (2005). *School leadership that works: From research to results.* Alexandria, VA: Association for Supervision and Curriculum Development.

Maxwell, J. C. (1998). *The 21 irrefutable laws of leadership: Follow them and people will follow you.* Nashville, TN: Thomas Nelson.

McCourt, F. (2005). *Teacher Man.* New York: Scribner.

McFarland, L. J., Senn, L. E., & Childress, J. R. (1994). *21st century leadership: Dialogues with 100 top leaders.* New York: Leadership Press.

McKenna, P. (2004). *Change your life in seven days.* London: Bantam Press.

McMullan, B. (1994). Charters and restructuring. In M. Fine (Ed.), *Chartering urban school reform: Reflections on public high schools in the midst of change.* New York: Teachers College Press.

McWhorter, D. (2001). *Carry me home. Birmingham, Alabama: The climatic battle of the civil rights movement.* New York: Touchstone.

Mead, M. (2001). *Letters from the field, 1925-1975.* New York: Harper Colophon Books.

Meier, D. (1995). *The power of their ideas: Lessons for America from a small school in Harlem.* Boston: Beacon Press.

Meier, D., Sizer, T. R., & Sizer, N. F. (2004). *Keeping school: Letters to families from principals of two small schools.* Boston: Beacon Press.

Merriam-Webster. (2005). *Webster's collegiate dictionary.* (11th ed.). Springfield: MA: Author.

Merriam-Webster. (2000). *Webster's third new international dictionary.* Springfield: MA: Author.

Metz, M. H. (2003). *Different by design: The context and character of three magnet schools.* New York: Teachers College Press. (Original work published 1986)

Miller, M. (2003). *The two percent solution.* New York: Public Affairs

Mink, O. G. (Ed.). (1993). *Change at work: A comprehensive management process for transforming organizations.* San Francisco: Jossey-Bass.

Monroe, L. (1997). *Nothing's impossible: Leadership lessons from inside and outside the classroom.* New York: Times Books.

Murphy, J. (2005). *Connecting leadership and school improvement.* Thousand Oaks, CA: Corwin Press.

Murphy, J., & Hallinger, P. (1993). *Restructuring schooling: Learning from ongoing efforts.* Thousand Oaks, CA: Corwin Press.

National Association of Elementary School Principals. (2001). *Leading learning communities: NAESP standards for what principals should know and be able to do.* Alexandria, VA: Author.

National Center for Effective Schools. (1989). *A conversation between James Comer and Ronald Edmonds: Fundamentals of effective school improvement.* Dubuque, IA: Kendall/Hunt.

National Commission on Excellence in Education. (1983). *A nation at risk.* Washington, DC: Author.

The 9/11 Commission. (2002). *Final report of the National Commission on Terrorist Attacks Upon the United States: Authorized edition.* New York: Norton.

Noguera, P. A. (2003). *City schools and the American Dream: Reclaiming the promise of public education.* New York: Teachers College Press.

Ogden, E. H., & Germinaro, V. (1995). *The nation's best schools: Blueprint for excellence* (Vol. 2). Lancaster, PA: Technomic.

Osteen, J. (2004). *Your best life now: 7 steps to living at your full potential.* New York: Warner Faith.

O'Toole, J. (1999). *Leadership a to z: A guide for the appropriately ambitious.* San Francisco, CA: Jossey-Bass.

Ouchi, W. G. (2003). *Making schools work: A revolutionary plan to get your children the education they need.* New York: Simon & Schuster.

Panasonic Foundation. (2006). *Strategies for school system leaders in district-level change, Atlanta, GA: Mobilizing the system around instruction* (Vol. 12, pp. 10–15). Secaucus, NJ: Author.

Panasonic National School Change Awards. (n.d.). 2000–2007 Nominations have been received from schools in the following states. Retrieved November 13, 2007 from http://www.npli.org/nsca/winners.html

Peters, T. (2003). *Re-imagine: Business excellence in a disruptive age.* London: Dorling Kindersley.

Popkewitz, T. S., Tabachnick, B. R., & Wehlage, G. (1982). *The myth of educational reform: A study of school responses to a program of change.* Madison: University of Wisconsin.

Ravitch, D. (2000). *Left back: A century of failed school reforms.* New York: Simon & Schuster.

Raubinger, F. M., Rowe, Piper, West. (1969). *The development of secondary education.* New York: Macmillan.

Reeves, D. (2002). *The leader's guide to standards: A blueprint for educational equity and excellence.* San Francisco: Jossey-Bass.

Reeves, D. B. (2004). *The daily disciplines of leadership: How to improve student achievement, staff motivation, and personal organizations.* San Francisco: Jossey-Bass.

Reich, R. B. (2000). Your job is change. *Fast Company, 39,* 150.

Rogers, C., & Freiberg, H. J. (1994). *Freedom to learn* (3rd ed.). New York: McMillan College.

Rogers, M. B. (1998). *Barbara Jordan: American hero.* New York: Bantam.

Rogoff, B. (1991). Social interaction as apprenticeship in thinking: Guidance and participation in spatial planning. In L. B. Resnick, J. M. Levine, & S. Teasley (Eds.), *Perspectives on socially shared cognition.* Washington: APA Press.

Sapolsky, R. M. (2004). *Why zebras don't get ulcers* (3rd ed.). New York: Henry Holt.

Sarason, S. B. (1990). *The predictable failure of educational reform.* San Francisco: Jossey-Bass.

Sarason, S. B. (2002). *Educational reform: A self-scrutinizing memoir.* New York: Teachers College Press.

Schein, E. H. (1992). *Organizational culture and leadership.* San Francisco, CA: Jossey-Bass.

Schein, E. (1999). How to set the stage for a change in organizational culture. In P. M. Senge, A. Kleiner, C. Roberts, G. Roth, R. Ross, & B. Smith (Eds.), *The dance of change: The challenges to sustaining momentum in learning organizations* (pp. 334–344). New York: Doubleday/Currency.

Schlechty, P. C. (2004). *Shaking up the schoolhouse: How to support and sustain educational innovation.* San Francisco: Jossey-Bass.

Schmoker, M. (1996). *Results: The key to continuous school improvement.* Alexandria, VA: Association for Supervision and Curriculum Development.

Schmoker, M. (2001). *The results handbook: Practical strategies from dramatically improved schools.* Alexandria, VA: Association for Supervision and Curriculum Development

Schmoker, M. (2006). *Results now: How we can achieve unprecedented improvement in teaching and learning.* Alexandria, VA: Association for Supervision and Curriculum Development.

Schools That Stretch. (2001, May, 21). *Time, 157,* 71.

Schwahn, C. J., & Spady, W. G. (1998). *Total leaders: Applying the best future-focused change strategies to education.* Arlington, VA: American Association of School Administrators.

Senge, P. (2006). *The fifth discipline: The art and practice of the learning organization.* New York: Currency Doubleday.

Senge, P., Cambron-McCabe, N., Lucas, T., Smith, B., Dutton, J., & Kleiner, A. (2000). *Schools that learn: A fifth discipline fieldbook for educators, parents, and everyone who cares about education.* New York: Doubleday.

Senge, P. M., Kleiner, A., Roberts, C., Ross, R. B., & Smith, B. J. (1994). *The fifth discipline handbook: Strategies and tools for building a learning organization.* New York: Doubleday.

Sergiovanni, T. J. (1992). *Moral leadership: Getting to the heart of school improvement.* San Francisco: Jossey-Bass.

Sergiovanni, T. J. (1996). *Leadership for the schoolhouse: How is it different? Why is it important?* San Francisco: Jossey-Bass.

Shaw, G. B. (1949). *Selected plays with prefaces.* New York: Penguin.

Shinohara, R. (2000, December 24). Schools make strides: Efforts bring big gains in test scores [Electronic version]. *Anchorage Daily News,* B1.

Simmons, J. (2006). *Breaking through: Transforming urban school districts.* New York: Teachers College Press.

Sizer, T. R. (1984). *Horace's compromise: The dilemma of the American high school.* Boston: Houghton Mifflin.

Sizer, T. R. (1991). No pain, no gain. *Educational Leadership, 48*(8), 32–34.

Sizer, T. R. (2004). *The red pencil: Convictions from experience in education.* New Haven, CT: Yale University Press.

Smith, F., & Smith, L. (1993). *Advocacy design center training and technical assistance proposal.* Unpublished manuscript.

Smith, K. K. (1982). Philosophical problems in thinking about organizational change. In P. S. Goodman, R. G. Burgess, J. Hockey, C. Hughes, H. Phtiaka, C. J. Pole, & A. Sanday (Eds.), *Change in organizations* (pp. 316–374). San Francisco: Jossey-Bass.

Smith, L. (1977). *The American dream.* Glenview, IL: Scott Foresman.

Smith, L. (1999, February 17). This is a *nice* private public school: How one district redefined itself through a high school. *Education Week.*

Smith, L. (2001a, February 7). Can we schools really change? *Education Week.*

Smith, L. (2001b, October 3). What are schools for? We should seize this moment to define our purposes. *Education Week.*

Smith, L. (2002, February). In the aftermath, what's the purpose? *The School Administrator.*

Smith, L. (2005, May 18). Sleeping with the enemy: Two views of leadership development. *Education Week.*

Smith, P. J. (Ed.). (2000). *Onward! Twenty-five years of advice, exhortation, and inspiration from America's best commencement speeches.* New York: Scribner.

Smith, W. F., & Andrews, R. L. (1989). *Instructional leadership: How principals make a difference.* Alexandria, VA: Association for Supervision and Curriculum Development.

Spady, W. (2001). *Beyond counterfeit reforms: Forging an authentic future for all learners.* Lanham, MD: Scarecrow Press.

Sparks, D. (2005). *Leading for results: Transforming teaching, learning and relationships in schools*. Thousand Oaks, CA: Corwin Press.

Sternberg, R. J. (2006, February 22). Creativity is a habit. *Education Week, 25*, 64.

Thomas, E. (2005, September 12). The Lost City—what went wrong: Devastating a swath of the south, Katrina plunged New Orleans into agony. *Newsweek*. Article retrieved November 13, 2007 from Newsbank Inc. database.

Tichy, N. M., with Cohen, E. (1997). *The leadership engine: How winning companies build leaders at every level*. New York: HarperBusiness Essentials.

Tucker, M. S., & Coddings, J. B. (1998). *Standards for our schools: How to set them, measure them, and reach them*. San Francisco: Jossey-Bass.

Tyack, D., & Cuban, L. (1995). *Tinkering toward utopia: A century of public school reform*. Cambridge, MA: Harvard University Press.

Wagner, T. (2000). *How schools change: Lessons from three communities revisited* (2nd ed.). New York and London: RoutledgeFalmer.

Wagner, T. (2002). *Making the grade: Reinventing America's schools*. New York: RoutledgeFalmer.

Wagner, T., & Kegan, R. (2006). *Change leadership: A practical guide to transforming our schools*. San Francisco: Jossey-Bass.

Wallis, C., Steptoe, S., & Miranda, C. A. (2006, December 18). How to Bring Our Schools Out of the 20th Century. *Time, 168*. Article retrieved November 13, 2007 from Newsbank Inc. database.

Washington, J. M. (1986). *A testament of hope: The essential writings and speeches of Martin Luther King, Jr*. New York: HarperCollins.

Watzlawick, P., Weakland, J. H., & Fisch, R. (1974). *Change: Principles of problem formation and problem resolution*. New York: Norton.

Welch, J. (with Welch, S.). (2005). *Winning*. New York: Harper Business.

Whitaker, K. S., & Moses, M. C. (1994). *The restructuring handbook: A guide to school revitalization*. Boston: Allyn & Bacon.

Wiggins, G., & McTighe, J. (2005). *Understanding by design, expanded* (2nd ed.). Alexandria, VA: Association for Supervision and Curriculum Development.

Williams, J. (1999, October 3). Having pushed for charter status, MPS school now must prove itself. *Milwaukee Journal Sentinel*, p. 1.

Yaverbaum, E. (2006). *Leadership secrets of the world's most successful CEOs*. New York: Barnes & Noble.

Zimbalist, R. A. (2005). *The human factor in change*. Lanham, MA: ScarecrowEducation.

Zmuda, A., Kuklis, R., & Kline, E. (2004). *Transforming schools: Creating a culture of continuous improvement*. Alexandria, VA: Association for Supervision and Curriculum Development.

Credits

Permission to reprint excerpted material has been granted for the following:

Chapter 1, p. 25, excerpt from *The Human Side of School Change: Reform, Resistance and the Real-Life Problems of Innovation*, by Robert Evans. Reprinted with permission of John Wiley & Sons, Inc.

Chapter 12, p. 173, excerpt from *Children of Crisis*, by Robert Coles. Reprinted with permission of Little, Brown and Company.

Chapter 13, p. 182, excerpt from *The Great Earthquake and Firestorms of 1906: How San Francisco Nearly Destroyed Itself*, by Philip Fradkin. Copyright © 2006 by Philip Fradkin, University of California Press. Reprinted with permission.

Chapter 14, p. 201, excerpt from *Leadership for the Schoolhouse: How Is It Different? Why Is It Important?*, by Thomas J. Sergiovanni. Reprinted with permission of John Wiley & Sons, Inc.

Chapter 15, pp. 216–217, excerpt from *Dynamic Instructional Leadership to Support Student Learning and Development: The Field Guide to Comer Schools in Action*, by Edward T. Joyner, Michael Ben-Avie, and James P. Comer. Reprinted with permission.

Index

CORWIN PRESS

The Corwin Press logo—a raven striding across an open book—represents the union of courage and learning. Corwin Press is committed to improving education for all learners by publishing books and other professional development resources for those serving the field of PreK–12 education. By providing practical, hands-on materials, Corwin Press continues to carry out the promise of its motto: **"Helping Educators Do Their Work Better."**